Logging in Action

Get the eBook FREE!

(PDF, ePub, Kindle, and liveBook all included)

We believe that once you buy a book from us, you should be able to read it in any format we have available. To get electronic versions of this book at no additional cost to you, purchase and then register this book at the Manning website.

Go to https://www.manning.com/freebook and follow the instructions to complete your pBook registration.

That's it!
Thanks from Manning!

Logging in Action

WITH FLUENTD, KUBERNETES AND MORE

PHIL WILKINS
FOREWORDS BY CHRISTIAN POSTA
AND ANURAG GUPTA

MANNING
SHELTER ISLAND

Manning Publications Co.	Development editor: Katie Sposato Johnson
20 Baldwin Road	Technical development editors: Sam Zaydel
PO Box 761	Review editor: Aleksandar Dragosavljević
Shelter Island, NY 11964	Production editor: Andy Marinkovich
	Copy editor: Carrie Andrews
	Proofreader: Melody Dolab
	Technical proofreaders: Kerry Koitzsch
	Typesetter and cover designer: Marija Tudor

ISBN 9781617298356
Printed and bound by CPI Group (UK) Ltd, Croydon, CR0 4YY

contents

foreword

Software is the lifeblood of most industries today and can be a differentiator for those companies that can iterate quickly and find customer value before their competitors. Some of the recent trends that allow large organizations to move fast include the adoption of cloud platforms and microservice architectures. While some of the trends have evolved, one thing has remained constant: when things go wrong, we need to quickly understand where to look to fix the problem. Microservices and ephemeral cloud infrastructure (containers, etc.) exacerbate this problem.

I vividly remember working on a particularly nasty distributed problem for a client a few years back wherein a set of services would communicate with each other to provide some business function, and after six days (almost on the dot!), the set of services would all come crashing down. The resulting outage caused significant revenue loss for this client. The client decided to restart all of the services one by one after four days to avoid the problem.

After observing the system for a few days, I noticed that the memory usage of all of the services involved in the call graph was growing significantly, so I worked with the client to safely capture memory and thread dumps to understand what was happening. I determined that a particular buffer was getting filled, but when looking through the code it was very difficult to identify why this was happening. The system included both blocking and nonblocking code on various threads, which made it difficult to work with. I had to turn to a tried-and-true foundation of working with distributed systems to help diagnose the issue: logging events.

After a few days spent diligently poring over many hundreds of thousands of log lines across the various services, I was able to see that a certain combination of messages that flowed through the system triggered a memory leak in all of the services, which would eventually cause an "OOM" or out-of-memory event in the services.

Although logging helped significantly in this endeavor, it was not easy. The logging was not consistent across the services, the timestamps were wrong, and the technology used to pull the logs from the machines would sometimes fail, crash, or corrupt the log files. We also lost valuable log data as the services were restarted after four days because the client could not take an outage. If the client had a better logging and observability architecture, a lot of this would have been simplified and would have reduced the time to pinpoint the OOM issue.

In this book, Phil Wilkins does an amazing job of conveying the principles of good logging patterns and demonstrates this with concrete technology and examples using a ubiquitous log collection and aggregation technology called Fluentd. Fluentd is used to collect, unify, and stream logging data from a variety of systems to a centralized data store, which can then be used for proper analysis. Phil walks the reader through building a logging system, taking into account such things as timestamps, structured human-readable data, and more complex things such as routing and massaging the logging data.

If you're building distributed systems such as microservices architectures, you will want to seriously consider your logging and observability architecture to support your day-to-day operations. This book will be a useful companion as you embark on your journey.

—CHRISTIAN POSTA, VP, Global Field CTO at Solo.io

I started my Fluentd journey seven years ago by integrating the project as the core piece of Microsoft Azure's Log Analytic Linux agent. The initial learning curve was challenging; however, the benefits we received from a growing community, plugin ecosystem, and ease of extensibility made the project a favorite within Azure environments. I then jumped to Treasure Data, where I managed the project, and afterward joined Elastic, where I learned of other logging toolsets. After admiring Fluentd from afar, I finally left Elastic, started Calyptia, a company built around the Fluentd ecosystem, and became a project maintainer.

When starting as a maintainer, I immersed myself in the community, surveying users about their pains and where we could do better. The community highlighted their knowledge gaps on getting started and where to find in-depth explanations of certain topics, and asked for more concrete examples.

In a happy coincidence, I also met Phil Wilkins while chatting with the community and had the opportunity to read his work *Logging in Action*. Phil has immense talent for deciphering complex topics and providing easy-to-understand visuals and instruction. *Logging in Action* fills many of the community's gaps with architecture details and deep step-by-step explanations.

Users who are brand-new to the observability space or already running Fluentd in production will gain value from maximizing Fluentd's performance with a deep dive on Fluentd's plugin architecture and on multiworker/multithread architecture. All of these examples accompany simple configuration and line-by-line explanations to customize in your environment.

Beyond the basics of getting started, *Logging in Action* goes into important real-world use cases and business value. Some of my favorites include reducing log volume, which can reduce costs for users who are using expensive backends, as well as how to use Fluentd to route and send data to multiple destinations. Both use case examples would have made my role much easier in previous years.

With Fluentd in its tenth year of development and users deploying the ecosystem's projects over 2 million times a day with Docker, it is hard to find a modern-day Kubernetes service or cloud provider without reference to these essential tools. I highly recommend using *Logging in Action* as a getting-started guide or refresher, or as a way to optimize your logging journey.

—ANURAG GUPTA,
FLUENT MAINTAINER AND CO-FOUNDER, CALYPTIA

preface

In some ways, this book has been in development for as long as I have worked in the software industry. This may sound odd, given that my career in IT started in the early '90s. I learned early on the importance of logging and translating error events into diagnoses and problem resolution. Lessons came from being a young lead developer on a critical product development running round-the-clock system testing. If something wasn't shown on the displays, it was assumed to be a presentation system problem, so get Phil—he needs to fix things now, even if it is some antisocial time of day or night. The reality was that the presentation subsystem was rarely at fault. The error originating from one of many complex backend systems sent erroneous data or tried to communicate using the wrong version of the interface. The better I made the logging to help show what had or had not been sent to the display system, the fewer the calls received.

Over the years, I've seen the constant drive to deliver functionality and features over giving the nonfunctional aspects the attention sometimes needed. Functional goals will always override the nonfunctional considerations. As software developers, we can be our own worst enemies when it comes to monitoring and logging. Writing logging events isn't that exciting when our code runs sweetly and passes all our unit tests. The functionality is complete and within the agreed time as far as the decision-makers are concerned, so why spend more time on the solution?

The reality is that we often collect logs and stick them in a dark place until something starts to go wrong. Logging will never be a sexy subject, but it is essential, and when done well, it can allow us to do some clever stuff. Good logging makes it possible for machine learning and artificial intelligence to be used for pattern recognition or to directly notify the right person to address the issue. You could go as far as detecting a log event and then trigger housekeeping processes to avoid a problem.

IBM used to call the ideas of self-protecting and self-healing processes *autonomics*—sound more fun now?

My open source background started about the same time as I switched to using Java (release 1.4 had just come out), starting with libraries such as Log4J. This progressed to larger open source solutions like JBoss v3 application server, and then working with Fuse (Apache CXF, Camel, ServiceMix, and ActiveMQ) before RedHat acquired the businesses, building and providing services for these frameworks. One of the great things about truly open-source solutions are the vendor-agnostic characteristics, which means it can have adaptors and plugins covering a diverse set of sources, making it easy to integrate. An architecture that lends itself well to integrating things will encourage such an ecosystem to thrive, and that's what Fluentd has.

The last thread of the story comes from my views on knowledge sharing. I've seen people use the idea of "knowledge is power" as a reason to withhold as much as possible, forcing people to go to individuals who make themselves indispensable. I've always interpreted this idea in an almost diametrically opposite way. I don't want to be indispensable, as it means you're back to being called upon day and night. Better to share your knowledge with all. Make your investment in developing knowledge worthwhile; people are far more likely to appreciate it and come back to you in the future (on your terms). It wasn't until I got involved with Oracle middleware and its user community, and later partner community, that I found a like-minded group of people who encouraged my writing and sharing. My journey as an author really got going.

My initial "serious" encounters with Fluentd occurred when I looked at the CNCF ecosystem to see what solutions were in the incubator. CNCF-incubated projects suggest possible future technology evolution. In Fluentd, I found a tool that offered far more than just letting Splunk hoover up log files. Fluentd creates opportunities to move log management to exciting places and address many significant log management challenges in a hybrid and multicloud space. However, I felt it was underrepresented in terms of explaining and illustrating Fluentd's capability and potential in a cohesive way, and thus this book was born. This might suggest that the Fluentd documentation is terrible, but far from it. The online documentation is, however, a dictionary, not a guide. It doesn't address the questions of what to look for when applying configuration and why.

acknowledgments

This book has been my first solo writing adventure and my first with Manning, and it has reminded me that there is a lot more effort that goes into a good book than meets the eye. But I hope you'll agree that the prodding and encouragement from the Manning editorial team means this is a book that will deliver for you.

I'd like to thank everyone at Manning for their support, particularly Katie Sposato Johnson and Andrew Waldron, who have been with me all the way through this adventure, and Carrie Andrews for finally whipping the content into shape.

In writing this book, we've had the support of volunteer reviewers and MEAP readers. Their feedback has been of great help and insight. Along the way, Anurag Gupta and Eduardo Silva Pereira, as technical and product leads for Fluentd and Fluent Bit, have reached out and taken the time to discuss Fluentd and Fluent Bit with me and contribute to the reviewing process. Thank you all for the time and feedback.

My journey as an author wouldn't have started without support and encouragement over the years. Those involved in my journey to becoming an Oracle Ace Director (think Java Rock Stars or Microsoft MVPs for, in my case, Oracle Integration and Cloud) have been central to this journey. By extension, to friends and colleagues past and present at Capgemini and Oracle—as always, many thanks, and I hope we'll get a chance to enjoy food and drink together again as it becomes safe to travel again.

Lastly, and most importantly, this book would have never happened without the support and understanding from my wife, Catherine, and our two sons, Christopher and Aaron, when I've spent evenings and weekends at the computer rather than in their company. All my love to you.

To all the reviewers: Alex Saez, Andrea C. Granata, Andres Sacco, Clifford Thurber, Conor Redmond, Elias Rangel, George Thomas, Joel Holmes, John Guthrie,

Kanak Kshetri, Kent R. Spillner, Kerry E. Koitzsch, Mario-Leander Reimer, Michael Bright, Michal Rutka, Raymond Cheung, Satej Kumar Sahu, Sau Fai Fong, Sidharth Masaldaan, Simeon Leyzerzon, Stefan Hellweger, Suresh Koya, Trent Whiteley, Vamsi Krishna, and Zoheb Ainapore, your suggestions made this a better book.

about this book

Logging in Action was written to help people get the most out of Fluentd and think about how logging can make our lives easier. Yes, the book focuses on Fluentd, but it is one of the most influential logging tools, as you will see.

The time spent developing software is such a small fraction of the life of the code that we produce and that needs to be kept operating. The weaker the logging, the harder it will be to understand and care for these systems in 20 or 30 years. Consider this: in 2020, Reuters has been quoted as stating that there are about 220 billion lines of COBOL code (www.bmc.com/blogs/cobol-trends); the Linux kernel was released in 1991, so software hangs around. Well-written logs and maximizing the logging tools and frameworks can make an enormous contribution to helping. You don't need to be a superstar hotshot developer or a sysadmin versed in the dark arts of kernel configuration to benefit from this book; as the author, I don't consider myself to be either of these.

Fluentd and various other technologies, such as Prometheus, are strongly associated with cloud-native solutions. But don't let this put you off; even if you're working with COBOL 77 on a mainframe, you still need to know what is going on. Tools like Fluentd have simply approached the same problems of monitoring, measuring, and alerting in a manner that can also address the demands that cloud-native can add (integration into containers, hyper scaling, and very highly distributed solutions crossing data centers and hosting vendors). Given this, much of the book focuses on the problem of logging regardless of location. Fluentd addresses the challenges of containers, hyper scaling, and so on, so we engage with these problems in the most advanced part of the book.

Everyone comes with preconceived ideas about what logging and monitoring is and how it should be used. Those preconceptions are influenced by our day jobs as a developer, sysadmin, database admin, security specialist, and so on. I hope this book helps you see other perspectives you've not considered. For example, when looking at logs, we often think about a cure rather than prevention. I hope this book will get you considering ideas that will help adopt preventative, or at least more responsive, approaches when handling log events.

Who should read this book

Logging in Action is for anyone involved in the practical tasks of developing, configuring, or running IT solutions, such as those on the support team battling to keep an archaic piece of undocumented software that no one dares touch running through the day. For the architect who is thinking about reducing the run costs for a system to release future funding on the next cool enhancement. For the developer writing code who doesn't want to be called at 3:00 a.m. to sort out a problem because logs aren't clear about what is going wrong and causing code to fail. For anyone in the IT industry who recognizes that it's time to "pay it forward" and try to ease the pain of understanding or preventing IT problems. Ultimately, if you want to get more out of your logging, this book should provide you with something.

How this book is organized

The book has four parts that cover eleven chapters and five appendices. The chapters take you through how to do things, and the appendices provide lots of reference material and additional supporting resources and tools.

Part 1

Part 1 lays out the big ideas, detailing the architecture of Fluentd and the use cases and opportunities Fluentd can support, as well as the prerequisites for deploying Fluentd. We conclude with the section with the classic hands-on "Hello World" example:

- *Chapter 1* starts with the basics of the elevator pitch for logging unification, touring through the background and fundamental ideas behind logging and Fluentd. We explore the different use cases and the different perspectives on logging, and examine ELF and EFK software stacks, as well as the differences and commonalities among these things.
- *Chapter 2* goes through the makeup of a log event, how time is important (particularly for distributed solutions), the architecture of Fluentd, and how this influences decisions. Next, we cover the footprint needed to deploy and run a basic Fluentd configuration. We conclude by following the tradition of creating the Fluentd equivalent of a "Hello World" program.

Part 2

Part 2 gets down to the details of working with Fluentd, illustrating the mechanics around capturing log events, routing, filtering, and outputting events. We provide the practical steps that turn the handling of log events from shifting data to making the logs more meaningful and, crucially, actionable and/or measurable:

- *Chapter 3* is all about capturing log events. We look at the most common sources, such as log files, and illustrate the nuances of processing such data. How can we extract more meaning from log events using parsers? And, of course, if we are monitoring everything else, how do we monitor the monitor?

- *Chapter 4* explores this question: Having captured events, what are we going to do with them? We examine buffers to help with I/O performance but ultimately put the log events into storage, such as structured files or repositories like a NoSQL database. We then look at approaches that support post-event analysis (e.g., mining events within Elasticsearch), and also explore how to be more proactive, spotting important events and being notified about them through Slack the moment they occur.

- *Chapter 5* covers who wants the log events, and how we get the events to the right places? Security people want all the data in their specialist data mining toolkit. Operations do not want the logs clogging up the environment, but they want anything that helps them see production issues and get meaningful data to the right people.

- *Chapter 6* looks at getting more meaning from logs. Let's turn logs from data to information. Do we need to inject additional information into a log event to give it valuable context? If so, how?

PART 3

Part 3 takes us into the most advanced aspects of Fluentd, looking at deployment, performance, and scaling in both classic deployment scenarios and containerized environments. We address the challenge of building our own plugins to handle the niche situations where an existing plugin doesn't meet our needs:

- *Chapter 7* addresses how Fluentd can be applied to scale (either statically or dynamically) and how it can operate in distributed multiserver and clustered environments, including on-premises only, hybrid, and multicloud factors. We also look at how to incorporate resilience into a deployment so log events continue to flow.

- *Chapter 8* looks at configuring Fluentd within Kubernetes and Docker to capture events from the applications and listen to the log events generated by these platform technologies themselves.

- *Chapter 9* addresses those who wish to add to Fluentd's community with their own plugins or need to develop something to deal with their own niche problem that doesn't have a plugin to help already. This is the one chapter where having some development experience will be beneficial.

PART 4

Part 4 explores the issue that Fluentd, and what it can do with logs, is only as good as the log events that are created. We examine what makes good log events. Producing log events to file systems is not the optimal solution, so we explore different ways to get log events to Fluentd more effectively:

- *Chapter 10* describes the effective use of log classification, the kinds of information that can increase the value and use of log events, and how we make the information available. This includes taking into account the implications of logging sensitive data.
- *Chapter 11* looks at logging frameworks and how they can simplify handling log events in different languages. The chapter examines how log events can be sent to Fluentd using techniques that are more direct than log files. Avoiding this step gains efficiency and flexibility in our setup. We take a tour of how many logging frameworks are organized and connect such frameworks directly to Fluentd rather than stepping via log files, including how this can be done without the application getting locked into using Fluentd.

APPENDICES

The appendices contain the content that will be helpful for quick reference when working with Fluentd, along with many resources to help you learn more about related subjects and helpful tools. Outside of Fluentd and the LogSimulator, we cover the installation of the products used to help demonstrate various aspects of Fluentd. We cover this in the appendices to avoid any disruption to the book's flow:

- *Appendix A* takes you through installing the different tools and the configuration needed to run all the examples, scenarios, and exercises in the book if you want to get down and dirty.
- *Appendix B* helps with manipulating times and dates and formulating regular expressions that can differ because of programming language differences. This appendix provides handy lookups to address these issues.
- *Appendix C* addresses the fact that Fluentd lives in a world of plugins, and this should help you identify plugins that can help but haven't been used in the chapters. This isn't an exhaustive list, but it calls out some plugins that are likely to be handy sooner or later.
- *Appendix D* tells a story of how we've applied logging management to deliver significant improvements to large organizations. To protect the innocent, I've fudged some details. However, if you're trying to help your organization adopt better logging and monitoring practices, this should offer some ideas.
- *Appendix E* addresses the reality that logging and Fluentd touch on many aspects of IT. Rather than trying to cover everything in detail, as that would result in a book so big we'd never be able to pick it up, we've identified a variety of external resources we think can help.

About the code

This book contains many examples of Fluentd configuration and source code, both in numbered listings and in line with standard text. In both cases, the source code is formatted in a `fixed-width font like this` to separate it from ordinary text.

We've restricted the book to showing only the relevant sections of a configuration file in most cases. All the listing titles provide a reference to the complete code or configuration. The book doesn't include configuration or code annotations, but we have left them in the original source files to make the code compact and easy to read on the page. In rare cases, even this was not enough, and listings include line-continuation markers (➥).

Source code for the examples in this book is available for download from the publisher's website at www.manning.com/books/logging-in-action or via the GitHub repository at https://github.com/mp3monster/LoggingInActionWithFluentd. I hope that over time we'll get to add additional examples into this repository.

liveBook discussion forum

Purchase of *Logging in Action* includes free access to liveBook, Manning's online reading platform. Using liveBook's exclusive discussion features, you can attach comments to the book globally or to specific sections or paragraphs. It's a snap to make notes for yourself, ask and answer technical questions, and receive help from the author and other users. To access the forum, go to https://livebook.manning.com/#!/book/logging-in-action/discussion. You can also learn more about Manning's forums and the rules of conduct at https://livebook.manning.com/#!/discussion.

Manning's commitment to our readers is to provide a venue where a meaningful dialogue between individual readers and between readers and the author can take place. It is not a commitment to any specific amount of participation on the part of the author, whose contribution to the forum remains voluntary (and unpaid). We suggest you try asking the author some challenging questions lest his interest stray! The forum and the archives of previous discussions will be accessible from the publisher's website as long as the book is in print.

about the author

PHIL WILKINS has spent over 30 years in the software industry working for and with a diverse range of businesses and environments, from multinationals to software startups, from radar to retail, and commercial health care. He started out as a developer on real-time solutions and has worked through technical leadership roles, primarily in Java-based environments.

Phil has joined Oracle as a Technology Evangelist having previously worked for Capgemini as a Consulting Architect and Technology Evangelist specializing in cloud integration, API design, and non-functional considerations such as logging and monitoring. He was part of a multi-award-winning PaaS team in the UK using vendor-specific and open-source technologies; his client-facing role with well-known UK and international brands, where he provided internal support to delivery teams. His work with delivery teams focused on technical expertise, developing and defining best practices, and leading innovation initiatives. He is TOGAF certified.

Outside of his daily commitments, Phil actively works to support the developer community in various ways, including as a co-organizer of the London Oracle Developer Meetup, author of journal articles and blogs, and presenter at conferences in the UK and around the world. Phil's contributions to the community for open source and PaaS have been recognized since 2019 by Oracle with the accreditation as an Oracle Ace Director.

about the cover illustration

The figure on the cover of *Logging in Action* is "Fille Bratzke à Udinskoi Ostrog," or a Bratzke girl in Udinskoi Ostrog, from a book by Jacques Grasset de Saint-Sauveur published in 1797. Each illustration is finely drawn and colored by hand.

In those days, it was easy to identify where people lived and what their trade or station in life was just by their dress. Manning celebrates the inventiveness and initiative of today's computer business with book covers based on the rich diversity of regional culture centuries ago, brought back to life by pictures from collections such as this one.

Part 1

From zero to "Hello World"

Any good thriller starts by introducing its primary protagonists. Their motivations, backgrounds, and strengths and weaknesses are presented. The environment in which the key players operate is shown in the first 20 minutes.

This is what the first part of the book is about. The first chapter introduces our hero, Fluentd (and sibling Fluent Bit); we set the scene with the context, the use cases, and so on. If you are still in the process of discovering what Fluentd is about or thinking about the things that will help you make a case to your colleagues for adopting Fluentd, there is plenty of fuel for thought here.

If chapter 1 is about our principal player, then chapter 2 looks at the environments in which Fluentd can operate. We will progress through the first practical steps by installing Fluentd and keep with the time-honored tradition established by Brian Kernighan, with the first solution being "Hello World."

Introduction to Fluentd

This chapter covers

- Examining use cases for logs and log events
- Identifying the value of log unification
- Differentiating between log analytics and unified logging
- Understanding monitoring concepts
- Understanding Fluentd and Fluent Bit

Before getting into the details of Fluentd, we should first focus on the motivations for using a tool such as Fluentd. How can logging help us? What are log analytics, and why is log unification necessary? These are among the questions we will work to answer in this chapter. We'll highlight the kinds of activities logging can help or enable us to achieve.

Let's also take a step back and understand some contemporary thinking around how systems are measured and monitored; understanding these ideas will mean we can use our tools more effectively. After all, a tool is only as good as the user creating the configuration or generating log events to be used.

As we do this, it is worth exploring how Fluentd has evolved and understanding why it holds its position within the industry. If you are considering Fluentd as a possible tool or looking to make a case for its adoption, then it is helpful to understand its "origin story," as this will inform how Fluentd may be perceived.

1.1   Elevator pitch for Fluentd

Given that you're looking at this book, we presume you have at least heard of Fluentd and probably have a vague sense of what it is. Let's start with the "elevator pitch" as to what Fluentd and Fluent Bit are.

The primary purpose of Fluentd and its sibling Fluent Bit is to capture log events from a diverse range of possible sources (infrastructure such as network switches, OS, custom applications, and prebuilt applications, including Platform as a Service and Software as a Service). It then gets those events to an appropriate tool where the log events can be processed to extract meaning and insight, and possibly trigger actions. Fluentd's primary job is not to perform detailed log analytics itself, although it can derive meaning, and deeper analysis could be incorporated into its configuration if needed.

By unifying the log events from all the sources of logs impacting the operation of our solution, we have the opportunity to see the big picture. For example, was the error in the database the cause of an error returned to a user by the application, or was the database error a symptom of the operating system not being able to write to storage?

1.1.1   What is a log event?

We've described Fluentd in terms of log events, so what qualifies as a *log event*? A log event is best described as the following:

- Log events are humanly readable information that is primarily textual in nature. The textual information can range from unstructured to highly structured.
- Each log event has a place in time, defined with a timestamp (usually absolute 01:00:00 1 Jan 1970, but could be relative +0.60), or time can be inferred by the log event's position in a series of events.
- Each event also has an explicit or implicit association to a location that can be associated with a component running in a location that may be physical or logical.

Let's illustrate the point. Anyone with some coding experience will probably recognize the screenshot shown in figure 1.1 as an extract of log output. In this case, the output is generated by Fluentd. As you can see, there is a timestamp for the event; a location, which comes from the host the events are occurring on; and some additional semistructured content.

```
  port 24224
  tag "catCall"
</source>
<match *>
  @type stdout
</match>
</ROOT>
2021-07-15 20:57:16 +0100 [info]: starting fluentd-1.12.0 pid=25836 ruby="2.6.4"
2021-07-15 20:57:16 +0100 [info]: spawn command to main:  cmdline=["C:/Ruby26-x6
4/bin/ruby.exe", "-Eutf-8", "C:/Ruby26-x64/bin/fluentd", "-c", "Chapter2/Fluentd
/HelloWorld.conf", "--under-supervisor"]
2021-07-15 20:57:18 +0100 [info]: adding match pattern="*" type="stdout"
2021-07-15 20:57:18 +0100 [info]: adding source type="http"
2021-07-15 20:57:18 +0100 [info]: #0 Oj is not installed, and failing back to Ya
jl for json parser
2021-07-15 20:57:18 +0100 [info]: adding source type="forward"
2021-07-15 20:57:18 +0100 [info]: #0 starting fluentd worker pid=10160 ppid=2583
6 worker=0
2021-07-15 20:57:18 +0100 [info]: #0 listening port port=24224 bind="0.0.0.0"
2021-07-15 20:57:18 +0100 [info]: #0 fluentd worker is now running worker=0
2021-07-15 20:58:03.361723600 +0100 myTag: {"Hello":"World"}
```

Figure 1.1   Log output from Fluentd

1.1.2   *Fluentd compared to middleware*

Those who have worked with middleware (e.g., Apache Camel, MuleSoft, Oracle SOA Suite) will appreciate the idea of describing Fluentd as an enterprise service bus specialized in logs. Figure 1.2 suggests this, with the concept of input and output and capabilities to route and transform the log events. This will become ever more apparent as the book progresses.

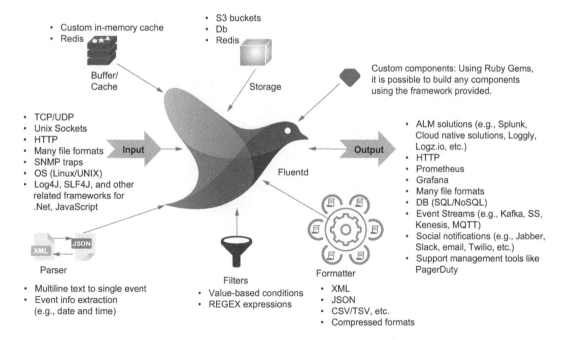

Figure 1.2   Illustration showing different types of Fluentd plugins and their relationship to the core

NOTE   If you'd like to explore this analogy further, you might consider reading the liveBook version of *Open-Source ESBs in Action* by Tijs Rademakers and Jos Dirksen (Manning, 2008) at http://mng.bz/Nx6n.

DEFINITION   *Middleware* is a generic term covering software that provides services to software applications beyond those available from the operating system. Often this entails connecting different pieces of software. It can sometimes be described as "software glue."

DEFINITION   An *enterprise service bus* is a specific category of middleware for passing data in a near-real-time manner between pieces of software. This usually includes the sequencing of the execution of the different software components as well.

1.2   Why do we produce logs?

We create log entries for a wide range of reasons. Some of the use cases for logs are only needed a fraction of the time but are invaluable when needed. Nearly every use case we can think of will fall into one of the following categories:

- *Debugging*—Knowing which parts of the code are being executed in a scenario makes it easy to isolate a bug. Yes, we have debuggers, and so on, but often it's just as easy to drop a few log lines in to help. Some of these log messages will be left in to provide assurance that things are running fine during production. Other lines of log messages may be disabled while we're not developing and testing software. Note that we would never recommend trying to connect to a production environment with a debugger. Allowing a production system to log information intended for debugging should be done with an understanding of the possible consequences (later in the book, we'll explore why this is so).

- *Unexpected data values or abnormal conditions occurring*—When code encounters data values that are out of bounds, sometimes it is better to flag and keep going, as you would see when
  - Using the default condition in a switch statement, when the code should have a value you have allowed for in the switch. But as a result of a change or bug elsewhere, your code needs to gracefully handle the situation and make it known (e.g., the classic problem of a presentation layer [UI] differing from the backend supported data values):

```
switch (caseSwitch)
  {
      case 1:
         // do something expected
         break;
      case 2:
         // do something expected
         break;
      default:
         System.Diagnostics.Debug.Write("Unexpected " + caseSwitch);
         // unexpected path - log this as it may be indicative
```

```
    // of a bug
        break;
}
```

- Applying defensive coding. For example, before using an object variable, checking that it isn't null—a standard action when first loading configuration data to ensure everything is as expected.
- Reporting when the code handling connection issues experiences an error, and you're going to fall back and try again. This is so we can understand the cause of a slow response that impacts user experience from the logs.

- *Audit and security*—We live in a world where internal and external actors try to get hold of data for illegitimate use. To help us watch for misuse, we need to know what is going on. Events need to be recorded, if not reported. Sometimes this is to search for abnormal behavior patterns, and other times to show that the system did everything as it should. We often see this kind of use case referred to as *forensic logging* or *application security monitoring* and *security information and event management* (SIEM). Bringing log events together that can create an audit trail is important. A single out-of-norm event may be insignificant. But when you can see the same kind of event reoccurring regularly in an unusual manner, over time it may point to something more suspicious.

Logging, security, and log forensics

For further insight into forensic logging, this article provides some insights into the realities of using logs: http://bit.ly/Fluentd-ForensicLogging. And this Gartner article adds additional color to this landscape: http://bit.ly/AppSecurityMonitoring.

The National Institute of Standards and Technology (NIST) also provides an excellent guide on logging for security purposes in "Guide to Computer Security Log Management" (http://mng.bz/ExWd). While the title may suggest that the content is for a security specialist, it does offer a good entry into this application of logging for anyone in the IT industry.

- *Root cause analysis*—Sometimes we see a problem, but the cause isn't apparent. Often this is because we are looking only at the logs from a small set of components. For example, an application based on its logs appears to slow down over time, but there is no evidence of a memory leak. Only when we bring logs together from all the sources can we identify a cause and separate other problems as side effects. For example, our application could be fine. Still, we use another service on the same server, which never releases CPU threads properly, resulting in the server slowly running out of resources to run all applications. But this can't be seen until all the information is presented together.
- *Determining the cause of performance issues*—Tools such as Prometheus (https://prometheus.io/) and Grafana (https://grafana.com/) are well known for

gathering metric data to provide insight into the performance of software being run. While the data may show you what is happening, it doesn't necessarily tell you why. It is textual logs that describe what is happening—whether that is database query logs or application thread traces.

- *Anomaly detection*—While a system may appear to operate perfectly fine and yields the expected results when a solution is tested, anomalies occur in the results during the system's regular operation. Logging can facilitate the detection of such issues by helping to find correlations in the log events when anomalies arise, providing an indicator of the cause.

  An example of this was the occurrence of the Intel Pentium FDIV bug in the 1990s, where an error in the design of specific Pentium processors meant that while the software ran perfectly, some calculations in specific conditions produced an incorrect result. If we log events such as the outcomes of important calculations even when the software is running as expected, it becomes easier to spot any possible anomalies and examine activities to identify the origin of the anomaly (for more detail, see https://en.wikipedia.org/wiki/Pentium_FDIV _bug).

  Another example of an anomaly that can be seen is running our apps in production environments where we share resources with other processes. Our test environments show that everything is fine, but in production, we experience out-of-memory errors. These scenarios can result from test conditions being subtly different than production, where we may have been able to use more memory than is available in production conditions. Seeing what else is running and the details around the errors can help diagnose resource conflict issues. Not as high profile as a chip flaw, but still an issue that can be challenging to isolate.

- *Operational effectiveness and troubleshooting*—Mature, well-produced log events can include the use of error codes. An error code can be linked to a particular problem and guidance on how to resolve the issue.

- *Determine when to trigger subsequent actions*—Use log events to recognize specific needs and initiate processes automatically instead of requiring manual intervention.

  This can be particularly helpful for legacy states where the software and hardware environments are fragile and poorly understood but operationally critical; people become risk-averse to change (or may not even be able to implement change for off-the-shelf solutions). Therefore, to implement tasks like preventive measures for errors, we need to implement solutions outside the application being monitored. This could be simply watching for completion messages reporting success, at which point the next operation or error prevention can be started.

1.3   Evolving ideas

Ideas around log management and the application of logging have been evolving a fair bit over the last four or five years; this is partly driven by the rapid progression of containerization. Docker and Kubernetes and the effective growth in individual small services (microservices/macroservices/mini-services) to support dynamic and hyper-scaling mean environments and deployed applications are far more transient in nature. Other factors such as broader adoption to varying degrees of DevOps have also evolved. The net result is that a couple of concepts have developed that are worth noting.

1.3.1   Four golden signals

Observability was probably the first of the modern monitoring concepts to develop. Discussions around observability started to gain mainstream recognition around 2016 and showed up in what have become referential texts, such as Google's site reliability engineering (SRE) guide (available at https://landing.google.com/sre/sre-book/ toc/). The idea isn't new; it's just been well defined.

Observability essentially states that we should track or observe and measure what software is doing to manage and understand a system. Industry thinking has evolved this premise to the tracking of four specific signals, often referred to as the *four golden signals* of SRE: latency, errors, traffic, and saturation. These four signals are sometimes referred to as *metrics*, *measures*, or *indicators* (the language is used interchangeably; personally, the term *signal* feels very binary, and life is rarely that). Here is what the signals mean:

- *Latency*—How long it's taking to address a request. A growing latency indicates potential performance issues from the increasing demand of need, or lack of performance tuning, for software or configuration.
- *Errors*—Problems that can impact the service and the frequency, and whether they are self-recovered (e.g., not getting a DB connection means fall back and try again). Fluentd will come into its own handling errors, as we will see as we progress through the book.
- *Traffic*—Increased traffic can indicate growing demand or malicious intent, depending on the gain or loss of effectiveness if traffic drops.
- *Saturation*—Reflects how full or heavily used a system is (e.g., CPU and disk utilization). Once a system passes a certain saturation threshold, performance degradation will be experienced as the operating system has to dedicate more effort to manage its limited resources.

While deriving all four signals from logs alone is not desirable (e.g., service degradation would require us to hold multiple performance measures over time and compare them), halfway-decent logging can yield the signals given the use of timestamping. Latency could be derived by the time difference between the first and last log events occurring; for example, throughput could be indicated through volumes of log entries.

1.3.2   *Three pillars of observability*

Another perspective of observability that has become popular in the industry relates to the character of the things we monitor. The type of information gathered when monitoring can be described by one of several definitions. As a result, observability is made up of three pillars, or core ideas:

- *Metrics*—Typically numerical and quantify the state of things. We then regularly sample the data points in the environment (e.g., CPU utilization).
- *Logs*—Primarily textual but event-based, therefore having characteristics of time and description (e.g., Simple Network Management Protocol [SNMP] traps).
- *Traces*—Tracking execution flows and the time it takes for transactions and sub-transactions to execute different steps. Trace logs are largely numerical, being made up of timestamps as code executions enter and leave different parts of the solution. To provide these times with context, identifiers, such as transaction ID and the entry and exit points, are identified.

Everyone will be familiar with metrics, as we have all at some point needed to see how hard a CPU is working or have experienced constraints because of a lack of memory or how much storage is available on our hard disks.

Tracing is probably most strongly associated with the OpenTracing initiative (https://opentracing.io/) and the Cloud Native Computing Foundation (CNCF) project Jaeger (https://jaegertracing.io/). OpenTracing has combined with a project called OpenCensus (https://opencensus.io/) to form OpenTelemetry (https://open telemetry.io/). Yet logging may contribute to this space, as specific log entries may act as a measuring point within a trace—particularly within legacy solutions. There is the risk that people will merge thinking about tracing with logging. It is often desirable to correlate trace performance information back to logs, so logs can be used as a key diagnostic tool in determining where the low performance occurs. However, the tooling available to each pillar has distinct differences and strengths. We can see this by considering Jaeger's visualization of execution paths (traces) versus Fluentd's ability to parse log events and trigger actions. While these CNCF projects have brought tracing to the fore, the idea isn't new, and many service bus solutions (such as Oracle SOA Suite and MuleSoft) have some sort of mechanism for tracing. The difference is that OpenTracing and OpenTelemetry are trying to drive standardization.

We are seeing signs that these standards are being adopted by open source implementation frameworks and commercial solutions. How does this relate to Fluentd? Depending upon the log output, it can represent a means to trace execution (e.g., record a transaction, an identifier, an execution point in the codebase, and a time). In other words, a trace is a specialized log. This relationship and the deployment models being supported make Fluentd and Fluent Bit capable of being part of an Open-Telemetry solution. As a result, the OpenTelemetry Protocol (OTLP) is being incorporated into Fluentd. All these measures play a part at different levels of a solution (infrastructure to business logic), as figure 1.3 illustrates.

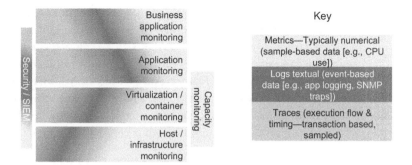

Figure 1.3   Three pillars of observability as applied to a solution stack

The definitions for the layers are as follows:

- *Business application monitoring*—This presents pure abstracted business application monitoring or business activity monitoring (BAM) and relates to the measurement of application/business tasks described by things like Business Process Execution Language (BPEL).
- *Application monitoring*—This reflects traditional monitoring of applications and middleware/workflow technologies such as Oracle's SOA Suite or Microsoft's BizTalk underpinning BPEL implementations.
- *Virtual machine/container monitoring*—This measures whether the engine that shares host computing services gives appropriate levels of resources to the guest environment(s). It monitors to ensure that the virtualized hardware is running smoothly.
- *Host/infrastructure monitoring*—This detects hardware problems, such as storage capacity, overheating CPUs, fan failures, and so on.

NOTE   More information about BAM can be found in the liveBook version of *Activiti in Action* by Tijs Rademakers (Manning, 2012) at http://mng.bz/DxgR.

Of these two concepts, I believe the four signals are better considered as measures. By measuring the data that each signal describes, the signal will indicate whether something is right or wrong. More importantly, do the changes in the signals being received show a trend or pattern that at least means that the solution being monitored is not degrading anymore? Ideally, we want a trend indicating continued improvement. Regardless, this information will not give you information on the root problem. For example, signals showing a highly saturated system won't tell you why the system is saturated, which can occur if code is stuck in an infinite loop. For this, you still need to understand what the software is doing. This is not to say signals are wrong; they are, without a doubt, the best way to provide a cue that there's an issue. But it is through the lens of the three pillars, I believe, that a deeper appreciation of what is or isn't happening can be achieved with the sight of cause and effect in the way software is behaving.

You may have observed that, in the reasons for logging (for debugging, audit, etc.), various activities will be handled by more than one or two individuals in an organization. Once an organization grows beyond a certain size, we have specialists working in different areas. The specialization of roles brings pressure for different tooling. While many monitoring tools have plugin features, and so on, they may not support every individual need. This can mean we end up with multiple tools in an Enterprise IT landscape, and in some organizations, people and organization politics will further complicate the IT tooling landscape. Yet, they all need a blend of data from the same source systems.

1.4   Log unification

Fluentd, Logstash, and other related tools are sometimes referred to as *log unification tools*. But what is meant by this, and what value(s) should a unification tool have? Let's look more closely at the value of unification and differentiate it from some other associated ideas.

The Cambridge English Dictionary describes *unification* as "the act or process of bringing together or combining things or people" (http://mng.bz/lax2). This is what we use Fluentd for—collecting log events from diverse sources and bringing them together with a single tool so the log events can be processed and sent to the appropriate endpoint solutions(s).

This ability is essential, as it provides many significant benefits; we have touched on some of these when looking at the application of logs. As we bring these value points together, we can roughly group them into log sourcing and log-based insights.

The log sourcing benefits include the following:

- It eases the task of locating and retrieving logs and log events. Through a single platform, locating relevant log events becomes far easier. We can route the log events to a convenient location/tool, rather than needing to access multiple platforms with potentially many different locations and ways of accessing the log events.
- With virtualization, containerization, and more recently functions as a service, the hosting of logic becomes transient, so the means to easily gather log information before it is lost is more critical than ever. Using Fluentd, we can configure lightweight processes into these transient environments that push log events to a durable location.
- A single technology brings logs events together regardless of the source or target. As a result, log event management becomes easier and more accessible. We don't have to master how all the different ways to log events can be captured and stored (e.g., Syslog, SNMP, Log4J, and the many other log forms and protocols), as Fluentd makes this easier.
- Operating systems are complex, made up of many discrete processes and applications. Often, discrete components come with their own logs. We need to bring these together to trace an event through the different components. Some

of this has been solved with operating systems and network equipment adopting a small group of standards like Syslog and SNMP traps.

It would be easy to think that Syslog and SNMP can meet all our logging needs. But software is more than a bunch of OS components that can use SNMP or Syslog, so we need to bring these sources together at another level of unification. For example, Syslog is predominantly a Linux solution; its use of UDP means there is a risk of event loss, and UDP has size limits. The data structures and predefined values are infrastructure-centric, to name a few of the Syslog constraints.

- In the era of the network and the internet, our applications pass events through many different managed devices, creating a real change in the number of places where our communications could be disrupted. Unifying the log events at this scale of distribution brings the problem to manageable proportions.

The log-based insights include the following:

- It is easier to create holistic view(s) of log events, allowing us to see the cause and effect more easily.
- With logs unified into an analytics platform, the data can be capitalized on with processes such as
  - Searching across all the logs in one accessible location
  - Identifying trends and patterns in the production environment
  - Extracting analytical data enabling forecasting future likely behavior
  - Looking at user behavior to determine if the systems are subject to misuse or patterns of malicious actions
- A unification platform creates the opportunity for us to move from a reactive, post-event analysis approach to identifying issues and then proactively acting on them as they occur. This potentially can extend to a position where we identify warning signs and proactively perform actions to avoid a problem. The ability to become proactive comes from the unification tool's ability to filter, route, and apply meaning to log events.
- Infrastructure as a Service and Platform as a Service have brought whole new levels of dynamic change and routing complexity. As a result, the unifying of logs reduces the scale of the challenge of tracking what could be impacting our solution.

While we have discussed the why and what of log unification, we should also differentiate it from other concepts associated with processing log events, particularly log analytics.

NOTE For more information about SNMP, see the liveBook version of *Software Telemetry* by Jamie Riedesel (Manning, 2021) at https://livebook.manning .com/book/software-telemetry/chapter-2/v-9/point-11605-169-174-1.

1.4.1   *Unifying logs vs. log analytics*

Many tools in the logging space come into the category of log analytics, where the focus is on applying data-analysis techniques such as pattern searching, using complex rules across many data records. Such processing is often associated with big data and search engine technologies. The best known of these is probably Splunk, as a purely commercial product, and Elasticsearch, as an open source solution with commercial options.

The log events need to be ingested into an analytics engine to enable log analysis to be performed. Such analytical processes may include event correlation (e.g., determining which systems or components generate the most errors or when the fault frequency relates to a particular event during the day). Getting log events into the engine can be done manually if necessary. Typically, analytics products like Splunk have tools to harvest or aggregate the log events using one of the more common protocols in the analytics engine. These services are then deployed to multiple locations to gather different log sources. This is a simple act of aggregation, as the harvesting is not intelligent; there is no possibility of handling the log events effectively until they are in the analytics engine. Harvesters typically don't have the same levels of connectivity and configuration seen with unification tools.

The differentiator is that a log analytics engine's strength is applying search and computational science to many logs, not the gathering and routing of log events. Whereas the strength of unification tools is sourcing and delivering the log events, it typically has relatively simplistic analytical capabilities such as event counts over time.

Both technologies have some standard capabilities, regarding the transformation/ application of meaning to the data (i.e., the process of data becoming usable information). Without these abilities, neither solution can be very effective. Both technologies have strong event-filtering capabilities, but are applied in different ways.

> **DEFINITION**   *Log routing* is when log events are taken and then directed through a middleware tool, such as Fluentd, to the applications that need those log events.

> **DEFINITION**   *Log aggregation* means log events are taken and sent to a central location to be processed.

1.5   *Software stacks*

The industry has been talking about software stacks since 2000 (some have attributed this term to David Axmark and Michael "Monty" Widenius, cofounders of MySQL), when the best-known stack was named: the LAMP (Linux, Apache, MySQL, PHP) stack. By *software stack*, we mean a standard combination of products (typically open source) used together to deliver software solutions. Another well-known stack is MEAN (MongoDB, Express, AngularJS, Node.js). A complete list of stacks can be found at https://en.wikipedia.org/wiki/Solution_stack.

> **Software stacks or solution stacks**
>
> It is worth noting that people often use the terms *software stack* and *solution stack* interchangeably. In most cases, this is reasonable; the stack provides a complete solution, such as log management; we just need to apply the configuration.
>
> But it isn't valid in cases where the stack provides all the elements on which a solution can be built; the MEAN stack contains all the components to build a lot of solutions, but you have to add your own software to the MEAN stack to deliver a solution.

1.5.1 ELK stack

The best-known stack within the software landscape for log processing is ELK (Elasticsearch, Logstash, Kibana). This combination of products provides the ability to perform log analytics with Elasticsearch, visualization through Kibana, and log routing and aggregation with Logstash. The ELK stack has fitted together so well because all three components, while open source, have been developed by Elastic (www.elastic.co), which has been successful, like Red Hat, with an open source–based business model.

While a single vendor for these components leads to them being neatly integrated and complementing each other's features, it also means that development effort can be heavily influenced by the vendor's business model and objectives. For Elastic, this is to sell more services and enterprise extensions to the different parts of the ELK stack. This issue can be addressed by the open source product being governed by an external and neutral organization such as Apache, CNCF, or the Linux Foundation. But ELK is not subject to such governance.

Unfortunately, Logstash, as part of this stack, has been impacted by the perception that it is biased to Elasticsearch as a target solution for log events (which may or may not be valid). Logstash does have plugins for products other than Elasticsearch. However, it could be argued that these plugins have had to come from vendors wanting to compete with Elasticsearch in the ELK stack, or Elastic has had to implement them to remain competitive. In comparison to Elastic, the founders of Fluentd didn't have their own analytics product as a preferred location for log events to be sent. We could also consider the adoption of Fluentd by CNCF as an implicit recognition of being free from these biases. It also helps that the community around Fluentd has produced more plugins, making it more flexible than Logstash.

This has led to a variant stack known as EFK that is gaining traction (Elasticsearch, Fluentd, Kibana). As Fluentd has plugins for Elasticsearch and Kibana, this alternate stack is viewed as equally capable but with greater flexibility for unification. OpenShift, for example, adopted EFK to manage log events (see http://mng.bz/YwDj).

As shown in figure 1.4, both ELK and EFK have lightweight, smaller variants of the unification capability. Beat's relationship to Logstash is the same as Fluent Bit's relationship to Fluentd (more on Beats and Fluent Bit later in this chapter).

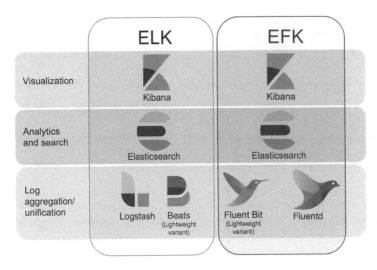

Figure 1.4   ELK vs. EFK software stacks, illustrating how the stacks differ and which products are involved in each stack

1.5.2   *Comparing Fluentd and Logstash*

In table 1.1, we have tried to draw out the differentiators of the two products. Both have a lot in common, which is why it is possible to replace Logstash with Fluentd in the stack. However, there are differences worth highlighting.

Table 1.1   Fluentd and Logstash comparison

Aspect	Fluentd	Logstash
Primary contributor and product governance	Treasure Data governed by CNCF	Elastic
Commercially supported versions	Yes	Yes (more robust option, as support can cover the full stack)
Plugins available	~500	~200
Configuration style	Declarative—use of tags	Procedural—use of if-then-else constructs.
Performance	Comparatively (to Logstash) lower memory footprint	Comparatively (to Fluentd) higher memory footprint
Caching	Highly configurable cache options with file and memory caching out the box	In-memory queue with a fixed size
Language/run-time machine	CRuby—no run time required for core	JRuby with dependency on Java run time (JVM)

1.5.3 *The relationship between Fluentd and Fluent Bit*

Fluentd has a small C-based kernel, but the bulk of the product is built using Ruby. This brings a bit of a tradeoff. The core tradeoff with Ruby is that it runs on an interpreter (although several variants utilize the Java Virtual Machine, Truffle, and so on, instead of the original interpreter, such as JRuby, used by Logstash). Ruby uses a packaging tool known as Gems to provide additional libraries and even applications. To enable Fluentd to be used in Internet of Things (IoT) situations, a smaller resource footprint is needed for devices like a smart meter or Raspberry Pi. The objective of creating a minimal footprint version of Fluentd led to the creation of Fluent Bit. Fluent Bit provides a subset of the Fluentd features, focusing on taking log events and routing them to a more centralized location. The log events can then be processed (filtered, transformed, enriched, etc.) more effectively—as you would expect of Fluentd. Table 1.2 the differences between Fluentd and Fluent Bit.

Table 1.2 Fluentd vs. Fluent Bit

Aspect	Fluentd	Fluent Bit
Development language	Written using C & Ruby	Written using C to minimize the deployment footprint
Dependencies	Dependency upon RubyGems	No dependencies (unless customized)
Storage and memory footprint	Memory requirements ~20 MB, depending upon configuration and plugins	~150 Kb
Plugins available	Able to leverage approximately 300 prebuilt and third-party plugins	Restricted to the in-built plugins and 30 other extensions. Input / Output CPU stats / FluentdTreasure Kernel messages / HTTP Memory stats / Library Serial interfaces / Elasticsearch TCP / InfluxDB Log Files / NATS Docker / Statistics MQTT / Treasure Data Service
OS support	Prebuilt installers for a wide range of OSes covering most flavors of Windows, OS X, Linux	A number of small-footprint Linux variants based on CentOS, Debian (and derivatives, such as Raspbian), and Ubuntu for x86 and AArch processors have been built. Other OSes such as BSD-based Unixes may be supported, but there are no guarantees for plugins.

Despite these differences, Fluent Bit and Fluentd are more than capable of working together, as we'll see later in the book. IoT isn't the only use case that lends itself well to the use of Fluent Bit. When considering microservices, small footprints and rapid startup times are highly desirable for some containers. We'll explore the deployment possibilities later in the book for microservices and the use of Fluentd or Fluent Bit.

1.5.4   *The relationship between Logstash and Beats*

The relationship between Beats and Logstash does differ a bit from that between Fluentd and Fluent Bit. For a start, the Beats are actually a set of individual small foot-print components collecting data for one thing. Each individual Beat solution is built upon a Go library called *libbeat*, compared with Logstash's use of Java. The Beats family are made up of the following:

- *Filebeat*—Collects log files (with specific modules to handle Apache, server logs, etc.)
- *Packetbeat*—Collects network packet data (DNS, HTTP, ICMP, etc.)
- *Metricbeat*—Collects server metrics
- *Heartbeat*—Provides an uptime monitor
- *Auditbeat*—Collects audit events to monitor activities through systemd (http://mng.bz/6Z9o) and Auditd (http://mng.bz/oa5d) on Linux
- *Winlogbeat*—Integrates into Windows OS to run PowerShell scripts and Sysmon, among others
- *Functionbeat*—Works with serverless solutions, currently just on AWS (Amazon Web Services)

The libbeat library has been made available as open source. It has made it a lot easier (and given the assurance of code independence) for third parties, including the open source community, to build more Beat solutions using the framework. All the beats use a shared data structure definition to communicate the data collected.

1.6   *Log routing as a vehicle for security*

With infrastructure becoming increasingly configuration-driven rather than being physical boxes and cables, the points where data can have ingress and egress to an environment can increase quickly, as it is simply a case of configuring new points where data can come and go. It is preferable that the number of points at which data passes between public and private networks be limited—this is just one of many reasons for having backend (or reverse) proxies. With logging agents in the pure aggregation model, each node wants to talk directly to the point of aggregation. This can be mitigated if the solution can tolerate network proxies. But would it not be better to use a proxy that better understands what is being routed, such as Fluentd?

> **DEFINITION**   *Proxies* are servers that retrieve resources on behalf of a client from one or more servers. The retrieved resources are then returned to the requestor, appearing as originating from the proxy server itself. Proxies are described as a backend or reverse if deployed closer to the server performing the computation rather than the (usually lightweight) client. Proxies are usually implemented to optimize network load by implementing traffic caching and applying security by controlling where data enters and leaves a network.

The log routing capabilities of Fluentd, as we'll see, allow us to use Fluentd nodes as routers/consolidators of logs, meaning we can control network exposure, as well as several other considerations.

Security considerations within Fluentd go beyond configuring routing to control network points for ingress and egress of logs in networks. Fluentd supports the use of SSL/TLS certificates, so that the data being sent between Fluentd nodes or between Fluentd and other networked services (e.g. MongoDB) is secure. This increases security by making checks for authenticity and the ability to encrypt the data. Today, security needs to be an aspect of everything we do, rather than a bolt-on; we'll address such issues directly where appropriate throughout the book.

1.7 Log event life cycle

Another perspective worth considering is the life cycle of a log event. When a software component of some kind generates a log entry, to get value from it, it needs to be passed through a life cycle, shown in figure 1.5.

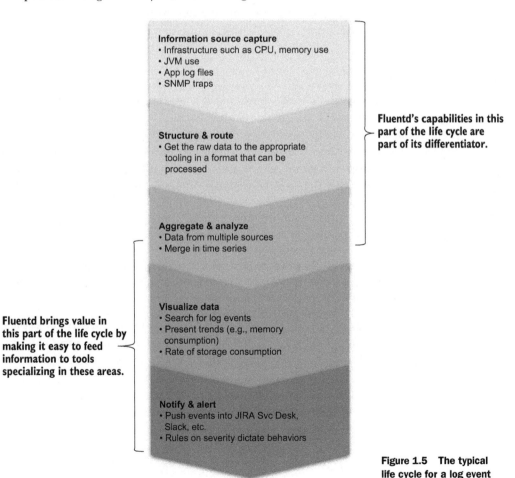

Figure 1.5 The typical life cycle for a log event

As figure 1.5 shows, we start with capturing the log event (*information source capture*), and as the event flows down, it gains more meaning and value. Based on what we've already discussed, any log unification tool, including Fluentd, is most effective with the information source capture and the *structure and route* phases. The *aggregate and analyze* phase will see features for analysis focusing on individual events but will lean on aggregating and analyzing aggregated logs. *Visualize data* is the product's weakest area. Given these tools' routing and connectivity capabilities, the *notify and alert* phase is easily realized by connecting suitable services. Not only that, but there is also the potential for this phase to be moved upward, as we don't always need the analytics products to decide whether it is necessary to notify and alert.

As shown in the figure, tools like Fluentd support the upper half of the life cycle very well (from capture to aggregate and some of the analyze stage). The lower half is well supported by log analytics (*aggregate and analyze, visualize data, notify and alert*).

1.8 Evolution of Fluentd

In this section, we will look at the events that led to the creation of Fluentd and its rapid growth in adoption. Figure 1.6 shows a timeline of key events in the evolution of Fluentd.

1.8.1 Treasure Data

Fluentd's origins go back to 2011 when *big data*, through the use of Hadoop, was impacting mainstream IT. As a Silicon Valley startup, Treasure Data was established to create value around Hadoop-based processing of semi-structured data. Treasure Data found it needed a tool to help it capture data from multiple sources and ingest the data into a Hadoop data store. As a result, it set about building Fluentd and made it available as free and open source software (FOSS) using the Apache 2 License (www.apache.org/licenses/LICENSE-2.0). This made it easy to build upon, extend, and exploit the tool. As a result, developers (other than just those working for Treasure Data) contributed to and extended Fluentd.

> **NOTE** To learn more about Hadoop, check out the liveBook version of *Mastering Large Datasets with Python* by John T. Wolohan (Manning, 2020) at http://mng.bz/do2o.

In 2013, Fluentd got a big boost due to the recommendation by AWS for data collection across and onto their platform. This was further helped by Google using Fluentd with its BigQuery product and then incorporating Fluentd into its monitoring solution.

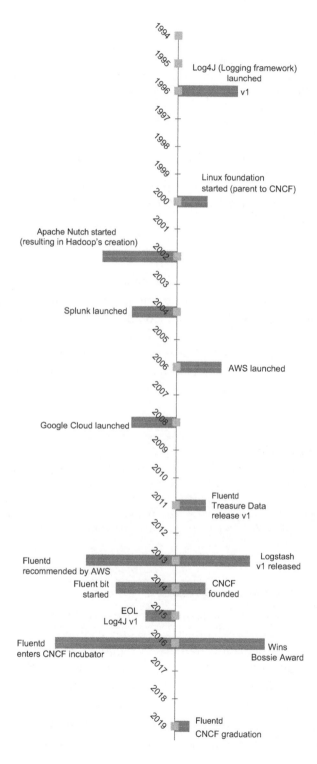

1994

1995 Log4J (Logging framework) launched

1996 v1

1997

1998

1999 Linux foundation started (parent to CNCF)

2000

Apache Nutch started (resulting in Hadoop's creation) 2001

2002

2003

Splunk launched 2004

2005

2006 AWS launched

2007

Google Cloud launched 2008

2009

2010

2011 Fluentd Treasure Data release v1

2012

Fluentd recommended by AWS 2013 Logstash v1 released

Fluent bit started 2014 CNCF founded

EOL Log4J v1 2015

Fluentd enters CNCF incubator 2016 Wins Bossie Award

2017

2018

2019 Fluentd CNCF graduation

Figure 1.6   Timeline of events that have influenced Fluentd

Treasure Data background

Treasure Data was founded in 2011 to deliver business value using big data technologies such as Hadoop. However, Sadayuki Furuhashi and the team at Treasure Data found they needed a tool to help them capture and ingest data and set about building Fluentd. It was made available as open source in October 2011. Since 2011, Treasure Data has developed several specialist areas such as Customer Information Systems and the Internet of Things (IoT).

Treasure Data has since been acquired by the microprocessor company Arm (and, in turn, Arm was acquired by NVIDIA) and spun out to be a business in the SoftBank Group Corp. However, Fluentd is still important to Treasure Data, and the team continues to be very active committers to GitHub for several important open source projects, including Fluentd and Fluent Bit.

1.8.2   CNCF

The next major event for Fluentd was its adoption by the Cloud Native Computing Foundation (CNCF). CNCF's existence was strongly influenced by Google in conjunction with the Linux Foundation to give Kubernetes a vendor-neutral home. Kubernetes is designed to run multiple containers across one or more servers, with containers hosting one or more different applications. Not to mention that containers can be started and torn down on the different servers as needed. From this, it is clear that corralling and routing log data is a critical challenge that can be answered well by Fluentd's capabilities.

Fluentd's history with the CNCF

Google donated Kubernetes to the CNCF and made it possible for competing enterprises to bring together and collaborate more effectively on Kubernetes and its ecosystem. Like CNCF's parent, the Linux Foundation, all its projects are open source and supported by many contributors. Fluentd was among the first projects after Kubernetes to come under the CNCF's governance and, as a result, was an early graduate.

1.8.3   *Relationship to major cloud vendors PaaS/IaaS*

Infrastructure as a Service (IaaS) and Platform as a Service (PaaS) solutions have influenced and been influenced by CNCF projects. It is only natural that those technologies have the best chance of being incorporated or supported by cloud platform offerings. When it comes to Fluentd, we have seen the major vendors (AWS, Azure, Google, Oracle, DigitalOcean, Alibaba, etc.) do one of the following:

- Directly leverage Fluentd for their own needs (e.g., Google, Oracle)
- Package it up as part of a larger offering (Bitnami, Google Stackdriver)
- Expose their various services to being accessible as inputs or outputs to their services (AWS—S3, RDS, CloudWatch, Beanstalk, etc.)

For example, AWS has output plugins for its storage services. AWS's CloudWatch solution can both receive and send log information to Fluentd. As we have seen, Google embraced Fluentd early on.

Beyond the IaaS cloud offerings, there is a range of specialist PaaS services for performing log analytics, ranging from Loggly (www.loggly.com) to Datadog (www.datadoghq.com). These vendors have provided plugins into Fluentd, so it becomes effortless for customers to route log data to these services.

All of this has contributed to driving plugin development for Fluentd (see figure 1.2) and organizations committing to support Fluentd. Plugin development particularly has propelled the Fluentd differentiation, with a rich catalog covering more sources and targets than just about any other competition (we will summarize the plugins later in this chapter and provide references with the latest and greatest plugins). With greater support and engagement, more organizations are attracted to working with Fluentd. As the saying goes, "many eyes make all bugs shallow," so more adoption typically means more eyes, resulting in a robust and reliable solution. This is, of course, one of the foundational arguments for open source software. If this kind of cycle continues long enough, we see solutions becoming de facto answers to common problems. While, at the time of this writing, Fluentd hasn't reached that stage yet, it is very much on its way.

1.9 Where can Fluentd and Fluent Bit be used?

Fluentd and Fluent Bit can be used or adapted to almost any situation, from running in containers to being deployed on IoT devices to mainframe solutions. As we have seen, Fluent Bit's footprint is small enough to operate on a vast range of IoT devices, which is reflected in part by Arm's acquisition of Treasure Data. Fluentd and Fluent Bit together cover at least 90% of the OS platforms in use today. As already discussed, Fluentd works well with cloud offerings, but it is not bound to the cloud and can work in more traditional virtualized or dedicated server deployments.

The more relevant question should be, will deploying Fluentd or Fluent Bit make your job easier? Should you use Fluent Bit or Fluentd?

Using Fluentd and Fluent Bit, from a basic laptop or desktop machine, to servers, physical and virtual, running Windows and Linux OSes, can be done without any worries. This means that as we get hands-on in the rest of the book, putting Fluentd into action should be possible. The possible exception is chapter 8, when we run Kubernetes and Docker, which will need a bit more power, but we're still talking about a midrange desktop or laptop. But understanding the limits of Fluentd can help beyond that.

1.9.1 Platform constraints

Beyond the OS and hardware, platform constraints are minimal. The most basic environment just needs to be able to run the Ruby engine. Ruby is supported by a range of standard package-based installations (yum, Homebrew, apt, RubyInstaller for Windows, to name a few). Making the installation for all the standard OSes is straightforward, and the package managers should help resolve any dependency issues. But for the less common environments, Ruby also provides a "from source" installation guide (www.ruby-lang.org/). If there isn't a prebuilt installation option for Fluentd itself—a rare situation given the prebuilt installers covered (RPM, Deb, MSI, and RubyGems)—then the Fluentd website (https://fluentd.org) provides details of how to achieve an installation from the source code.

Depending upon the configurations that need to be established, Fluentd has additional plugins that may be required. Fluentd plugins are typically deployed using Ruby-Gems (an open source package manager for Ruby components; https://rubygems.org/). Gems can be installed from a local location if you need stringent network controls.

Optionally, there are prebuilt solutions that can be deployed to Docker and Kubernetes if preferred. We will address the question of deployment of Fluentd as part of Kubernetes later in the book.

The last option—while we believe it is possible, we haven't heard of it being tried—is the creation of a platform-native binary of Fluentd through the use of GraalVM (https://www.graalvm.org/docs/getting-started/). GraalVM is a next-generation language virtual machine that incorporates Java (JVM) and several other language interpreter packs, including Ruby (https://github.com/oracle/truffleruby). But GraalVM also can create platform native binaries for Java and the other supported languages as well.

With Fluentd deployed, it needs to read one or more configuration files that tells Fluentd (typically installed as a daemon process in production) what it should do.

> **DEFINITION**   A *daemon* is a computer program that runs as a background process and is usually started and stopped by the operating system when it starts up and shuts down. This term is more commonly associated with Linux- and Unix-based operating systems. Often, applications designed to operate this way will have their name end with a *d*; for example, *syslogd* is a daemon that implements system logging (Syslog) in Linux. In Windows operating systems, these processes are referred to as *Windows services*.

So, any deployment location needs to be able to read the file and ideally allow updates to the file for Fluentd. Fluent Bit can use a configuration file or even interpret the configuration from a command-line parameter.

1.10 *Fluentd UI-based editing*

Fluentd does have a browser-delivered user interface. Figure 1.7 illustrates one of the UI screens to give a sense of what it is like.

When it comes to working with Fluentd's UI, it can perform a range of tasks such as

- Editing the configuration file
- Managing a Fluentd instance in terms of stopping and starting
- Getting plugins patched or installed
- Inspecting Fluentd's logs

We will focus directly on the configuration file for this book, as this will help explore the more complex nuances and is more mature than the UI. We'll take a brief tour of the UI in chapter 2 once we have completed the installation of Fluentd.

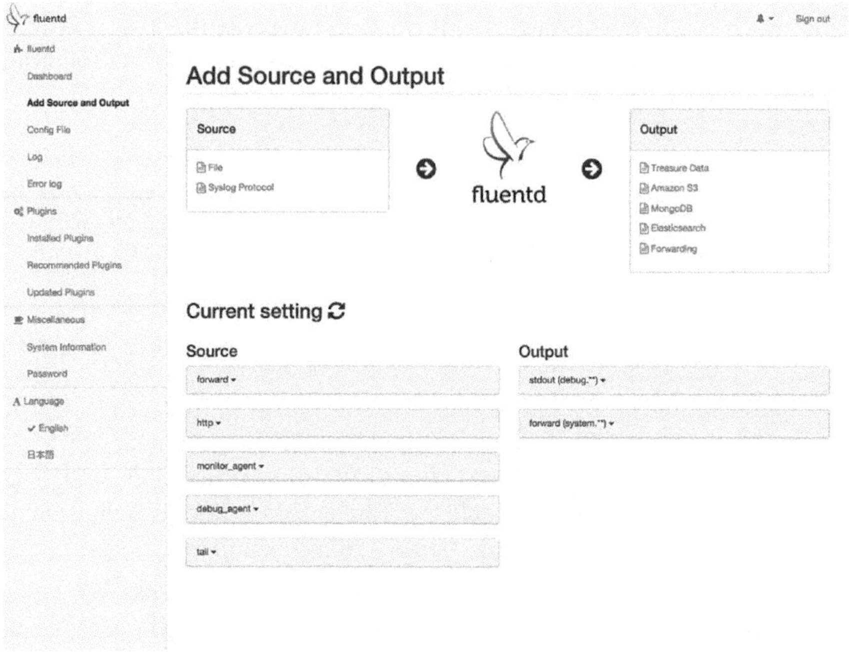

Figure 1.7 Part of the Fluentd UI

In addition to the web-based UI, there is an additional plugin for Microsoft's Visual Studio Code that will help with syntax highlighting when editing configuration files. The plugin can be used to help address typical issues like missing brackets. This plugin can be downloaded from within Visual Studio Code or from http://mng.bz/ GOeA. Other editors, such as Sublime Text, also have open source packages/plugins to support the syntax editing of the Fluentd configuration file.

UI for Fluent Bit?

Given the intention to make Fluent Bit's footprint as small as possible, incorporating a UI would go against that principle. Typical Fluent Bit uses are to source the log events and forward them to the point of aggregation where more processing of events can happen (e.g., Fluentd or a log analytics tool). This means the configurations should be comparatively simple, and the need for a UI is limited. The case for an integrated UI would go against the minimized footprint goal.

1.11 Plugins

As mentioned earlier, Fluentd's plugins in the breadth and depth of coverage outweigh most if not all competition. We cannot cover every possible plugin in the following chapters, so we'll focus on those that help illustrate core ideas and represent cases that most Fluentd deployments are likely to encounter.

But given the scope of plugins, it is worth getting a sense of what is available and what could be achieved. Fluentd plugins can be grouped into the following categories, and with each category, we have provided some examples:

- Inputs
  - *File storage*—AWS S3, text files (HTTP log files, etc.)
  - *Data(base) source*—MongoDB, MySQL, generic SQL (for all ANSI SQL DBs)
  - *Event sources*—AWS Kinesis, Kafka, AWS CloudWatch, GCP Pub/Sub, RabbitMQ
  - *OS*—System, HTTP Endpoint, dstat, SNMP
  - *App servers*—IIS (Internet Information Services), WebSphere, Tomcat
- Outputs
  - *File storage*—AWS S3, Google Cloud Storage, File
  - *Database storage*—BigQuery, MongoDB, InfluxDB, MySQL, SQL Server
  - *Event storage*—Kafka, Google Stackdriver, AWS CloudWatch, Prometheus
  - *Log analytics tools*—Splunk, Datadog, Elasticsearch
  - *Notifications*—Slack, Mail, HipChat, Twitter, Twilio, PagerDuty
- Log/Event Manipulation (parsers, filters, and formatters)
  - *Map*—Log format mapper
  - *Numeric Monitor*—Generates stats relating to logs
  - *Text to JSON*
  - *Key/Value Parsing*
  - *GeoIP*—Translating IP addresses to geographic location based on published information (for more information on the use of GeoIP, see the liveBook version of *Securing DevOps* by Julien Vehent (Manning, 2018) at http://mng.bz/raJJ.
  - *JWT*—Working with JSON Web Tokens (more background on this can be found in the liveBook version of *OpenID Connect in Action* by Prabath Siriwardena (Manning, 2022) at http://mng.bz/VlMy.
  - *Redaction*—The masking of data so sensitive data values can't be seen by those not authorized to do so
  - *Formatters*—The means to lay out the data into different structures and potentially different notations (e.g., XML to JSON)
- Storage
  - *Caching*—Redis, Memcached
  - *Persistent storage*—Local file, SQL databases, S3 Block storage

- *Service Discovery*—Configuration to find other nodes that understand Fluentd's comms mechanisms

NOTE A complete list of available Fluentd plugins is managed at www.fluentd .org/plugins/all.

1.12 How Fluentd can be used to make operational tasks easier

Throughout this chapter, we have examined a number of the scenarios and use cases that Fluentd can help with. As we progress through the book, we will introduce scenarios and look at increasing complexity.

1.12.1 Actionable log events

Rather than waiting until log events are collected together before anything is done with the content, it is possible to create configurations so that as they are received, they can be processed. Such processing could include filtering to find the events that require immediate attention. If a system logs an event that typically only occurs shortly before the solution fails—for example, the OS goes into a panic state (for more on kernel panic, see https://wiki.osdev.org/Kernel_Panic)—then as soon as that event is detected, we could send a message to someone responsible for handling such events via near real-time channels like PagerDuty or Slack (we will illustrate the Slack scenario in chapter 4). But actionable log events can easily extend further, such as triggering a script to perform automated remediation (e.g., purging or archiving older log files so storage isn't exhausted).

1.12.2 Making logs more meaningful

The actionable event can also be extended to provide a means by which log events can be made more meaningful. In larger, long-lived organizations, there are legacy solutions that are still business-critical (they are typically very large and embody lots of logic to ensure compliance to requirements that very few people understand). As a result, the replacement cost can be huge, and no one wants to take on the risk of making modifications, even to improve log messages to make support easier. But such problems can be addressed; those innocent-looking log messages that are harbingers of doom if someone doesn't execute some remediation soon can be modified to have things like error codes attached. Ops people can then easily find the operational protocol.

The application of meaning can go further; some logs will have structures that don't align to standard formats, such as JSON and XML. But Fluentd can be used to impose structure quickly and early, so downstream, the log events can be handled more efficiently. If an application accidentally logs sensitive data, the sooner such information is removed or masked, the better. Otherwise, all downstream log-processing solutions have to implement a far more stringent security setup, because they will be receiving sensitive data such as credit card data (PCI compliance), personal data (General Data Protection Regulation), or data subject to similar legislation. If such issues become a problem, and the source of their logs can't be fixed, Fluentd can filter out or modify the log event to mask such content.

1.12.3 Polyglot environments

Over the last 10 years, there has been an explosion of different programming languages. As a result, we often talk about *polyglot* environments where many different languages are used in an end-to-end solution; for example, R or Python may be used to extract deep meaning from data, while web interfaces could be written in JavaScript. Backend solutions could be Java, Scala, Clojure, dot Net (.NET), and PHP. Thick client applications working with the same backend could be written with C#, VB.Net, or Swift. In these types of environments, we need an agnostic solution of the implementation language of applications. Fluentd provides this, but many languages have libraries that allow log events to be passed in an optimized manner directly to Fluentd.

1.12.4 Multiple targets

The multiple targets issue embodies the fact that it is common to have teams dedicated to specific tasks in larger organizations, such as information security. Different teams want to use different tools to support their specialism—for example, algorithms are particularly good at detecting patterns indicating malicious security activities.

1.12.5 Controlling log data costs

Log events, like any operational data, need storage and consume network capacity when moved, which results in costs. That cost can be noticeable when large volumes of uncompressed or unfiltered text exit a cloud provider's network and are communicated over a business's internet connection. Yet, at the same time, we don't want to be overly parsimonious with logging; otherwise, we will never appreciate what is happening. Fluentd can help with this by filtering and storing some log events locally where the log events have limited value. But the log information that can be of further help can get sent onward to a central location. Not only that, but the transmission can also be optimized through compression mechanisms (bulk log events can be highly compressed).

1.12.6 Logs to metrics

Previously we introduced the three pillars of observability (logs, traces, metrics). In some cases, we want to get metrics, such as how many occurrences of a log event occur, or which process is alive or dead by looking at logs for signs of life (i.e., whether events have been created). With the plugins, it is possible to generate such measures and share such data with Prometheus and Grafana.

This can be extended through the possibility of Fluentd monitoring its own deployed nodes—when you get into complex distributed use cases, this can also be highly desirable. After all, Fluentd is just another piece of software and is therefore as vulnerable to bugs as any other code.

1.12.7 *Rapid operational consolidation*

Company mergers and acquisitions can drive the need to consolidate operational resources, such as operational teams. Such consolidation will happen quicker than any process to consolidate major IT systems. We can easily direct log data to current operational support team tools to monitor and reduce the time and effort to absorb new systems into the operations organization through log unification.

Summary

- Key concepts influencing modern thinking around monitoring come from ideas such as Google's four golden signals and the three pillars of observability.
- Log analytics differs from log unification by focusing on a platform to mine the log data. In contrast, log unification is about bringing logs together and directing the content to necessary tools.
- Fluentd and Fluent Bit started as open source initiatives from Treasure Data before coming under the governance of the CNCF.
- Fluentd and Fluent Bit are not aligned to any analytics platform. Considering the association with CNCF has helped the adoption of Fluentd by IaaS and PaaS vendors as either a part of a monitoring product or service or as supporting connectivity between Fluentd and their product.
- Fluentd has seen strong adoption in the microservices space, but it can fit equally well with a legacy landscape.
- Fluentd has a broad range of plugins available and a framework that enables custom plugins to be developed when needed.
- Fluent Bit trades off the highly pluggable nature for a tiny optimized footprint.
- Both Fluentd and Fluent Bit can support the majority of platforms with prebuilt artifacts. Both are open source solutions; it is possible to build the kernel and plugins on just about any conceivable platform.
- The application of logging is wide-ranging and offers value during the software's entire life cycle.
- Fluentd supports a wide range of use cases, from debugging distributed solutions to operational monitoring.
- Understand how Fluentd fits into the EFK software stack, and what the differences are between the ELK and EFK software stacks.

2

Concepts, architecture, and deployment of Fluentd

This chapter covers

- Outlining Fluentd's architecture and core concepts
- Reviewing prerequisites and deployment of Fluentd, Fluent Bit, and Fluent UI
- Executing basic configurations of Fluentd and Fluent Bit
- Introducing configuration file structure

Chapter 1 looked at the theory, industry trends, and use cases that Fluentd can help us with. This chapter discusses how Fluentd works, including deploying and running the simplest of configurations to implement the traditional developer's "Hello World."

2.1 Architecture and core concepts

When you're driving a car, it is a lot easier when you have some basic appreciation of how the vehicle is powered (e.g., gas, diesel, electric, liquefied petroleum gas). The mental models that come with such understanding mean we can learn what to expect—whether we can expect to hear the engine rev, whether it's possible for the engine to stall, and how the gears work (if there are any). For the same reason, before we start working with Fluentd and Fluent Bit, it is worth investing time in understanding how these tools work. Based on this, we should run through some of the building blocks of Fluentd that will help with the mental models.

2.1.1 *The makeup of a log event*

Chapter 1 introduced the concept of log events. Understanding how Fluentd defines a log event is the most crucial thing in appreciating how Fluentd works, so let's look at its composition. Each log event is managed as a single JSON object comprised of three mandatory, nonrepeating elements, as described here and shown in figure 2.1:

- *Tag*—Each log event has a tag associated with it. The tags are typically linked to the source initially through the configuration but can be subsequently manipulated within the configuration. Fluentd can apply conditional operations (routing, filtering, etc.) to the log events as necessary by using the tags. When using the HTTP interface, the tag can be defined in the call, as we will see.
- *Timestamp*—This is derived from the log information or is applied by the input plugin. This ensures that the events are kept in series, an essential consideration when unifying multiple log sources and potentially trying to understand the sequence of events across components. This data is held as nanoseconds from epoch (1 January 1970 00:00:00 UTC).
- *Record*—The record is the core event information after separating out the time. This means we can address the log content without worrying about locating the timestamp for the event and the tag needed for basic controls, as we'll see later in the book. This provides an immediate benefit; whenever a log event is passed in from a Fluentd-aware adaptor, we can avoid initial parsing for the time. It is

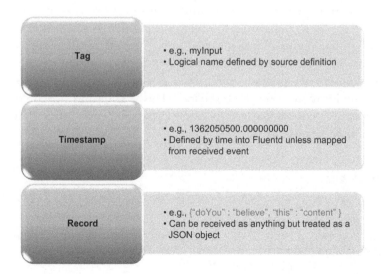

| Tag | • e.g., myInput
• Logical name defined by source definition |

| Timestamp | • e.g., 1362050500.000000000
• Defined by time into Fluentd unless mapped from received event |

| Record | • e.g., {"doYou" : "believe", "this" : "content" }
• Can be received as anything but treated as a JSON object |

Figure 2.1
Makeup of log event

possible to translate the record into further detailed structures to make it easier to process. We see how to apply more meaning to the data later in the book.

Once captured, other plugins can then work with the existing tags to modify, add, and extend them as necessary. When working with the tags, they can have wildcards and other logic applied to them. For example, if we have several separate logs associated with one solution (call them subsystems 1, 2, and 3), we could tag each log file as App .Subsystem1, App.Subsystem2, and App.Subsystem3. The processing of the logs could then be addressed by using a wildcard (e.g., App.*). We can set the filter to be more specific for handling only a specific subsystem's log events (e.g., App.Subsystem2).

2.1.2 *Handling time*

Given the importance of timestamps in the logs, all systems that need to work together must report against a common clock/time. In addition, the time must *not* be subject to movements for daylight savings. Without this, every time the clocks go back, logs will get out of sync. When clocks are moved forward, the logs will see an irregular period of no log events being recorded. This can trigger anomalies if any time-based analysis (analysis for event throughput, measurement of meant time between errors, watching for heartbeat events, etc.) is performed.

This consideration is compounded by the fact that systems may be working together across multiple time zones. Therefore, all systems need to run against a collectively agreed upon time. The typical solution to this is to link systems to Coordinated Universal Time (UTC). However, when we need to have millisecond precision on the timestamps across multiple servers to ensure correct order, something is required to keep them in sync.

Time synchronization is handled by linking servers to a common time source and then using a protocol to request a time to align. This protocol is known as *Network Time Protocol* (*NTP*). When configuring a server, it is highly recommended to ensure that NTP is configured. Many technologies and service providers offer a free standard NTP service to synchronize with. There is a limit to this; the duration for the current time to reach different servers can differ by a few milliseconds or nanoseconds (depending on the location of the NTP service). This is known as *clock* or *time skew*. Despite best efforts, log entries may very occasionally appear out of step when aggregating across multiple servers.

NTP and clock skew

More specific detail on NTP and clock skew can be found at www.ietf.org/rfc/rfc1305 .txt.

Most operating systems provide an NTP client process (or daemon) that can be activated (if not defaulted to be active) and configured to sync with an NTP server. The closer the NTP server, the lower the risk of skew.

2.1.3   *Architecture of Fluentd*

Fluentd's operations are prescribed by a configuration file (which may include other configuration files, but this will be addressed later in the book). The configuration file describes how and, in some cases, when a plugin should be applied. A good number of plugins are incorporated into the core of Fluentd, so they require no additional installation—for example, the tail plugin that operates a bit like the Linux `tail -f` command. For those less familiar with Linux/Unix utilities, the `tail -f` command provides the means to see on the console what is being added to a file as it occurs.

In chapter 1, we introduced the idea of plugins and illustrated them with some examples. Before we build on this and examine the types of plugins in more detail, we should clarify a point of terminology. If you read the Fluentd documentation, it refers to *directives*; these can overlap with plugin types. But the relationship between types of plugins and a directive is not one-to-one in nature, as plugins can have supporting or helper relationships and therefore not a directive. Later in the chapter, as we look at the "Hello World" example, we'll see the directives and plugins, and how Fluentd knows where to pick up a configuration file.

The following list focuses on the core plugin types and where they map to directives we have identified. In addition to this, we have highlighted the more common plugin interrelationships:

- *Input*—In terms of the configuration file, the input plugins will correlate to a *source* directive. An input can leverage *parser* plugins that can take the raw log text and assert structural meaning. For example, they can extract key values from the message text, such as log event classifications needed for later processing. Inputs range from files to data stores to direct API integrations.
- *Output*—As a type of plugin, these provide us with the means to store (e.g., file, database) or connect to another system (including another Fluentd node) to pass on the log events. The output plugin aligns with the *match* directive within the configuration file—something that is not obvious at this stage but, as we illustrate the use of Fluentd, will become more apparent. The output plugin can leverage *formatter, filter, buffer,* and *service discovery* plugins. The more generic input plugins have an equivalent output.
- *Buffer*—The buffer plugin type focuses on the batching up and temporary caching of log events so that the I/O workload can be optimized. This issue will be addressed in more depth as we progress through the book.
- *Filter*—This plugin type applies rules through which we can control where log events can go. This plugin is engaged with the *output* plugin.
- *Parser*—This plugin's task is to take the log event, extract key values, and apply additional needed structure to the captured content. This is key when taking content from sources such as log files, which will start effectively as a single line of text. This can range from *regex* and *grok* to domain-specific logic.
- *Formatter*—When content is output, it needs to be produced so that the data can be handled by the consuming component. For example, structure the content

so it can be consumed by Prometheus or Grafana, which expect specific structures or a humanly readable message for PagerDuty. As a result, the formatter plugin gets used by the output plugins within the *match* directives.

- *Storage*—As we will see shortly, the performance and efficiency of Fluentd is a tradeoff with the way we need to handle log events. Storing log events means we can keep the events (often temporarily) until they need to be processed. Temporary storage, such as caches, can give us performance gains, but at the risk of losing the event in a failure. Some storage options are therefore more durable to mitigate such a risk. We will use storage plugins in several different ways throughout the book.
- *Service discovery*—When this plugin is used, it typically works in tandem with the output plugin. Its purpose is to help connect to other Fluentd nodes, as we will explore later in the book. This type of plugin addresses how the target servers are identified/found within a network, from a list of server IPs in a reloadable config to using specific parts of a DNS record.

In figure 2.2, we represent the core Fluentd building blocks, along with supporting elements that exist to help the extension, adoption, and use of Fluentd. Note that the

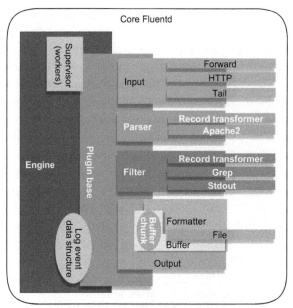

Figure 2.2 View of the Fluentd architecture illustrating the core building blocks and optional support resources available depending on your context

specific plugins implemented in the diagram are only a subset of those built in the standard deployment and a fraction of those deployable and used by Fluentd. As we progress through the book, all of these building blocks will be examined in depth, from configurations to tune the engine to how the plugin base provides the foundations for controlling all plugin behavior. But appreciating the different blocks and their relationships will help from the outset.

2.1.4 *Fluent configuration execution order*

There are a couple of essential rules that need to be understood when working with Fluentd and Fluent Bit configuration files. While we will explore these points in more depth with illustrations in the book, mainly when we address routing in chapter 5, these points are fundamental to the design and implementation of a Fluent configuration, so it is worth calling them out now:

- *Log events are consumed only once* within a Fluentd or Fluent Bit instance unless Fluentd is told to explicitly copy the log event (using a feature within the core of Fluentd, which we will address later in the book). This sequencing is illustrated in figure 2.3.

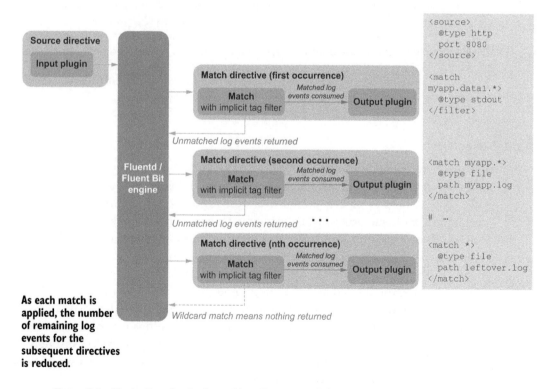

Figure 2.3 Illustration of order impact in a Fluentd configuration

- *The order in which operations are defined within a configuration file is significant.* The first directive that matches an event will become the consumer unless that event is copied. Therefore, as a general practice
  - When you want all log events to undergo common operations, define those directives early in the configuration, but copy them for later targeted directives.
  - Catch-all directives should be late in the configuration.
  - Targeted directives should precede the catch-all directives.

- *Fluentd by default is single-threaded.* This helps to ensure that time series is not compromised. Fluentd can be configured to run in a concurrent manner (multiprocess rather than threaded) by changing the configuration, and we will look at that later in chapter 7. It does mean that if you create a complex series of log event operations, it's possible that Fluentd cannot process events as fast as they are created. This means a bottleneck has been made. There are strategies for avoiding this, but this will further complicate the whole process.

Single vs. Multithreaded

The challenges of multithreading are varied, from coordination overhead when more threads are running than processor cores to mutual thread-locks (two threads waiting for each other). When it comes to time-series events, keeping things in sequence or correcting order is important. If not carefully applied, multithreading can create race conditions that may lead to events getting out of sequence. To better understand race conditions, an excellent source is https://devopedia.org/race-condition -software.

2.1.5   Directives

Previously, we mentioned directives within Fluentd, and it is easy to mix up directives and plugins. Directives provide a framework for grouping plugins to achieve a logical task, such as outputting log events to a destination. You'll see that directives are declared in the same way as XML elements by being started and ended with angle brackets. It is possible to supply attributes within the element, such as tag filtering, as is the case with of the `match` example. Within the directive, we then identify the plugin and supply its configuration as name-value pairs. As we get to more sophisticated examples, you'll see that we can nest things, including helper plugins.

If a command or plugin must be called directly by the logic that makes Fluentd process a stream of log events, then it is a directive. While this is very abstract at this stage, the idea and subtlety will become more apparent as we progress through the book and its examples. As figure 2.4 illustrates, we can visualize the directives, plugins, and helper plugins that appear in configuration files.

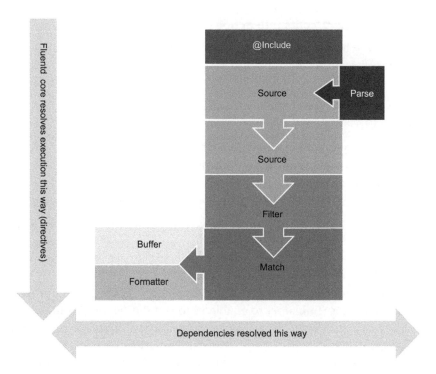

Figure 2.4   Relationships between Fluentd directives in the context of Fluentd's execution order (central column—Source, Filter, Match) and native plugins (parser, buffer, formatter)

The directives illustrated in figure 2.4 are summarized in table 2.1. We will examine each of these directives in depth in part 2 of this book.

Table 2.1   Fluentd directives

Directive	Description
source	The *source* directive tells Fluentd to receive/source log events, as we've just seen.
match	This is about matching log events to other operations, including the output of log events.
filter	This controls which events should be handled by one or more processes—typically referred to as a pipeline.
@include	This tells Fluentd to bring in other configuration files to assemble a complete set of operations, just as import or include statements do in conventional code.
label	The label provides a grouping mechanism for log events, which provides significantly more capability than just using tags.
system	This tells Fluentd how to configure and behave internally (e.g., the setting of log levels).

2.1.6   *Putting timing requirements into action*

If you want to see how much you have absorbed so far, try answering these questions. The answers follow these questions.

1   What are the three key elements of a log event within Fluentd/Fluent Bit?
2   What is the recommended time zone to connect time servers with?

ANSWERS

1   We introduced these in section 2.1.1; the elements of a log event are
   - *Timestamp*—Representation of the log event occurrence
   - *Record*—The body of the log event
   - *Tag*—Associated with each log entry and used to route the log event

2   As you may recall, in section 2.1.2, we recommend linking your NTP servers using UTC.

2.2   *Deployment of Fluentd*

In this section, we will deploy Fluentd and tools such as the LogGenerator (sometimes referred to as the LogSimulator) to enable us to run the "Hello World" scenario and the subsequent examples and exercises. All the configuration files for Fluentd and the simulator can be found in the book's GitHub repository (http://mng.bz/Axyo). Within the repository, each chapter has its own set of folders. Note that the configuration files in the repository will differ slightly from those shown in the configuration examples in the book, so they can include helpful additional comments. We assume that the complete code and configuration samples will be downloaded either from Manning or via our GitHub repository for the book. Each chapter folder contains subfolders for code, configurations, and solutions. The LogGenerator (more on this later) has been downloaded from GitHub (https://github.com/mp3 monster/LogGenerator) and copied into the root folder for the chapters (e.g., the root shown in figure 2.5).

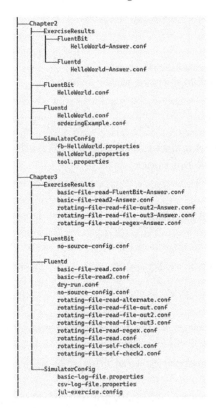

Figure 2.5   Directory structure used in the book for examples and solutions

NOTE   As Fluentd, Fluent Bit, and the LogSimulator are used throughout the book, we have incorporated the instructions within the chapter. In later chapters, where we use other utilities and products for one or possibly two chapters, we have provided the instructions in appendix A.

2.2.1 *Deploying Fluentd for the book's examples*

We already established in chapter 1 that Fluentd and Fluent Bit are both very capable when it comes to the means to deploy onto diverse platforms. That creates an interesting challenge for this book. Do we describe deploying Fluentd and Fluent Bit onto the widest variety of platforms or focus on just one? Do we make you work with Docker and bundle everything up in an image?

The approach we took in this book was to support Windows first; this is predicated on the fact that in trying, prototyping, and experimenting with Fluentd, you are likely using a desktop or laptop computer rather than an enterprise server. Windows is the most dominant OS on desktop and laptop machines, so it makes sense to focus on that environment.

However, to make it easier to take the guidance in this book to enterprise servers, or if you're fortunate enough to have a Mac or you're a committed Linux fan and have installed your favorite flavor of Linux OS, we have highlighted differences between Linux and Windows. The majority of instructions will include the Linux equivalent. Those working with Linux or macOS will most likely know that Linux is just the kernel and that the layers above this, such as the UI layer, and installation managers differ across the Linux flavors. This means you may need to tweak the commands provided to work on your particular flavor of OS.

Docker image

It is possible to also download a prepared Docker image made available via Docker Hub (https://hub.docker.com/r/fluent/fluentd/) or directly from the Fluentd GitHub site (https://github.com/fluent/fluentd-docker-image). For production environments, this approach is worth considering and is explored further in chapter 8. In most of the book, utilizing Docker will simply add additional effort unless you're entirely conversant with using Docker.

2.2.2 *Deployment considerations for Fluentd*

When considering the deployment of Fluentd into production, we need to consider *volume metrics*—that is, the amount of log data needing to be captured, filtered, routed, and stored. In part 3 of the book, we will focus on the ability of Fluentd and Fluent Bit to be scaled out and distributed. But to start with, let us assume that we are working in an environment that does not demand such levels of scaling. Even in a simple deployment, we should be aware that the computing effort for log processing should be less than the computing effort for the core application. Remember, each time log events are stored or transmitted, the operation generates a lot of I/O activity, which carries a computational overhead. If you are familiar with low-level computer operations, you will appreciate that every process comes with an overhead:

- Every network message is topped and tailed with routing, verification, and details such as the size of the message.

- Every file write requires the use of the hardware to locate a chunk of physical storage that can be used, record the details of the block of storage used, and mechanically position the writing device for physical media.

The more we can group log events in a cache and transmit them as a block, the more efficient the use of resources is. Like all things in life, there is a tradeoff. We cache before writing to storage, which means the data is slower reaching the end of the log event processing. The longer data is working through a process, the more likely that a power loss or component failure will result in data loss. For this chapter, we only need to make sure our environment has enough resources to run; considerations of performance versus the risk of data loss aren't necessary.

2.2.3   *Fluentd minimum footprint*

Fluentd resource requirements are minimal (see table 2.2) by modern machine specs, but are worth noting when dealing with small footprint setups.

Table 2.2   Fluentd minimum hardware footprint

RubyInstaller size	130 MB
Ruby installed storage needs (with DevKit)	(80 MB for basic Ruby, plus 820 MB for the DevKit 1 GB)
Memory required	~20 MB
Fluentd additional storage	300 KB
Ruby minimum version	Ruby 2.x (against Fluentd v1.x)

2.2.4   *Simple deployment of Ruby*

To get ready to run Fluentd, we need to first install Ruby. This is best done with the latest stable version of Ruby using your operating system's package framework. Links to the different installation packages can be found via www.ruby-lang.org. For Windows, we do this by going to the Downloads page that has links to the relevant artifact. For Windows, we get taken to https://rubyinstaller.org to retrieve the RubyInstaller. When we get to chapter 8, we will need to do a bit of development, so we should install the software development kit (SDK) version of Ruby (shown as Ruby+DevKit on the website).

Once downloaded, run the installer; it will then take you through the steps to define the preferred location, and it will also ask if you want to install Mysys—say yes. Mysys is needed for RubyGems with a low-level C dependency, such as plugins interacting with the OS. Several development-related tools, such as MinGW, allow Ruby development to use Windows C native libraries. This means we should have Mysys, and we recommend taking the complete installation with MinGW to support any possible development requirements later.

> **NOTE**   Additional information about DevKit is available in the liveBook version of *Rails4 in Action* by Ryan Bigg, et al. (Manning, 2015) at http://mng.bz/ZzAR.

The installer should add Ruby to the Windows PATH environment variable. (Appendix A provides details on the PATH environment variable.) When checking, you need to confirm that the bin folder for Ruby is included. If the Ruby directory path is not in the PATH environment variable, we need to follow the instructions in appendix A to add the full Ruby path. Once set, it should be possible to execute the command ruby -version, and Ruby will display the installed version once the path has been amended.

> **NOTE** It is worth noting an open source package manager for Windows called Chocolatey (https://chocolatey.org/), which feels more like a Linux package manager. Chocolatey can be used as an alternative means to install Ruby.

For Linux users, all the major Linux OSes have a relevant package manager with a recent stable installation—from Homebrew for macOS to apt, yum, pkg, and others. When there is an option, as with Windows, it is worth installing everything to support the development activities undertaken in chapter 9. Like Windows, we need to confirm the path has been correctly set using the instructions in appendix A. We also can verify Ruby using the same command, ruby -version. In addition, we need to verify whether the package manager has included the RubyGems package manager. Check this by running the command gems help. This will return the gems help information or fail. If this fails, then the following steps are needed (replacing x.y.z in the next steps with the latest stable version):

```
wget http://production.cf.rubygems.org/rubygems/rubygems-x.y.z.tgz
tar xvf rubygems*
ruby setup.rb
```

2.2.5 *Simple deployment of Fluentd*

Fluentd can be installed in a variety of different ways. Treasure Data (introduced in chapter 1) provides a Windows installer for Fluentd, but it should be noted that the installer introduces a prefix of *td* into file and folder names. The Treasure Data installer also includes additional plugins not included in the standard installer.

There is a wealth of ways to install Fluentd and its dependencies with different benefits and nuances. We will install Fluentd using RubyGems for the following reasons:

- Gems package installer is platform-neutral, so the installation process is the same for Linux, Windows, and many other environments.
- Gems are the easiest way to install plugins not included in the core of Fluentd.
- We have Gems installed (needed to help install Ruby dependencies), so we can keep our approach consistent.

To install Fluentd this way, we simply need to run the following command:

```
gem install fluentd
```

As long as you have connectivity to https://rubygems.org/, then relevant Gems, including dependencies, will safely download and install. These sites may need to be accessed through a proxy server or a local gems server in enterprise environments. The installation can be tested by running the following command:

```
fluentd --help
```

This will display the help information for Fluentd. It should also be possible to see the Fluentd and other gems installed in the deployment location `lib\ruby\gems\2.7.0\gems\` (and the equivalent path for other OSes).

In addition to the core Fluentd, the installation also provides some secondary tools, some of which we will use throughout the book. The major tools provided are summarized in table 2.3

Table 2.3   Fluentd support tools provided with an installation

Fluentd tool	Tool description
`fluent-binlog-reader`	Fluentd can create binary log files (giving compression and performance benefits)—for example, when file caching. This utility can be used to read the file and generate readable content.
`fluent-ca-generate`	This is a utility for creating basic (self-signed) certificates that can be used to encrypt communications between Fluentd/Fluent Bit nodes.
`fluent-cat`	The `fluent-cat` tool provides a means to inject a single log message into Fluentd; it does require the forward plugin to be configured. For example: `echo '{"message":"hello"}' | fluent-cat debug.log --host localhost --port 24224` This command would send a log event to the local Fluentd instance configured to listen on port 24224 using the forward plugin. We can use this to help test the routing, filtering, and output steps. But, crucially, it does not allow us to check the input plugin configurations (hence the LogSimulator).
`fluent-debug`	This is a utility to help with remote debugging, used in conjunction with the Ruby tooling.
`fluent-gem`	This is essentially an alias to the Ruby `gem` command, which will list all the gems available.
`fluent-plugin-config-format`	This provides the means to interrogate a plugin to obtain details of the configuration parameters the plugin will support. The output could be characterized as a README document. As some plugin implementations may support multiple types of plugin (e.g., input and output), it is necessary to specify the plugin type. For example (on both Windows and Linux), the command `fluent-plugin-config-format -f txt input tail` will retrieve the text format of the tail output plugin's configuration details. This utility is ideal for being included within a continuous integration pipeline for custom-built plugins, as it can generate documentation in several formats.
`fluent-plugin-generate`	This generates a code skeleton for plugin development. The template includes a Gem file, README, stubbed Ruby code for the plugin, and a skeleton test framework.

A COUPLE OF OS DIFFERENCES

Linux- and Unix-based operating systems support a framework of *interrupt signals.* These signals can be sent to an application to control their behavior. Perhaps the most commonly known of these is SIGHUP. Fluentd can use these signals to trigger operations such as reloading the configuration file without needing to restart. Table 2.4 summarizes the essential interrupts and their impact.

Table 2.4   Linux signals and how Fluentd will react to them

Linux signal	Effect on Fluentd
SIGINT or SIGTERM	This tells Fluentd to gracefully shut down so that it clears everything in memory, and any file buffering is left in a clean state. If another process is calling Fluentd, it is better to stop that process first, as it can prevent the shutdown from completing.
SIGUSR1	This tells Fluentd to ensure that all of its cached values, including its log events, are flushed to storage and then refresh the file handles to the file storage. This is then repeated based on a system environment variable called *flush_interval*.
SIGUSR2	Secures and gracefully handles the reloading of the configuration. It can be considered graceful as it ensures any cache is safely stored before reloading the configuration, so no log events are lost.
SIGHUP	This interrupt is most known for forcing a configuration to reload. It performs the same operations as SIGUSR2 but also flushes its internal logs, so no internal log information is lost.
SIGCONT	This signal will get Fluentd to record its internal status—thread information, memory allocation, and so on.

Sending Linux kill commands to a Fluentd process—for example, `kill -s USR1 3699`, where `3699` represents the process ID for Fluentd—will result in Fluentd interpreting the signal as a SIGUSR1 signal. At present, there is no Windows-equivalent way to send these signals, although several change requests have been submitted to the project for such features.

FILE HANDLES

Within a Linux file system, the number of file handles that can be used at any one time can be controlled, unlike Windows, which has these limits driven entirely by the OS version and architecture (e.g., 32 or 64 bit). Additionally, Linux uses file handles for real files, but these handles also represent things like network connections. *The default number of file handles can be restrictive for Fluentd.* It is not unusual to adjust the number of file handles held open in production environments. Manipulating the file-handle limits can be done by editing configuration files or using the Linux `ulimit` command. More detail can be found at https://linuxhint.com/linux_ulimit_command/. The number of file handles shouldn't be a problem for the examples and scenarios provided, but when ramping up the volume in a production context, it is something to be aware of. The correct number of file handles depends on the number and speed of files being written, the number of network ports being supported, and so on.

2.2.6   *Deploying a log generator*

Ideally, we want to prove our configuration for input plugins and confirm configuration for things like log rotation. We want a configuration-driven utility that can continuously send log events. We have one available at https://github.com/mp3monster/ LogGenerator and will be using this in the subsequent chapters. This tool provides several helpful features for us:

- Take an existing log file, replay the log events from an existing log file, write them with current timestamps, and write the logs with the same time intervals as the logs had when originally written.
- Take a test log file that describes the time gap and log body, and play it back with the correct intervals between events.
- Write log files based on a pattern, meaning different log formats can be generated.
- Send the logs via the Java logging framework to simulate an application using a logging framework.

The LogGenerator GitHub repository includes extended documentation on how the tool can be used. The utility is written using Groovy, which means at its heart is Java and the use of standard Java classes and libraries. Groovy adds several conveniences over Java. Specifically, it executes as a script to keep development quick and easy, meaning tweaking it for your own needs is easy; it includes some convenience classes that make working with REST and JSON very easy. Not everyone wants to install Groovy or modify the script. As a result, we have taken advantage of Groovy's relationship with Java to compile and package it to a JAR file, making it possible to be executed without installing Groovy if preferred. The JAR is available to download from GitHub as well.

JAVA INSTALLATION

To install Java, you can either use a package manager or retrieve and download from www.java.com/en/download/. The tool's implementation has been done so that Java 8 or later will work. Still, you need the Java Development Kit (JDK) rather than the Java Runtime Environment (JRE). Once Java is downloaded and installed, you need to ensure that the correct version is set up in your PATH environment variable and JAVA_HOME. We assume that you do not have any other applications using Java and are dependent on a different Java version. If this is the case, we recommend writing a script to set these variables each time you start a new console to run the LogGenerator; this approach is illustrated for the Groovy setup. You can check which version of Java is in use with the command java -version.

GROOVY INSTALLATION

If you want to use the LogSimulator from the prepared JAR, you can skip this section, but if you want to use the Groovy version, see how it works, or modify it, you'll need the following steps. With the prerequisite Java installed, we can now install Groovy (download from https://groovy.apache.org/download.html or install it using a package manager). As with Java, you also want Groovy to be set on the PATH environment variable and GROOVY_HOME setup. You can confirm whether Groovy is suitably installed using the command `groovy --version`. The following code fragments are example scripts for ensuring environment variables are set up. This is the Windows setup:

```
set JAVA_HOME=C:\Program Files\Java\jdk1.8.0_221
set PATH=%JAVA_HOME%\bin;%PATH%
echo Set Shell to Java
java -version
set GROOVY_HOME=C:\Program Files\Groovy-3.0.2\
set PATH=%GROOVY_HOME%\bin;%PATH%
echo Set Shell to Groovy
groovy --version
```

The Linux version of this script would be

```
export JAVA_HOME=/usr/lib/jdk1.8.0_221
export PATH=$JAVA_HOME/bin:$PATH
echo Set Shell to Java
java -version
export GROOVY_HOME=/usr/lib/Groovy-3.0.2
export PATH=$GROOVY_HOME/bin;$PATH
echo Set Shell to Groovy
groovy --version
```

The simulator uses a properties file to control its behavior and uses a file that describes a series of log entries to replay. We will use this in later chapters to see how log rotation and other behaviors can work. Each book chapter has a folder containing the relevant properties files and log sources to help with that chapter, as shown in figure 2.5. With the LogSimulator copied into the download root folder as previously recommended, run this command:

```
groovy LogSimulator.groovy Chapter2\\SimulatorConfig\\tool.properties
```

We can see an example of the console output when running the LogSimulator as a Groovy application in figure 2.6.

Figure 2.6 LogSimulator example output when in verbose mode, using the HelloWorld-Verbose.properties file and Fluentd running with the associated HelloWorld.conf file

RUNNING LOGSIMULATOR AS A JAR

To use the JAR version of the LogSimulator, the JAR file needs to be downloaded into the parent directory of all the chapter resource folders. Then the command can have the Groovy LogSimulator.groovy element replaced with `java -jar LogSimulator.jar`, so the command would appear as

```
java -jar LogSimulator.jar Chapter2\\SimulatorConfig\\tool.properties
```

We will assume you've installed Groovy and run the LogGenerator using the Groovy command for the rest of the book. But as you can see, the only difference is the part of the command that uses Java or Groovy and the JAR or Groovy file. The GitHub repository includes all the details on how the JAR file is generated if you wish to extend the tool and re-create the jar file.

LOGSIMULATOR IN MORE DETAIL

If you would like to know what is going on in more depth, then edit the tool.properties file and change the `verbose` property from `false` to `true`. This will display to the console log entries that are defined in the file small-source.txt. All the properties for the simulator are explained in the documentation at https://github.com/mp3 monster/LogGenerator.

2.2.7 Installing Postman

An easy-to-use tool is needed to send single log events to exercise the Fluentd configuration in our "Hello World" scenario. While utilities such as cURL can be used, we have elected to use Postman with its friendly UI and ability to work across multiple platforms. Postman is a well-known tool that supports most environments (Windows, macOS, Linux, etc.). Postman is free for individual use, and the binary can be retrieved from www.postman.com/downloads/.

For Windows, this is an installer that will resolve the appropriate file locations. For Linux, the download is a tarred gzip file that will need to be unpacked (e.g., `tar -xvf Postman-linux-x64-8.6.2.tar.gz`). Once Postman is installed/untarred, ensure that it can be started—for Windows, this can be done with the installed links.

2.3 Bringing Fluentd to life with "Hello World"

Now that we've looked at the architecture of Fluentd and deployed it into an environment, let's bring this to life.

2.3.1 "Hello World" scenario

The "Hello World" scenario is very simple. We will use the fact that Fluentd can receive log events through HTTP and simply see the console record the events. To start with, we will push the HTTP events using Postman. The next step will be to extend this slightly to send log events using the LogSimulator.

2.3.2 *"Hello World" configuration*

Before running the example, let us quickly look at the configuration file (see listing 2.1). As you can see, we have provided some comments within the configuration file. Within a configuration file, we can comment anywhere by leading with a hash (#) character. The configuration between <system> and </system> are instructions to Fluentd on how its internals should work; in this case, use Info-level logging. Then we have used a *source* directive to define the origins of log events using the built-in HTTP plugin capability that the @type identifies. The following name-value pairs are then treated as attributes or properties for that plugin. For example, here we have defined the use of port 18080 to receive log events.

We then define an output using the *match* directive. The asterisk in the *match* directive is a wildcard, telling the *match* directive that any tag can be processed by the output plugin, in this case, standard out, which will appear in the console. The configuration file used in this example is stripped to the bare minimum, defining just the input and output parameters for each plugin and a couple of illustrative comments.

Listing 2.1   Chapter2/Fluentd/HelloWorld.conf

```
# Hello World configuration will take events received on port 18080 using
# HTTP as a protocol

# set Fluentd's configuration parameters      Set the default log level for Fluentd—
<system>                                      because we have set the level to info, this is
    Log_Level info             ◄─────────     not strictly necessary, as that is the default.
</system>

# define the HTTP source which will provide log events    This is a source
<source>                                               ◄─┘ directive.
    @type http                                  ◄──────────┐  @type indicates
    port 18080     ◄──┐ Lines following a plugin define      │  the plugin type.
</source>              │ configuration parameters for that plugin.

# accept all log events regardless of tag and write them to the console
<match *>          ◄──┐ The match directive defines which log
    @type stdout      │ events will be allowed into the plugin.
</match>
```

2.3.3 *Starting Fluentd*

As the Fluentd service is in our PATH, we can launch the process with the command fluentd anywhere. However, the tool will look in different places without a parameter defining the config location, depending on the environment and installation process. For Windows and Linux, Fluentd will try to resolve the location /etc/fluent/fluent.conf. For Windows, this will fail unless the command is run within a Linux subsystem. We are not using the default to start Fluentd. We need to navigate the shell to wherever you have downloaded the configuration file or include the full path to the configuration file as the parameter. Then run the following command:

```
fluentd -c HelloWorld.conf
```

To run the Fluentd command from the root of the downloaded resources, which will be the norm for the rest of the book, the command would be

```
fluentd -c ./Chapter2/Fluentd/HelloWorld.conf
```

This command will start Fluentd, and we will see the information displayed on the console as things start up, including the configuration being loaded and checked. When running Fluentd or Fluent Bit on Windows, depending upon the permissions for your user account, you may get a prompt, as shown in figure 2.7. This prompt occurs because Fluentd and Fluent Bit will, by default, expose access points to the network.

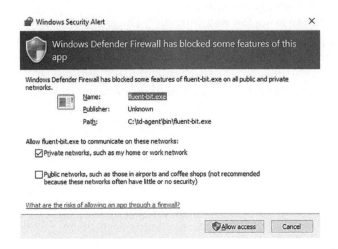

Figure 2.7   Windows prompting to allow Fluentd or Fluent Bit (depending on what is being started) access to use the network

We should, of course, allow access. Without it, both Fluentd and Fluent Bit will fail. Within a Linux environment, the equivalent security controls are established through IPTables rules and possible SELinux configuration. As Linux environments can vary more than Windows, it is worth having a good Linux reference to help set up and troubleshoot any restrictions. Manning has several such titles, such as *Linux in Motion* by David Clinton (www.manning.com/livevideo/linux-in-motion).

The next step is to send a log event using Postman. Once Postman has started, we need to configure it to send a simple JSON payload to Fluentd. Figure 2.8 shows the settings in the header.

Figure 2.8   Defined JSON payload to send to Fluentd using Postman

We also need to set the Body content, as we're going to use a POST operation. By selecting Body (and the Raw option) on the screen, we can then key into the body field {"Hello" : "World"}. With this done, we're ready now to send. We see this configuration in figure 2.9.

Figure 2.9 Setting the message body in Postman

Click the Send button in Postman. Figure 2.10 shows the result. You may have noticed that in the API call, we have not defined a time for the log event; therefore, the Fluentd instance will apply the current system time.

```
CMD Light - fluentd  -c Chapter   ×    +   ∨                         —   □   ×

E:\dev\github\LoggingInActionWithFluentd>fluentd -c Chapter2\Fluentd\HelloWorld.
conf
2021-07-29 16:58:15 +0100 [info]: parsing config file is succeeded path="Chapter
2\\Fluentd\\HelloWorld.conf"
2021-07-29 16:58:15 +0100 [info]: gem 'fluent-plugin-elasticsearch' version '4.3
.3'
2021-07-29 16:58:15 +0100 [info]: gem 'fluent-plugin-elasticsearch' version '2.1
2.5'
2021-07-29 16:58:15 +0100 [info]: gem 'fluent-plugin-mongo' version '1.5.0'
2021-07-29 16:58:15 +0100 [info]: gem 'fluent-plugin-s3' version '1.5.0'
2021-07-29 16:58:15 +0100 [info]: gem 'fluent-plugin-slack' version '0.6.7'
2021-07-29 16:58:15 +0100 [info]: gem 'fluent-plugin-td' version '1.1.0'
2021-07-29 16:58:15 +0100 [info]: gem 'fluentd' version '1.12.0'
2021-07-29 16:58:16 +0100 [info]: Oj is not installed, and failing back to Yajl
for json parser
2021-07-29 16:58:16 +0100 [info]: using configuration file: <ROOT>
  <system>
    Log_Level info
  </system>
  <source>
    @type http
    port 18080
  </source>
  <source>
    @type forward
    port 24224
    tag "catCall"
  </source>
  <match *>
    @type stdout
  </match>
</ROOT>
2021-07-29 16:58:16 +0100 [info]: starting fluentd-1.12.0 pid=13668 ruby="2.6.4"
2021-07-29 16:58:16 +0100 [info]: spawn command to main: cmdline=["C:/Ruby26-x6
4/bin/ruby.exe", "-Eutf-8", "C:/Ruby26-x64/bin/fluentd", "-c", "Chapter2\\Fluent
d\\HelloWorld.conf", "--under-supervisor"]
2021-07-29 16:58:17 +0100 [info]: adding match pattern="*" type="stdout"
2021-07-29 16:58:18 +0100 [info]: adding source type="http"
2021-07-29 16:58:18 +0100 [info]: #0 Oj is not installed, and failing back to Ya
jl for json parser
2021-07-29 16:58:18 +0100 [info]: adding source type="forward"
2021-07-29 16:58:18 +0100 [info]: #0 starting fluentd worker pid=22116 ppid=1366
8 worker=0
2021-07-29 16:58:18 +0100 [info]: #0 listening port port=24224 bind="0.0.0.0"
2021-07-29 16:58:18 +0100 [info]: #0 fluentd worker is now running worker=0
2021-07-29 16:58:22.466085600 +0100 : {"Hello":"World"}
```

Figure 2.10 Fluentd output after sending the REST event—note the last line showing the output of the received event

While this configuration is as "useful as a chocolate teapot," as the expression goes, it does illustrate the basic idea of Fluentd—the ability to take log events and direct them (explicitly or implicitly) to an output. Let's finish this illustration by using the LogSimulator to create a stream of log events.

A new shell window is required to run the LogSimulator. Within the shell, you will need to navigate to where the configurations have been downloaded. Within each of the chapter's folders is a folder called SimulatorConfig. Depending upon the chapter, you will find one or more property files. Inside the property file, you'll find a series of key-value pairs that will control the LogSimulator's behavior. This includes referencing the log file to replay or test data. These references are relative, meaning we need to be in the correct folder—the parent folder to the chapters—to start the simulator successfully. We can then start the LogSimulator with the command

```
groovy LogSimulator.groovy Chapter2\SimulatorConfig\HelloWorld.properties
```

or, if you choose to use the JAR file

```
java -jar LogSimulator.jar Chapter2\SimulatorConfig\HelloWorld.properties
```

Remember to correct the slashes in the file path for Linux environments. The Log-Simulator is provided with a configuration that will send log events using a log file source using the same HTTP endpoint. This will result in each of the log events being displayed on the console.

2.4   *"Hello World" with Fluent Bit*

Fluent Bit, as previously mentioned, is written in C/C++, making the footprint very compact. The downside of this is that it requires more effort to build Fluent Bit for your environment. You will need to be comfortable with the Gnu Compiler Collection (GCC) (https://gcc.gnu.org/), which is typically available on Linux platforms, or the cross-platform C compiler Clang (https://clang.llvm.org/), which can work in a GCC mode. For this book, we aren't going to delve any further into the world of C/C++ compilation. This means downloading one of the prebuilt binaries or using one of the supported package managers, such as apt and yum. For Windows, Treasure Data has provided Windows binaries (available at https://docs.fluentbit.io/manual/installation/windows). Because the binaries are provided by Treasure Data, the created artifacts make use of the prefix *td*. For simplicity and alignment to the basic version of Fluent Bit, we recommend downloading the zip version. We have used the zip download approach for our examples.

Unpack the zip file to a suitable location (we will assume `C:\td-agent`) as the location. To make life easier, it is worth adding the bin folder (e.g., `C:\td-agent\bin`) into the `PATH` environmental variables, as we did with Fluentd.

We can check that Fluent Bit has been deployed with the following simple command:

```
fluent-bit --help
```

This will prompt Fluent Bit to display its help information on the console.

2.4.1   *Starting Fluent Bit*

The obvious assumption would be that as long as we limit our Fluentd configuration file to the plugins available in a Fluent Bit deployment, we can use the same configuration file. Unfortunately not—while the configuration files are similar, they aren't the same.

We'll explore the difference in a while. But to get Fluent Bit running with our "Hello World" example, let's start things with a configuration file previously prepared, using the command

```
fluent-bit -c ./Chapter2/FluentBit/HelloWorld.conf
```

As a result, Fluent Bit will start up with the configuration provided. Unlike Fluentd, Fluent Bit's support for HTTP is more recent and may not have all the features you want, depending on when you read this. Therefore, it is possible to match Fluentd for HTTP in our scenario of sending JSON. If you bump up against HTTP feature restrictions, then you can at least drop down to using the TCP plugin (HTTP is a layer over the TCP protocols). Both Fluent Bit and Fluentd support HTTP operations for capturing status information and HTTP forwarding. The only downside of working at the TCP layer is that we can't use Postman to send the calls. You can create the same effect with other tools that know how to send text content to TCP sockets. For Linux, utilities such as *tc* can do this. In a Windows environment, there isn't the same native tooling. It is possible to create a Telnet session using tools such as PuTTY (www.putty.org), and LogSimulator includes the ability to send text log events to a TCP port. For Fluent Bit, let's use Postman for HTTP and use the LogSimulator for TCP. Starting with TCP, the following command will start the LogSimulator, providing it with a properties file and a file of log events to send. As we have already installed this tool, we can start it up. Using a separate shell (with the correct Java and Groovy versions), we can run the command

```
groovy LogSimulator.groovy Chapter2\SimulatorConfig\fb-HelloWorld.properties
    .\TestData\small-source.json
```

We can now expect to see the shell running the LogSimulator reporting the sent events to the console. The log events will be sent at varying time intervals (the console should look something like the screenshot in figure 2.11).

At the same time, Fluent Bit in the other console will start reporting the receipt and sending to its console the JSON payloads received. This is shown in figure 2.12.

Figure 2.11   Simulator console output at the end of the log event transmission

Figure 2.12   Example Fluent Bit console output

You may have noticed a lag between the simulator starting and seeing Fluent Bit displaying events. This reflects that one of the configuration options is the time interval when the cache of received log messages is flushed to the output. As we will discover later in the book, this is one of the areas that we can tune to help performance.

NOW WITH HTTP

The difference between the TCP and HTTP configurations is small, so you can either make the changes to the `Chapter2/FluentBit/HelloWorld.conf` or use the provided configuration file `Chapter2/FluentBit/HelloWorld-HTTP.conf`. The following shows the changes that need to be applied:

- In the Input section, change the `Name tcp` to `Name http`.
- As we have been using port 18080 for HTTP in Postman, let's correct the port in the configuration, replacing `port 28080` with `port 18080`.

Save these changes once applied. To see how Fluent Bit will work now, stop the current Fluent Bit process if it's still running. Then restart as before, or using the provided changes, start with

```
fluent-bit -c ./Chapter2/FluentBit/HelloWorld-HTTP.conf
```

Once running, use the same Postman settings to send the events as we did for Fluentd.

2.4.2 *Alternate Fluent Bit startup options*

Fluent Bit can also be configured entirely through the command line. This makes an effective way to configure Fluent Bit, as it simplifies the deployment (no mapping of configuration files needed). However, this does come at the price of readability. For example, we could repeat the same configuration of Fluent Bit with

```
fluent-bit -i tcp://0.0.0.0:28080 -o stdout
```

If you run this command with the simulator as previously set up, the outcomes will be the same as before. Fluent Bit, like Fluentd, isn't tied to working with a single source of log events. We can illustrate this by adding additional input definitions into the command line. While running in a Windows environment, let's add the `winlog` events to our inputs. For Linux users, you could replace the `winlog` source with `cpu` and ask Fluent Bit to tell us a bit more about what it is doing by repeating the same exercise, but with the command

```
fluent-bit -i tcp://0.0.0.0:28080 -i winlog -o stdout -vv
```

This time we will see several differences. First, when Fluent Bit starts up, it will give us a lot more information, including clearly showing the inputs and outputs being handled. This results from the `-vv` (more on this in the next section). As the log events occur, in addition to our log simulator events, the `winlog` information will be interleaved.

FLUENTD AND FLUENT BIT INTERNAL LOGGING LEVELS

Both Fluentd and Fluent Bit support the same command-line parameters that can control how much information they log about their activities (as opposed to any log-level information associated with a log event received). In addition to being controlled by the command line, this configuration can be set via the configuration file. Both tools recognize five levels of logs, and when no parameter or configuration is applied, the midlevel (info) is used as the default log level. Table 2.5 shows the log levels, the command-line parameters, and the equivalent configuration setting. The easiest way to remember the command line is -v is for *verbose* and -q is for *quiet*; more letters increase verbosity or quietness.

Table 2.5 Log levels recognized by Fluentd and Fluent Bit

Log level	Command line	Configuration setting
Trace	-vv	Log_Level trace
Debug	-v	Log_Level debug
Info		Log_Level info
Warning	-q	Log_Level warn
Error	-qq	Log_Level error

> **NOTE** Trace level setting will occur only if Fluent Bit has been compiled with the *build flag* set to enable trace. This can be checked using the Fluent Bit help command (fluent-bit -h or fluent-bit --help) to display a list of the build flags and their settings. Trace-level logging should be needed only while developing a plugin.

2.4.3 *Fluent Bit configuration file comparison*

Previously we mentioned that the Fluentd and Fluent Bit configurations differ. To help illustrate the differences, table 2.6 offers the configuration side by side.

Table 2.6 Fluentd and Fluent Bit configuration comparison (using the HTTP configuration of Fluent Bit)

Fluent Bit	Fluentd

<pre># Hello World configuration will take 	
events received
# on port 18080 using TCP as a protocol 	
 	
[SERVICE]
    Flush   1
    Daemon   Off
  Log_Level   info</pre>
	<pre># Hello World configuration will take
	events received on port 18080 using
	# HTTP as a protocol
	
	# set Fluentd's configuration parameters
	<system>
	    Log_Level info
	</system></pre>

<pre># define the TCP source which will provide 	
log events
[INPUT]
    Name   http
    Host   0.0.0.0
    Port   18080</pre>
	<pre># define the HTTP source which will
	provide log events
	<source>
	    @type http
	    port 18080
	</source> # after a directive</pre>

<pre># accept all log events regardless of tag 	
and write
# them to the console 	
[OUTPUT]
    Name stdout
    Match *</pre>
	<pre># accept all log events regardless of tag
	and write them to the console
	<match *>
	    @type stdout
	</match></pre>

If you want to play spot the difference, then you should have observed the following:

- Rather than directives being defined by opening and closing angle brackets (`<>`), the directive is in square brackets (`[]`), and the termination is implicit by the following directive or end of the file.
- `SERVICE` replaces the *system* for defining the general configuration.
- `@type` is replaced by the `Name` attribute to define the plugin to be used.
- *Match*, rather than being the name of the directive with a parameter in the directive, becomes `Output`. The *match* clause is then defined by another name-value pair in the attributes.
- Older versions of Fluent Bit didn't support HTTP, so events would need to be sent using events using TCP, but the events received can still be in JSON format.

When looking at the configurations side by side, the details aren't too radically different, but they are significant enough to catch people out.

2.4.4   *Fluent Bit configuration file in detail*

Looking more closely at the configuration file and the rules that are applied, we've just seen there are some similarities, and there are some differences. In the following listing, we have highlighted a few key rules.

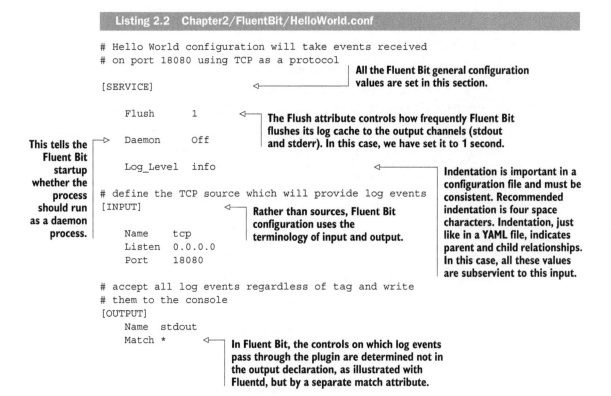

Listing 2.2   Chapter2/FluentBit/HelloWorld.conf

```
# Hello World configuration will take events received
# on port 18080 using TCP as a protocol

[SERVICE]                                          All the Fluent Bit general configuration
                                                   values are set in this section.

    Flush      1                                   The Flush attribute controls how frequently Fluent Bit
                                                   flushes its log cache to the output channels (stdout
    Daemon     Off                                 and stderr). In this case, we have set it to 1 second.

    Log_Level  info                                Indentation is important in a
                                                   configuration file and must be
# define the TCP source which will provide log events   consistent. Recommended
[INPUT]                                            indentation is four space
                        Rather than sources, Fluent Bit   characters. Indentation, just
    Name    tcp         configuration uses the     like in a YAML file, indicates
    Listen  0.0.0.0     terminology of input and output.   parent and child relationships.
    Port    18080                                  In this case, all these values
                                                   are subservient to this input.

# accept all log events regardless of tag and write
# them to the console
[OUTPUT]
    Name  stdout
    Match *                 In Fluent Bit, the controls on which log events
                            pass through the plugin are determined not in
                            the output declaration, as illustrated with
                            Fluentd, but by a separate match attribute.
```

This tells the Fluent Bit startup whether the process should run as a daemon process.

As with Fluentd, ordering within the configuration file is important, particularly in `match` statements—for example, if we added the following configuration fragment immediately before the current `OUTPUT` declaration:

```
[OUTPUT]
    Name file
    Path ./test.out
    Match *
```

Suppose the configuration appeared as follows:

```
# send all log events to a local file called test.out
[OUTPUT]
    Name file
    Path ./test.out
    Match *

# accept all log events regardless of tag and write
# them to the console
[OUTPUT]
    Name  stdout
    Match *
```

Should we expect logs to appear in the log file, stdout (i.e., console), or both? The answer is that events will appear only in the file. This is because we match all events in both outputs; then it is the first output definition in the configuration that gets the events (i.e., the log file, with a wildcard `match` attribute; no log events will make it to `stdout`).

2.4.5 *Putting the dummy plugin into action*

To test out some of the details, see if you can implement the following configuration change. Within both Fluentd and Fluent Bit is a built-in input plugin called *dummy*. Modify the respective HelloWorld.conf files and incorporate the source, and then start up Fluentd and Fluent Bit, in turn, to see what outcomes you get. The result of the exercise is included at the end of the chapter.

ANSWER

Rather than filling the pages with configuration files, the answer configurations can be found in the downloaded folders Chapter2/ExerciseResults/Fluentd/HelloWorld-Answer.conf and Chapter2/ExerciseResults/FluentBit/HelloWorld-Answer.conf.

2.5 *Fluentd deployment with Kubernetes and containers*

So far, we have looked at the deployment of Fluentd and Fluent Bit as you might approach the requirement with only minimal consideration to how the host is working (native deployments, virtualization, and containerization). We have referenced some of the mechanisms that would allow us to further automate or containerize these tools. As discussed in chapter 1, Fluentd has a strong association with containerization and the use of Kubernetes. We'll briefly look at how Fluentd is configured in a

Kubernetes context; when we get to part 3 of the book, we'll look at details such as scaling and containerization in depth.

Establishing a deployment of a Kubernetes environment and containerization warrants its own book (we recommend *Kubernetes in Action*, 2nd edition by Marko Lukša; www.manning.com/books/kubernetes-in-action-second-edition). It is, however, worth looking at how things operate in principle; as we work through the configuration of Fluentd in the following chapters, you will be able to appreciate how the configuration could relate to a Kubernetes deployment. It may also prompt ideas on how and what you may wish to monitor with Fluentd when it comes to the microservices themselves.

2.5.1 *Fluentd DaemonSet*

Fluentd is one of the options for incorporating log management into a Kubernetes environment. This is typically achieved by defining configuration files. The Kubernetes configuration files tell Kubernetes how pods (collections of containers that work together) and containers should be run across one or more worker nodes (servers providing compute power to a Kubernetes cluster). Within Kubernetes, we can describe different ways for pods to be deployed, such as ReplicaSets, Jobs, and DaemonSets. For example, it is possible to define things such that a Fluentd container will be executed on each worker node to collect log events from all the local containers running on that node. This type of configuration within Kubernetes is known as a *DaemonSet* and is a typical configuration for Kubernetes to have for Fluentd. As we'll see later in the book, this isn't the only way to deploy Fluentd, nor are we limited to one deployment model. In the next listing, we can see an example DaemonSet configuration for applying a configuration file and parameters for routing log events to another Fluentd node.

Listing 2.3   Chapter2/Out-of-the-box Fluentd DaemonSet designed for forwarding

```
apiVersion: apps/v1

kind: DaemonSet
metadata:
  name: fluentd
  namespace: kube-system
  labels:
    k8s-app: fluentd-logging
    version: v1
spec:
  selector:
    matchLabels:
      k8s-app: fluentd-logging
      version: v1
  template:
    metadata:
      labels:
        k8s-app: fluentd-logging
        version: v1
    spec:
      tolerations:
      - key: node-role.kubernetes.io/master
```

◁── **Tells Kubernetes whether the pod should run on the master (controlling node)**

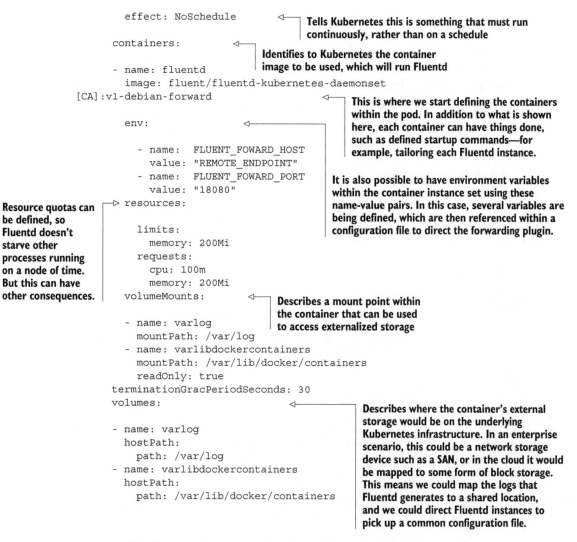

```
          effect: NoSchedule                          Tells Kubernetes this is something that must run
                                                      continuously, rather than on a schedule
      containers:
                                          Identifies to Kubernetes the container
                                          image to be used, which will run Fluentd
      - name: fluentd
          image: fluent/fluentd-kubernetes-daemonset
[CA]:v1-debian-forward
                                                      This is where we start defining the containers
          env:                                        within the pod. In addition to what is shown
                                                      here, each container can have things done,
                                                      such as defined startup commands—for
          - name:   FLUENT_FOWARD_HOST                example, tailoring each Fluentd instance.
            value:  "REMOTE_ENDPOINT"
          - name:   FLUENT_FOWARD_PORT                It is also possible to have environment variables
            value:  "18080"                           within the container instance set using these
                                                      name-value pairs. In this case, several variables are
          resources:                                  being defined, which are then referenced within a
                                                      configuration file to direct the forwarding plugin.
          limits:
            memory: 200Mi
          requests:
            cpu: 100m
            memory: 200Mi
          volumeMounts:                      Describes a mount point within
                                             the container that can be used
          - name: varlog                    to access externalized storage
            mountPath: /var/log
          - name: varlibdockercontainers
            mountPath: /var/lib/docker/containers
            readOnly: true
      terminationGracPeriodSeconds: 30
      volumes:
                                             Describes where the container's external
      - name: varlog                         storage would be on the underlying
        hostPath:                            Kubernetes infrastructure. In an enterprise
          path: /var/log                     scenario, this could be a network storage
      - name: varlibdockercontainers         device such as a SAN, or in the cloud it would
        hostPath:                            be mapped to some form of block storage.
          path: /var/lib/docker/containers   This means we could map the logs that
                                             Fluentd generates to a shared location,
                                             and we could direct Fluentd instances to
                                             pick up a common configuration file.
```

Resource quotas can be defined, so Fluentd doesn't starve other processes running on a node of time. But this can have other consequences.

NOTE The DaemonSet comes from http://mng.bz/nYea.

It should be noted that it is possible within an infrastructure hosting Kubernetes nodes to run processes such as Fluentd directly on the underlying platform. While this eliminates the abstraction layer of Kubernetes (and the associated overhead), it also removes the opportunity to use Kubernetes to manage and monitor that Fluentd is running. We recommend this only in very unusual circumstances.

NOTE DaemonSets are defined to provide basic operations on every worker node. This could be sending log events directly to Elasticsearch (as part of an EFK stack as discussed in chapter 1) or forwarding logs to various cloud vendor log analytics solutions, such as AWS CloudWatch. These can be found in the Fluentd GitHub (http://mng.bz/2jng).

Figure 2.13 illustrates how the Kubernetes configuration can work using a Daemon-Set. Typically, the DaemonSet configuration would be held in a shared configuration repository or file system and then passed to Kubernetes through a tool like kubectl, the standard Kubernetes CLI tool. We have assumed that the Fluentd configuration resides on a shared file system and is therefore mounted by the Fluentd container to allow access. Another approach would be to pass the configuration using the Daemon-Set YAML file or simply wire directly into the Docker image. The log consumers that the Fluentd configuration has within the DaemonSet could direct the log events to Elasticsearch, or to a file system outside the cluster that the Kubernetes configuration has made accessible. We will explore more about this when we get to scaling Fluentd.

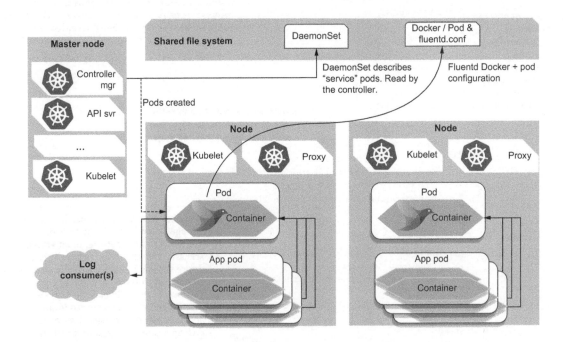

Figure 2.13   A deployment model of Fluentd within Kubernetes as a DaemonSet. Each distinct server in the Kubernetes cluster has its own pod with a container running Fluentd.

2.5.2   *Dockerized Fluentd*

Like just about any application, in addition to manually installing or automating a manual install through tools like Ansible (www.ansible.com), it is possible to deploy Fluentd or Fluent Bit using the Docker container engine. Predefined Fluentd Docker files (i.e., the files that tell Docker how to build an executable image) are provided in the GitHub repository (https://github.com/fluent/fluentd-docker-image), which include addressing different host OS factors (e.g., Debian to Windows). Fluent Bit also has a smaller set of predefined Docker files in GitHub (https://github.com/fluent/fluent-bit). The

GitHub repositories contain the configuration files and scripts. The realized images are held in Docker Hub and can be found at https://hub.docker.com/u/fluent for Fluentd and https://hub.docker.com/r/fluent/fluent-bit for Fluent Bit.

2.6 Using Fluentd UI

We have managed to install and run Fluentd and Fluent Bit. But in both cases, the control has been through the command line. Fluentd can also run with a web UI. The web UI is served from the same process that executes Fluentd's core logic if it is installed.

2.6.1 Installing Fluentd with UI

The installation will trigger Fluentd to download and install a series of additional gems. This is because it provides the means to incorporate several plugins beyond the basic ones provided. This does mean the installation takes longer than just installing Fluentd. The commands to install the UI are

```
gem install -V fluentd-ui
fluentd-ui setup
```

Once the installation is complete, we can start the UI up with the following command:

```
fluentd-ui start
```

This will start up a Fluentd node, which includes a web server. The web UI can be accessed by opening port 9292 (i.e., pointing your browser to `localhost:9292` will present you with the login screen).

Securing Fluent-UI with HTTPS

The Fluentd UI is run using HTTP; no SSL/TLS certificate is used on a default installation. This is unlikely to be an issue in development/experiment environments. But running without SSL/TLS and at least basic credentials is far from recommended when it comes to production. This can be addressed in several ways:

- Implement a *reverse proxy* in front of Fluentd-ui using Nginx or the Apache Server—a common approach to securing web content not protected by SSL/TLS certificates (documentation on how to do this is available at http://mng.bz/Ywne). It also means an additional process is running in your environment, with the need to have networking configured so that the reverse proxy isn't bypassed.
- For its web layers, Fluentd UI uses the Ruby on Rails framework (https://rubyonrails.org/) and the Ruby application server Puma (https://puma.io). Therefore, it is possible to configure Puma with an SSL/TLS certificate. Applying the configuration needs Ruby code changes and startup parameters with a knock-on for the Fluent code base. This is undesirable, as any update will mean reapplying those changes.
- We wouldn't recommend the use of Fluentd UI in production. This may seem like avoiding a problem rather than addressing it. However, there is a lot of merit

(continued)

in this. For production environments, you want to have Fluentd configuration files controlled through tools such as Git. This means not empowering users with a UI in production that can make configuration changes. It is better to get users to make controlled changes that can then be rolled out securely. If you're running Fluentd in a microservices or distributed environment, allowing changes only from the controlled configuration file provides the means to drive environment consistency and reduce the chance of "configuration drift."

Again, we recommend using Fluentd UI only for experimentation purposes and not in production. Given this, the following will provide enough insight to enable you to appreciate what the UI supports.

By default, the login username is *admin,* and the password is *changeme.* Once logged in, the UI presented will look something like figure 2.14. Differences can occur as the UI has reactive and responsive characteristics, resulting in the layout adjusting based on the device used to view the UI.

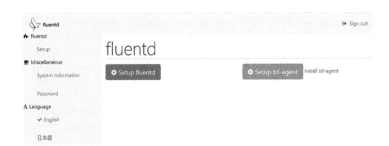

Figure 2.14   UI when Fluentd UI starts without any configuration

We need to provide some configuration values for the Fluentd node to perform with. Clicking Setup Fluentd will take us to a UI through which we can configure the behavior. Figure 2.15 illustrates some of the relevant configuration needed.

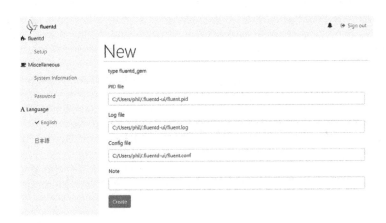

Figure 2.15   Fluentd UI for setting the configuration locations

The configuration fields are set with default values. Switch the Config File option to point to the existing HelloWorld.conf file used to run Fluentd. You may wish to also provide alternative locations for the process identifier (PID) and log files. As soon as we click the Create button in the UI, the server process will start if the locations and files can be written to and read from. The UI then switches to a different home page, as shown in figure 2.16.

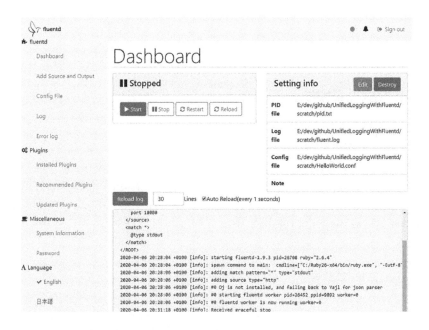

Figure 2.16 Fluentd UI once the backend is running

The navigation menu on the left is now a lot richer. The Fluentd submenu provides options for working with the configuration file, accessing logs, and any error logs. The logs shown are the same as the console output. The navigation menu lets us see the details of Installed Plugins, Recommended Plugins, and Updated Plugins.

The core of the screen is given over to the live log being produced by the server with controls for starting and stopping operations and the current configuration. The Config File options will show us the configuration file being used and the ability to edit the configuration file directly. If the UI options for configuration become an issue, you can resort to traditional editing. The Add Source and Output options allow web pages that capture plugin configurations using the UI as a guided, form-based presentation for modifying configuration values. As figure 2.17 illustrates, the UI does provide a nice logical flow for setting up the plugins and their configuration values.

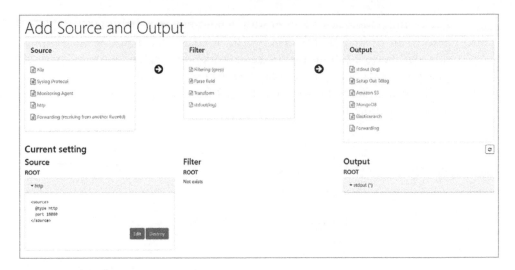

Figure 2.17   Fluentd UI defining inputs and outputs

Clicking on one of the Source, Filter, or Output elements will navigate you to a UI for configuring that type of plugin. For example, selecting a File source presents you with a file picker UI (as shown in figure 2.18).

Figure 2.18   Fluentd UI file picker as part of the File plugin configuration

Summary

- Log events are composed of a tag, a timestamp, and a record that holds the core log event.
- Using NTP for machine time synchronization is crucial when bringing multiple server logs together to ensure correct log ordering.
- Fluentd and Fluent Bit can be deployed in most environments, as infrastructure requirements are very small and application dependencies are minimal. If necessary, you can compile these tools to work in niche situations.
- There are a variety of ways for deploying Fluentd, including deploying Ruby and RubyGems and then retrieving Fluentd as a gem.

- Deployment of the LogSimulator to quickly mimic sources of log events just requires Java, but to customize the tool, you need Groovy as well.
- Fluentd can be used with Kubernetes and Docker logging, as well as with traditional environments. We can retrieve standard configurations for this for Kubernetes deployment.
- When deployed on a Linux host, Fluentd can respond to signals such as SIGINT to shut down gracefully and SIGUSR2 to reload the configuration file.
- Fluentd UI is one of the additional tools available with Fluentd. This provides a web front to visualize the configuration of a Fluentd environment and observe what Fluentd is doing. Other tools include the ability to generate certificates and list available plugins.
- The order of how configurations are defined in a configuration file is important.
- Fluentd's and Fluent Bit's own logging can be configured to different log levels.
- Fluentd and Fluent Bit configurations are similar but not the same.

Part 2

Fluentd in depth

In part 1, we introduced Fluentd and Fluent Bit, we explored what drives the adoption of these tools, and we covered the problems both Fluentd and Fluent Bit are best suited to address. We also took the time to understand the differences between Fluentd and Fluent Bit. From here on, we will focus primarily on Fluentd.

In the following part, we will dig into what Fluentd can do and how to configure it. In doing so, we'll tackle some scenarios that most users will likely encounter sooner or later—for example, how to capture log events from a log file as they are added by another log application, including handling challenges such as log rotation. Chapter 3 starts with capturing log events, focusing on sources such as files, as this is one of the most common sources of log events. Chapter 4 takes us into storing log events in different destinations, such as databases and social/collaboration tools. This includes dealing with the parsing and formatting of events. Chapters 5 and 6 show the different aspects of log event routing, duplication, and log attribute injection.

By the end of part 2, we will have covered enough ground for you to build configurations for most use cases. This allows us to go into part 3, where we will focus on the challenges of Docker, Kubernetes, scaling, performance, and use cases requiring specialist plugins.

Using Fluentd to
capture log events

This chapter covers

- Configuring Fluentd for the input of log files
- Examining the impact of stopping and starting during file reading by Fluentd
- Using parsers to extract more meaning from log events
- Self-monitoring and external monitoring of Fluentd using APIs

With the conceptual and architectural foundations set up, and having run a simple configuration, we're ready to start looking at the capture of log events in more detail. In this chapter, we're going to focus on capturing log events. But before we do, let's look at how we can check that our Fluentd configuration is correct.

Setting up to follow and try the configurations

A quick note about how we're presenting code in the book. To avoid the book becoming bloated with code and Fluentd configuration files, we've included only the configuration and code parts relevant to the subject being discussed. But the files

(continued)
referenced in the downloads and GitHub repository are the complete configurations (https://github.com/mp3monster/LoggingInActionWithFluentd).

The repository includes both complete configurations and partial configuration files so you can implement configuration yourself. Along with this are scenarios and solutions to the scenarios that will allow you to try out your understanding of ideas in the book.

If you have skipped the initial chapters, you need to ensure you have the Log-Simulator installed and configured (details in Chapter 2) or have the basic setup as documented at https://github.com/mp3monster/LogGenerator and including any troubleshooting tips.

3.1   Dry running to check a configuration

When developing Fluentd configurations, we don't want to set up a test to discover that the configuration is incorrect. Just as we do when developing code, we use a means to check code before we try running the solution. This becomes more important as the configuration or code becomes more complex.

Dry running a configuration file gets Fluentd to load the configuration and confirm that it can execute it, based on syntactical correctness and whether the attributes are recognized and the values provided are valid. The dry-run option is part of the Fluentd command line. To use the dry-run capability, we just add `--dry-run` to the command-line parameters. Any configuration errors are reported in the console output; for example:

```
2020-04-17 11:08:51 +0100 [error]: config error file="Chapter3/Fluentd/basic-
    file-read2.conf" error_class=Fluent::ConfigError error="'path' parameter
    is required"
```

This dry run shows that a plugin is missing a mandatory attribute; in this case, the failed plugin configuration needs a path attribute.

Solving structural errors

If the error is more "structural" in nature, such as omitting a start or end to a declarative block—for example, `</parse>` being missed when there is a `<parse>` declaration—then we're most likely to see a `backtrace` (stack trace) error. Fluentd will complete the backtrace error with what it thinks is missing. The suggestion may be incorrect in these circumstances, and a missing syntactical element elsewhere is the cause. The easiest way to sort out these kinds of issues is to ensure you have applied good indentation and start matching up start and end blocks.

Successful execution of the dry run will result in Fluentd stopping gracefully. If you are running with the default logging level, then the following kind of message is displayed:

```
2020-04-17 10:53:24 +0100 [info]: finsihed dry run mode
```

As this is classed as *info,* if you have configured Fluentd to be quieter, you will not see a message, just Fluentd coming to a stop without any errors.

Fluent Bit currently does not have a comparable feature, partly because the expectation is for simpler configurations. The ability to provide the Fluent Bit configuration entirely via the command line communicating an error will be more challenging. If your goal is to supply Fluent Bit with the configuration using the command line, we recommend that you start working with a file until the configuration is complete and valid. Then strip the new line and redundant whitespace—something that can be done with tools online (e.g., browserling.com) or just *awk* and *sed* on a Linux host. This should allow you to reduce the configuration to a single line, ready for use.

3.1.1 *Putting validating Fluentd configuration into action*

As the nominated team Fluentd expert, you have been asked to check several configurations. This is an opportunity to try the dry-run feature to evaluate whether the configuration is valid and fix it if necessary (if you need to fix a configuration, it might be worth making a copy of the original configuration). The configuration files to validate are the following:

- `Chapter3/Fluentd/basic-file-read.conf`
- `Chapter3/Fluentd/dry-run.conf`

No one wants to become the person who fixes everyone's Fluentd configurations, so you might consider how to share the answers to the following questions with your colleagues:

1 How do you know that the configuration file is valid?
2 How do you know when a configuration is faulty?

ANSWERS

1 You should have found that `Chapter3/Fluentd/basic-file-read.conf` is valid already. We know that this configuration file is fine, as when the dry-run mode is used, the console output will not report any error messages and should terminate cleanly. The process will terminate with the following message (assuming the log levels haven't been set higher than info):

```
2020-04-17 10:53:24 +0100 [info]: finsihed dry run mode
```

2 The console logging output will report an error reflecting the configuration issue identified for `Chapter3/Fluentd/dry-run.conf`. We should see the following message with the details:

```
2020-04-17 10:54:00 +0100 [error]: config error file="Chapter3/Fluentd/
basic-file-read2.conf" error_class=Fluent::ConfigError error="Missing
'@type' parameter on <source> directive"
```

3.2 *Reading log files*

Log files are the most common source of log events when it comes to applications. While it is inefficient, file creation and consumption are the oldest ways for data to be shared between processes, including events. As a result, the *File* plugin is part of the set of core plugins.

The first step is constructing a file source in a Fluentd configuration file. This can be done by adding the following fragment into a copy of the `Chapter3/Fluentd/no-source-config.conf` (or using `Chapter3/Fluentd/basic-file-read.conf`):

Listing 3.1   Chapter3/Fluentd/basic-file-read.conf illustrating a file tail

```
                        The file source plugin is called tail,
<source>                as it behaves a bit like the Linux
  @type tail       ◁───  command of the same name.
                                         Defines the file(s)
  path ./Chapter3/basic-file.*   ◁───  to be captured
  read_lines_limit 5   ◁─┐
                          Maximum number of lines that should
  tag simpleFile          be read before the events are read
  <parse>          ◁─┐    before starting to process them

    @type none      Every file processor needs to know how to convert the text line
  </parse>          input into a log event. There are several standard parsers provided
</source>           by Fluentd, from predefined formats to expression processors.
```

As the configuration extract shows, we have told Fluentd to use any file it finds in the chapter 3 folder with a name starting with `basic-file` and read its contents without any form of parsing. Before starting Fluentd, we run the simulator so we can see what is produced. This can be done using the command

```
groovy LogSimulator.groovy ./Chapter3/SimulatorConfig/basic-log-
    file.properties ./TestData/small-source.txt
```

What we should see is the creation of a file called `basic-log.txt` in the chapter 3 folder. The folder will contain only the message part of our source file (`TestData/small-source.txt`).

With the log file generated, we can now start Fluentd to see what happens. This is done with the command (remembering that we are using relative paths as explained in chapter 2)

```
fluentd -c ./Chapter3/Fluentd/basic-file-read.conf
```

When Fluentd starts up, we'll see the console output showing the configuration file. Soon after, it will detect the file and start sending it to the console as log events.

3.2.1   *Putting the adaption of a Fluentd configuration to Fluent Bit into action*

Your team has decided that the current configuration requirements are simple enough to use Fluent Bit rather than Fluentd. As part of preparing to deploy your solution in a container, you need to copy the `Chapter3/FluentBit/no-source-config.conf` file. Then apply the appropriate configuration changes and run Fluent Bit to test the configuration.

ANSWER

Fluent Bit is started using the command `fluent-bit -c <configuration file>`. The configuration you will have produced should look like the configuration in `Chapter3/ExerciseResults/basic-file-read-FluentBit-Answer.conf`.

The simulator can be started with the command

```
groovy LogSimulator.groovy ./Chapter3/SimulatorConfig/basic-log-
    file.properties ./TestData/source.txt
```

The log events should be displayed on the console as a result.

3.2.2 *Rereading and resuming reading of log files*

If Fluentd was to stop (or needed to be stopped), but the application continued to write log events, then when Fluentd restarts, it will collect all log events it finds rather than only those written after Fluentd stopped. This behavior may be acceptable in a microservice where Fluentd is within the same container as the application logic, and as a result of Fluentd stopping, the Kubernetes pod is shut down. A fresh instance of the container is then started. But in many cases, this isn't enough. Fortunately, this has been considered, and Fluentd has the means to track its progress through the log file(s). If the configuration does not track its position to resume where it left off, then a warning is displayed like this:

```
2020-04-14 17:07:09 +0100 [warn]: #0 'pos_file PATH' parameter is not set to
    a 'tail' source.
2020-04-14 17:07:09 +0100 [warn]: #0 this parameter is highly recommended to
    save the position to resume tailing.
```

If you want to eliminate this warning, because you don't need to continue where you left off, then an additional attribute in the configuration needs to be added to the tail statement:

```
read_from_head true
```

In many cases, particularly with more traditional deployments, we will definitely want to resume where the last log event was read. We should introduce an attribute that tells Fluentd to record its progress through log files with

```
pos_file ./Chapter3/basic-file.pos
```

The `pos_file` attributed is used by the tail plugin to specify a file where the plugin can record its progress through the log file(s). When Fluentd restarts, the `pos_file` is examined as part of the startup to determine where to pick up from. But the `pos_file` alone will not ensure that existing log entries are picked up the first time Fluentd is started. To ensure that all log events are collected from the start, we need to use the `read_from_head` attribute and set it to be `true`.

3.2.3 *Configuration considerations for tracking position*

Some design issues need to be considered when using position files, such as the one used by the tail plugin when the `pos_file` is defined. These considerations include the following:

- *Avoid sharing the files across different tail configurations.* Sharing a file like this runs the risk of an I/O collision, as two different threads try to write their position information at the same time, resulting in file corruption. This also applies to setting up multiple worker threads (we'll examine this in detail when looking at Fluentd scaling).

- *You want the* `pos_file` *entry to exist only for as long as the log files exist.* If the log files are deleted, then the tracker file needs to be deleted. Otherwise, on a restart, the plugin can't work out where to resume file processing correctly. This can be tricky in a containerized environment, as the file system may be entirely local and therefore as transient as the container. This can be overcome if the log files have their part of the file system mapped to durable storage outside the container.

RECOMMENDATION If possible, when using position tracker files, hold them in the same folder as the log file(s) that they are used to track. This raises the chance that the tracker and log files will be handled consistently (i.e., retained or treated transiently). When the log files are purged, the chance of the `pos_file` being purged at the same time is better.

NOTE There is some divergence between Fluentd and Fluent Bit when it comes to the use of `pos_file`. Fluent Bit doesn't have a `pos_file` attribute; instead, it used `DB` as the attribute for this task.

Try to rerun the Fluentd configuration with the changes just described applied to the current configuration file (or run Fluentd with `Chapter3/Fluentd/basic-file -read2.conf`, which includes the position file in the configuration).

3.2.4   *Wildcards in the path attribute*

You may have noticed that the configuration has a wildcard (i.e., asterisk, "*") instead of a file extension in the path declaration. Fluentd will accept the use of wildcards in the same way the operating system will. As a result, it is possible to read multiple files through a single *source* directive (or configuration if you prefer).

This can be simply illustrated if you have run the previous case configuration. By running that configuration, you should have a file called `basic-file.txt` and `basic -file-read2.pos_file` in the Chapter 3 folder. Delete the `pos_file` and then copy `basic-file.txt` to `basic-file.log`. Rerun Fluentd with the same configuration file as last time. In the log output, you will have two entries saying `#0 following tail of ./Chapter3/basic-file.txt` and `#0 following the tail of ./Chapter3/ basic-file.log`. If you open the `pos_file`, you will see that each file has a line.

NOTE If you try to delete the pos file while Fluentd is still running, Fluentd will still be holding a handle to the file, which prevents deletion. Therefore, always shut down the Fluentd process first.

This means that wildcards must be used with care; it can be advantageous if an application creates multiple logs in the same place that need to be captured. The other use case where this can be of enormous help is if you elastically scale solutions such as web servers with all the servers configured to log to a high-performance network storage device. We can set the Fluentd configuration to target a single folder location rather than having a Fluentd configuration for each server's log files.

In this latter case, if each web server has its log file and new web servers are started after Fluentd, we need to detect the new log files. By default, Fluentd checks every 60 seconds for files matching the `path` attribute. This can be tuned using the attribute called `refresh_interval` using a time expression; for example, `refresh_interval 5s` means checking every 5 seconds. As a result, those new web server log files will be picked up on the subsequent scan. This provides a simple way to accommodate autoscaling.

3.2.5 *Expressing time*

When defining time as an interval, such as when you need to specify a task frequency, Fluentd has a time data type with an associated notation for setting these attribute's values. For time data type attributes, we can represent the time values as shown in table 3.1.

Table 3.1 Notations for expressing values of time type in Fluentd configurations

Interval	Character	Examples
Seconds	s	10s → 10 seconds 0.1s → 100ms
Minutes	m	1m → 1 minute 0.25m → 15 seconds
Hours	h	24h → 24 hours 0.25h → 15 minutes
Days	d	1d → 1 day 0.5d → 12 hours

The number provided will be treated as an integer. If the value is not an integer, it will be processed as a float representing a fraction of the time period. This notation applies to nearly all standard Fluentd and Fluent Bit plugin properties used for expressing time intervals.

3.2.6 *Controlling the impact of wildcards in filenames*

As we have just discussed, the use of wildcards can be powerful, but it also comes with risks, such as picking up unwanted files. There are several strategies that we can apply to control the risks of wildcards.

EXPLICIT LISTING

If all the filenames are known in advance, the `path` attribute can be populated as a comma-separated list of files. The files will be processed in the same way as the wildcard path matching multiple files—each file will be read and a pos entry recorded if we are recording read progress. The `path` attribute could look something like this:

```
path Chapter3/structured-rolling-log.0.log, ChapterN/another-rolling-log.0.log
```

As with many other plugins, it is possible to change the delimiter of each entry in the path. This is done by setting the attribute `path_delimiter` (e.g., `path_delimiter = ';'`), allowing us to get around any strange file-naming issues.

LOG SEQUENCING BY DATED FOLDERS

Some solutions allow you to configure logging so that folders contain all the logs for a particular period (all logs for a day, month, etc.). This makes it easier to manage multiple logs covering long periods. Fluentd is, therefore, able to process the structure of such file paths using date elements (e.g., `Chapter3/2020/08/30/app.log`). To achieve this effect, we need to modify the configuration to look like

```
path Chapter3/%Y/%m/%d/*.log
```

In the section "Expressing dates and times" in appendix B, there is a table that describes the different escape sequences, such as `%Y`, `%m`, and `%d`, shown in the preceding example.

Configuration errors

Fluentd is good at indicating errors in its configuration. Typically they are published as warnings in the Fluentd output with an explanation. For example, adding `%B` into the filename would yield `./Chapter3/structured-rolling-logMay.0.log not found. Continuing without tailing it`. This makes sense; the file does not exist. Another example of error handling is using escape sequences for incorrect date attributes, resulting in Fluentd treating the values as normal text and reporting errors.

USING FILE EXCLUSIONS

Another approach is to exclude files by providing a list of files that should never be considered using the `exclude_path` attribute. This attribute works just like the `path` attribute, so it can use wildcards or comma-separated lists. For example:

```
exclude_path: ./Chapter3/*.zip, ./Chapter3/threadDump*.txt
```

This declaration would prevent any files with .zip or thread dump files from being collected from the folder. This is a good way to mitigate the risk of accidentally picking up files that shouldn't be captured—for example, if an application's logging may also generate stack dump files or documents intended to be sent to a vendor for analysis in the same file location as normal logs.

ONLY CONSIDER RECENTLY CHANGED FILES

We can tell the plugin to only consider files that have changed within a certain time frame. So, we could assume that any files generated/changed soon after installation or a restart contain log events worth collecting; this is done by setting the attribute `limit_recently_modified` to a time-interval value. For example:

```
limit_recently_modified: 2m
```

The `limit_recently_modified` attribute is another instance of a time data type, so it can be configured in the way we just described.

Controlling which log files are examined by using the change duration can help in several ways:

- If a lot of log files are retained in the same location (as would be the case for log rotation—more on this shortly), then we can control how far back we go in processing files.
- In real-time use cases, such as log events from the equipment on a manufacturing line, if the log event is not captured within a specific time frame, then the log event becomes redundant, as nothing can be done. So why waste time processing log events that are effectively out of date?
- If the available compute capacity is small, and there is a large backlog of logs to be caught up on, you can create a condition where you never catch up to the currently generated events. Limiting how far backlog file processing can go reduces the risk of this scenario.

The use of this configuration needs to be carefully considered, along with the frequency of checking for new files. If the refresh interval is longer than the `limit_recently_modified` attribute, then by the time new files are identified, they may well have fallen out of the time frame of the limit.

3.2.7 *Replacing wildcards with delimited lists in action*

Back up the configuration file `Chapter3/Fluentd/basic-file-read2.conf`. Copy `basic-file.txt` to a file called `basic-file.log`, and then copy the file again so that this copy is called `basic-file.out`. Modify the path in the Fluentd configuration so that the wildcard is not in the path, and, using the comma notation, add the .txt and .out files.

Run Fluentd and the simulator as we did earlier using the commands

- `groovy LogSimulator.groovy ./Chapter3/SimulatorConfig/basic-log-file.properties ./TestData/source.txt`
- `fluentd -c Chapter3/Fluentd/basic-file-read2.conf`

REPLACING WILDCARDS WITH DELIMITED LISTS SOLUTION

The change to the configuration file should result in the attribute looking like `Chapter3/Fluentd/basic-file-read2-Answer.conf`. As with the wildcard run, the output will contain two log files (you can see this from the `pos_file` and by reviewing the console output). But the additional third file was not processed.

3.2.8 *Handling log rotation*

Log rotation is a common solution to allowing a substantial level of logging to be collected without logs files becoming so large that they are too difficult to work with or endlessly consume space. Log rotation also simplifies the process of purging older content rather than trimming a file; you simply delete the oldest log.

The *tail* input plugin can handle log rotation. The out-of-the-box approach is to define the configuration so that the path explicitly identifies the lead file in the rotation (e.g., `path ./Chapter3/structured-rolling-log.0.log`). By excluding wildcards from the folder that contains the log, rotation means that as files are rotated, they will not get picked up by the folder rescan. With this, we add the attribute `rotate_wait`. This attribute stipulates a period during which the current file, which will have been rotated to `./Chapter3/structured-rolling-log.1.log`, continues to be read. This is necessary, as the log writer may not have finished flushing content to the first file before creating the new file, possibly resulting in the final content of the older file being missed. So, awareness of how long it may take the writer to complete is important; if this isn't known, you need to allow enough time so that logs aren't being generated so fast that you can never catch up. We have created a setup to illustrate the behavior. Listing 3.2 shows the input configuration.

Rotate_wait: Suggested configuration

Every case is different and is dependent upon how the log writer mechanism works. For backend servers, we have typically looked at 30 seconds as a reasonable tradeoff. This is based on not wanting to get too far behind with the logs, as catchup can create spikes in workload (as we catch up with the log events on an active server), and if we experience a node issue, there is a fair chance we'll have caught the events leading up to the catastrophic event.

Listing 3.2   Chapter3/Fluentd/rotating-file-read.conf

```
<source>
  @type tail
  path ./Chapter3/structured-rolling-log.0.log

  rotate_wait = 15s

  read_lines_limit 5
  tag simpleFile
  pos_file ./Chapter3/rotating-file-read.pos_file
  read_from_head true

  <parse>
    @type none
  </parse>
</source>
```

Note the absence of a wildcard, although we could also use ./*/ structured-rolling-log.0.log as long as the other chapter folders are still clean.

Our rotation control with a decent amount of time expressed as an elapsed time using the notation described in section 3.2.5

Ensures we read from the beginning of the file. However, this will only be the beginning of the current rotation.

We can run this configuration with the console command from the folder where all the book's chapter folders have been downloaded to

```
fluentd -c ./Chapter3/Fluentd/rotating-file-read.conf
```

In a second console, run the following command:

```
groovy LogSimulator.groovy ./Chapter3/SimulatorConfig/jul-log-file.properties
    ./TestData/medium-source.txt
```

The LogSimulator runs with a configuration that leverages the *standard Java utility logging* framework (part of the core of Java) to provide the log rotation behavior. Java's logging works like a wide range of logging frameworks (logging frameworks are explored further in part 4). The simulator has been configured to loop over a data set several times. To make it easy to observe this behavior, the simulator adds a line counter for each line in the file. The iteration counter is added to the front of each message. So, if you track the output, you will see that all the lines are in the correct sequence as they come out of Fluentd. If you are quick enough, you will also observe log messages like this on the console:

```
2020-04-24 16:29:42.966831500 +0100 simpleFile: {"message":"2020-04-24--
    16:29:42 INFO   com.demo  (36-1) Heres a picture of me with REM. Thats
    me in the corner"}
2020-04-24 16:29:42 +0100 [info]: #0 detected rotation of ./Chapter3/
    structured-rolling-log.0.log; waiting 15 seconds
2020-04-24 16:29:42 +0100 [info]: #0 following tail of ./Chapter3/structured-
    rolling-log.0.log
```

Note the value (36-1) in the first of these lines; this is reflecting the line number and iteration number, respectively, from the LogSimulator configuration, with the line number being the line from the source log and the iteration being the count of how many times we've fed the log entries through for Fluentd to pick up. The rest of the first line reflects the log message. The following two lines tell us Fluentd is aware of the rotation file changes, but before ensuring that it is reading from the new lead file, it will continue to monitor the current file for any final content to be flushed.

> **WARNING** If Fluentd must restart but the application continues to run, and the logs rotate before Fluentd recovers, then the use of read_from_head true will take only log events from the start of the current rotation. A result of any logs between Fluentd stopping and the latest rotation will not get captured. This impact can be mitigated by ensuring that Fluentd will automatically restart if it fails and making the time to typically fill a log more than the time for Fluentd to fail and recover.

There is an alternative approach if it is necessary to use wildcards within a single folder using several attributes:

- refresh_interval—Controls the frequency at which the list of files that should be detected by the wildcard can be renewed.
- limit_recently_modified—This prevents older log files that may be picked up because of the wildcard from being used as long as they haven't changed in the period defined.
- pos_file_compaction_interval—This is an interval between each visit to the position tracker file to have its entries tidied up. Depending upon the configuration, the pos file can accumulate entries that then become redundant. As the position file is regularly read and updated, the fewer the entries in the file, the more efficient handling the position file will be. Given this, it is best to periodically do some housekeeping.

This approach depends on the log file being regularly written to; otherwise, the logging will "stutter." As a rule, a log file is out of scope for capture if the last update was older than the `limit_recently_modified` value. As before, we have a config file containing the input as shown in the next listing.

Listing 3.3   Chapter3/Fluentd/rotating-file-read-alternate.conf

```
<source>
  @type tail
  path ./Chapter3/structured-rolling-*.*.log
  read_lines_limit 5
  refresh_interval 30s

  limit_recently_modified 5s

  pos_file_compaction_interval 15s
  tag simpleFile
  pos_file ./Chapter3/rotating-file-read.pos_file
  read_from_head true
  <parse>
    @type none
  </parse>
</source>
```

The path has wild cards now.

The time interval to check to sweep for new log files if logs need to be set, as explained in section 3.2.5

To avoid accidentally reading the older logs, we identify a period in which the file must change.

The cleanup interface

As with the previous illustration, the Fluentd instance can be fired up with

```
fluentd -c ./Chapter3/Fluentd/rotating-file-read-alternate.conf
```

For the log events to track, you can use the same configuration as the last time:

```
groovy LogSimulator.groovy ./Chapter3/SimulatorConfig/jul-log-file.properties
     ./TestData/medium-source.txt
```

> **WARNING**   As with the main way to handle log rotation, it is possible to lose logs. In addition, if the `limit_recently_modified` attribute is set to be too short, the new log file is picked up as the current file has a final flush or file-handle closed, which may include any final log entries to be written to storage. These final file operations can impact the file change stamp, triggering Fluentd's file scan to detect the older log file as being in scope. This will potentially result in overlapping log entries as older log events are collected after more recent ones.

3.3   *Self-monitoring*

In the previous section, there are scenarios in rotating logs where there may be an outside chance of losing log events. But Fluentd, like any good application, logs events about its activity. This means it is possible to use Fluentd to monitor its well-being by tracking its log events. In addition to Fluentd's logs, there are other ways to obtain health information, as we will see.

3.3.1   *HTTP interface check*

Fluentd provides an HTTP endpoint that will provide information about how the instance is set up, as the following listing shows.

Listing 3.4 Chapter3/Fluentd/rotating-file-self-check.conf

```
<source>
  @type monitor_agent        The address to bind to
  bind 0.0.0.0               (i.e., the local server)
  port 24220                 The port to be used
</source>                    for this service
```

With the Fluentd running with the provided configuration (fluentd -c Chapter3/ Fluentd/ rotating-file-self-check.conf), start up Postman as we did in chapter 2. Then configure the address to be 0.0.0.0:24220/api/plugins.json. As you can see in the bind attribute, as with other plugins, this relates to the DNS or IP of the host, and the port attribute matches the port part of the URL. The interface could be described as {bind}:{port}/api/plugins.json. Unlike in chapter 2, where the operation was a POST, we need the operation set to be GET. Once done, click the send button, and we will see an HTTP representation of the running configuration returned, as highlighted in figure 3.1.

As you can see in figure 3.1, the URL and the result are highlighted. If you prefer the results to be represented using label tab-separated values (*ltsv*), just omit the

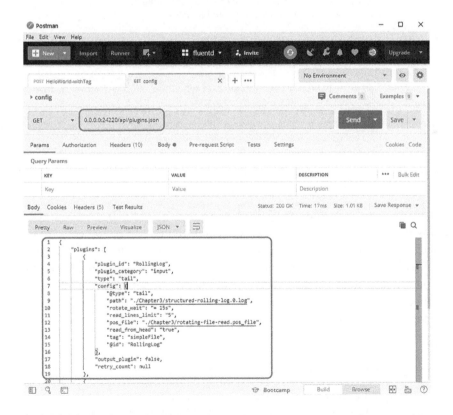

Figure 3.1 Postman illustrating the outcome of invoking the Fluentd API made available by including the monitor_agent plugin

.json from the URL. The URL can also handle several additional parameters when the output is set to be JSON. For example, adding to the URL ?debug=1 will yield a range of additional state information (note the value for debug does not matter; it is the presence of a parameter that is significant). The full set of parameters available to use as part of the monitoring agent URL is described in table 3.2.

Table 3.2   URI parameters available for calling the monitor_agent API

URI Parameter	Description	Example
debug	Will get additional plugin state information to be included in the response. The value set for the parameter does not matter.	?debug=0
with_ivars	The use of this parameter is sufficient for the instance_variables attribute to be included in the response. We will discuss the instance variables when we develop our plugin later in the book.	?with_ivars=false
with_config	Overrides the default or explicit setting include_config. The value provided must be true in lowercase; all other values are treated as false.	?with_config=true
with_retry	Overrides the default or explicit setting include_config. The value provided must be true or false in lowercase; all other values are treated as false.	?with_retry=true
tag	This filters the returned configuration to return only the directives linked to the tag name provided.	?tag=simpleFile
@id	This filters the response down to a specific directive. If the configuration doesn't have an explicit ID, then the value will be arbitrary.	?id= in_monitor_agent
@type	Allows the results to be filtered by plugin type.	?id=tail

We can also get the basic state of the plugins periodically reported within Fluentd by adding the tag and emit_interval attributes to the source directive. We can see the impact if we run the configuration with these values set using fluentd -c Chapter3/Fluentd/ rotating-file-self-check2.conf (or you can try editing and adding the attributes to the previous configuration yourself). With Fluentd up and running, we will start to see some status information every 10 seconds, like the following fragment published:

```
2020-05-01 17:10:04.041641100 +0100 self:
    {"plugin_id":"in_monitor_agent","plugin_category":"input","type":"monito
    r_agent","output_plugin":false,"retry_count":null}
```

As the information is tagged, we can direct this traffic to a central monitoring point, all of which saves on needing to script the HTTP polling. By incorporating the source in the following listing into the configuration file (before the match), the information gets fed to the same output.

```
<source>
  @type monitor_agent
  bind 0.0.0.0
  port 24220
  @id in_monitor_agent          Tells the monitor_agent to include configuration
  include_config true           information in the output of the agent

  emit_interval 10s             How frequently the monitoring_agent
                                should run its self-checking and output
</source>
```

3.4   *Imposing structure on log events*

So far, we have only looked at the most simplistic log files; however, very few log files are like this. The more structured they are, the better we can apply more meaning to log events, and it becomes easier to make the events actionable within Fluentd or downstream solutions. This means changing the type of parser from none to using one of the provided plugins. It is worth noting that we can group parsers into two general categories:

- *Product-specific parsers*—Some products are so heavily used that parsers have been produced specifically for them, rather than using a generic parser with detailed configuration. Apache and Nginx are examples of this. The benefit of these is a typically more straightforward configuration, and performance is higher as code is optimized to process just that specific log structure.
- *Generic parsers*—These can be grouped by either
  - Supporting a specific type of file notation (e.g., CSV, LTSV, discussed shortly)
  - Using highly configurable parser technology (e.g., Grok, Regex)

  These parsers are highly configurable, but at the same time, they are a lot more complex to configure. The more configurable and flexible the parser is, the less efficient the parsing of each event.

Out of the box, there is a range of parsers coving these categories. In addition to the pass-through parser (referred to as *none*), other parsers include CSV and JSON, along with specific parsers for web server monitor files. These are complemented with the other community (open source) provided parsers. Section 3.4.1 describes the core parsers, how they work, and when they can help. Section 3.4.2 continues with a couple of community-provided parsers also worth knowing about; these do not reflect the sum totality of all the possible parsers but are the ones we believe are worth knowing about.

Having reviewed the different options, we will apply one of the most commonly used parsers—Regex—to log events.

3.4.1   *Standard parsers*

APACHE2

Apache and *Nginx* are the two most dominant web servers in production today, with Apache having been available since the mid-1990s. In the process of applying monitoring within an enterprise, there is a good chance you'll encounter an Apache server, even if it is wrapped up as part of a larger product. This parser and the Nginx parser are designed to take standard web server logs that record the requests and responses that are processed. Recording details the following:

- Host
- User
- Method (HTTP POST, GET, etc.)
- URI
- HTTP request and response codes
- Payload size
- Referrer
- Agent

APACHE_ERROR

In addition to the core Apache log files, we also need to capture separate errors and associated diagnostic and debug information for CGI scripts, and so on. The information captured covers

- Level (e.g., warning, error)
- PID: process identifier
- Client associated with the error (e.g., browser, application)
- Error message

NGINX

This parser handles standard Nginx access logs that capture the HTTP calls received. At the heart of the plugin, it applies a regular expression to capture the message elements. This means that modifying the Nginx configuration would necessitate changes to this parser for a Regex and adapt the standard Regex accordingly. The attributes captured are

- *Remote*—Remote address
- *User*—Remote user
- *Method*—HTTP verb post, get, etc.
- *Path*—URL being used that Nginx is handling
- *Code*—HTTP code
- *Size*—Buffer size
- *Referrer*—Provided identity of the referrer when a call is referred
- *Agent*—Usually the browser type
- *Http_x_forwarded_for*—If forwarding has occurred, the HTTP header information recording the forwarding steps is held by this element.

NOTE More information about the Nginx logging can be obtained from http://mng.bz/1joX

CSV

The CSV parser is a rapid parser using, by default, a comma to delimit each field. The parser by default works by using Ruby's own CSV processor (see http://mng.bz/J12o).

Alternatively, an optimized quick parser (which is restricted to recognizing the use of quotes to allow the delimiter to be used as usual and multiple quotes as an escape pattern [e.g., """]) can be used by setting the attribute `parser_type` to `fast`.

An optimized string parser to apply meaning to a CSV string will always be better than trying to apply meaning by performing our string processing or using a Regex parser.

The `keys` attribute then takes a list of field names. The `time_key` attribute identifies which of the keys to use as the timestamp for the log event. The delimiter can be changed from a comma to something else using the delimiter attribute.

The following illustrates a CSV parser using the optimized option, rather than the default:

```
<parse>
  @type csv
  keys message, trans_id, time, host
  time_key time
  parser_type fast
</parse>
```

When applied to a log entry, `"my quoted message, to you"`, `124`, `2020/04/15 16:59:04`, `192.168.0.1` would produce an internal representation of

```
time: 1586966344
record:
{
  "message" : "my quoted message, to you",
  "trans_id" : "124",
  "host" : "192.168.0.1"
}
```

JSON

This treats the received log event as a JSON payload. There is a trend of treating log events as JSON structures to aid in meaning without creating considerable overheads in the log file size. This trend is even reflected in Fluentd; as you may remember, Fluentd treats log events as JSON objects.

It will look for a root element called `time` to apply as a log event timestamp. The tag associated with the log event can be found in the root element as the `tag`. Nested JSON structures are not, by default, processed. The parser could easily process the following structure, although additional attention would be needed to enable `nested1` to be processed as JSON in the following JSON fragment:

```
{
  "time" : "",
  "tag" : "myAppTag.Source1"
  "field1" : "blah",
  "field2" : "more blah",
  "fieldNested" :
  {
    "nested1": "nested blah"
  }
  "fieldn": "enough of the blah"
}
```

If desired, it is possible to change the JSON parser implementation for an alternate Ruby implementation. However, the default parser has shown up across multiple benchmarks as being the most performant.

TSV

This is very similar to the CSV parser. The key difference is there is no support for escaping and quoting values. It assumes a default delimiter as a tab character (or the escape sequence \t). As with the CSV parser, the TSV parser can have the delimiter changed (*delimiter* attribute). It also expects attributes of keys and time_key to define the JSON mapping and timestamp. It does offer one additional optional attribute called null_value_pattern, which, if set, will result in any value found to contain that value to replace the value in the JSON with an empty string. For example, null_value_pattern '-' would mean that a line like afield\t123\t-\tother-Field would result in

```
{
  "field1"  : "afield",
  "field2" : "123",
  "field3" : "",
  "field4" :"otherField"
}
```

LTSV

Label tab separated value (LTSV) is a variation on the tab-separated value. The key difference is that each tab-separated value is prefixed by a label and a label-delimiting character in the form of a colon. This means the values have semantic meaning, and value order is not important. As a result, there is no need for masses of comma separators for empty values, as you can see in CSV files. It can be argued that this is more efficient and tolerant than JSON in terms of logging data (e.g., no additional quotes, characters, braces), and only three characters are reserved—tab, label delimiter, and new line. Additional characters are not legal in JSON. For example, host-name:localhost/tip:127.0.0.1 (note tab is represented by /t in the middle of the example) has two labels—hostname and ip. LTSV is documented in detail at http://ltsv.org/ and includes links to helpful tools.

As with the TSV parser, we can modify the delimiter so characters other than the tab can be used. In addition, the attribute label_delimiter can be used to change the default (colon) label delimiter.

MSGPACK

MessagePack is an open source standard and library that describes inline the payload allowing content to be removed or shortened. The format is supported in several parts of Fluentd (which is unsurprising, considering it was developed by the same team responsible for Fluentd).

It works by providing a short field and value descriptors. As a result, compression can be achieved by stripping out redundant characters such as quotes, whitespace, and so on.

This format can be used for communication between Fluentd and Fluent Bit nodes and is worth using when crossing networks, particularly with additional dynamic HTTP-based compression (more at https://msgpack.org/ and www.website-optimization.com/speed/tweak/compress/). For example, the JSON fragment {"Fluentd": 1, "msgPackSupport":true} would be reduced to the hex

```
82 a7 46 6c 75 65 6e 74 64 01 ae 6d 73 67 50 61 63 6b 53 75 70 70 6f 72 74 c3
```

which is 26 bytes and a compression of 68%.

Given this efficiency, it is worth considering using msgpack when you're sharing log events that cross wide area networks, cloud providers, and so on, as those networks will cost more based on data volume and can be subject to bandwidth and latency issues.

MULTILINE

Unfortunately, not all logs are elegant such that a single line represents a single event, as is the case when handling stack traces and stack dumps. The *multiline* plugin addresses this by defining multiple regular expressions (Regex). The regex expressions allow the log line to be parsed and tease out the log elements wanted. For this to work, the plugin requires a Regex to identify the first line of a multiline log event (and, by implication, the end of this log entry). This Regex is specified with an attribute-name of format_firstline. After this attribute, up to 20 additional regex formats can be defined in numerical sequence.

See the following for how the Regex works, but the configuration follows the pattern

```
@type multiline
format_firstline <regex expression>
format1 <regex expression>
format2 <regex expression>
…
formatN <regex expression>
</parse>
```

The multiline plugin as a parser is currently only available with the *tail* input plugin because of the unique interactions between the two plugins.

If the application's logging framework can be configured to not produce multiline output (e.g., Log4J 2 can support this in its pattern configuration), then it is worth at least considering. This is because the multiline parser isn't as efficient as most single-line parsers. Another strategy to avoid the multiline parser is for log events like stack traces to be written to separate files. Separate files mean that we can use the multiline parser on just a subset of all log events.

NONE

This can be used where a parser must be defined (e.g., in the tail plugin). But no parsing is applied, and the entire log line forms the Fluentd record. The time of reading is set to be the time value for the log event.

REGEX

Regex parser is probably the most powerful parser option available, but as a result, it is also the most complex. In section 3.4.3, we will drill into the use of Regex in more depth.

SYSLOG

Syslogs are most commonly generated by OS and infrastructure processes, but nothing prevents applications from using the format. The original unofficial structure of a syslog entry was formalized by the IETF as *RFC 3164* (https://tools.ietf.org/html/rfc3164). This was then superseded by *RFC 5424* (https://tools.ietf.org/html/rfc5424) in 2009. As some hardware can take many years before being replaced, Fluentd can handle both standards. By default, Fluentd will assume the original standard, but you can tell Fluentd to use the later standard, or use the payload to work it by setting the `message_format` attribute with one (*rfc3164*, *rfc5424*, *auto*). If you know which format will be handled, it is better to explicitly define it in the configuration. Doing so removes the overhead of having to evaluate each event before parsing. If a single endpoint is consuming both event types, you may have to accept the overhead.

The plugin has two different algorithms for processing the events—string processing logic and a regular expression (`regexp`). Currently, the default is *regex*, but in the future, this will be changed to default to the string option, which is faster than the `regexp` algorithm. If you wish to force the algorithm, the attribute `parser_type` needs to be set with either *regexp* or string.

3.4.2   *Third-party parsers*

In addition to the core parsers, there are some third-party parsers. The following ones are only a subset of the possible options. However, these are either certified or have been heavily downloaded, so they are likely to have benefited from extensive use and, given that the code is open source, benefited from Linus's Law. Given enough eyeballs, all bugs are shallow—Eric Raymond).

MULTIFORMAT PARSER PLUGIN FOR FLUENTD

This attempts to use different format patterns in the defined order to get a match. This is available from http://mng.bz/wnoO.

Grok parser for Fluentd

This uses a Grok-based approach to pull details from a log entry. It includes multiline support. This is available from https://github.com/fluent/fluent-plugin-grok-parser. The benefit of using the Grok parser is that Grok is used by Logstash as a filtering and parsing mechanism; therefore, it is a relatively small step to leverage Grok predefined patterns and switch between using Logstash and Fluentd.

3.4.3   *Applying a Regex parser to a complex log*

As previously noted, the Regex or regular expression parser is probably the most powerful and the hardest to use. In most applications of Regex, the outcome is normally a single result, a substring, or a count of occurrences of a string. However, when it comes to Fluentd, we need the regex to produce multiple values back, such as setting the log event time, breaking down the payload to the first level of elements in the JSON event body. Let's take a Regex expression and break it down to highlight the basics. But before we can do that, we need to work with a realistic log entry. Let's run up the log simulator configuration for this, using the command

```
groovy LogSimulator.groovy Chapter3/SimulatorConfig/jul-log-file2.properties
    ./TestData/medium-source.txt
```

Note that this is a slightly different configuration from the last example, so we can see a couple of possibilities within Fluentd. Looking at the output file generated (still `structuredrolling-log.0.log`), the payload that is being sent now appears as

```
2020-04-30--20:10:52 INFO   com.demo   (6-1) {"log":"A clean house is the sign
    of a broken computer"}
```

In this output line, we can see the applied timestamp, with to-the-second accuracy, then a space followed by the log level, more space, and then a package name, followed by the numbering scheme, as previously explained. Finally, the core log entry is wrapped as a JSON structure. When we parse the message, we need to strip away that JSON notation, as it should not be in the JSON structure we want.

The goal is to end up with a structure as follows in Fluentd, so we can then use the values for future manipulation:

```
{
  "level":"INFO",
  "class":"com.demo",
  "line":33,
  "iteration":1,
   "msg":"What is an astronauts favorite place on a computer? The Space bar!"
  }
```

Here is the regular expression, with character positions added below it, to make it easy to precisely reference each piece:

```
(?<time>\S+)\s(?<level>[A-Z]*)\s*(?<class>\S+)[^\d]*(?<line>[\d]*)
1234567890123456789012345678901234567890123456789012345678901234567
0         1         2         3         4         5         6

\-(?<iteration>[\d]*)\)[\s]+\{"log":"(?<msg>.*(?="\}))
89012345678901234567890123456789012345678901234567890123
  7         8         9        10        11        12
```

As part of the expression, we need to use Regex's ability to define groups of text. The scope of a group is defined by open and closing brackets (e.g., characters 1 and 12). To assign some source text to a JSON element, we need to use ?<name>, where the name is the element name to appear in the JSON. It should be the values `level`, `class`, `line`, `iteration`, and `msg` in our case. In addition to this, we also need to capture the log event time with the default `time` value. This can be seen between characters 2 and 8, for example, and between 16 and 23. Immediately after this, we can use the Regex notation to describe the text to be captured. For this, we use `\S` (characters 9 and 10), which means a non-whitespace character; by adding a + (character 11), we are declaring that this should happen one or more times. We will need to provide the parser with additional configuration, as we will need to declare how to break this part of the message into a specific time.

The first character not to match the pattern is the space between the time and the log level—so we use the Regex representation for a single space (characters 13 and 14) and then start the group for the log level.

The expression defines the log level, which we know will be formed by one or more alphabetic uppercase characters. The use of the square brackets denotes a choice of values (characters 24 and 28). We could list all the possible characters within the brackets, but for readability, we've opted to indicate between capital A and capital Z; the hyphen between A and Z (character 27) denotes that this is a range. As the log level word will be multiple characters, we use the asterisk to note multiple. That completes the log level. So, outside the group, we need to denote the multiple whitespace characters—that is, \s* (starting at 31).

We can follow the same basic pattern used for the date and time for a path or class string. This can be seen between characters 34 and 46. To pass along the line to the following meaningful characters, we have defined a range with the Regex expression \d (characters 49 and 50), which means a numeric digit. However, by adding the circumflex (^), we negate the following value—in this case, any non-numeric character. This means that we will skip over the whitespace and the opening bracket.

The groups for the line and iteration are the same—multiple digits required with a hyphen between the two groups. The hyphen is escaped (character 68) because it has meaning to Regex. We can see the same character escape for the curly bracket at character 95.

After the curly bracket starts the log detail, we know what the text is, so we can put it into the expression (starting at character 97). This underlines the importance of being exact in the expression, as non-escaped code characters will get treated as literals and therefore will be expected to be found where they occur in the Regex. If the literal character is not found as expected by the Regex, then the string being processed will be rejected.

The next new Regex trick is the use of the dot (character 112). This denotes any character; when combined with a following asterisk, then the expression becomes multiple occurrences of any character. This makes for an interesting challenge—how do we stop the closing quotes and bracket from being consumed into the msg group? This is by using a subgroup definition containing ?= (characters 115 and 116). This describes a look ahead for the following sequence when you find that sequence and then stop allocating text to the current group. As a result, the match expression is " }, but as a curly bracket has Regex meaning, we have to escape it with another slash. This does mean that any characters after this will be ignored.

In appendix B, we have included details of the Regex expressions, so you have a quick reference for building your expressions. Please note that if you research Regex elsewhere, while there is a high level of commonality in implementations, you will find subtle differences. Keep in mind that the Regex here is implemented using the Ruby language.

To complete the parser configuration, we need to tell the parser which named grouping represents the date and time (often shortened to *date-time* or *date-time-group* [DTG]) and how that date-time is represented. In our case, the date and time can be expressed using the pattern of %Y-%m-%d--%T. As the time element is standard, we can use one of the short circuit formats (%T) described in appendix B. Finally, let's piece all this information together and define the parser attributes (listing 3.6).

> ### Regular expression processing is a rich and complex capability
>
> There are entire books devoted to the subject and many more with dedicated chapters. Here we have only scratched the surface, giving just enough to help you understand how it works within the Fluentd context. It might be worthwhile investing in a book to help. This link may also help: www.rubyguides.com/2015/06/ruby-regex/.

NOTE When the parser expression fails during processing, Fluentd will generate a warning log entry.

Listing 3.6 Chapter3/Fluentd/rotating-file-read-regex.conf—parse extract

```
<parse>                          We have changed the parser type          The expression needs to
  @type regexp        ◁—┘        here to regexp for regular expressions.  be provided between
                                                                          forward slashes. It is
  Expression /(?<time>\S+)\s(?<level>[A-Z]*)                              possible to add extra
\s*(?<class>\S+)[^\d]*(?<line>[\d]*)\-(?<iteration>[\d]*)\)               controls after the trailing
    [\s]+\{"log":"(?<msg>.*(?="\}))/                              ◁—      slash, as we will see.

  time_format %Y-%m-%d--%T                                    ◁—         time_format allows us to
  time_key time    ◁—┐  time_key is used to tell Fluentd which           define the date-time
                      │  extracted value to use for the timestamp.       format more concisely.
</parse>              │  By default, it will use a value called time,
                      │  so technically this is redundant.
```

This configuration can be run by restarting the simulator, as we did to get an example value, and then starting Fluentd with the configuration

```
fluentd -c Chapter3/Fluentd/rotating-file-read-regex.conf
```

As Fluentd outputs the processed stream of events to console, you will see entries like this:

```
2020-04-30 23:29:47.000000000 +0100 simpleFile:
    {"level":"","class":"INFO","line":"50","iteration":"1","msg":"The truth
    is out there. Anybody got the URL"}
```

Each line printed by Fluentd to the console will take the date and time of the log event, the time zone offset, the event tag, and the payload as a correctly structured JSON, with the time omitted. Notice how the nanoseconds are all 0. This is because we have given Fluentd a log time that does not have nanosecond precision; therefore, that part of the timestamp is left at 0.

More importantly, you will note that all the JSON values are quoted, so they will be treated as strings. This may not be an issue. But having come this far, it would be a shame not to define the data types correctly. It may well enable downstream activities, such as extrapolating additional meaning, to be more effective. The defining of non-string data types is straightforward. We need to add the attribute types within the parser construct, which takes a comma-separated list with each defined value described in the format *name:type*. In our use case, we would want to add `types line:integer, iteration:integer`. The complete list of types supported are

- *string*—Can be defined explicitly, but is the default type
- *bool*—Boolean
- *integer*—Representation for any whole number (i.e., no decimal places)
- *float*—Represents any decimal number
- *time*—Converts the value into the way that Fluentd represents time internally. We can extend this to describe how the time should translate. For example:
  - *date:time:%d/%b/%Y:%H:%M—Defining the formatting of the representation*
  - *date:time:unixtime—Timer from 1 Jan 1970 in integer format*
  - *date:time:float—The same epoch point, but the number is as float*
- *array*—A sequence of values of the same type (e.g., all strings, all integers)

The handling of the array requires the values to have a delimiter to separate each value. The delimiter by default is a comma, but it can be changed by adding a colon and the delimiter character. For example, a comma-delimited array could be defined as `myList:array`. But if I wanted to replace the delimiter with a hash, then the expression would be `myList:array:#`.

The last manipulation of the JSON involves whether we would like the date time-stamp to be included in the JSON; after all, it was in the body of the log event. This can easily be done by adding `keep_time_key true` to the parser attributes.

We can add the changes described (although the provided configuration has these values ready but commented out, so you could just uncomment them and rerun the simulator and Fluentd as before). As a result of these changes, the log entries will appear like this:

```
2020-05-01 00:14:25.000000000 +0100 simpleFile: {"time":"2020-05-01--
    00:14:25","level":"","class":"INFO","line":75,"iteration":1,"msg":"I
    started a band called 999 megabytes we still havent gotten a gig"}
```

If you look at the JSON body now, our numeric elements are no longer in quotes, and the timestamp appears in the JSON payload.

Evaluating/checking Regex expressions

Regex expressions can be challenging; the last thing we want to have to do is run logs throughout the Fluentd environment to determine whether the expression is complete or not. To this end, Fluentd UI configuration for tail supports Regex validation.

In addition, there is a free web tool called Fluentular (https://fluentular.herokuapp
.com/) that will allow you to develop and test expressions.

Some IDEs, such as Microsoft's Visual Studio Code, have Regex tools to help visualize the Regex being built—for example, Regexp Explain (http://mng.bz/q2YA). The
completed Regex can be seen in the following figure.

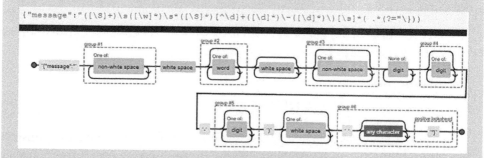

**Visualization of a regular expression (Regex) using Regexp Explain in visual code to help you
understand how a parser should process a log event. This can also be done with https://
regexper.com/.**

If you look carefully, you will note that the `?<element name>` is missing; however,
it is easy to see where these pieces need to be added, as the core parts have been
grouped. If the grouping is used, it becomes easy to port the expression into Fluentd
and add the elements.

3.4.4 *Putting parser configuration into action*

This exercise is designed to allow you to work with the parser. The simulator configuration `Chapter3/SimulatorConfig/jul-log-file2-exercise.properties`
has some differences to the previous worked example. Copy the Fluentd configuration file used to illustrate the parser (`Chapter3/Fluentd/rotating-file-read-
regex.conf`). Then, modify the parser expression so that all the input values are
properly represented as JSON elements of the log event, rather than just the payload
as defaulted by Fluentd. A variation of the log simulator configuration can be run
using the command

```
groovy LogSimulator.groovy Chapter3/SimulatorConfig/jul-log-file2-
    exercise.properties ./TestData/medium-source.txt
```

Run the revised Fluentd configuration and determine whether your changes have
been effective.

ANSWER

The parser configuration should appear like the code shown in the following listing.

Listing 3.7   Chapter3/ExerciseResults/rotating-file-read-regex-Answer.conf

```
<parse>
  @type regexp
  Expression /(?<time>\S+)\s(?<level>
[A-Z]*)\s*(?<class>\S+) [^\d]*(?<iteration>[\d]*)\-(?<line>[\d]*)\][\s]+
\{"event":"(?<msg>.*(?="\,))/
  time_format %Y-%m-%d--%T
  time_key time
</parse>
```

A complete configuration file is provided at `Chapter3/ExerciseResults/` `rotating-file-read-regex-Answer.conf`.

Summary

- Fluentd's configuration can be validated using the `dry_run` option without needing to start a proper deployment.
- Log events held in log files can be wide-ranging in format, from unstructured to fully structured. Fluentd's ability to consume log events from files allows it to accommodate this level of diversity.
- Fluentd can handle log file complexity—the processes applied to log files can be complex, such as handling log rotation and tracking where to resume if Fluentd is stopped and started.
- A wide range of logging event sources can be handled as a result of Fluentd's plugin model and broad community and vendor support.
- Input plugins can use a range of out-of-the-box parsers (e.g., CSV, Regex, LTSV, web server standard files) to apply structure and meaning to the log event.
- Developing configurations for regular expressions (regex) can be challenging, but tools exist to ease this challenge (e.g., Fluentular, designed specifically for Fluentd; Regexp Explain; and others).
- In addition to monitoring other systems using plugins, Fluentd can be configured to provide the means to be monitored via methods such as enabling and using an HTTP endpoint to check Fluentd.

Using Fluentd
to output log events

This chapter covers

- Using output plugins for files, MongoDB, and Slack
- Applying different buffering options with Fluentd
- Reviewing the benefits of buffering
- Handling buffer overloads and other risks of buffering
- Adding formatters to structure log events

Chapter 3 demonstrated how log events can be captured and how helper plugins such as parsers come into play. But capturing data is only of value if we can do something meaningful with it, such as delivery to an endpoint formatted so the log events can be used—for example, storing the events in a log analytics engine or sending a message to an operations (Ops) team to investigate. This chapter is about showing how Fluentd enables us to do that. We look at how Fluentd output plugins can be used from files, as well as how Fluentd works with MongoDB and collaboration/social tools for rapid notifications with Slack.

This chapter will continue to use the LogSimulator, and we will also use a couple of other tools, such as MongoDB and Slack. As before, complete configurations are available in the download pack from Manning or via the GitHub repository, allowing us to focus on the configuration of the relevant plugin(s). Installation steps for MongoDB and Slack are covered in appendix A.

4.1   *File output plugin*

Compared to the *tail* (file input) plugin, we are less likely to use the file output plugin, as typically we will want to output to a tool that allows us to query, analyze, and visualize the events. There will, of course, be genuine cases where file output is needed for production. However, it is one of the best options as a stepping-stone to something more advanced, as it is easy to see outcomes and the impact of various plugins, such as parsers and filters. Logging important events to file also lends itself to easily archiving the log events for future reference if necessary (e.g., audit log events to support legal requirements). To that end, we will look at the file output before moving on to more sophisticated outputs.

With the file output (and, by extension, any output that involves directly or indirectly writing physical storage), we need to consider several factors:

- Where can we write to in the file system, as dictated by storage capacity and permissions?
- Does that location have enough capacity (both allocated and physical capacity)?
- How much I/O throughput can the physical hardware deliver?
- Is there latency on data access (NAS and SAN devices are accessed through networks)?

While infrastructure performance isn't likely to impact development work, it is extremely important in preproduction (e.g., performance testing environments) and production environments. It is worth noting that device performance is essential for the file plugin. Other output plugins are likely to be using services that will include logic to optimize I/O (e.g., database caching, optimization of allocated file space). With output plugins, we have likely consolidated multiple sources of log events. Therefore, we could end up with a configuration that has Fluentd writing all the inputs to one file or location. The physical performance considerations can be mitigated using buffers (as we will soon see) and caching.

4.1.1   *Basic file output*

Let's start with a relatively basic configuration for Fluentd. In all the previous chapters' examples, we have just seen the content written to the console. Now, rather than a console, we should simply push everything to a file. To do this, we need a new `match` directive in the configuration, but we'll carry on using the file source for log events.

To illustrate that an output plugin can handle multiple inputs within the configuration, we have included the self-monitoring source configuration illustrated in the previous chapter, in addition to a log file source. To control the frequency of log events generated by the Fluentd's `self_monitor`, we can define another attribute called `emit_interval`, which takes a duration value—for example, 10s (10 seconds). The value provided by `emit_interval` is the time between log events being generated by Fluentd. Self-monitoring can include details like how many events have been processed, how many worker processes are managed, and so on.

At a minimum, the file output plugin simply requires the `type` attribute to be defined and a path pointing to a location for the output using the `path` attribute. In the following listing, we can see the relevant parts of our `Chapter4/Fluentd/rotating-file-read-file-out.conf` file. The outcome of this configuration may surprise you, but let's see what happens.

> **Listing 4.1 Chapter4/Fluentd/rotating-file-read-file-out.conf—match extract**

```
<source>
  @type monitor_agent
  bind 0.0.0.0
  port 24220
  @id in_monitor_agent
  include_config true
  tag self
  emit_interval 10s
</source>

<match *>
    @type file                              ⟵  Changes the plugin
    path ./Chapter4/fluentd-file-output          type to file
</match>                                                       The location of the
                                                         ⟵  file to be written
```

The outcome of using this new `match` directive can be seen if the LogSimulator and Fluentd are run with the following commands:

- `fluentd -c ./Chapter4/Fluentd/rotating-file-read-file-out.conf`
- `groovy LogSimulator.groovy ./Chapter4/SimulatorConfig/jul-log -output2.properties ./TestData/medium-source.txt`

The easy presumption would be that all the content gets written to a file called `fluentd-file-output`. However, what has happened is that a folder is created using the last part of the path as its name (i.e., `fluentd-file-output`), and you will see two files in that folder. The file will appear with a semi-random name (to differentiate the different buffer files) and a metadata file with the same base name. What Fluentd has done is to implicitly make use of a buffering mechanism. The adoption of a buffer with a default option is not unusual in output plugins; some do forgo the use of buffering—for example, the *stdout* plugin.

4.1.2 Basics of buffering

Buffering, as you may recall from chapter 1, is a Fluentd helper plugin. Output plugins need to be aware of the impact they can have on I/O performance. As a result, most output plugins use a buffer plugin that can behave *synchronously* or *asynchronously*.

The synchronous approach means that as log events are collected into *chunks*, as soon as a chunk is full, it is written to storage. The asynchronous approach utilizes an additional queue stage. The queue stage interacting with the output channel is executed in a separate thread, so the filling of chunks shouldn't be impacted by any I/O performance factors.

The previous example had not explicitly defined a buffer; we saw the output plugin applying a default to using a file buffer. This makes more sense when you realize that the file output plugin supports the ability to compress the output file using gzip, increasing effectiveness the more content you compress at once.

In figure 4.1, we have numbered the steps. As the arrows' varying paths indicate, steps in the life cycle can be bypassed. All log events start in step 1, but if no buffering is in use, the process immediately moves to step 5, where the physical I/O operation occurs, and then we progress to step 6. If there is an error, step 6 can send the logic back to the preceding step to try again. This is very much dependent upon the plugin implementation but is common to plugins such as database plugins. If the retries fail or the plugin doesn't support the concept, some plugins support the idea of a secondary plugin to be specified.

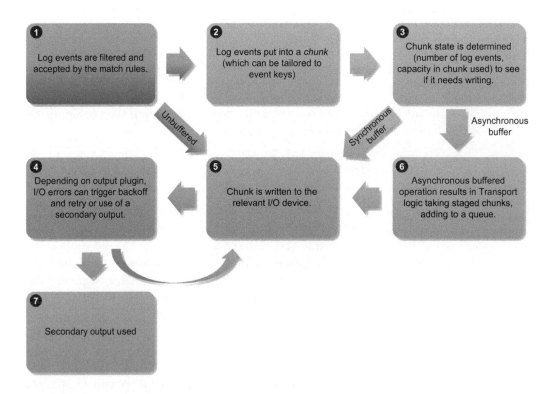

Figure 4.1   Log event passing through the output life cycle (e.g., the italic steps are only used when things go wrong)

A secondary plugin is another output plugin that can be called (step 7). Typically, a secondary plugin would be as simple as possible to minimize the chance of a problem so that the log events could be recovered later. For example, suppose the output plugin called a remote service from the Fluentd node (e.g., on a different network, in a separate server cluster, or even a data center). In that case, the secondary plugin could be a simple file output to a local storage device.

> **NOTE** We would always recommend that a secondary output be implemented with the fewest dependencies on software and infrastructure. Needing to fall to a secondary plugin strongly suggests broader potential problems. So the more straightforward, less dependent it is on other factors, the more likely that the output won't be disrupted. Files support this approach very well.

If buffering has been configured, then steps 1 through 3 would be performed. But then the following action would depend upon whether the buffering was asynchronous. If it was synchronous, then the process would jump to step 5, and we would follow the same steps described. For asynchronous buffering, the chunk of logs goes into a separate process managing a queue of chunks to be written. Step 4 represents the buffer operating asynchronously. As the chunks fill, they are put into a queue structure, waiting for the output mechanism to take each chunk to output the content. This means that the following log event to be processed is not held up by the I/O activity of steps 5 onward.

Understanding gzip compression

Gzip is the GNU implementation of a ZLIB compression format, defined by IETF RFC's 1950, 1951, and 6713. Zip files use an algorithm known as Lempel-Ziv coding (LZ77) to compress the contents. In simple terms, the algorithm works by looking for reoccurring patterns of characters; when a reoccurrence is found, that string is replaced with a reference to the previous occurrence. So the larger the string occurrences identified as reoccurring, the more effective reference becomes, giving more compression—the bigger the file, the more likely to find reoccurrences.

Out of the box, Fluentd provides the following buffer types:

- *Memory*
- *File*

As you may have realized, the path is used as the folder location to hold its buffered content and contains both the content and a metadata file. Using file I/O for the buffer doesn't give much of a performance boost in terms of the storage device unless you establish a *RAM disk* (aka, *RAM drive*). A file-based buffer still provides some benefits; the way the file is used is optimized (keeping files open, etc.). It also acts as a staging area to accumulate content before applying compression (as noted earlier, the more data involved in a zip compression, the greater the compression possible). In addition, the logged content won't be lost as a result of some form of process or hardware failure, and the buffer can be picked back up when the server and/or Fluentd restart.

NOTE   RAM drives work by allocating a chunk of memory for storage and then telling the OS's file system that it is an additional storage device. Applications that use this storage believe they are writing to a physical device like a disk, but the content is actually written to memory. More information can be found at www.techopedia.com/definition/2801/ram-disk.

With buffers in many plugins being involved by default, or explicitly, we should look at how to start configuring buffer behaviors. We know when the events move from the buffer to the output destination, how frequently such actions occur, and how these configurations impact performance. The life cycle illustrated in figure 4.1 provides clues as to the configuration possibilities.

4.1.3   *Chunks and Controlling Buffering*

As figure 4.1 shows, the buffer's core construct is the idea of a chunk. The way we configure chunks, aside from synchronous and asynchronous, will influence the performance. Chunks can be controlled through the allocation of storage space (allowing for a reserved piece of contiguous memory or disk to be used) or through a period. For example, all events during a period go into a single chunk, or a chunk will continue to fill with events until a specific number of log events or the chunk reaches a certain size. Separation of the I/O from the chunk filling is beneficial if there is a need to provide connection retries for the I/O, as might be the case with shared services or network remote services, such as databases.

In both approaches, it is possible through the configuration to set attributes so that log events don't end up lingering in the buffer because a threshold is never fully met. Which approach to adopt will be influenced by the behavior of your log event source and the tradeoff of performance against resources available (e.g., memory), as well as the amount of acceptable latency in the log events moving downstream.

Personally, I tend to use size constraints, which provides a predictable system behavior; this may reflect my Java background and preference not to start unduly tuning the virtual machine.

Table 4.1 shows the majority of the possible controls on a buffer. Where the control can have some subtlety in how it can behave, we've included more elaboration.

Table 4.1   Buffer configuration controls

Attribute	Description
timekey	This is the number of seconds each chunk will be responsible for holding (by default, 1 day). The time attribute of a log_event then determines which chunk to add the event to. For example, if our timekey was set to 300 (seconds) and the chunk started on the hour, then when an event timestamped 10:00:01 arrived and further events arrived every 30 seconds, an additional 9 more events would be held in the first chunk. The next chunk would hold events that started arriving after 10:05:00, so the next event would be 10:05:01.

Table 4.2 Buffer configuration controls *(continued)*

Attribute	Description
timekey	If we had additional out-of-order events arriving before 10:05 (e.g., with time-stamps 10:03:15 and 10:03:55), but they didn't arrive until 10:04:31, then they would still be added to the first chunk.
	This behavior can be further modified by the timekey_wait attribute.
timekey_wait	This is the number of seconds after the end of a chunk's storage period before the chunk is written. This defaults to 60 seconds.
	Extending our timekey example, if this value was set to 60s (60 seconds), then that chunk would be held in memory until 10:06 before being flushed. If another event was received at 10:05:21 with a timestamp of 10:04:49, this would go in our first chunk, not the chunk covering the received time.
chunk_limit_size	This defines the maximum size of a chunk, which defaults to 8 MB for memory and 256 MB for a file buffer. The chances of increasing this threshold are small, but you may consider reducing it to limit the maximum footprint of a container or constraints of an IoT device. Remember that you can operate multiple chunks.
chunk_limit_records	This defines the maximum number of log events in a single chunk. If the size of log events can fluctuate wildly in size, this will need to be considered. A number of large logs could create a very large chunk, creating risks around memory exhaustion and varying durations for writing chunks.
total_limit_size	This is the limit of storage allowed for all chunks before the new events received will be dropped with error events lost accordingly.
	This defaults to 512 MB for memory and 64 GB for file.
chunk_full_threshold	Once the percentage of the buffer's capacity exceeds this value, the chunk is treated as full and moved to the I/O stage. This defaults to 0.95. If log events are very large relative to the allocated memory, you may consider lowering this threshold to ensure more predictable performance, particularly if you limit the queue size.
queued_chunks_limit_size	This defines the number of chunks in the queue waiting to be persisted as required. Ideally, this should never be larger than the flush_thread_count.
	The default value is 1.
compress	This accepts only the values of either text (default) or gzip. When gzip is set, then compression will be applied. If other compression mechanisms are introduced, the options available will expand.
flush_at_shutdown	This tells the buffer whether it should write everything to the output before allowing Fluentd to shut down gracefully. For the memory buffer, this defaults to true but is false for a file, as the contents can be recovered on startup. We recommend setting it to true in most cases, given that you may not know when Fluentd will restart and process the cached events (if it can).
flush_interval	This is a duration defining how frequently the buffered content should be written to the output storage mechanism. This means we can configure behavior centered on either volumes or time intervals. This defaults to 60 seconds (60s).

Table 4.2   Buffer configuration controls *(continued)*

Attribute	Description
flush_mode	Accepted values are • default—Uses lazy if chunk keys are defined, otherwise interval • lazy—Flush/write chunks once per timekey. • interval—Flush/write chunks per specified time via flush_interval. • immediate—Flush/write chunks immediately after events are appended into chunks.
flush_thread_count	The number of threads to be used to write chunks. A number above 1 will create parallel threads—this may not be desirable depending on the output type. For example, if a connection pool to a database can handle multiple connections, more than 1 is worth considering. But more than 1 on a file could create contention or write collisions. This defaults to 1.
flush_thread_interval	The length of time the flush thread should sleep before looking to see if a flush is required. Expressed as a number of seconds in floating-point format and defaults to 1.
delayed_commit_timeout	When using the asynchronous I/O, we need to set a maximum time to allow the thread to run before we assume it must be experiencing an error. If this time is exceeded (default 60s), then the thread is stopped. This needs to be tuned to take into account how responsive the target system is. For example, writing large chunks to a remote database will take longer than writing small chunks to a local file system.
overflow_action	If the input into the buffer is faster than we can write content out of the buffer, we will experience an overflow condition. This configuration allows us to define how to address that problem. Options are • throw_exception—Throw an exception that will appear in the Fluentd log as a BufferOverflowError; this is the default. • block—Block input processing to allow events to be written. • interval—Flush/write chunks per specified time via flush_interval. • drop_oldest_chunk—Drop the oldest chunk of data to free a chunk up for use. • Throwing exceptions may be okay when an overflow scenario is never expected, and the potential loss of log events is a risk worth taking. But in more critical areas, we would suggest consciously choosing an alternative, such as interval.

We can amend the configuration with the understanding of buffer behavior (or use the prepared one). As we recommend flushing on shutdown, we should set this to true (flush_at_shutdown true). As we want to quickly see the impact of the changes, let's set the maximum number of records to 10 (chunk_limit_records 10) and the maximum time before flushing a chunk to 30 seconds (flush_interval 30). Otherwise, if we have between 1 and 9 log events in the buffer, they'll never get flushed if the sources stop creating log events. Finally, we have added an extra layer of protection in our configuration by imposing a time-out of the buffer write process. We can see this in the following listing.

Listing 4.2 Chapter4/Fluentd/rotating-file-read-file-out2.conf—match extract

> By default, the file buffer doesn't flush on shutdown, as events won't be lost by stopping the Fluentd instance. However, it is desirable to see all events completed at shutdown. There is the risk that a configuration change will mean the file buffer isn't picked up on restart, resulting in log events effectively being in limbo.

```
<match *>
    @type file
    path ./Chapter4/fluentd-file-output
    <buffer>
     flush_at_shutdown true

      delayed_commit_timeout 10
      chunk_limit_records 10

      flush_interval 30

    </buffer>
</match>
```

> As we understand our log content and want to see things happen very quickly, we will use several logs rather than the capacity to control the chunk size, which indirectly influences how soon events are moved from the buffer to the output destination.

> As the buildup of self-monitoring events will be a lot slower than our file source, forcing a flush on time as well will ensure we can see these events come through to the output at a reasonable frequency.

To run this scenario, let's reset (delete the `structured-rolling-log.*` and `rotating-file-read.pos_file` files and the `fluentd-file-output` folder) and run again, using each of these commands in a separate shell:

- `fluentd -c Chapter4/Fluentd/rotating-file-read-file-out2.conf`
- `groovy LogSimulator.groovy Chapter4/SimulatorConfig/jul-log-file2.properties ./TestData/medium-source.txt`

Do not shut down Fluentd once the log simulator has completed. We will see that the folder `fluentd-file-output` is still created with both buffer files as before. But at the same time, we will see files with the naming of `fluentd-file-output.<date>_<incrementing number>.log` (e.g., `fluentd-file-output.20200505_12.log`). Open any one of these files, and you will see 10 lines of log data. You will notice that the log data is formatted as a date timestamp, tag name, and then the payload body, reflecting the standard composition of a log event. If you scan through the files, you will find incidents where the tag is not `simpleFile` but `self`. This reflects that we have kept the source reporting on the self-monitoring and matches with our `simpleFile`, which is tracking the rotating log files.

Finally, close down Fluentd gracefully. In Windows, the easiest way to do this is in the shell: press CTRL-c once (and only once), and respond yes to the shutdown prompt (in Linux, the interrupt events can be used). Once we can see that Fluentd has shut down in the console, look for the last log file and examine it. There is an element of timing involved, but if you inspect the last file, chances are it will have less than 10 records in it, as the buffer will have flushed to the output file whatever log events it had at shutdown.

Buffer sizing error

If you set a buffer to be smaller than a single log event, then handling that log event will fail, with an error like

```
emit transaction failed: error_class=Fluent::Plugin::Buffer
::BufferChunkOverflowError error="a 250bytes record is larger than
buffer chunk limit size" location="C:/Ruby26-x64/lib/ruby/gems/2.6.0/
gems/fluentd-1.9.3-x64-mingw32/lib/fluent/plugin/buffer.rb:711:in `block
in write_step_by_step'"
```

4.1.4   *Retry and backoff*

The use of buffers also allows Fluentd to provide a retry mechanism. In the event of issues like transient network drops, we can tell the buffer when it recognizes an issue to perform a retry rather than just losing the log events. For retries to work without creating new problems, we need to define controls that tell the buffer how long or how many times to retry before abandoning data. In addition to this, we can define how long to wait before retrying. We can stipulate retrying forever (attribute `retry_forever` is set to `true`), but we recommend using such an option with great care.

There are two ways for retry to work using the `retry_type` attribute—through either a fixed interval (`periodic`) or through an exponential backoff (`exponential_backoff`). The exponential backoff is the default model, and each retry attempt that fails results in the retry delay doubling. For example, if the retry interval was 1 second, the second retry would be 2 seconds, the third retry 4 seconds, and so on. We can control the initial or repeated wait period between retries by defining `retry_wait` with a numeric value representing seconds (e.g., 1 for 1 second and 60 for 1 minute).

Unless we want to retry forever, we need to provide a means to determine whether or not to keep retrying. For the periodic retry model, we can control this by number or time. This is done by either setting a maximum period to retry writing each chunk (`retry_timeout`) or a maximum number of retry attempts (`retry_max_attempts`).

For the backoff approach, we can stipulate a number of backoffs (`retry_exponential_backoff_base`) or the maximum duration that a backoff can go before stopping (`retry_max_interval`).

Suppose we wanted to configure the buffer retry to be an exponential backoff starting at 3 seconds. With a maximum of 10 attempts, we could end up with a peak retry interval of nearly 26 minutes. The configuration attributes we would need to configure are

```
retry_exponential_backoff_base 3
retry_max_times 10
```

The important thing with the exponential backoff is to ensure you're aware of the possible total time. Once that exponential curve gets going, the time extends very quickly. In this example, the first 5 retries would happen inside a minute, but intervals really start to stretch out after that.

4.1.5 *Putting configuring buffering size settings into action*

You've been asked to help the team better understand buffering. There is an agreement that an existing configuration should be altered to help this. Copy the configuration file `/Chapter4/Fluentd/rotating-file-read-file-out2.conf` and modify it so that the configuration of the buffer chunks is based on the size of 500 bytes (see appendix B for how to express storage sizes).

Run the modified configuration to show the impact on the output files.

As part of the discussion, one of the questions that came up is if the output plugin is subject to intermittent network problems, what options do we have to prevent the loss of any log information?

ANSWER

The following listing shows the buffer configuration that would be included in the result.

> **Listing 4.3 Chapter4/ExerciseResults/rotating-file-read-file-out2-Answer.conf**

```
<match *>
    @type file
    @id bufferedFileOut
    path ./Chapter4/fluentd-file-output        Note that we've retained the delay
    <buffer>                                     and flush time, so if the buffer stops
                                                 filling, it will get forced out anyway.

        delayed_commit_timeout 10
        flush_at_shutdown true        Size-based constraint
        chunk_limit_size 500          rather than time-based
        flush_interval 30
    </buffer>
</match>
```

A complete configuration file is provided at `Chapter4/ExerciseResults/rotating-file-read-file-out2-Answer.conf`. The rate of change to the log files is likely to appear different, but the same content will be there. To address the question of mitigating the risk of log loss, several options could be applied:

- Configure the retry and backoff parameters on the buffer to retry storing the events rather than losing the information.
- Use the capability of defining a *secondary* log mechanism, such as a local file, so the events are not lost. Provide a means for the logs to be injected into the Kafka stream at a later date. This could even be an additional source.

4.2 *Output formatting options*

How we structure the output of the log events is as important as how we apply structure to the input. Not surprisingly, a formatter plugin can be included in the output plugin. With a formatter plugin, it's reasonable to expect several prebuilt formatters. Let's look at the out-of-the-box formatters typically encountered; the complete set of formatters are detailed in appendix C.

4.2.1   *out_file*

This is probably the simplest formatter available and has already been implicitly used. The formatter works using a delimiter between the values `time`, `tag`, and `record`. By default, the *delimiter* is a tab character. This can only be changed to a comma or space character using the values `comma` or `space` for the attribute delimiter; for example, `delimiter comma`. Which fields are output can also be controlled with Boolean-based attributes:

- `output_tag`—This takes a true or false value to determine whether the tag(s) are included in the line (by default, the second value in the line).
- `output_time`—This takes true or false to define whether the time is included (by default, the first value in the line). You may wish to omit the time if you have it incorporated into the core event record.
- `time_format`—This can be used to define the way the date and time are used in the path. If undefined and the timekey is set, then the timekey will inform the structure of the format. Specifically:
  - 0...60 seconds   then `'%Y%m%d%H%M%S'`
  - 60...3600 seconds then `'%Y%m%d%H%M'`
  - 3600...86400 seconds then `'%Y%m%d%H'`

NOTE If the formatter does not recognize the attribute value set, it will ignore the value provided and use the default value.

4.2.2   *json*

This formatter treats the log event record as a JSON payload on a single line. The timestamp and tags associated with the event are discarded.

4.2.3   *ltsv*

As with the `out_file` formatter and the parser, the limiters can be changed using *delimiter* (each labeled value) and `label_delimiter` for separating the value and label. For example, if delimiter was set to `delimiter ;` and `label_delimiter =` was set, then if the record was expressed as `{"my1stValue":" blah", "secondValue": "more blah", "thirdValue": "you guessed – blah"}`, the output would become `my1st Value=blah; secondValue= more blah; thirdValue=you guessed – blah`.

As the values are label values, the need for separating records by lines is reduced, and therefore it is possible to switch off the use of new lines to separate each record with `add_newline false` (by default, the value is set to true).

4.2.4   *csv*

Just like ltsv and `out_file` the delimiter can be defined by setting the attribute `delimiter`. The attribute has a default, which is a comma. Additionally, the csv output allows us to define which values can be included in the output using the `fields` attribute. If I use the record again to illustrate if my event is `{"my1stValue":" blah", "secondValue":" more blah", "thirdValue":"you guessed – blah},` and I set the fields attribute to be the `secondValue, thirdValue` fields, then the output would be `"more blah", "you guessed - blah"`. If desired, the quoting of each value can be disabled with a Boolean value for `force_quotes`.

4.2.5 *msgpack*

As with the *msgpack* parser, the formatter works with the MessagePack framework, which takes the core log event record and uses the MessagePack library to compress the content. Typically, we would only expect to see this used with HTTP forward output plugins where the recipient expects MessagePack content. To get similar compression performance gains, we can use gzip for file and block storage.

> **NOTE** You may have noticed that most formatters (`out_file` being an exception) omit adding the time and keys from the log event. As a result, if you want those to be carried through, it will be necessary to ensure that they are incorporated into the log event record or that the output plugin utilizes the values explicitly. Adding additional data into the log event payload can be done using the *inject* plugin, which can be used within a *match* or *filter* directive. We will pick up the inject feature when we address filtering in chapter 6.

4.2.6 *Applying formatters*

We can extend our existing configuration to move from the current implicit configuration to being explicit. Let's start with the simplest output using the default `out_file` formatter, using a comma as a delimiter (`delimiter comma`) and excluding the log event tag (`output_tag false`). We will continue to use the same sources as before to demonstrate the effect of formatters. This `out_file` formatter configuration is illustrated in the following listing.

Listing 4.4 Chapter4/Fluentd/rotating-file-read-file-out3.conf—formatter configuration

```
<match *>
   @type file
   @id bufferedFileOut
   path ./Chapter4/fluentd-file-output
   <buffer>
      delayed_commit_timeout 10          To reduce the number of files being
      flush_at_shutdown true             generated, we have made the number
      chunk_limit_records 50        ◁─┘  of records a lot larger per file.

      flush_interval 30
      flush_mode interval
   </buffer>                             We explicitly define the output formatter
   <format>                             to be out_file, as we want to override the
      @type out_file         ◁─┘       default formatter behavior.

      delimiter comma         ◁─────────┐ Replace the tab delimiter
      output_tag false    ◁──┐          │ with a comma.
   </format>                 │  Exclude the tag
</match>                     │  information from
                            │  the output.
```

Assuming the existing log files and outputs have been removed, we can start the example using the following commands:

- `fluentd -c Chapter4/Fluentd/rotating-file-read-file-out3.conf`
- `groovy LogSimulator.groovy Chapter4/SimulatorConfig/jul-log-file2.properties ./TestData/medium-source.txt`

Open up one of the `fluent-file-output.*` files, and the changes will be immediately obvious with the loss of tab-based separation, as it has been replaced by a comma. The tag information will also be missing.

4.2.7   Putting JSON formatter configuration into action

Your organization has decided that as standard practice, all output should be done using JSON structures. This approach ensures that any existing or applied structural meaning to the log events is not lost. To support this goal, the configuration file `/Chapter4/Fluentd/rotating-file-read-file-out3.conf` will need modifying.

ANSWER

The format declaration in the configuration file should be reduced to look like the fragment in the following listing.

> **Listing 4.5   Chapter4/ExerciseResults/rotating-file-file-out3-Answer.conf**

```
<format>
@type json
</format>
```

A complete example configuration to this answer can be found in `/Chapter4/ExerciseResults/rotating-file-read-file-out3-Answer.conf`.

4.3   Sending log events to MongoDB

While outputting to some form of file-based storage is a simple and easy way of storing log events, it doesn't lend itself well to performing any analytics or data processing. To make log analysis a practical possibility, Fluentd needs to converse with systems capable of performing analysis, such as SQL or NoSQL database engines, search tools such as Elasticsearch, and even SaaS services such as Splunk and Datadog.

Chapter 1 highlighted that Fluentd has no allegiance to any particular log analytics engine or vendor, differentiating Fluentd from many other tools. As a result, many vendors have found Fluentd to be an attractive solution to feed log events to their product or service. To make adoption very easy, vendors have developed their adaptors.

We have opted to use MongoDB to help illustrate the approach for getting events into a tool capable of analytical processing logs. While MongoDB is not dedicated to textual search like Elasticsearch, its capabilities are well suited to log events with a good JSON structure. MongoDB is very flexible and undemanding in getting started, so don't worry if you've not used MongoDB. The guidance for installing MongoDB can be found in appendix A.

Summary of MongoDB

We do not want to get too sidetracked by the mechanics of MongoDB, but it's worth summarizing some basic ideas. Most readers will be familiar with relational databases and their concepts. The role of the database structure in both MongoDB and a relational DB is analogous. Within a database schema is a set of tables. In MongoDB, the nearest to this is a *collection*. Unlike a relational database, a collection can contain pretty much anything, which is why it is sometimes described as using a *document model*. You could say that each entry in a collection is roughly comparable to a record in a table containing a DB-assigned ID and a BLOB (binary large object) or text data type. Commonly the row or document of MongoDB is a structured text object, usually JSON. MongoDB can then search and index parts of these structures, making for a flexible solution. For Fluentd, it means we can store log events that may have different record structures.

More recent versions of the MongoDB engine provide the means to validate the content structure going into a collection. This provides some predictability in the content. If this is used, then we can exploit Fluentd to structure the necessary payload.

In addition to controlling how strictly the contents must adhere to a structure for each document, Mongo also incorporates the idea of *capped size*. This feature allows us to set limits on the amount of storage used by the collection, and the collection operates as a FIFO (first in, first out) list.

When you want to empty a table in a relational database, it is often easier to simply drop and re-create the table. The MongoDB equivalent is to delete the collection; however, if this is the only collection within the database, the database will be removed by MongoDB. There are two options: only delete the collection's contents and keep the collection, or create a second empty collection so the database is not empty.

You can discover a lot more with the book *MongoDB in Action* by Kyle Banker, et al. (www.manning.com/books/mongodb-in-action-second-edition).

4.3.1 Deploying MongoDB Fluentd plugin

The MongoDB input plugin is provided in the Treasure Data Agent build of Fluentd but not in the vanilla deployment. If we want Fluentd to work with MongoDB, we need to install the RubyGem if it isn't already in place.

To determine whether the installation is needed and perform installations of gems, we can use a wrapper utility that leverages the RubyGems tool called *fluent-gem*. To see if the gem is already installed, run the command `fluent-gem list` from the command line. The command will show the locally installed gems, which contain Fluentd and its plugins. At this stage, there should be no indication of a *fluent-plugin-mongo* gem. We can, therefore, perform the installation using the command `fluent -gem install fluent-plugin-mongo`. This will retrieve and install the latest stable instance of the gem, including the documentation and dependencies, such as the MongoDB driver.

4.3.2   *Configuring the Mongo output plugin for Fluentd*

Within a match, we need to reference the `mongo` plugin and set the relevant attributes. Like connecting to any database, we will need to provide an address (which could be achieved via a *host* [name] and *port* [number on the network]) and user and password, or via a *connection string* (e.g., `mongodb://127.0.0.1:27017/Fluentd`). In our example configuration, we have adopted the former approach and avoided the issue of credentials. The database (schema) and collection (table comparable to a relational table) are needed to know where to put the log events.

Within a MongoDB output, there is no use of a formatter, as the MongoDB plugin assumes all content is already structured. As we have seen, without configuration, a default buffer will be adopted. As before, we'll keep the buffer settings to support only low volumes so we can see things changing quickly. We can see the outcome in the following listing.

> **Listing 4.6   Chapter4/Fluentd/rotating-file-read-mongo-out.conf—match configuration**

```
<match *>
    @type mongo                    Mongo is the
    @id mongo-output               plugin name.
    host localhost                              Identifies the MongoDB host server. In our dev setup,
                                                that's simply the local machine; this could alternatively
                                                be defined by using a connection attribute.
                                   The port on the target server to communicate
                                   with. We can also express the URI by combining
    port 27017                     hostp, port, and database into a single string.

                                         As a MongoDB installation can support multiple
    database Fluentd                     databases, we need to name the database.

                                     The collection within the database we want to add log
    collection Fluentd               events to—a rough analogy to an SQL-based table

    <buffer>
                                         Buffer configuration to ensure the log events
        delayed_commit_timeout 10    are quickly incorporated into the MongoDB
        flush_at_shutdown true
        chunk_limit_records 50
        flush_interval 30
        flush_mode interval
    </buffer>
</match>
```

Mongo vs Mongo replica set plugins

If you've looked at the Fluentd online documentation, you may have observed two output plugins, *out_mongo* and *out_mongo_replset*. The key difference is that the *replset* (replica set) can support MongoDB's approach to enable scaling, where additional instances of Mongo can be defined as replicas of a master. When this happens, the ideal model is to directly write activity to the master, but read from the replicas. In terms of configuration differences, a comma-separated list of nodes is needed rather than naming a single host. Each node represents a node in the replica group (e.g.,

```
nodes 192.168.0.10:27017, 192.168.0.20:27017, 192.168.0.30:27017).
```
The replica set name is also needed (e.g., `replica_set myFluentReps`). More information on the Mongo replica set mechanism is documented at https://docs.mongodb.com/manual/replication/.

Ensure that the MongoDB instance is running (this can be done with the command `mongod --version` in a shell window or by attempting to connect to the server using the Compass UI). If the MongoDB server isn't running, then it will need to be started. The simplest way to do that is to run the command `mongod`.

With Mongo running, we can then run our simulated logs and Fluentd configuration with the commands in each shell:

- `groovy LogSimulator.groovy Chapter4/SimulatorConfig/jul-log-file2-exercise.properties ./TestData/medium-source.txt`
- `fluentd -c Chapter4/fluentd/rotating-file-read-mongo-out.conf`

Mongo plugin startup warning

When Fluentd is started up with the MongoDB plugin, it will log the following warning: `[mongo-output]`. Since v0.8, invalid record detection will be removed because mongo driver v2.x and API spec don't provide it. You may lose invalid records, so you should not send such records to the Mongo plugin.

This essentially means that the MongoDB driver being used does not impose any structural checks on the payload (which the collection may be configured to require). As a result, if strong checking is being applied by the MongoDB engine, it may drop an update, but the information will not get passed back through the driver, so Fluentd will be none the wiser, resulting in data loss. For the more common application of Fluentd, it is better not to impose strict checks onto the payload. If this isn't an option, then a filter directive could identify log events that will fail MongoDB's checks.

With the log events being created and consumed by Fluentd, using Compass, navigate into the Fluentd database, and click the Fluentd collection. This will provide a view of the collection, as illustrated in figure 4.2.

VIEWING LOG EVENTS IN MONGODB

To see how effective MongoDB can be for querying the JSON log events, if you add the expression `{"msg" : {$regex : ".*software.*"}}` into the FILTER field and click FIND, we'll get some results. These results will show the log events where the `msg` contains the word software. The query expression tells MongoDB to look in the documents, and if they have a top-level element called `msg`, then evaluate this value using the regular expression.

If you examine the content in MongoDB, you will see that the content stored is only the core log event record, not the associated time or tags.

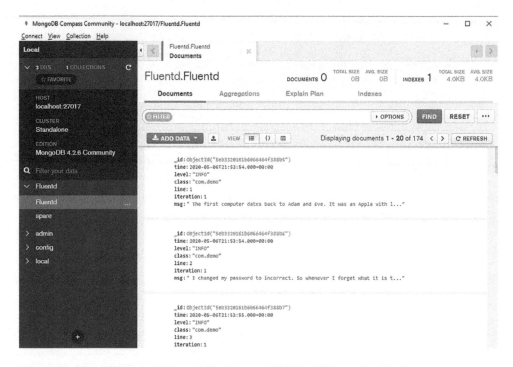

Figure 4.2   MongoDB is viewed through the Compass UI tool, with logged content.

To empty the collection for further executions of the scenario in a command shell, run the following command:

```
mongo Fluentd --eval "db.Fluentd.remove({})".
```

The mongo plugin has a couple of other tricks up its sleeve. When the attribute `tag_mapped` is included in the configuration, the tag name is used as the collection name, and MongoDB will create the collection if it does not exist. This makes it extremely easy to separate the log events into different collections. If the tag names have been used hierarchically, then the tag prefix can be removed to simplify the *tag_mapped* feature. This can be defined by the `remove_tag_prefix` attribute, which takes the name of the prefix to remove.

As collections can be established dynamically, it is possible to define characteristics within the configuration; for example, whether the collection should be capped in size.

In this configuration, we have not formally defined any username or password. This is because in the configuration of MongoDB, we have not imposed the credentials restrictions. And incorporating credentials in the Fluentd configuration file is not the best practice. Techniques for safely handling credentials within Fluentd configuration, not just for MongoDB but also for other systems needing authentication, are addressed in chapter 7.

4.3.3 *Putting MongoDB connection configuration strings into action*

Revise the configuration to define the connection by a connection attribute, not the host, port, and database used. This is best started by copying the configuration file `Chapter4/fluentd/rotating-file-read-mongo-out.conf`. Adjust the run commands to use the new configuration. The commands should look something like this:

- `groovy LogSimulator.groovy Chapter4/SimulatorConfig/jul-log-file2-exercise.properties ./TestData/medium-source.txt`
- `fluentd -c Chapter4/fluentd/my-rotating-file-read-mongo-out.conf`

ANSWER

The configuration of the MongoDB connection should look like the configuration shown in the following listing.

Listing 4.7   Chapter4/ExerciseResults/rotating-file-read-mongo-out-Answer.conf

```
<match *>
    @type mongo
    @id mongo-output
    connection_string mongodb://localhost:27017/Fluentd        ◄─┐

    collection Fluentd                      Note the absence of the host, port, and
    <buffer>                                database properties in favor of this. You
        delayed_commit_timeout 10           could have used your host's specific IP
        flush_at_shutdown true              or 127.0.0.1 instead of localhost.
        chunk_limit_records 50
        flush_interval 30
        flush_mode interval
    </buffer>
</match>
```

The example configuration can be seen at `Chapter4/ExerciseResults/rotating-file-read-mongo-out-Answer.conf`

Before we move on from MongoDB, we have focused on the output use of MongoDB so it can be used to query log events. But MongoDB can also act as an input into Fluentd, allowing new records added to MongoDB to be retrieved as log events.

4.4 *Actionable log events*

In chapter 1, we introduced the idea of making log events actionable. So far, we have seen ways to unify the log events. To make log events actionable, we need a couple of elements:

- The ability to send events to an external system that can trigger an action, such as a collaboration/notification platform that Ops people can see and react to log events or even invoke a script or tool to perform an action
- Separating the log events that need to be made actionable from those that provide information but require no specific action

The process of separating or filtering out events that need to be made actionable is addressed later in the book. But here, we can look at how to make events actionable without waiting until all the logs have arrived in an analytics platform and running its analytics processes.

4.4.1   Actionable log events through service invocation

One way to make a log event actionable is to invoke a separate application that can perform the necessary remediation as a result of receiving an API call. This could be as clever as invoking an *Ansible Tower* REST API (http://mng.bz/Nxm1) to initiate a template job that performs some housekeeping (e.g., moving logs to archive storage or tell Kubernetes about the internal state of a pod). We would need to control how frequently an action is performed; plugins such as *flow_counter* and *notifier* can help. To invoke generic web services, we can use the HTTP output plugin, which is part of the core of Fluentd. To give a sense of the art of the possible, here is a summary of the general capabilities supported by this plugin:

- Supports HTTP *post* and *put* operations
- Allows proxy in the routing
- Configures content type, setting the formatter automatically (a formatter can also be defined explicitly)
- Defines headers so extra header values required can be defined (e.g., API keys)
- Configures the connection to use SSL and TLS certificates, including defining the location of the certificates to be used, versions, ciphers to be used, etc.
- Creates log errors when nonsuccessful HTTP code responses are received
- Supports basic authentication (no support for OAuth at the time of writing)
- Sets time-outs
- Uses buffer plugins

4.4.2   Actionable through user interaction tools

While automating problem resolution in the manner described takes us toward self-healing systems, not many organizations are prepared for or necessarily want to be this advanced. They would rather trust a quick human intervention to determine cause and effect than rely on an automated diagnosis where a high degree of certainty can be difficult. People with sufficient knowledge and the appropriate information can quickly determine and resolve such issues. As a result, Fluentd has a rich set of plugins for social collaboration mechanisms. Here are just a few examples:

- IRC (Internet Relay Chat) (https://tools.ietf.org/html/rfc2813)
- Twilio (supporting many different comms channels) (www.twilio.com)
- Jabber (https://xmpp.org)
- Redmine (www.redmine.org)
- Typetalk (www.typetalk.com)

- PagerDuty (www.pagerduty.com)
- Yammer (www.microsoft.com/en-gb/microsoft-365/yammer)
- Slack (https://slack.com/)

Obviously, we do need to include the relevant information in the social channel communications. A range of things can be done to help that, from good log events that are clear and can be linked to guidance for resolution, to Fluentd being configured to extract relevant information from log events to share.

4.5   *Slack to demonstrate the social output*

Slack has become a leading team messaging collaboration tool with a strong API layer and a free version that is simply limited by the size of conversation archives. As a cloud service, it is a great tool to illustrate the intersection of Fluentd and actionable log events through social platforms. While the following steps are specific to Slack, the principles involved here are the same for Microsoft Teams, Jabber, and many other collaboration services.

If you are already using Slack, it is tempting to use an existing group to run the example. To avoid irritating the other users of your Slack workspace as a result of them receiving notifications and messages as you fill channels up with test log events, we suggest setting up your own test workspace. If you aren't using Slack, that's not a problem; in appendix A, we explain how to get a Slack account and configure it to be ready for use. Ensure you keep a note of the API token during the Slack configuration, recognizable by the prefix `xoxb`.

Slack provides a rich set of configuration options for the interaction. Unlike MongoDB and many IaaS- and PaaS-level plugins, as Slack is a SaaS service, the resolution of the Slack instance is both simplified and hidden from us by using a single `token` (no need for server addresses, etc.). The `username` isn't about credentials, but how to represent the bot that the Fluentd plugin behaves as; therefore, using a meaningful name is worthwhile. The `channel` relates to the Slack channel in which the messages sent will be displayed. The general channel exists by default, but you may wish to create a custom channel in Slack and restrict access to that channel if you want to control who sees the messages. After all, do you want everyone within an enterprise Slack setup to see every operational message?

The `message` and `message_keys` attributes work together with the message using `%s` to indicate where the values of the identified payload elements are inserted. The references in the `message` relate to the JSON payload elements listed in the `message_keys` in order sequence.

The `title` and `title_keys` work in a similar way to `message` and `message_keys`, but for the title displayed in the Slack UI with that message. In our case, we're just going to use the `tag`. The final part is the `flush` attribute; this tells the plugin how quickly to push the Slack messages to the user. Multiple messages can be grouped up if the period is too long. To keep things moving quickly, let's flush every second.

Edit the existing configuration provided (`Chapter4/Fluentd/rotating-file -read-slack-out.conf`) to incorporate the details captured, in the Slack setup. This is illustrated in the following listing.

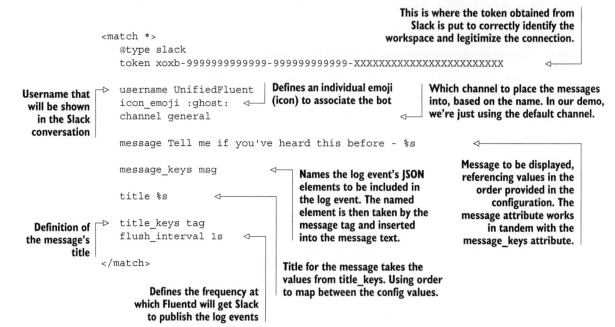

Listing 4.8   Chapter4/Fluentd/rotating-file-read-slack-out.conf—match configuration

This is where the token obtained from Slack is put to correctly identify the workspace and legitimize the connection.

```
<match *>
  @type slack
  token xoxb-9999999999999-999999999999-XXXXXXXXXXXXXXXXXXXXXX
  username UnifiedFluent
  icon_emoji :ghost:
  channel general

  message Tell me if you've heard this before - %s

  message_keys msg

  title %s

  title_keys tag
  flush_interval 1s
</match>
```

Username that will be shown in the Slack conversation

Defines an individual emoji (icon) to associate the bot

Which channel to place the messages into, based on the name. In our demo, we're just using the default channel.

Message to be displayed, referencing values in the order provided in the configuration. The message attribute works in tandem with the message_keys attribute.

Names the log event's JSON elements to be included in the log event. The named element is then taken by the message tag and inserted into the message text.

Definition of the message's title

Title for the message takes the values from title_keys. Using order to map between the config values.

Defines the frequency at which Fluentd will get Slack to publish the log events

Before running the solution, we also need to install the Slack plugin with the command `fluent-gem install fluent-plugin-slack`. Once that is installed, we can start up the log simulator and Fluentd with the following commands:

- `fluentd -c Chapter4/Fluentd/rotating-file-read-slack-out.conf`
- `groovy LogSimulator.groovy Chapter4/SimulatorConfig/social-logs.properties ./TestData/small-source.txt`

Once this is started, if you open the *#general* channel in the web client or app, you will see messages from Fluentd flowing through.

All the details for the Slack plugin can be obtained from https://github.com/ sowawa/fluent-plugin-slack. Our illustration of Slack use is relatively straightforward (figure 4.3). By using several plugins, we can quickly go from the source tag to routing the Slack messages to the most relevant individual or group directly. Alternatively, we have different channels for each application and can direct the messages to those channels.

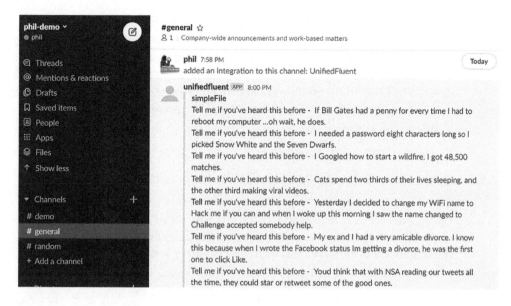

Figure 4.3   Our Fluentd log events displayed in Slack

4.5.1   *Handling tokens and credentials more carefully*

For a long time, good security practice has told us we should not hardwire code and configuration files with credentials, as anyone can look at the file and get sensitive credentials. In fact, if you commit to GitHub, it will flag with the service provider any configuration file or code that contains a string that looks like a security token for a service GitHub knows about. When Slack is told and decides it is a valid token, then be assured that it will revoke the token.

So how do we address such a problem? There are a range of strategies, depending upon your circumstances; a couple of options include the following:

- Set the sensitive credentials up in environment variables with a limited session scope. The environment variable can be configured in several ways, such as with tools like Chef and Puppet setting up the values from a keystore.
- Embed a means to access a keystore or a secrets management solution, such as HashiCorp's Vault, into the application or configuration.

The configuration files may not look like it is possible to secure credentials based on what we have seen so far in the book. We can achieve both of these approaches for securely managing credentials within a Fluentd configuration file, as Fluentd allows us to embed Ruby fragments into the configuration. This doesn't mean we need to immediately learn Ruby. For the first of these approaches, we just need to understand a couple of basic patterns. The approach of embedding calls to Vault is more challenging but can be done.

The notation to embed the Ruby code is to prefix the Ruby code with `"#{` and close it with `}"`. Ruby's core language provides us with a set of classes and static operations, providing a lot of flexibility to access information such as environment variables. Environment variables can be accessed using the ENV class (https://ruby-doc.org/core-2.5.0/ENV.html). So if we created an environment variable called `slack-token`, then rather than including the token directly in the configuration, we could replace the setting of the attribute with

```
token "#{ENV['slack-token']}"
```

4.5.2   *Externalizing Slack configuration attributes in action*

The challenge is to set up your environment so that you have an environment variable called *SlackToken*, which is set to hold the token you have previously obtained. Then customize `Chapter4/Fluentd/rotating-file-read-slack-out.conf` to use the environment variable, and rerun the example setup with the commands

- `fluentd -c Chapter4/Fluentd/rotating-file-read-slack-out.conf`
- `groovy LogSimulator.groovy Chapter4/SimulatorConfig/social-logs.properties ./TestData/small-source.txt`

Confirm that log events are arriving in Slack.

ANSWER

By setting up the environment variable, you'll have created a command that looks like either

```
set slack-token= xoxb-9999999999999-999999999999-XXXXXXXXXXXXXXXXXXXXXXXX
```

or for Windows or Linux

```
Export slack-token= xoxb-9999999999999-999999999999-XXXXXXXXXXXXXXXXXXXXXXXX
```

The configuration will now have changed to look like the example in the following listing.

Listing 4.9   Chapter4/rotating-file-read-slack-out-Answer.conf—match configuration

```
<match *>
   @type slack
   token "{ENV["slack-token"]}"
   username UnifiedFluent
   icon_emoji :ghost:
   channel general
   message Tell me if you've heard this before - %s
   message_keys msg
   title %s
   title_keys tag
   flush_interval 1s
</match>
```

4.6 *The right tool for the right job*

In chapter 1, we highlighted the issue of different people wanting different tools for a range of reasons, such as the following:

- To perform log analytics as different tools and to have different strengths and weaknesses
- To multicloud, so specialist teams (and cost considerations of network traffic) mean using different cloud vendor tools
- To make decisions that influence individual preferences and politics (previous experience, etc.)

As we have illustrated, Fluentd can support many social platforms and protocols. Of course, this wouldn't be the only place for log events to be placed. One of the core types of destination is a log analytics tool or platform. Fluentd has a large number of plugins to feed log analytics platforms; in addition to the two we previously mentioned, other major solutions that can be easily plugged in include

- Azure Monitor
- Graphite
- Elasticsearch
- CloudWatch
- Google Stackdriver
- Sumo Logic
- Logz.io
- Oracle Log Analytics

Then, of course, we can send logs to a variety of data storage solutions to hold for later use or perform data analytics with; for example:

- Postgres, InfluxDB, MySQL, Couchbase, DynamoDB, Aerospike, SQL Server, Cassandra
- Kafka, AWS Kinesis (time series store/event streaming)
- Storage areas such as AWS S3, Google Cloud Storage, Google BigQuery, WebHDFS

So, the question becomes, what are my needs and which tool(s) fit best? If our requirements change over time, then we add or remove our targets as needed. Changing the technology will probably raise more challenging questions about what to do with our current log events, not how to get the data into the solution.

Summary

- Fluentd has an extensive range of output plugins covering files, other Fluentd nodes, relational and document databases such as MongoDB, Elasticsearch, and so on.

- Plugin support extends beyond analytics and storage solutions to collaboration and notification tools, such as Slack. This allows Fluentd to drive more rapid reactions to significant log events.
- Fluentd provides some powerful helper plugins, including formatters and buffers, making log event output configuration very efficient and easy to use.
- Log events can be made easy to consume by tools such as analytics and visualization tools. Fluentd provides the means to format log events using formatter plugins, such as out_file and json.
- Buffer helper plugins can support varying life cycles depending on the need, from the simple synchronous cache to the fully asynchronous. With this, the buffer storage can be organized by size or number of log events.
- Buffers can be configured to flush their contents not just on shutdown, but also on other conditions, such as new events being buffered for a while.

Routing log events 5

So far in this book, we have seen how to capture and store log events. But in all the examples, routing was simply all events going to the same output. However, this can be far from ideal. As described in chapter 1, we may want log events to go to different tools, depending on the type of log event. It may be desirable to send a log event to multiple locations or none. In this chapter, we will, therefore, examine the different ways we can route events. In addition, we will look at some smaller features that can contribute to solving the challenges of routing, such as adding information into the log event to ensure the origin of the log event is not lost along the way.

Routing often aligns with how work is split among individuals or teams. As we will see, the use of inclusions supports how multiple teams can each work on their part of a Fluentd configuration without interrupting others and injecting specific

119

configuration values. For example, we have seen the security team needing to apply routing and filtering of log events to their tool (and exclude events they're not interested in). In contrast, the Ops team needs the log events in a different tool. With the routing and inclusion features, we can quickly achieve this.

The one aspect of routing we will not address in this chapter is the idea of forwarding log events to other Fluentd nodes, as that is best addressed when we look at scaling later in the book.

5.1   *Reaching multiple outputs by copying*

One way to get log events to all the correct output(s) is to ensure that all outputs receive the event, and each output includes one or more filters to stop unwanted content from being output. We'll focus on copying in this section and will address filtering later, as before we filter things, we need to get the log events to the right place.

As described in chapter 2, log events are, by default, consumed by the first appropriate match directive, containing the output plugin. To allow a log event to reach more than one output plugin within a match directive, we need to use the *copy* plugin (*@copy*).

Each destination is held within a *store* declaration defined with XML style tags `<store>` and `</store>` within the match directive. While *store* may not always seem intuitive as a plugin name (many outputs are for solutions we wouldn't associate with storage, like Grafana), it is worth remembering that more of the Fluentd plugins address the retrieval and storage of log events than anything else. The diagram in figure 5.1 illustrates how the directive and plugins relate to each other both logically and in the way the configuration file is written.

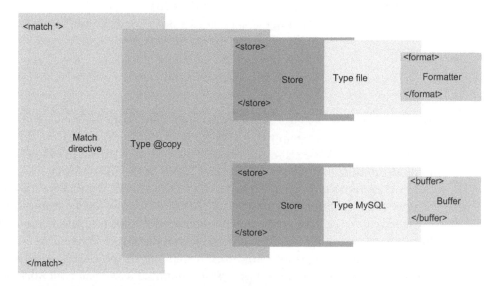

Figure 5.1   Visualization of the hierarchy of elements for a match directive using @copy and Store. Reading from left to right, we see the blocks of configuration with increasing detail and focus (i.e., Buffer or Formatter for a specific plugin type). The store configuration block can occur one or more times within the copy plugin.

Within each store configuration block, we can configure the use of a plugin. Typically, this is going to be an output plugin but could easily be a filter plugin. The store plugin's attributes can be configured just as they would if used directly within a match directive, as we have done previously. This includes using helper plugins, such as *buffers*.

To illustrate this, we're going to take a file input, and rather than send the log events from one file to another file, as we did in chapter 3, we will extend the configuration to send the output to both a file and a stdout (console). We can see a representation of this in figure 5.2.

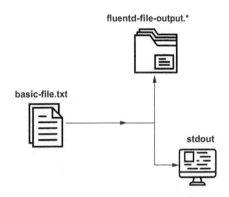

To implement this, we need to edit the `match` directive. The easiest way to do this is to first wrap the existing output plugin attributes within the `store` tags and then add the next `store` start and end tags. With the store start and end tags in place, each of the output plugins can be configured. Finally, introduce the *@copy* at the start of the `match` directive. The modified configuration is

Figure 5.2 Visualization of a configuration file using store and copy to send log events to multiple destinations

shown in the following listing, which contains the two `store` blocks, each holding an output plugin (`file` and `stdout`). You'll also see a third `store` block with the output plugin type of `null`, followed by an `@include` directive. We will explain these shortly.

Listing 5.1 Chapter5/Fluentd/file-source-multi-out.conf—copy to multiple outputs

```
<match *>
  @type copy          ◁─┐  Declaring the plugin
    <store>              │  to be used
      @type null
    </store>
    <store>           ◁─── Start of the store block—each store reflects the action to take. This is
                           often done to store a log event using a plugin or forward to another
      @type stdout         Fluentd node. In this case, we're simply writing to the console.
    </store>
    <store>           ◁─┐  Third store
      @type file         │  routes to a file
      @id bufferedFileOut
      tag bufferedFileOut
      path ./Chapter5/fluentd-file-output
      <buffer>
        delayed_commit_timeout 10
        flush_at_shutdown true
        chunk_limit_records 500
        flush_interval 30
        flush_mode interval
      </buffer>
      <format>
        @type out_file
```

```
      delimiter comma
      output_tag true
    </format>
  </store>
  @include additionalStore.conf
</match>
```

Let's see the result of the configuration. As this uses a file source, we need to run the LogSimulator as well. So, to run the example, the following commands are needed:

- `fluentd -c ./Chapter5/Fluentd/file-source-multi-out.conf`
- `groovy LogSimulator.groovy ./Chapter5/SimulatorConfig/`
  `log-source-1.properties`

After running these commands, log events will appear very quickly on the console. Once the buffer reaches the point of writing, files will appear with the name `fluentd-file-output.<date>_<number>.log`. It is worth comparing the content in the file to the console, as we have included additional attributes into the payload.

5.1.1   *Copy by reference or by value*

In most, perhaps even all programming languages, there is the idea of shallow and deep copying, sometimes called *copy by reference* (illustrated in figure 5.3) and *copy value* (illustrated by figure 5.4). Whichever terminology you are used to, *copy by reference* means that the copy of the log event is achieved by each copy referring to the same piece of memory holding the log event. If the log event is modified, then that change impacts all subsequent uses for all copies. *Copying by value* means grabbing a new piece of memory and making a wholesale copy of the content. This means if one copy is modified, the other will not be because it is an outright clone. While we have not yet seen a reason to do anything other than use the default behavior, in the next chapter, we'll see that it is possible to manipulate the contents of a log event.

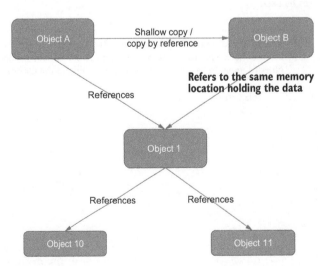

Figure 5.3   How objects reside in memory when copied by reference

As shown in figure 5.3, when Object B is created as a shallow copy of Object A, then they both refer to the same memory holding the inner object (Object 1). So if we change Object 1 when updating through Object B, we will impact Object A as well.

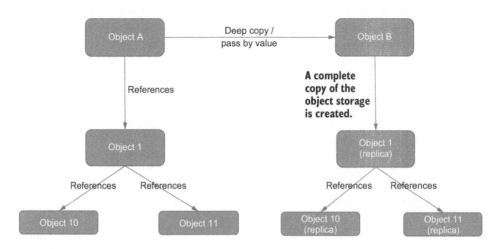

Figure 5.4 How objects reside in memory when copied by value

Within the copy configuration, we can control this behavior with the copy_mode attribute. Copy mode has several settings that range in behavior from a copy by reference to a copy by value:

- *no_copy*—The default state, and effectively copy by reference.
- *Shallow*—This deep-copies the first layer of values. If those objects, in turn, reference objects, they are still referencing the same memory as the original. Under the hood, this uses Ruby's *dup* method. While faster than a deep copy, the use of dup needs to be used with care; it is comparable to *no_copy* of nested objects.
- *Deep*—This is a proper copy by value, leveraging Ruby's *msgpack* gem. If in doubt, this is the approach we recommend.
- *Marshal*—When Ruby's msgpack cannot be used, then native language object marshaling can be used. The object is marshaled (serialized) into a byte stream representation. Then the byte stream is unmarshaled (deserialized), and an object representing the byte stream is produced.

How copy operations work

The following will help you better understand how copy behaviors work:

- Ruby dup (shallow copy): http://mng.bz/mxOP
- msgpack-ruby (deep copy): https://rubydoc.info/gems/msgpack
- msgpack serialization (marshal): https://ruby-doc.org/core-2.6.3/Marshal.html

Ideally, we shouldn't need to worry about copying by value, as log events are received in a well-structured manner with all the necessary state information, so content manipulation becomes unnecessary. Sadly, the world is not ideal; when using the copy feature, consider whether the default option is appropriate; for example, do we need to manipulate the log event for one destination and not another? The use of labels to create "pipelines" of log event processing will increase the possibility of needing to consider how we copy as well, as we will see later in this chapter.

Another consideration to be aware of is that when copying log events for different stores, if a log event can carry sensitive data, we may wish to redact or mask values for most cases, but not for the log events sent to the security department. If security does not wish to be impacted by any data masking or redaction, they will need a deep copy.

5.1.2 *Handling errors when copying*

In the example configuration we provided, both outputs are to the same local hardware, and it would need a set of unique circumstances that impacts one file and not the other. However, suppose the output is being sent to a remote service, such as a database or Elasticsearch. In that case, the chance of an issue impacting one output and not another is significantly higher. For example, if one of the destination services has been shut down or network issues prevent communication, what happens to our outputs? Does Fluentd send the log events to just the available stores, or to none of them unless they are all available?

Fluentd does not try to apply *XA transactions* (also known as *two-phase commit*), allowing an all-or-nothing behavior because the coordination of such transactions is resource-intensive, and coordination takes time. However, by default, it does apply the next best thing; in the event of one output failing, subsequent outputs will be abandoned. For example, if we copy to three stores called Store A, Store B, and Store C, which are defined in the configuration in that order, and we fail to send a log event to Store A, then none of the stores will get the event (see the first part of figure 5.5). If the problem occurred with Store B, then Store A would keep the log event, but Store C would be abandoned (see the second part of figure 5.5.).

But if you have a buffer as part of the output configuration, this may mask an issue, as the buffer may operate asynchronously and include options such as fallback and retry. As a result, an error, such as giving up retrying, may not impact the copy process, as described. Given this approach, there is the option to sequence the copy blocks to reflect the priority of the output.

The downside is that if you use asynchronous buffering with retries, the buffer will allow the execution to continue to the next store. But if it subsequently hits the maximum retries, it will fail that store, but subsequent store actions may have been successful.

How priority/order is applied should be a function of the value of the log event and the output capability. For example, the use of the output plugin allows a *secondary* helper plugin such as *secondary_file*. If the log events are so critical that they cannot be lost, it is best to prioritize the local I/O options first. If the log event priority is to get it to a remote central service quickly (e.g., Kafka or Splunk) and is failing, then that means the

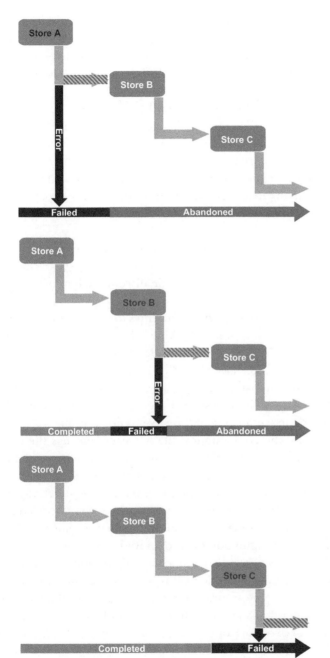

Figure 5.5 How a store error impacts a containing copy. The bar across the bottom of each diagram indicates which store would get the data value, which store failed, and which store was not actioned. For example, in the middle example, if Store B failed, then Store A will have got the log event, Store B wouldn't have the event, and Store C would not be communicated with.

event is of little further help elsewhere (e.g., Prometheus for contributing to metrics calculations); therefore, it's best to lead off with the highest priority destination.

Fluentd does offer another option to tailor this behavior. Within the `<store>` declaration, it is possible to add the argument `ignore_error` (e.g., `<store ignore_error>`). Then, if output in that store block does cause an error, it is prevented from cascading the error that would trigger subsequent store blocks from being abandoned. Using our example three stores again, setting `ignore_error` on Store A would mean that regardless of sending the event to Store A, we would continue to try with Store B. But if Store B failed, then Store C would not receive the event.

5.2   *Configuration reuse and extension through inclusion*

As Fluentd configurations develop, mature, and potentially introduce multiple processing routes for log events, our Fluentd configuration files grow in size and complexity. Along with this growth, we're also likely to discover that some configurations could be reused (e.g., different match definitions want to reuse the same filter or formatter), particularly when trying to achieve the ideal of *DRY* (Don't Repeat Yourself). So in this section, let's explore how to address the challenges of larger configuration files and maximize reuse.

We could try to solve this by ensuring that the Fluentd configuration actions appear in the correct order. The use of tags to filter events may work. This can get rather messy as an approach, and small changes could disrupt the flow of log events in unexpected ways.

The alternative is trying to massage configuration files to allow bits to be reused in different contexts. The first step is to isolate the Fluentd configuration that needs to be reused into its own file and then use the `@include` directive with a file name and path for wherever that configuration was needed. With the `include` statement, the referenced file is merged into the parent configuration file. This means we can reuse configurations and incorporate inclusions so that the Fluentd configuration doesn't need to be manipulated, so the sequencing of directives is not a problem.

During Fluentd's startup, the configuration file is parsed and has the inclusion directive replaced with a copy of the included file's contents. This way, we can include the same configuration file wherever it is needed. For example, if we have an enterprise-wide setup for Elasticsearch, then all the different Fluentd configurations can reference a single file for using the enterprise Elasticsearch, and changes, for instance, optimizing connection settings, can then be applied to one file. Everyone inherits the change when the configuration file is deployed.

An *inclusion* does not have to contain a complete configuration; it can easily contain a single attribute. An excellent example of this is where you want to reuse some common Ruby (e.g., retrieving some security credentials) logic into the Fluentd configuration, as we'll discuss later. Equally, an inclusion file may be used to inject a block of configuration, such as a `store` block or even an entire additional configuration file that could also be used independently. In listing 5.2, we have added several inclusions by introducing `@include additionalStore.conf` after the last `store` tag defines additional store configurations from a separate file. This means we could define a common destination for all our log events and repeat the configuration across this and other configuration files to log all events in a common place, and then allow the configuration to focus on the destinations.

Listing 5.2   Chapter5/Fluentd/file-source-multi-out2.conf—illustration of inclusion

```
<match *>
  @type copy
    <store>
      @type null
    </store>
    <store>
      @type stdout
    </store>
    <store>
      @type file
      @id bufferedFileOut
      tag bufferedFileOut
      path ./Chapter5/fluentd-file-output
      <buffer>
        delayed_commit_timeout 10
        flush_at_shutdown true
        chunk_limit_records 500
        flush_interval 30
        flush_mode interval
      </buffer>
      <format>
        @type out_file
        delimiter comma
        output_tag true
      </format>
    </store>
  @include additionalStore.conf

</match>

@include record-origin.conf
```

Incorporates the external file into the configuration providing an additional store declaration

Brings a complete configuration set that could be separately run if desired or could be reused

We have also added an inclusion directive referencing the file `record-origin .conf`. This illustrates the possibility that when multiple teams contribute functionality into a single run-time environment (e.g., a J2EE server), rather than all the teams trying to maintain a single configuration file and handling change collisions, each team has its own configuration file. But come execution time, a single configuration file uses inclusions to bring everything together. As a result, the Fluentd node needs to merge all the configurations together during startup. Within the `record-origin .conf` (if you review the content of `record-origin.conf`), we have introduced some new plugins, which we will cover later in the chapter.

Let's see the result of the configuration. As this uses a file source, we need to run the LogSimulator as well. So, to run the example, the following commands are needed:

- `fluentd -c ./Chapter5/Fluentd/file-source-multi-out2.conf`
- `groovy LogSimulator.groovy ./Chapter5/SimulatorConfig/log-source-1.properties`

NOTE It is important to remember that the content of an inclusion can have an impact on the configuration, which has the `include` declaration. So the placement and use of inclusions must be done with care, as the finalized order of directives and their associated plugins is still applicable, as highlighted in chapter 2.

If the path to the included file is relative in the `include` statement, then the point of reference is the file's location with the `include` directive. The `include` directive can use a comma-separated list, in which case the list order relates to the insertion sequence—for example, `@include file.conf, file2.conf` means `file.conf` is included before `file2.conf`. If the `include` directive uses wildcards (e.g., `@include *.conf`), then the order of insertion is alphabetical.

Figure 5.6 shows the dry-run output and highlights where `include` declarations have been replaced with the included configuration or configuration fragment contents.

```
<system>
  Log_Level info
</system>
<source>
  @type tail
  path "./Chapter5/annotated-file-1.txt"
  read_lines_limit 5
  tag "simpleFile"
  pos_file "./Chapter5/annotated-file.pos_file"
  read_from_head true
  <parse>
    @type "json"
    unmatched_lines
  </parse>
</source>
<match *>
  @type copy
  <store>
    @type "null"
  </store>
  <store>
    @type "stdout"
    <inject>
      hostname_key "hostName"
      worker_id_key "workerId"
      time_key "fluentdTime"
      time_type string
      localtime true
    </inject>
  </store>
  <store>
    @type "file"
    @id bufferedFileOut
    path "./Chapter5/fluentd-file-output"
    <buffer>
      delayed_commit_timeout 10
      flush_at_shutdown true
      chunk_limit_records 500
      flush_interval 30
      flush_mode interval
      path "./Chapter5/fluentd-file-output"
    </buffer>
    <format>
      @type "out_file"
      delimiter comma
      output_tag true
    </format>
  </store>
  <store>
    <store>
      @type "null"
      @id inclusion
    </store>
  </store>
</match>
</ROOT>
2020-10-19 08:08:57 +0100 [info]: starting fluentd-1.9.3 pid=10724 ruby="2.6.4"
```

Figure 5.6 Configuration file with the include resolved (highlighted in the box) as Fluentd starts up

NOTE As the process is a purely textual substitution, it does mean that the inclusion can easily be an empty placeholder file or a configuration fragment. If the inclusion is injected in the wrong place within a file, it can invalidate the entire configuration.

5.2.1 Place holding with null output

In listing 5.2, the additional inclusion fragment (`@include additionalStore .conf`) provided the configuration fragment shown in listing 5.3. This `store` definition uses the *null* output plugin; it simply discards the log events it receives.

Placing null plugins when working in an environment where different teams may wish to output log events to different tools allows developers to build a service to put the placeholder in the Fluentd configuration ready for the other team(s) to replace. In many respects, the use of null is the nearest thing to adding a TODO code comment.

NOTE TODO is a common tag used in code to flag when something still needs to be done.

Listing 5.3 Chapter5/Fluentd/additionalStore.conf—include configuration fragment

```
<store>
  @type null
  @id inclusion
</store>
```

5.2.2 Putting inclusions with a MongoDB output into action

Let's apply some of the insights to this scenario. Knowing where best to apply effort is best driven by analytical insights. Directing error events into a database makes it easy to get statistics over time showing what errors occur and how frequently. When combined with an appreciation of the impact of an error, the effort can be targeted with maximum value.

We need to apply this to `Chapter5/Fluentd/file-source-multi-out.conf`. To help with this, the work from chapter 4, where we used Fluentd with a MongoDB plugin, can be leveraged. We can capitalize on it to see the impact of copy errors and the use of the `ignore_error` option. To do this, create a copy of the `Chapter5/Fluentd/file-source-multi-out.conf` that can be safely modified. For simplicity, let's call this copy `Chapter5/Fluentd/file-source-multi-out-exercise .conf`. We need to replace the `@type  null` with the configuration for MongoDB output. The commands you will need to run the scenario are

- `fluentd -c ./Chapter5/Fluentd/file-source-multi-out-exercise.conf`
- `groovy LogSimulator.groovy ./Chapter5/SimulatorConfig/log-source-1.properties`

With the changes applied, we should be able to complete the following steps:

1 Check the configuration using the dry-run capability. This should yield a valid result.

2   Confirm that the modified configuration produces the desired result by starting MongoDB and rerunning the LogSimulator and Fluentd.

3   Verify the behavior is as expected if we cannot connect to MongoDB, and repeat the same actions for running the LogSimulator and Fluentd.

4   The previous step should have highlighted the absence of the `ignore_error` option. Modify the Fluentd configuration adding the `ignore_error` option to the console output configuration. Rerun the configuration and LogSimulator. Confirm that the desired behavior is now correct.

ANSWERS

1   The modified Fluentd configuration file should now look like `Chapter5/ExerciseResults/file-source-multi-out-Answer1.conf` and yield a successful dry run.

2   With MongoDB running, the database should continue to fill with events that reflect the content sent to the file, and the console will still display content.

3   With MongoDB stopped, the output plugin will start realizing errors, as there is no configuration to ensure the issue does not cascade to impact other plugins. None of the output streams will produce log events. This is because of the default position that subsequent output plugins should not be executed once an error occurs.

4   With the `ignore_error` added to the configuration, the configuration should now resemble `Chapter5/ExerciseResults/file-source-multi-out-Answer2.conf`. With the MongoDB still stopped, the MongoDB output will fail, but the failure will not stop output to the console but will inhibit output to the file.

5.3   *Injecting context into log events*

Providing more information and context can help us work with log events. To do this, we may need to manipulate the predefined log event attributes and capture additional Fluentd values. This section looks at this in more detail.

By injecting this information into the log event as identifiable log event attributes, we can then reference the values explicitly when trying to exclude directives with a filter, which will prevent log events from being processed any further in a sequence of events. For example, suppose log events associated with a specific host are deemed unnecessary to be forwarded by comparing the attribute set with the hostname. In that case, we can apply a filter with an exclude directive to stop the information from going anywhere.

The *inject* operation can only be used with match and filter directives, which is unfortunate, as we might want to apply it at the source. That said, it is not a significant challenge to overcome if desired, as we will see shortly. Using our example configuration `Chapter5/Fluentd/record-origin.conf`, we can see the injection at work in listing 5.4.

When configuring the injection of time data, it is possible to configure different representations of the time. This is covered by the `time_type` attribute, which accepts values for

- *String*—Allows a textual representation to be used and defers to the time_ format attribute for the representation. The time_format uses the standard notation, as described in appendix A.
- *Float*—Seconds and nanoseconds from the epoch (e.g., 1510544836 .154709804).
- *Unixtime*—This is the traditional seconds from epoch representation.

In listing 5.4, we have gone for the most readable format of the string. In addition to describing the time data format, it is possible to specify the time as *localtime* or as *UTC* time by including the attributes localtime and utc, which take Boolean values. Trying to set both attributes could be the source of a lot of problems.

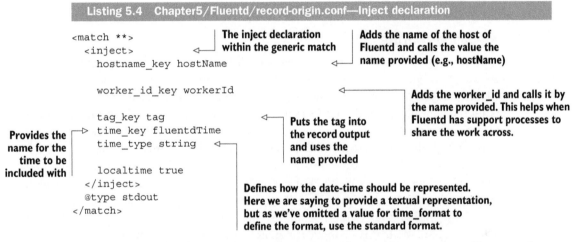

Listing 5.4 Chapter5/Fluentd/record-origin.conf—Inject declaration

The properties for the inject configuration relate to the mapping of known values like hostname, tag, and so on, to attributes in the log event record.

To see this configuration in action, we have used the monitor_agent and stdout, so all we need to do is run Fluentd with the command fluentd -c ./Chapter5/flu-entd/record-origin.conf. The outcome will appear in the console, something like

```
2020-05-18 17:42:41.021702900 +0100 self: {"plugin_id":"object:34e82cc",
  "plugin_category":"output","type":"stdout","output_plugin":true,"retry_coun
  t":0,"emit_records":4,"emit_count":3,"write_count":0,"rollback_count":0,"sl
  ow_flush_count":0,"flush_time_count":0,"hostName":"Cohen","workerId":0,"tag
  ":"self","fluentdTime":"2020-05-18T17:42:41+01:00"}
```

Within this output, you will see that the injected values appear at the end of the JSON structure using the names defined by the attributes; for example, "hostName": "Cohen", where Cohen is the PC used to write this book.

5.3.1 Extraction of values

If we can inject certain values into the log event's record, then it seems obvious that there should be a counter capability for extracting values from the record to set the tag and timestamp of the log event. This ability can be exploited by plugins that work with source, filter, and match directives. This gives us a helpful means to set tags dynamically based on the log event record content. Dynamically setting tags makes tag-based routing very flexible. For example, if the log event had an attribute called source, and we wanted to use that as a means to perform routing, we could use the *extract* operation. For example:

```
<inject>
  tag_key nameOfLogRecordAttribute
</inject>
```

Unfortunately, only a subset of the plugins available takes advantage of the *extract* helper. One of the core plugins that does incorporate this *exec*, which we have not covered yet. So as we explore tag-based routing in the next section, we'll use exec, and we will explore the interesting opportunities it offers.

5.4   *Tag-based routing*

In all the chapters so far, we have always had wildcards in the *match* declarations (e.g., <match *>), but we have had the opportunity to define and change the tag values at different stages. We have seen the tag being manipulated in contexts ranging from taking the tag value from the URI to setting the tag within the configuration and even extracting the tag from the log event record, as just discussed. We can use the tags to control which directives are actioned, which is the subject of this section.

We can control which directives will process and consume log events by defining the match values more explicitly. For example, a configuration for two inputs called AppA and AppB includes the tag attribute setting the respective tags to be AppA and AppB. Now, rather than match *, we set the directives to be <match AppA> and <match AppB>. With this change, the match directives will only process log events from the associated source.

In our example, to keep the sources simple, we have configured two occurrences of the dummy source plugin to generate log events. We have added additional attributes to control the behavior to repeat at different frequencies (with the rate attribute representing the number of seconds between each log event generated) and different messages (dummy attribute).

In the following listing, we show the key elements of the configuration (we have removed some configuration elements for clarity; this can be seen with the use of an ellipsis [. . .]).

Listing 5.5   Chapter5/Fluentd/monitor-file-out-tag-match.conf—tag matching

```
<source>

  @type dummy
  dummy {"hello from":"App A"}
  auto_increment_key AppACounter
  tag AppA
  rate 5
```

The first of two source definitions in this configuration file, but note that the port numbers are different, along with several other configuration attributes, so the sources are easy to distinguish.

```
</source>

<source>                    ◁─┐   The second self_monitor source configuration. Most
                             │   crucially, note the tag name differences between the sources.
  @type dummy
  dummy {"Goodbye from":"App B"}
  auto_increment_key AppBIncrement
  tag AppB
  rate 3                       The first of two match declarations. Note
</source>                      how we can use wildcard characters so
                         ◁─┘   partial name matching can be defined.
<match AppB>

    @type file             ◁──────────────────┐  File output configuration mapping to
                                               │  different output files for each match
    path ./Chapter5/AppB-file-output           │  (compare the path attributes)
    @id AppBOut
    <buffer> . . . </buffer>
    <format> . . . </format>
</match>                         The second match, this time
                         ◁─┘   without any wildcarding
<match AppA>
    @type file
    path ./Chapter5/AppA-file-output
    @id AppAOut
    <buffer> . . . </buffer>
    <format> . . . </format>
</match>
```

This setup can be run with the command

```
fluentd -c ./Chapter5/Fluentd/ monitor-file-out-tag-match.conf
```

The output files should reflect the different dummy messages, as the routing will have directed from the relevant source.

Despite the naming, it is still possible to use selective wildcarding with the tags. If we extend this example by adding an additional source and tagging it AppAPart2, we could catch AppA and AppAPart2. This is done by modifying the <match AppA> to become <match AppA*>. The log events captured from the new source would be incorporated into the AppA output.

This is illustrated in listing 5.6. If we do not want to reintroduce wildcard use, we can also utilize a comma-separated tag list in the match declaration; for example, <match AppA, AppAPart2>. To illustrate the wildcard behavior, this time we have introduced another source plugin called *exec*. The exec plugin allows us to call OS scripts and capture the result. We are simply using the more command (as it behaves the same way for Linux and Windows) within the exec statement.

> **Listing 5.6 Chapter5/Fluentd/monitor-file-out-tag-match2.conf—tag matching**

```
<source>                    ◁────────┐  Original source, which
  @type dummy                        │  remains unaltered
  dummy {"hello from":"App A"}
```

```
    auto_increment_key AppACounter
    tag AppA
    rate 5
</source>

<source>                               ⎤  The additional source, using
    @type exec              ⟵──────────┘  the exec source plugin
    command more .\TestData\valuePair.txt
    run_interval 7s
    tag AppAPart2
</source>
                          ⎤  The original AppB source,
<source>         ⟵────────┘  which remains unchanged
    @type dummy
    dummy {"Goodbye from":"App B"}
    auto_increment_key AppBIncrement
    tag AppB
    rate 3
</source>                              ⎤  The match for AppB
<match AppB> . . . </match>   ⟵───────┘  remains unmodified.

<match AppA*>                 ⟵──────────────      The original match for AppA has now been
                                                   modified to include the wildcard, which
                                                   means both AppA and AppAPart2 will be
    @type file                                     matched. This could described also be
    path ./Chapter5/AppA-file-output               expressed as <match AppA, AppAPart2>.
    @id AppAOut
    <buffer> . . . </buffer>
    <format> . . . </format>
</match>
```

This setup can be run with the command

```
fluentd -c ./Chapter5/Fluentd/ monitor-file-out-tag-match2.conf
```

The output files should reflect the different dummy messages, but the AppA output should now include the outcome of executing the OS command on a predefined test data file.

> ## Tag naming convention
>
> Despite using wildcard characters to help select tags for different directives regardless of the position, there is a convention normally applied. Tag naming typically follows a namespace-like hierarchy using the dot to break the hierarchy tiers (e.g., AppA.ComponentB.SubComponentC). Now the wildcard can filter the different namespaces (e.g., AppA.* or AppA.ComponentB.*). For example, if we had a web server hosting a domain with several different services, with each service potentially having one or more log outputs, we might see a convention of webserver.service.outputName in the tag convention.

5.4.1   *Using exec output plugin*

The exec plugin illustrated in listing 5.6 creates some interesting opportunities. When plugins cannot help us get the information required, we have several options:

- Build a custom plugin (which will be explored later in the book).
- Create an independent utility that can feed data to Fluentd directly via HTTP, UDP, forward plugins.
- Produce a small script that can be invoked by the exec plugin.

Using the exec plugin makes it easy to retrieve environment-specific information or perform things like grabbing web page output using utilities like *Wget* and *cURL*—a modern version of screen scraping. The latter is particularly interesting, as it is possible to extract information from web interfaces or web endpoints—for example, if a third party provided a microservice (which therefore has to be treated as a black box)—and could still be effectively monitored. If the third party has followed the best practice of providing a /health endpoint (see http://mng.bz/5KQz for more information), we could run a script to extract the necessary values from the response to a Wget or cURL call to /health.

The exec plugin does need to be used with some care. Each exec process is executed in its own thread so that it does not adversely impact the consumption of other logging events whenever triggered. However, if the process is too slow, then we could experience the following:

- The exec plugin will likely be triggered again before the last one has completed, which risks creating out-of-sequence events (due to how resources get shared across threads).
- Thread death could occur because there are too many threads demanding too many resources (this kind of issue could come about if the buffer ends up with too many threads).
- Events start being backed up, as logic will wait for threads to complete to allocate to another exec.

The takeaway is to think about what exec is doing; if it is slow or computationally demanding, then it's probably unwise to run it within Fluentd. We could consider independently running the exec process that writes the results to a file, and log management should be relatively lightweight compared to the core business process.

5.4.2   *Putting tag naming conventions into action*

A decision has been made by the team that the logging configuration should reflect a naming convention of the domain.service.source. The current configuration does not reflect the domain being called Demo, and the services are called AppA and AppB, with AppA having two components of Part1 and Part2. You have been asked to update the configuration file monitor-file-out-tag-match2.conf to align with this convention. Change the match directive for `AppA` so that only `Part1` is captured in the `AppA` file. Note the additional input, as the exec source is not yet needed in the output.

ANSWER

The outcome should result in a modified configuration that should look something like `Chapter5/ExerciseResults/monitor-file-out-tag-match-Answer.conf`. Note how the match condition has changed.

5.4.3   *Putting dynamic tagging with extract into action*

In section 5.3.1, we saw an explanation of how tags can be set dynamically. We should improve and rerun `monitor-file-out-tag-match2.conf` so that the exec sources set the tags based on the retrieved file value.

ANSWER

We should end up with a configuration that looks something like `Chapter5/ExerciseResults/monitor-file-out-tag-match-Answer2.conf`. Note that when we run this, the contents of the log events using the exec source will no longer reach the output because we've changed the tag, so it fails the match clause.

5.5   *Tag plugins*

There are plugins available to further help with routing using tags; let's look at some certified plugins outside the core Fluentd (table 5.1).

When plugins are described as "certified," it means they come from recognized and trusted contributors to the Fluentd community. As these plugins are not part of the core Fluentd, it does mean that to use these plugins, you will need to install them, just as we did for MongoDB in chapter 4.

Table 5.1   Additional tag-based routing plugins that can help with routing

Plugin name and link	Description
rewrite-tag-filter https://github.com/fluent/fluent -plugin-rewrite-tag-filter	With one or more rules in the `match` directive, the log event has a regular expression applied to it by the plugin. Then, depending on the result, the tag is changed to a specified value. The rule can be set such that you can choose whether the rewrite is applied to a true or false outcome from the regex. The log event is re-emitted to continue beyond the match event using the new tag if a successful outcome is achieved.
route https://github.com/tagomoris/ fluent-plugin-route	The route plugin allows tags to direct the log events to one or more operations, such as manipulating the log event and copying it to intercept it by another directive.
rewrite https://github.com/kentaro/fluent -plugin-rewrite	This enables tags to be modified using one or more rules, such as if an attribute of the log event record matches a regular expression. As a result, performing specific tasks based on the log event becomes very easy.

5.6   *Labels: Taking tags to a new level*

As we will see in this section, the label directive uses the basic idea of routing with tags and takes it to a whole new level. Ideally, we should be able to group a set of directives together clearly and distinctly for a particular group of log events, but this can become challenging. Labels allow us to overcome that. They have two aspects: first, an additional attribute using `@label` can be linked to a log event, in much the same way that tags are linked (although, unlike a tag, a label is not part of the log event data structure). Second, labels offer a directive (`<label labelName>...</label>`) that we use to group other directives (e.g., match and filter) that are executed in sequence. In effect, we are defining a pipeline of actions. To differentiate the two for the rest of the book, we will talk about labels as attributions to log events and directives as linking one or more directives together as a pipeline or a label pipeline.

There is one constraint for labels when compared to tags. It is possible to create a comma-separated list of tags (e.g., `<match basicFile,basicFILE2>`), but labels can have only a single label associated with that pipeline (e.g., `<label myLabel>`). You will find that trying to match multiple labels in the same way will result in an error—for example, `'find_label': common label not found (ArgumentError)`. This comes about as Fluentd does check that each label declaration can be executed during startup.

> **NOTE** Unlike tags, the naming convention is usually more functional in meaning.

5.6.1   *Using a stdout filter to see what is happening*

To help illustrate the point, we will introduce a special filter configuration. The important thing about filters with stdout, unlike match directives, is that even if the event satisfies the filter rule, it is emitted by the plugin to be consumed by whatever follows. This setup for a filter is a bit like a developer's `println` for helping to see what is happening during code development. We will look more closely at filters in the next chapter, but for now, let's see how the stdout plugin behaves in a filter.

The stdout plugin effectively accepts all events; thus, the following filter will let everything pass through and send the details to the console:

```
<filter *>
    @type stdout
</filter>
```

This configuration is typically referred to as *filter_stdout*. Using this as an additional step will help us illustrate the label pipeline behavior. This is another handy way of peeking at what is happening within a Fluentd configuration.

5.6.2   *Illustrating label and tag routing*

To illustrate a label-based pipeline, we have created a configuration that tails two separate files (from two different log simulators). The configuration of the simulator output results in two differing message structures (although both are derived from the same source data). To observe the differences, compare `basic-file.txt` and `basic-file2.txt` once the simulators are running.

The configuration will illustrate the use of a label being applied to one source and not another. Then, within the label "pipeline," one source (file) will be subject to both the stdout filter (as explained in section 5.6.1) and a file output that is separate from the output of the other file. This is illustrated in the following listing. As with other larger configurations, we have replaced sections with ellipses, so relevant aspects of the configuration are easier to read.

Listing 5.7   Chapter5/Fluentd/file-source-file-out-label-pipeline.conf label pipeline

```
<source>
  @type tail
  path ./Chapter5/basic-file.txt
  read_lines_limit 5
  tag basicFile
  pos_file ./Chapter5/basic-file-read.pos_file
  read_from_head true
  <parse> @type none </parse>
  @label labelPipeline

</source>

<source>

  @type tail
  path ./Chapter5/basic-file2.txt
  read_lines_limit 5
  tag basicFILE2
  pos_file ./Chapter5/basic-file-read2.pos_file
  read_from_head true
  <parse>  @type json </parse>
</source>
#### end - tail basic-file2

<label labelPipeline>

  <filter *>
    @type stdout
  </filter>

  <match *>
      @type file
      path ./Chapter5/label-pipeline-file-output
      @id otherSelfOut
      <buffer> . . . </buffer>
      <format> . . . </format>
  </match>

  <match *>
```

> Our source attaches a label to the events it creates; in this case, labelPipeline. This will mean the step operation performed on these events will be in the <label labelPipeline> block.

> This source is unlabeled. As a result, its log events will be intercepted by the next match blog that can consume the tag basicFILE2.

> At the start of the label block, any log events with a label that match will pass through this sequence of operations, assuming the processing allows the event to output from the plugin.

> Use the stdout filter to push the log events to stdout and output to the next plugin.

> Use the match to direct content to a file.

> We will never see any result from this stdout filter, as the preceding match will have consumed the log event. To send log events to both stdout and the file would require the use of the copy.

```
    @type stdout
  </match>
</label>
```
Defines the end of the label series of events

```
<match basicFILE2>
```
Outside of a label, the match will be applied to all no label events.

```
    @type file
    path ./Chapter5/alt-file-output
    @id basicFILE2Out
    <buffer> . . . </buffer>
    <format> . . . </format>
</match>
```

To run this configuration, we need to run the commands

- `fluentd -c Chapter5/Fluentd/file-source-file-out-label-pipe-line.conf`
- `groovy LogSimulator.groovy Chapter5/SimulatorConfig/basic-log-file.properties`
- `groovy LogSimulator.groovy Chapter5/SimulatorConfig/basic-log-file2.properties`

When running this setup, the log events can be seen in `basic-file.txt` and on the console. Additionally, there will be two more files, as the log content is output to `label-pipeline-file-output.*_*.log` and `alt-file-output.*_*.log` (wildcards represent the date and file increment number). Neither file should have tags mixing.

While the match expression defined continues to use a wildcard within the label pipeline, it is possible to still apply the tag controls on the directives within the pipeline. If you edit the configuration setting to align the match clause with `<match basicFILE2>`, you will see the logs displayed on the console but not in the file.

5.6.3 Connecting pipelines

As configurations become more sophisticated, you will likely need to create pipelines and link them together. This can be done using the *relabel* plugin. Relabel does what it says; it changes the label associated with the log event. As relabel is an output plugin, the log event can change the label and emit the log event rather than consume it. For example, you might have a label with several directives that can manipulate a log event into a human-friendly representation and send it to a social platform such as Slack. But before you use your label to do that, you may wish to take the log events through a labeled pipeline of filters that exclude all log events representing business-as-usual events.

As our Fluentd configuration structures become more complex with pipelines, it helps to visualize what is happening, as shown in figure 5.7. As you can see, we have now made the match that feeds the `alt-file-output` a labeled pipeline called `common`. To illustrate the use of relabel, the match in our original `labelPipeline` (as we saw in listing 5.7) has been modified. We have introduced a *copy* plugin to ensure that the log event goes to both the output and relabel (highlighting the store declaration can be done for more than just storage plugins). When we run this configuration, `alt-file-output` files will now contain both sources.

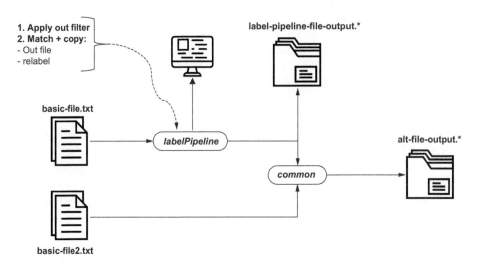

Figure 5.7   Label routing example, with two label pipelines connected (labelPipeline and common)

We can run the configuration using the commands

- `fluentd -c Chapter5/Fluentd/file-source-multi-out-label-pipelines.conf`
- `groovy LogSimulator.groovy Chapter5/SimulatorConfig/basic-log-file.properties`
- `groovy LogSimulator.groovy Chapter5/SimulatorConfig/basic-log-file2.properties`

The following listing shows the configuration with the application of `relabel`. Note the use of the ellipsis again, so you can focus on the key elements.

Listing 5.8   Chapter5/Fluentd/file-source-multi-out-label-pipelines.conf use of relabel

```
<source>
  @type tail
  path ./Chapter5/basic-file.txt
  read_lines_limit 5
  tag basicFile
  pos_file ./Chapter5/basic-file-read.pos_file
  read_from_head true
  <parse> . . . </parse>
  @label labelPipeline
```
This links this source's log events to a label, as we did in the previous example.

```
</source>

<source>
  @type tail
  path ./Chapter5/basic-file2.txt
  read_lines_limit 5
  tag basicFILE2
  pos_file ./Chapter5/basic-file-read2.pos_file
  read_from_head true
  <parse> . . . </parse>
  @label common          ◁──┐  Sets the second source to use the
                             │  common label rather than trust
</source>                    │  directives catching log events

<label labelPipeline>
    <filter *>
    @type stdout
  </filter>
                            Using the copy plugin within the match, we
  <match *>                 can cause the log event to be consumed
    @type copy     ◁──┘     by more than one output plugin.

    <store>                      The log event will get pushed
      @type file     ◁──┘        to a file output plugin first.
      path ./Chapter5/label-pipeline-file-output
      <buffer> . . . </buffer>
      <format> . . . </format>   As the copy directive is being used,
    </store>                     we can force the log event to be
    <store>            ◁─────────  processed by further operations.

      @type relabel     ◁──┐  Using the relabel plugin to change the log event's
                           │  label until this operation is 'labelPipeline'
      @label common    ◁──

                          The label is now set to be common; as
    </store>              we leave this match and label block,
  </match>                the event will be consumed by the
                          label directive called common.
</label>

<label common>      ◁──  The label common starts, which will now receive log events from both
                         sources. One source's event comes directly, and another passes
  <match *>              through the labelPipeline before reaching the common pipeline.
    @type file
    path ./Chapter5/alt-file-output
    <buffer> . . . </buffer>
    <format> . . . </format>
  </match>
</label>
```

5.6.4 *Label sequencing*

Unlike tags, the relative positioning of label directives does not matter, taking our current configuration shown in figure 5.7 as an example. While `labelPipeline` will trigger the use of the `common` label using relabel, the `common` label could be declared before the `labelPipeline`. The steps within a label pipeline are still sequential in execution. You can see and try this with the provided configuration file `Chapter5/Fluentd/file-source-multi-out-label-pipelines2.conf`. In the configuration, you can see

1 A relabel declaration that used to be for common, but has been changed to use the label `outOfSequence`. With it, we have moved the filter out to the new label section.

2 The `outOfSequence` label pipeline then redirects to the common, as we had previously and as illustrated in figure 5.8. The configuration file order actually reflects the appearance in the figure when reading the diagram left to right (ignoring the flow shown in the diagram).

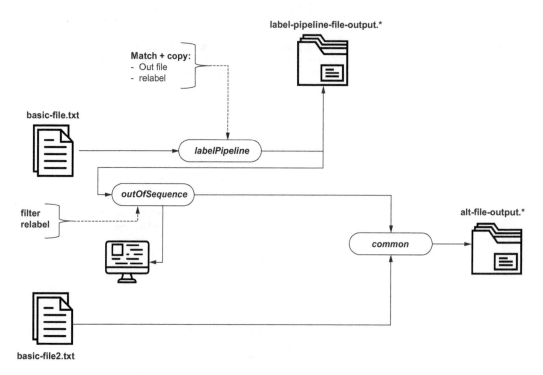

Figure 5.8   This configuration illustrates that labels are not order-sensitive.

The scenario can be executed using the commands

- `fluentd -c Chapter5/Fluentd/file-source-multi-out-label-pipelines2.conf`
- `groovy LogSimulator.groovy Chapter5/SimulatorConfig/basic-log-file-small.properties`
- `groovy LogSimulator.groovy Chapter5/SimulatorConfig/basic-log-file2-small.properties`

The simulator properties have been configured with a small data set to make it easier to confirm, and we do not get any accidental looping.

> **NOTE** While we have illustrated that labeling sections out of order is possible, we would not necessarily advocate it as good practice. As labels could be compared to *goto* statements in some respects, it is preferable to try to structure the configuration files to be as linear as practical.

5.6.5 *Special labels*

Fluentd's label feature includes a predefined `@Error` label. This means we can use the label directive to define a pipeline to process errors; those errors can be raised within our configuration or within a plugin executing the configuration. This does rely on the plugin implementation to use a specific API (`emit_error_event`). We can be confident that core Fluentd plugin implementations will use this API, but it might be worth checking to see if a third-party plugin uses the feature rather than simply writing to stdout. We will see this later in the book when we look at building our own plugin.

We could therefore build upon our existing Fluentd configuration steps to capture these errors. With this, we could do things like relabel the log event so that it gets picked up by a common pipeline or simply direct it to its own destination. In the next example, we've added a new label pipeline to our previous configuration that writes to its own file, as illustrated in the following listing.

Listing 5.9   Fluentd/file-source-multi-out-label-pipelines-error.conf using @Error

```
<source> . . . </source>

<source> . . . </source>

<label labelPipeline> . . . </label>

<label common> . . . </label>          The start of the pipeline using the predefined
                                       @Error label. As a result, any plugin that sets this
<label @Error>                    ◁──  label will have its error(s) handled in this pipeline.

  <match *>                    ◁──────  Matches all tags to write errors to file once
                                        log events are labeled with Error. But we
      @type file                        could get clever and handle errors associated
      path ./Chapter5/error-file-output with different tags differently. For example,
      <buffer> . . . </buffer>          specific tags that experience an error that
      <format>                          needs more urgent attention could be sent
        @type out_file                  to a notification or collaboration tool.
        delimiter comma
        output_tag true
      </format>
  </match>
</label>
```

> **TIP** It is always useful to create a simple generic pipeline for handling errors. The pipeline raises some sort of problem ticket, a social notification (e.g.,

Slack, Teams), or simply an email to notify the event within its own Fluentd configuration. Then use `include` as standard practice in all of your configurations. So, if you don't have any specific error-handling configuration, then the generic answer will kick in for you.

5.6.6   *Putting a common pipeline into action*

You have been asked to refactor the configuration referenced in listing 5.8 to have a single pipeline. This will allow the service to be incorporated into the main configuration through inclusion. This change will allow all of the different log event routes being developed by other teams to occur more safely. To help those teams, you should create an additional pipeline with a null output as a template.

ANSWER

The result actually involves three files. The core is `Chapter5/ExerciseResults/file-source-multi-out-label-pipelines-Answer.conf`. This uses `@include` to bring in the configurations `Chapter5/ExerciseResults/label-pipeline-Answer.conf`, which contains the refactored logic, and a template containing the null output defined by `Chapter5/ExerciseResults/label-pipeline-template-Answer.conf`.

Summary

- Fluentd provides a null output plugin that can be used as a placeholder for output plugins. The plugin will simply delete the received log events.
- Fluentd provides an exec plugin that allows us to incorporate the triggering of external processes, such as scripts, into the configuration. The external process can be invoked with arguments from the log event.
- Fluentd provides several mechanisms to route log events through a configuration. The simplest of these is using the tag associated with each log event.
- For more sophisticated routing where we want a "pipeline" of actions, Fluentd provides a label construct. The use of labels can also help us simplify the complexity in a configuration file when it comes to ordering configuration values.
- Fluentd provides naming conventions by using the conventions we can group and `namespace` tags. We can use wildcards in the configuration to group tags together.
- A Fluentd configuration can be assembled from multiple files through the use of the `@include` directive.
- If Fluentd experiences an error (e.g., can't connect to an instance of Elasticsearch), we can catch the error and perform actions using the custom `@Error` label.

Filtering and extrapolation 6

This chapter covers

- Applying filters to control log events
- Implementing the *record_transformer* filter
- Extrapolating information from log events
- Injecting environmental information into a log event
- Masking elements of log events to maintain data security

In chapter 5, we touched upon using the filter directive to send log events to standard out. Using filters this way, while helpful, is almost a sideshow to the full capability of the directive. The filter directive can help us to

- Filter out specific log events, so only particular log events go to particular consuming systems
- Filter out specific pieces of a log event message and allow us to record them as unique attributes of the log event (ultimately making it easier to apply logic with that data)

145

- Enrich the log events by amending the tag and timestamp to reflect the dynamic content of the log event record itself (e.g., adjusting for upstream caching of events)
- Further enrich log events; for example
  - Using plugins that can add geographical location information based on the public IP (known as GeoIP)
  - Attaching error guidance by identifying information in the log event(s) (e.g., if an error code is generic but the path to the code that generated it matched something, then annotate the log with a qualification, such as "root cause is DB connection error")
  - Adding contextual information, which can help you perform further analysis later (e.g., the Fluentd worker_id and server_id)
- Apply changes to address security considerations (e.g., anonymization, masking and redaction of any sensitive data that finds its way into log events)
- Calculate or extrapolate new data from the log event and its context (e.g., take two timestamps and calculate the elapsed time)
- Filter out log events that confirm everything is running as expected

This chapter will explore why we may want to filter log events in or out and how the filters are configured to do this. As filters can be used to manipulate event logs, we'll look at how this can be done, whether we should, and why we might want to do this.

6.1   *Application of filters*

We have just seen a brief summary of the breadth of possibilities for using filters; let's dig into some of these applications to better understand why we might want to use them.

6.1.1   *All is well events do not need to be distributed*

A lot of log information will actually indicate to us that things are running as they should. Getting these events is important; as noted management consultant and author Peter Drucker said, "You can't manage what you don't measure." Perhaps even more pertinent, Dag Hammarskjöld (economist and secretary-general of the United Nations) said, "Constant attention by a good nurse may be just as important as a major operation by a surgeon." In other words, we need to actively observe, quantify, and qualify the state to know everything is well. This steady, constant observation will allow us to make minor adjustments to keep things well, rather than needing skilled but major change.

But we do not need to share with everyone every log event that confirms things are fine. Like a heart monitor, when things are not right, the alarms and signals all go off to ensure everyone is aware help is needed. If everything is within expected parameters, the data doesn't go further than the monitor's display. For example, Elastic Beats can generate heartbeat log events, such as `2017-12-17T19:17:42.667-0500 INFO [metrics] log/log.go:110 Non-zero metrics in the last 30s:`

beat.info.uptime.ms=30004 beat.memstats.gc_next=5046416. This is probably a log message that doesn't need to be retained, or if retained, does not need to be
distributed and is instead logged locally for a short period.

If we are getting log events indicating all is well and unlikely to yield any more
insight, do we need to propagate the events to downstream systems? This will mean it
will be easier to see significant events. By filtering out mundane information, we are
also controlling costs. Physical infrastructure has a maximum amount of data it can
transmit before we need more hardware. We pay for public network capacity based on
bandwidth (i.e., data volume), so consuming the bandwidth distributing every "heartbeat" log event can accumulate cost with little gain—more networking hardware,
more bandwidth, and so on. Over the last couple of years, it has been observed that
the cost of data egress from cloud platforms can influence commercial decisions. In
other words, pushing data out of one cloud to another location costs money, and that
cost can become significant. But we don't want to cut off that one event in a hundred
that is important and worth transmitting.

6.1.2   *Spotting the needle in a haystack*

Filtering can be used to isolate those innocuous-looking events that are a warning of
more significant problems to come. These occur when someone has wrongly classified
what should be a warning log event as informational or even debug. The ability to
identify and flag these kinds of events is important when you can't get the logging to
generate more helpful events (e.g., off-the-shelf software, legacy solutions that no one
wants to touch).

6.1.3   *False urgency*

Sooner or later, we will encounter a situation where a warning or error log occurs, and
the issue escalates up the management chain. Lots of "shouting" starts about a problem that must trump all other priorities to be fixed. But ultimately, the consequences
of the issue and its impact don't require everything to be dropped; yes, an error
occurred, but it isn't the end of the world. What has been detected is a problem that
could have been handled by routine day-to-day operations tasks. With filters, we can
define rules that can help us separate the "world will end" events from the "please fix
me when you log in and direct the information accordingly" events.

Even better, if there are known operational steps to address an issue, we add the
reference to the remediation process to the log event. So when the alerts are triggered, they've got the remediation information linked to them. Unnecessary escala-
tion is avoided, actions that can compound a problem aren't taken, and so on.

6.1.4   *Releveling*

The previous application is when a log event can be generated and tagged with a log
level higher than it should be—for example, Error instead of Warning or Info. As
before, if people can't or won't fix the issue, then we can modify the log event as it gets
passed on. This is done by manipulating the log event to change the record's log level

to a less alarming and more accurate classification. Alternatively, tagging the log event with additional attributes with commentary shows this is a known incorrect log level.

6.1.5   Unimplemented housekeeping

As long as software development exists, business drivers will prioritize functional capabilities over nonfunctional ones such as housekeeping (archiving or deleting folders of processed files, etc.). When this is a characteristic of a legacy application, it is not unusual for people to fear changing anything to improve the system, such as cleaning up after itself. The typical result is that routine support processes are done manually, which we may then automate via scripts and just have to run in certain circumstances. Filtering out the indicators in logs alerting that housekeeping tasks need to be done (e.g., Fluentd capturing log events relating to disk space, for example) is a small step that triggers the execution of housekeeping tasks.

6.2   Why change log events?

Some filters allow us to modify log events. Why should we consider this, and how can this capability help us? Some might argue that modifying log events is also tampering with the "original truth," so should we even allow it?

6.2.1   Easier to process meaning downstream

When we process log events, we often need to extract more meaning from the logs provided. The log event is unstructured, semi-structured, or even structured but needs to be reparsed to a suitable data structure (e.g., reading JSON text files). The structure can help filter, route, create new reporting metrics, and measure using the log event data. Once we have invested the effort to extract meaning from a log event, why not make that easy to reuse downstream? In other words, apply the principle of DRY (don't repeat yourself). So, if you have extracted meaning and structure, don't make people do it again later. Simply pass the derived information with the log event.

6.2.2   Add context

To process an event correctly, we may need additional context. When trying to diagnose why an application is performing poorly, it isn't unusual to look at what else was happening around the events—for example, did the server have a large number of threads running? Sometimes it is easy to link this contextual data to the log event. The easiest way to associate additional context is to add it to the log event.

6.2.3   Record when we have reacted to a log event

We have already referred to the possibility that we initiate some sort of action due to a log event. In retrospect, it can be helpful to understand which event(s) triggered an action. Adding information to the triggering log event can be a more straightforward, acceptable action rather than correlating separate log events later to show cause and effect.

6.2.4 *Data redaction/masking*

When we are developing software, it is often helpful to log an entire data object being processed during the development phase. This isn't a problem during development and testing, as it's just test data. But if the data includes sensitive information, such as data that can be used to identify individuals (*PII*, personally identifiable information), as in health care or credit card use, for example, it can become a challenge. Any part of an IT system that handles such data becomes subject to a lot of legal, legislative, and contractual technical requirements. Such requirements come from international, national, and regional data laws such as

- *GDPR* (General Data Protection Register)
- *HIPAA* (Health Insurance Portability and Accountability Act) and other health care legislation
- *PCI DSS* (Payment Card Industry Data Security Standard)

You can add to this list that many companies may also wish to treat some financial accounting data with the same sensitivity. The obvious solution would be to fix the software so it doesn't log the data or limit the impact of such logging, limiting the "blast radius" of needing to apply extra extremely stringent controls, security mechanisms, and reporting. Fluentd provides an excellent means to address this:

- Remove or redact/mask the data from the logs. Masking is typically done by replacing sensitive values with meaningless ones. Redaction is removing information from sight by either deleting it from the communication, or simply never making it visible in logs, and so on. We can see data being masked on payment card receipts with asterisks or hash characters replacing your card number. Any approach to masking can be used as long as it can't be reversed to get back the original data.
- Co-locate Fluentd with the log source so that the amount of infrastructure subject to the elevated data security requirements is limited. The smaller the scope of elevated security, the smaller the "attack surface" (i.e., the smaller the number of servers and software components that may be subject to malicious attacks attempting to get the data, the better).
- Connect the main application's logging directly to Fluentd using *RPC* (remote procedure call) techniques rather than log files, so the log events are transient. We will see more on directly connecting applications to Fluentd in chapter 11.

Security not as a cost

It would be easy to read into what has been said here, concluding that security is an undesirable cost, and avoiding security is good. The reality is that today, security should be deemed an asset, and the application of security is a positive selling point. SaaS solution providers like Oracle do use their security as a virtue. The cost impact of data loss, particularly when the level of impact is not limited or understood, can

(continued)

easily outweigh the savings perceived of not having invested in securing against the risks. But the smaller the potential blast radius, the better. These days, a breach (malicious or accidental) is a matter of *when*, not *if*. The adage "assume the worst, hope for the best" is very appropriate.

6.3   *Applying filters and parsers*

In this section, we'll look at the practical configuration and use of filters and parsers to

- Manage the routing of log events
- Manipulate log events

To manipulate log events, we may need to impose or extract some meaning from them. To extract that meaning, we need to parse unstructured log event content, so we will need to touch upon the use of parsers.

6.3.1   *Filter plugins*

Filter as a directive is like a `match`, in so far as the directive can include tags in the declaration (e.g., `<filter myApp>` or `<filter *>`). The difference is that if the log event complies with the filter expression, rather than the log event being consumed, it can pass into the next part of the configuration without resorting to a copy action, as illustrated with the `match` directive in chapter 3.

Within the Fluentd core are the following filter plugins:

- *record_transformer*—The most sophisticated of the built-in filters; also provides a diverse set of options for manipulating the log event.
- *grep*—Provides the means to define rules about log event attributes to filter them out of the stream of events. Multiple expressions can be provided to define cumulative rules.
- *filter_parser*—Combines the capability of parser plugins with the filter.
- *stdout*—We have seen this plugin at work. Every event is allowed to pass through the filter but is also written to stdout.

Fluentd comes with a core set of filter plugins; in addition to this, there are community-provided filter plugins. Appendix C contains details of additional plugins that we believe can be particularly helpful.

6.3.2   *Applying grep filters*

The grep parser allows us to define a search expression and apply it to a named attribute in the log event. For example, we could extend our routing such that the events with log entries explicitly refer to computers in the text. This is the basis of the following scenario; while a computer reference is relatively meaningless, we could easily replace or extend it with a reference to a cataloged error code. For example, a WebLogic notification starts with `BEA-000`.

While we are demonstrating the use of the filter, let's use a different output plugin. Chapter 1 introduced EFK (Elasticsearch, Fluentd, Kibana), so we'll bring Elasticsearch into the mix to show more of this stack (appendix A provides instructions on how to install Elasticsearch). The Fluentd configuration we're going to use is shown in figure 6.1.

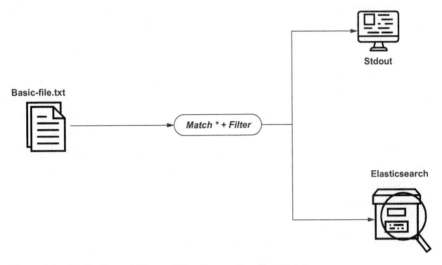

Figure 6.1 Application of filter and Elasticsearch as an output

We can apply a filter using the grep plugin, which will execute a regular expression whose result can be treated in a binary manner. The result will determine whether the log event is to be stored. This is all done by setting the directive to be `regexp`. We need to define the key, which is the log event's element to examine. In this case, we want to look at the core log event called `msg`. Once we've identified where to look, we need to provide a pattern for the regex parser to look for. Bringing this together with the attribute name gives us

```
<regexp>
    key msg
    pattern /computer/
</regexp>
```

With the filter defined, we need to send any matching log events to our installation of Elasticsearch. We do this using the `match` directive and a `@type` value of `elasticsearch`. The Elasticsearch plugin is incredibly configurable, with over 30 attributes covering behaviors ranging from caching control to determining how the log events are populated and indexed in Elasticsearch, and so on. We're not going to cover all of these, as we'd end up with a book explaining Elasticsearch, and for that, you'd be better off with *Elasticsearch in Action* by Radu Gheorghe, et al. (www.manning.com/books/elasticsearch-in-action); however, we should touch upon the most common attributes that you're likely to encounter.

As with the MongoDB connection, details must be provided to address the server (attributes `host` and `port`). Access credentials are likely to be required (*user* and *password*). As we haven't set up any such restrictions using the out-of-the-box deployment, we don't need to provide them. The *scheme* or type of communication, such as *http* or *https*, will dictate whether additional details will be needed (e.g., where the certificates to be used can be found); end-to-end SSL/TLS is always good security practice.

Once the means to connect to Elasticsearch have been defined, we need to declare where inside Elasticsearch the data should go (`index_name`) and what data to provide, such as whether to include the tag value in the core log event record (`include_tag_key`, `tag_key`). Remember, we also set how the data being passed is being represented. With the relationship between Elasticsearch and Logstash, it should come as no surprise that the plugin allows us to tell Fluentd to present the log events as Logstash would set the attribute `logstash_format` to `true`.

The Elasticsearch plugin also leverages helper caching plugins; thus, we need to consider how this can impact the behavior. For ease and speed, let's use a memory buffer being set to flush every 5 seconds by using the attribute `flush_interval 5s`. This configuration can be seen in the following listing.

Listing 6.1   Chapter6/Fluentd/file-source-elastic-search-out.conf

```
<filter *>           ←── Allows the filter to process any tag
  @type grep                           ←─┤ Defines the type of filter
  <regexp>        ←─────── Defines the field to apply the regular
                           expression to and then the expression,
    key msg                which needs to yield a binary result
    pattern /computer/
  </regexp>
</filter>           All log events that have passed through
                    the filter will now be processed by this
<match *>     ←──── match configured to write to file.

  @type elasticsearch    While we do not explicitly need to set the scheme, as it defaults
  host localhost         to http rather than https, it is worth including it to remind
  port 9200              ourselves of the low-security threshold in use. You could also
  scheme http     ←──┘   include the username and password as commented out as well.

  reload_on_failure true       Defines the index to be used; if
  index_name fluentd-book  ←── unspecified, it will default to Fluentd

  logstash_format false    ←─────┐
                                 │ Tells Elasticsearch to add to the named index,
                                 │ rather than it creating new ones using a timestamp
  include_tag_key true  ←──┘     name, as is the case for Logstash connectivity

  tag_key key            Shows we're telling the Elasticsearch plugin to
  <buffer>               include the log event tag in the data to be stored,
    flush_interval 5s    giving it the name key, as shown in the next attribute
  </buffer>
</match>
```

Let's see the result of the configuration. As this uses a file source, we need to run the LogSimulator as well. Assuming Elasticsearch is also running and ready, the following commands are needed to run the example:

- `fluentd -c ./Chapter6/Fluentd/file-source-elastic-search-out.conf`
- `groovy logSimulator.groovy ./Chapter6/SimulatorConfig/log-source-1.properties`

We can verify the records in Elasticsearch with the UI tool by reviewing the index contents, which we configured as `fluentd-book`. (Appendix A also covers the setting up of Elasticvue for this purpose.) You should find that the index contains the same log events that we sent to stdout.

Should filters modify log events?

The idea that we can change log events can be a contentious subject. If you change the original log event, are you modifying the original truth? To use a TV detective analogy, messing with the original log event is like tampering with a crime scene. Shouldn't Fluentd handle log events like the chain of custody for evidence? Generally, I would agree that the original log event should be retained unmodified. However, we often need to associate additional information to a piece of evidence (extending our analogy, a ballistics report would be attached to the relevant weapon). Rather than trying to keep the details separate, careful attachment of the details can be more helpful.

In the real world, the guidance we use is to keep a copy of the log event unaltered, with one exception—information security. If you need to mask or remove data, consider keeping an unadulterated copy somewhere safe that can be traced back to if necessary. Then any manipulated, extracted values can be kept along with the original. You might consider adopting a naming convention, so when those elements of a log event are manipulated, constructed, or enriched, the origin is clear.

6.3.3 Changing log events with the record_transformer plugin

Using a filter to control which log events are processed or not based on the log event's contents addresses many previously described scenarios. Modifying log events to add additional contextual information and derived values or to extract and record log event values in a more meaningful and usable manner helps with some of the other scenarios mentioned.

To illustrate how this can work, we're going to add to our log events new fields in addition to the standard ones, specifically the following:

- A field called `computer` containing the name of the host running Fluentd.
- Apply a prefix to the standard *message* of 'processed-' to illustrate the modification of existing values.
- The example log messages contain a JSON structure that includes a `name` attribute comprising `firstname` and `surname`. This combination could be

considered making the log data sensitive to PII rules, as it references an identifi-able individual. We will tease out the `firstname` and create a new log event attri-bute called `from` and delete the surname to address this. There should be no reason for the new attribute `from`; it does allow us to see how to copy elements.

Our log event message is structured and, when received, will look like

```
{"msg": "something about computers",
 "name":
    {
        "firstname": "Computer",
        "surname": "AI"
    },
 "age": 404
}
```

RECORD DIRECTIVE

The essential part of the filter definition is the `record` directive. Each line within the directive represents a field name and a field value. For example, if we wanted to add a new field called `myNewField` with a literal value of `aValue`, then we would configure the directive as follows:

```
<record>
  myNewField aValue
</record>
```

Just incorporating a design-time literal value isn't going to provide much value. To tell Fluentd that it needs to process a derived value, we need to wrap the expression within `${}`. We can reference the other fields within the log event by placing the name within the brackets (e.g., `${msg}`). To access the log event message, we use the notation `record["<field name>"]` (e.g., `record["msg"]`). Record is a reference to a function made available to use.

Within the characters `${}`, we are being allowed to use a small subset of Ruby objects, functions, and operators, including some provided by Fluentd. To allow this, we can include an attribute within the filter attribute `enable_ruby`; when this is set to `true`, it will allow the full power of the Ruby language to be used. This is defaulted to `false`, as it creates more work for the parser, such as ensuring that it can resolve depen-dencies, and so on; to keep things efficient, it's best not set to `true` unless necessary.

ACCESSING NESTED JSON ELEMENTS

To obtain the `firstname` element, we need to navigate the JSON structure within the message part of the log event. This can be done with either the standard *record* method—for example, `record["name"]["firstname"]`—which would traverse to the `firstname` as a child attribute but requires the attribute to be present. This can be a problem if part of the structure is optional, as any part of the path that is missing will trigger a run-time error. The alternative approach is to use a function called `dig` provided by the `record` operator. The syntax is remarkably similar; however, a nil result is provided rather than an error if the path does not exist. The `dig` function is record.dig ("msg", "name", "firstname"). This does require the *enable_ruby* to be set to work.

JSON ELEMENT DELETION

The record_transformer includes several attributes that allow the control of the composition of the log event elements. This can be done by using optional attributes in the configuration for listing elements to delete (remove_keys) or defining which elements (other than mandatory ones like tag) should remain (keep_keys). This includes the notation to traverse the JSON structure (which also works in other parts of the plugin). The order of attributes in the configuration is important. In our example, the remove_keys attribute needs to appear after the record directive; otherwise, we will find ourselves without an element to copy. To delete specific elements within a structure, we use the attribute remove_keys with the path through the object, such as $.name.surname. In the notation, $ (dollar sign) effectively represents the root of the log event. This is then followed by the attribute name using dot notation to traverse the structure. This does go back to the previous point of whether we can trust the path to exist. A single remove_keys attribute can be extended to more elements by making it a comma-separated list; for example, remove_keys $.name.surname, $.name.anotherName, $.somethingElse.

VALUE REPLACEMENT

The record operator includes a function that allows us to replace values in JSON elements. This is necessary for masking data and correcting values, such as the error message level, as described in section 6.1.4. This is done by referencing the element name and then invoking the function gsub followed by the parameters containing the value to replace and its replacement. For example, in our data set, the msg contains some occurrences of 'I'. Using the expression ${record["msg"] .gsub('I', 'We')}, the use of 'I' can be replaced with 'We'. In the following listing, we have included this expression. Rather than replacing the msg with the substituted string, a new attribute has been added to make the comparison easy.

Listing 6.2   Chapter6/Fluentd/file-source-transformed-elastic-search-out.conf

```
<filter *>
  @type record_transformer          Enables Ruby to support the record.dig
  enable_ruby true            ◁┘    approach of locating values
  <record>                                        Adds an attribute using the
    computer ${hostname}              ◁┘          known contextual values
    from ${record.dig("name", "firstname")}  ◁┐  Creates a new value by finding a
    msg processed ${record["msg"]}               sub-element and retrieving its value
    msg_gsub ${record["msg"].gsub('I ', 'We ')}  ◁┐
  </record>                                          Performs the string substitution
  remove_keys $.name.surname        ◁──────────┐    of 'I' with 'We'. A white space
</filter>                                            character is included to avoid
            Deletes the surname element to ensure   accidentally picking up
            we're not at risk with PII considerations  characters, in other words.
<filter *>
  @type stdout
```

Modifies the msg element by adding textual content

```
<inject>
    worker_id_key

</inject>
</filter>
```

The inject directive shown here allows the worker_id for the process to be added to the log event. The inject directive allows some different useful values to be added to provide additional context.

Let's see the result of the configuration. As this makes use of a file source, we need to run the LogSimulator. So, to run the example, the following commands are needed:

- `fluentd -c ./Chapter6/Fluentd/file-source-transformed-elastic -search-out.conf`
- `groovy logSimulator.groovy ./Chapter6/SimulatorConfig/log- source-1.properties`

Before starting the UI to review log events stored in the `fluentd-book-transformed` index in Elasticsearch, the changes from the `record_transformer` and the `inject` directive should be visible on the console because of the stdout filter.

PREDEFINED VALUES

The `record_transformer` also helps by providing some predefined values, including

- *Hostname*—The name of the computer host
- *Time*—The current time
- *Tag*—The current log event tag

With the Ruby flag enabled, we can extend the ability to get and set values to access any public class methods by using the `${}`. For example, using a method in a class would use `"${#<class>.<method>}"` where `<class>` is the name of the Ruby class and `<method>` is the corresponding public class method. `"#{Dir.getwd}"` will retrieve the current working directory.

6.3.4 *Filter parser vs. record transformer*

The `record_transformer` plugin provides us with the means to work with the log event as a JSON payload. If the log event is simply a single block of text, we will likely need to parse it to obtain meaningful values. In chapter 3, we introduced the use of parsers to extract meaning out of log events. The parsers we saw, like `regexp`, also work with the `filter` directive. As a result, where a `regexp expression` defines the parts of the string to capture as named values, the parser's behavior is extended such that the named elements will be made top-level log event attributes.

Let's take the same expression (included in the following listing) and put it into the context of the `filter` directive. The essential difference here is that we need to tell Fluentd which log event attribute to process before the parser definition. This means we can target a specific part of a log event. We can also use consecutive filters to break down nested structures if we wanted. In listing 6.3, we expect the output to result in additional attributes called `time`, `level`, `class`, `line`, `iteration`, and `msg`. Like the `record_transformer` plugin, we can determine whether the log event attribute that is processed is retained or not using the `reserve_data` configuration element. We can make the control a bit more nuanced by adding remove_key_name_field and setting it to true; Fluentd will remove the original attribute only if the parsing process was successful.

Listing 6.3 Chapter6/Fluentd/rotating-file-read-regex.conf—parse extract

```
<filter>
  @type parser
  key_name log                    Identifies the log event
                                  attribute to parse
  reserve_data true               Tells Fluentd to retain the existing
                                  value so if there are more attributes,
                                  we can retrieve them downstream
  <parse>
    @type regexp
    expression /
    (?<time>\S+)\s(?<level>[A..Z]*)\s*(?<class>\S+)[^\d]*(?<line>[\d]*)\-
    (?<iteration>[\d]*)\)[\s]+\{"log":"(?<msg>.*(?="\}))/
    time_format %Y-%m-%d--%T
    time_key time
    types line:integer,iteration:integer    Tells Fluentd what data type the
                                            extracted values should be, making
                                            further transformation easier
    keep_time_key true
  </parse>
</filter>
```

6.4 *Demonstrating change impact with stdout in action*

As the application generating logs already needs to be securely locked down to limit the impact of recording this information, the Fluentd installation will be collocated with the source. As manipulating log events is discouraged, the decision has been made to

- Add to the Fluentd configuration so that stdout outputs show the unmodified log event, so they can be observed in a contained but transient situation
- Allow the modified log events that are desensitized to go into Elasticsearch

Chapter6/Fluentd/file-source-transformed-elastic-search-out.conf is the starting point for making the required changes.

6.4.1 *A solution demonstrating change impact with stdout in action*

You can compare your configuration modifications to our implementation of the solution shown in Chapter6/ExerciseResults/file-source-transformed-elastic-search-out-Answer.conf. The fundamental changes are the positioning of the filters with the type set to stdout.

6.5 *Extract to set key values*

Sometimes we need to be clever and set the primary attributes of the log event (time and tag) more dynamically. This may be because we don't want to have a static value as part of the tag configuration (we typically set reflecting the source), but rather have it set dynamically reflecting an attribute of the log event. In doing so, we set ourselves up to filter more effectively with the match expressions. For example, we want the log event tag to reflect the name of a microservice, but we're collecting the log events from Kubernetes-level stdout, so a single feed will reflect from multiple services. As a result, we need to extract the value needed as the tag from the log event record.

When it comes to the timestamp, we may wish to adjust it to a time value in the log event, reflecting when the event occurred rather than when Fluentd picked the log event up. This may be necessary, as there is some latency between the event generation and Fluentd getting it.

The `extract` feature allows us to perform such a task. Unlike our filters and parsers, the `extract` directive can be incorporated into the `source`, `filter`, and `match` (out) plugins such as `exec`. The extract mechanism is very flexible in its use, but it is limited to only manipulate the tag and time log event attributes.

The `extract` parameters allow us to declare how to interpret the time value. The value to be used could be the time represented as seconds from epoch (midnight 1 Jan 1970 [UTC]). For example, `1601495341` is Wednesday, 30 September 2020 19:49:01. Another possible format can be the *ISO 8601* standard (more at www.w3.org/TR/NOTE-datetime).

Let's consider a simple example. We should set the tag using the value obtained by the exec source plugin. As with our previous use of `exec`, we've chosen a simple command that is easy to use or adapt to different OSes. We also get a structured object, so there are no distractions from needing to parse the payload before retrieving a value. The `source` directive needs to set the `tag` attribute to a value that won't come from our exec plugin.

To ensure we can see the impact of the data changing, let's set the `run_interval` to 10 seconds. This means the same file will be captured as the input but gives us time to save changes to the file between executions. Try changing the file when running the configuration. We've told the parser to ensure that the `exec` command is then treated as a JSON object.

Finally, we have included in the extract the `tag_key` attribute; this tells Fluentd which log event element should be retrieved and used to set the tag. We copy the contents of the log event element to another tag to preserve the original log event record. This attribute is called `keep_tag_key`, and we've elected to retain the captured payload unmodified. This is demonstrated in the following listing.

Listing 6.4   Chapter6/Fluentd/exec-source-extract-stdout.conf

```
<source>
  @type exec
  command more TestData\exe-src.json      Keeps the source capture
  run_interval 10s                        iterating so we can modify the
                                          payload and see the consequences

  tag exec
  <parse>
    @type json
```

```
  </parse>
  <extract>                          The extract
                                     directive
    tag_key msg                                   Identifies the name of the element
                                                  to use as the tag going forward
    keep_tag_key true                      Indicates we want to leave the retrieved
  </extract>                                log event content unmodified
</source>

<match *>
  @type stdout
</match>
```

To run this configuration, we need only run Fluentd with the command `fluentd -c ./Chapter6/Fluentd/exec-source-extract-stdout.conf`. Once Fluentd is running, change the value in the `TestData\exe-src.json` file and see how the change impacts the tag.

6.6 *Deriving new data values with the record_transformer*

With the ability to exclude log events from subsequent actions and extract specific values from log events, we can now consider the possibility of generating derived values and metrics. For example, we may want to understand how often errors occur, or which components or even which parts of the codebase are the source of most errors. While generating such measures using Elasticsearch or Splunk is possible, they are used sometime after the event analysis. If we want to be more proactive, we need to calculate the metrics more dynamically as the events occur.

In chapter 1, we introduced the idea that monitoring covers both textual-based contents and numeric metrics. Both log events and metrics are often, but not always, used within a time-based context (log events are seen in time order, and metrics often measure details such as a value over a period, such as CPU usage per second). Fluentd's core doesn't have the capabilities to generate time series–based metrics. However, some plugins written by the community, including the contributors to the core of Fluentd, can provide some basic numeric and time-series measures. As we'll see later, there are ways to address time-series data.

Time-series data points are not the only valuable numeric data that could be helpful. For example, how an alert is signaled may be a function of the transaction value (unit value × quantity) or how long or how many times a system has been retrying and failing with a database connection (current time − original error timestamp). The `record_transformer` can generate numeric metric values by taking data values and performing mathematical operations.

Using our example data set, we could consider replacing the age with the birth year, as the expression would be the current year minus age. For example:

```
<record>
  birthYr ${Date.today.year - record['age']}
</record>
```

While this may not be a very real-world example, it does show the art of the possible.

NOTE Quoting attributes needs to be done with care. If wrongly used, you will experience odd behaviors, where some log event attributes are found and others are not. When using the `record['xxxx']` approach, you need to use single quotes. Double quotes are necessary when using the dig method—that is, `record.dig("xxxx")`.

6.6.1 *Putting the incorporation of calculations into a log event transformation into action*

Some people hold the view that adopting birth years is less personal than age. This means you've been asked to amend the logged data that is stored downstream. The case has been made that the birth year is added, and the age attribute is removed. The `Chapter6/Fluentd/file-source-transformed-elastic-search-out.conf` configuration file has been identified as the starting point to incorporate the necessary changes. The same test source (`./Chapter6/SimulatorConfig/log-source-1.properties`) can be used to exercise the configuration. To make it easy to identify output from this scenario, change the `index_name` in your match configuration.

ANSWER

Our implementation of the configuration can be seen in `Chapter6/Exercise-Results/file-source-transformed-elastic-search-out-Answer2.conf`. The essential changes are the inclusion of `birthYr ${Date.today.year - record['age']}` in the `record` directive and after the `remove_keys $.age` directive. The results can be examined in the contents of Elasticsearch using the UI as previously described.

6.7 *Generating simple Fluentd metrics*

Fluentd has an excellent partner project under the control of the CNCF in *Prometheus* (https://prometheus.io/), whose role is to handle and create metrics-based data. Prometheus is typically also associated with Grafana for the visualization of such data. Prometheus and Grafana are associated with microservices. Like Fluentd, there aren't any real constraints or reasons for not using such tools outside of a microservice ecosystem.

> **The partnership of Fluentd and Prometheus**
>
> Given the mention of Prometheus, it is worth seeing how Fluentd can fit in with Prometheus's architecture and broader metrics and monitoring ecosystem. As the following figure shows, Fluentd can relate to Prometheus at several points.
>
> As the figure shows, Fluentd has several possible relationships with Prometheus, covering
>
> - A data feed into the Push Gateway as a source from which Prometheus can calculate metrics.
> - A feed of Fluentd internal metrics in a Prometheus format ready to be processed by the server (no preparation step needed from the Push Gateway). This is achieved using the *monitor_agent* plugin.
> - A channel for recording alerts for metrics via the Alert Mgr.

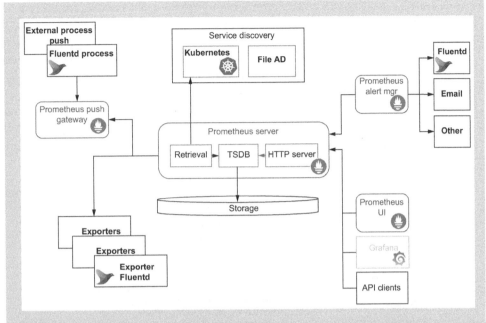

Prometheus architecture and how Fluentd can relate to it

The Prometheus plugin for Fluentd (installed with `fluent-gem install fluent-plugin-prometheus`) provides several measure options. The Prometheus plugin allows us to create metric values in the `filter` and `match` directives.

More about the Prometheus plugin can be found at https://github.com/fluent/fluent-plugin-prometheus, and information about Prometheus can be found at https://prometheus.io. There are also several books on the subject, such as Manning's *Microservices in Action* by Morgan Bruce and Paulo A. Pereira (2018) (www.manning.com/books/microservices-in-action), which can also help.

Prometheus's value lies in processing event series data and extracting and providing metrics data. If we can easily avoid sending every log event to Prometheus (or any other tool) to calculate basic metrics, there is an obvious case for not doing it. After all, why pass all this data around? As previously mentioned, there are community plugins to support time-series measures. The currently available plugins we think are worth considering for these kinds of requirements are

- fluent-plugin-datacounter (http://mng.bz/voX7)
- fluent-plugin-numeric-counter (http://mng.bz/4j9w)

Both plugins work in a similar fashion. The data counter will count log events based on matches to regular expressions. The numeric counter is looking to apply numeric meaning to the values. For example, we could use the numeric counter to count log events if an event attribute has a value in the range of one to ten. Both count over a defined period and emit log events based on the occurrences.

For instance, in our previous illustration of filtering, we isolated log events that referred to the word *computer* in the msg attribute of the event. We could change this to record how many log events every minute include a reference to *computer*, rather than filter these log events in or out.

In listing 6.5, we have amended the configuration so that the log event's element to examine is msg, as specified by the count_key attribute. We've only defined a single expression using pattern1 and used count_interval using the standard Fluentd notation as to the duration over which to count—in this case, 1 minute.

Listing 6.5   Chapter6/Fluentd/file-source-counted-elastic-search-out.conf

```
<match *>                          Defines the match directive
  @type datacounter       ◁──┘  to use the datacounter plugin
  @id counted
   tag counted                   Tells the plugin which element
  count_key msg           ◁──┘  of the log event to examine
  count_interval 1m       ◁──┐
  aggregate all                  Defines the period over
  output_messages yes            which we are counting events
  pattern1 p1 computer    ◁──┐
                                 By providing a numeric sequence of
</match>                         patterns, we can include the individual
                                 patterns.

<match *>
  @type elasticsearch
  host localhost
  port 9200
  index_name fluentd-book-counted
  scheme http
  logstash_format true
  reload_on_failure true
  include_tag_key true
  tag_key tag
  <buffer>
    flush_interval 5s
  </buffer>
</match>
```

Typically, we would not expect a match directive to allow any events onward without using a copy plugin. However, as the plugin utilizes the underlying emitter helper plugin, it can consume the matched log events and emit new events to be consumed downstream. To run this configuration, we need to install the fluent-gem by executing the command fluent-gem install fluent-plugin-datacounter.

The way threads and timing are handled within the plugin means that while there are inbound log events, the calculated values are not written to Elasticsearch. As a result, depending on the timing, you might not see the metrics written immediately.

As with the previous Elasticsearch scenarios, it is easier to see what is stored by changing the index name; for example, `fluentd-book-counted`. Assuming Elasticsearch is ready and running, we can run the scenario with the following commands:

- `fluentd -c ./Chapter6/Fluentd/file-source-counted-elastic-search-out.conf`
- `groovy logSimulator.groovy ./Chapter6/SimulatorConfig/log-source-1.properties`

6.7.1   *Putting log event counting into action*

The LogSimulator provides the means to set and change the rate at which log events are played through. Try changing the `count_interval` in the Fluentd configuration file and altering the LogSimulator configuration to send the log events through at different speeds (`SimulatorConfig/log-source-1.properties`). Add a pattern to the `datacounter` to locate occurrences of `Unix` in the message.

ANSWER

The changing of the LogSimulator speed will result in changing numbers of log events being counted. Changing the period of the count is varied by modifying the `count_interval` attribute in the configuration file. The second pattern defined in the `match` directive should look like `pattern2 p2 Unix`.

Summary

- Fluentd filters can isolate specific log events that need actions to be triggered, such as executing a housekeeping script.
- The application of `record_transformation` in a filter creates the possibility of modifying events to add, remove, and mask the content, including a look at cases as to why it helps to modify log events.
- Applying Fluentd transformation plugins to remove and mask sensitive data in log events enables us to limit the impact of requirements to satisfy regulations (from additional auditing to additional work to establish a higher level of security configuration).
- Fluentd provides the means to navigate JSON data structures, such as a transformed log event payload. As a result, we can apply more intelligence to event handling. For example, if a log event's customer attributes identify a high-value customer, we could also signal the CRM system in addition to signaling Ops.
- The tag, time, and record values of an event can be manipulated. The `extract` and `inject` features can ensure they reflect meaningful values—for example, changing the tag to reflect the log event record so routing and filtering using tags can be more dynamic.
- There are pros and cons of manipulating log events, from impacting an accurate record of what happened or having meaningful log data for downstream

use. Understanding the potential applications of the logs can help us determine the best course (e.g., use in possible legal actions needs unaltered logs).

- Fluentd can play several roles in a CNCF's Prometheus deployment, from feeding specific events and their event attributes to Prometheus to capturing the Prometheus output data and assisting in monitoring Prometheus.

Part 3

Beyond the basics

In Part 2, we worked through the core features, from source and matching directives to filtering, routing, and log event transformation and manipulation. We also saw some common sources and targets, from log files to Elasticsearch, MongoDB, and Slack. With this, we have enough knowledge to develop monitoring solutions to address many needs. But eventually, we will find ourselves needing to look beyond the basics.

We have made references to Cloud Native, Docker, and Kubernetes throughout the book but have not invested too much in the specifics of configuring Fluentd into these environments. This is mainly because it is worth appreciating that Fluentd is more than just a utility for Kubernetes. Before we specifically address logging with Docker and Kubernetes, we should first handle how Fluentd can scale, as this will inform aspects of how we can support containerization.

When we look at Docker and Kubernetes, we will address how Fluentd supports containerized applications and how we capture the log events from these technologies and the challenges they can bring.

Finally, we take on the challenge of what to do when existing plugins can't help us deal with esoteric or archaic applications or platforms with their custom ways of exposing data to be logged. Perhaps it is an application with an overly complex data structure, or maybe we need a custom parser to process it efficiently instead of using a regular expression. Maybe the only way to get log events is to call an application API. Whatever the problem, we need to develop our own plugins. So we'll build a custom plugin to understand how to address such a problem and reveal the heart of Fluentd's extensibility.

Performance and scaling

7

This chapter covers

- Tuning Fluentd to maximize resources using workers
- Deploying Fluentd with fan-in and -out patterns
- Using deployment patterns for scaling
- Implementing high availability and deployments
- Using Fluentd with microservice patterns

In previous chapters, we worked with just a single Fluentd instance. Still, we live in a world of distribution, virtualization, and containerization, which typically needs more than a single instance. In addition to distribution considerations, we need to support elasticity through scaling up (adding more CPUs or memory to a server to support more processes and threads) and scaling out (deploying additional server instances to have workload distributed via load balancing) to meet fluctuating demands (along with the reverse scale down and in). Enterprises demand resilience to handle failure and disaster scenarios. To provide good availability, we should at least have an active server and a standby server deployed, with both servers using configuration files that are kept synchronized. Configuration synchronization makes it possible to start up the standby server on short notice if the first instance fails (active-passive). In the more demanding cases, active-active deployments are needed with servers spread across multiple data centers; this is very conventional as a deployment pattern. A single server solution in the enterprise space is a rarity.

This chapter will explore the techniques and features available to let us scale Fluentd up using worker processes and resource management, and scale out with multiple Fluentd nodes. With scaling out, we can also factor in increased options for resilience. As Fluentd needs only a small footprint, we can implement some of the techniques and features to scale Fluentd on our desktop.

7.1 *Threading and processes to scale with workers*

One of the ways we can scale a Fluentd deployment is to use its ability to spawn additional child processes (workers) to exploit the fact that modern machines have multiple CPU cores available to run concurrent processes. Before configuring any scaling, it is vital to understand how Fluentd is impacted by its implementation with Ruby and how Ruby handles threads. Ruby has a *Global Interpreter Lock* (GIL), which means that while a process is not I/O bound, it will block other jobs (see appendix E for more detail on GIL and Ruby threading). Therefore, any computationally intensive tasks are best performed in separate OS processes and use the OS to provide more effective resource sharing. Some plugins do this for you (e.g., the AWS S3 plugin when using gzip compression), but not all, so we must be very mindful of this for performance optimization. Without that separation, the Fluentd process will effectively be locked until the process has completed or released the thread. Generally, Fluentd as a vehicle for routing log events is more likely to be I/O bound—whether that I/O is network-based or is ultimately storage (even if that is indirectly through physical storage for a database of some sort).

Fluentd addresses the thread locking constraint by launching separate processes, known as *workers*. By default, Fluentd has one worker and one controller process, but we can configure the number of workers. This effectively takes advantage of the fact that the OS typically allocates processes to CPUs and swaps between processes to give them a fair proportion of the CPU's compute capacity. As shown in figure 7.1, each worker will pick up and execute `source`, `filter`, and `match` directives, depending upon the configuration.

> **NOTE** When there are more processes than CPU cores, the processor will swap between the processes. More processes will mean more swapping. The activity of swapping requires a small amount of effort. If you have too many running processes, you'll spend more effort swapping processes than performing any meaningful work.

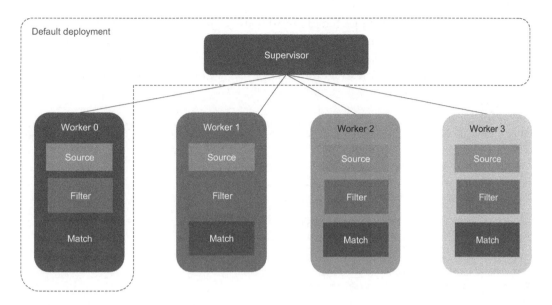

Figure 7.1 Default deployment and how new workers are managed

7.1.1 Seeing workers in action

The best way to understand the behavior of worker processes is to configure an example and see what actually happens. The most straightforward way to illustrate workers is to create a variation of the Hello World configuration. We will establish multiple workers and attribute to the workers the application of the dummy source plugin. Using the dummy source plugin means the source doesn't have I/O dependencies impacting behavior. The relevant match directives then push the output to stdout. Using a filter, we can inject into the log event which worker was involved in the process, building on what we learned in the previous chapter.

Let's define how many workers we will use and add this into the system directive alongside the log_level attribute we have been setting. This is done by setting the attribute workers in the *system* directive.

To define explicitly what each worker does, we wrap the directives in a directive of <worker x> where x represents the numeric worker ID that will execute the directives. For example, <worker 2> would use the third worker (IDs start at 0). If we want to effectively allocate more resources (i.e., workers) to a specific set of directives, we can specify a range of workers in the directive. For example, <worker 1-3> would allocate workers 1, 2, and 3 to perform the same activities. All workers will get directives not assigned. So worker 0 in our configuration would process only these directives.

In listing 7.1, we have defined four workers and have deliberately left the subsequent directives outside of the worker configuration. The result of this is that every worker will pick up the configuration. This means we can share a common output—but this has to be handled with care, as it can have undesirable side effects. These side effects can range from losing events to storage corruption, such as the problem of multiple processes trying to write to the same file. In our example, we're just applying a filter to extract the `worker_id`, add it to the log event, and send it to `stdout` (console).

Listing 7.1   Chapter7/Fluentd/dummy-stdout-multiworker.conf—illustrating workers

```
<system>
  log_level info
  workers 4                          ◁──┐ Declares the number
</system>                               │ of workers

<worker 0>                          ◁──┐ Activities specific
  <source>                             │ to worker 0
    @type dummy
    tag w0
    auto_increment_key counter
    dummy {"hello":"from worker 0"}
  </source>
</worker>

<worker 1-2>                        ◁──┐ Defines activities
  <source>                             │ for two workers
    @type dummy
    tag w1
    auto_increment_key counter
    dummy {"hello":"from worker 1-2"}
  </source>
</worker>

<worker 3>
  <source>
    @type dummy
    tag w2
    auto_increment_key counter
    dummy {"hello":"from worker 3"}
  </source>
</worker>                           ┌ Defines a source outside of the
                                    │ workers—we should see this
<source>                        ◁──┘ being picked up by all workers.
  @type dummy
  tag w-any
  auto_increment_key counter
  dummy {"hello":"from workerless"}
</source>

<filter *>
  @type record_transformer
  enable_ruby
  <record>
    worker_id ${ENV['SERVERENGINE_WORKER_ID']}  ◁──┐ Uses a filter to add the ID of the
  </record>                                         │ worker involved in that log event
</filter>
```

```
<match *>
  @type stdout
</match>
```

This configuration can be started up with the command

```
fluentd -c Chapter7/Fluentd/dummy-stdout-multiworker.conf
```

Before examining the stdout console, it is worth seeing what is happening in terms of processes. With a command console in Windows or a Linux shell, the following appropriate command should be run:

```
Windows: tasklist /fi "IMAGENAME eq Ruby.exe"
Linux: ps -ef | grep ruby
```

These commands will show you the Ruby processes, which will include Fluentd processes. As a result, you should see five processes listed if Fluentd is the only Ruby solution running. If other Ruby solutions are running, we can differentiate them, as the Fluentd processes will have identical or very nearly identical start times. The processes are made up of four workers and one controller process.

> **TIP** We can make processes easier to identify by using the `process_name` attribute in the `<system>` configuration (e.g., `process_name Fluentd`).

With the Fluentd processes having been run for a while, we'll want to shut things down. This is a little more complex to do now, as we have multiple processes. For Windows, this can be done with the command line `taskkill /IM Ruby.exe /F`, and the Linux equivalent is `pkill -f ruby` as long as you don't have any other Ruby processes running. If you have other Ruby processes running, you'll have to isolate the processes and manually kill each one.

Looking through the stdout results from having run Fluentd with the `dummy-stdout-multiworker.conf` configuration file, you should be able to see that the following has occurred (but be aware there is a level of arbitrary behavior):

- Log events with the tag `w-any` will appear with any of the `worker_id` entries.
- Logs linked to tag `w0` (including `"hello":"from worker 0"`) will only be linked to `"worker_id":"0"`.
- Logs linked to tag `w1` (including `"hello":"from worker 1-2"`) will only be linked to `"worker_id":"1"` or `"worker_id":"2"`.

7.1.2 *Worker constraints*

When using workers, there are some constraints that need to be considered. This relates to how processes can share (or not) resources such as file handles. So if you allocate multiple workers to a Fluentd configuration that writes to file output, the file needs to be separated, as only one worker can use one file properly. We can solve this by setting the file path to include the `worker_id`; for example, `path "logs/#{worker_id}/${tag}/%Y/%m/%d/logfile.out`.

Sharing ports among workers can be realized when the plugin uses the *server* helper plugin or when the plugin can natively handle the sharing of ports. The *forward* plugin is an example of native port management. As each process cannot use the same port, a reliable mechanism to overcome this and select suitable ports is needed. When the server helper plugin is used, it will then allocate consecutive ports to each worker. So if we had specified the use of four workers and then defined the use of a *monitor_agent* plugin with a port set to 30000, then worker 0 uses port 30000, worker 1 uses 30001, worker 2 uses 30002, and so on. If you are using workers, ensure that the ports being used are well separated. Separating the ports will avoid potential port collisions because the algorithm assigns the same port to different plugin instances across multiple workers. For example, specifying ports 30000 and then 30002 to different plugins, but then introducing four workers, would see ports 30002 and 30003 trying to be used by two different plugins.

7.1.3   Controlling output plugin threads

The threading behavior of output plugins can be controlled through the use of a property called `num_threads`. This value defaults to one. Increasing the number of threads can potentially increase the performance, as it allows context switching between threads to occur when a thread is blocked. As a result, any in-process latency can be used more effectively. But this won't overcome the constraints of GIL.

You could consider using such a configuration for output plugins where the configuration distributes the workload to several different destinations, as one thread works until it ends or has to stop for I/O. Then the next thread, not I/O bound, will be allowed to work. This all means we gain performance—rather than waiting for the I/O to release and the execution to continue, we swap the thread being executed to where work can be done.

Tuning the use of threads is difficult, as you must know how processes perform in order to recognize the potential for threads to wait on something such as I/O. With the thread switching overhead, there is a point at which it is more effective to wait on I/O rather than swap threads. This can also be compounded by the potential level of process switching at the OS level. Correctly tuning threads can often come down to running realistic workloads and measuring performance, then comparing test runs with different threading configurations to see where performance actually starts to drop off.

7.1.4   Memory management optimization

Another area that can be tuned is the Ruby VM layer. This means tuning the garbage collection and memory block allocation. To tune at this level, you need to have a good understanding of the specifics of the Ruby implementation, along with tooling to help you analyze how the configuration is impacting performance. In appendix E, we provide resources that can help with Ruby.

7.2 Scaling and moving workloads

Chapter 4 looked at the output plugins' ability to work with buffers, which will provide us with a means to optimize the performance around each I/O activity, particularly with the memory buffer. Beyond buffers and the tuning of threads and workers, the scaling options are about workload distribution. This could be achieved by

- Feeding the log events to an event stream technology like Kafka.
- Using tools such as Redis or Memcached for large-scale caches.
- Taking advantage of Fluentd's ability to pass log events to other Fluentd nodes. This ability provides the opportunity to move the workload to dedicated Fluentd nodes, either fanning out if the workload needs a lot of additional computing power, or, more likely, fanning in, bringing lots of log events from many smaller nodes down to one or two Fluentd instances.

In the following sections, we'll look at the fan-in (sometimes referred to as *concentrator* or *aggregator networks*) and fan-out deployments, as they are implemented using the same core set of plugins.

Fluentd's compute footprint is so small, we can run some configurations to illustrate the setup on a single machine.

7.2.1 Fan-in/log aggregation and consolidation

The most likely scenario for deploying multiple Fluentd and Fluent Bit nodes is supporting concentrator networks (fan-in), particularly in a containerized environment. This model describes two or more Fluentd nodes collecting log events and passing the events to a central Fluentd/Fluent Bit instance. For example, as we'll see later in this section, log events may originate at the Fluentd nodes at the tip of each "spine" of the fan. The log events are filtered as needed, and then events flow down the spine to the center of the fan—hence the name *fan-in* or *concentrator*.

Let's first start with log aggregation in a more generic form relevant to traditional virtualized or native hardware environments, which can also work in a containerized deployment. Then we'll see how this can vary with containers.

FAN-IN RELATION TO APPLICATION ARCHITECTURE AND DEPLOYMENT

Environments that handle high volumes and/or need a high level of resilience will see application software distributed across multiple servers. We can configure servers so a single Fluentd instance can see every server's log files or deploy a Fluentd (or Fluent Bit) instance on each server. Opening a server so parts of the file system can be accessed from another server creates challenges with security. Each server having a Fluentd node is a more robust and secure model to adopt. The better security comes from the fact that data flows outward from Fluentd to locations it knows about and with log events determined okay to share. This is illustrated in figure 7.2.

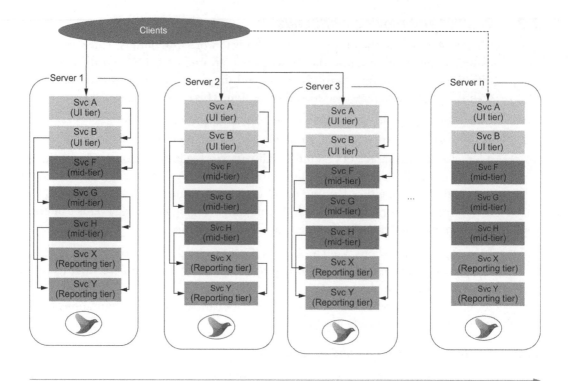

Scaling by adding and removing full-stack servers

Figure 7.2 Illustrating scaling using the full-stack model, where each server has all the features deployed. As a result, call sequences are more likely to remain within a server.

Scaling out can be implemented by the following:

- Each server holding a complete solution stack (presentation layer, mid-tier, and sometimes even the backend storage).

  When this occurs, you are likely to track a single request and response from end to end within the logs of a single server. But linking multiple request responses from a single client to the same backend (known as *server affinity*) can bias workload to specific servers. This can impact the effectiveness of dynamic scaling, as the new node(s) only taking on new clients.

- Segmenting the solution into logical parts and allocating parts to one or more specific servers. We often talk about this as an N-tier model with servers dedicated to running a tier, such as the presentation tier; other servers deployed with business logic tier; and other servers for persistence tier; and so on. We can see in figure 7.3 an N-tier or three-tier deployment. Each of the different-colored verticals represents a tier—UI or presentation tier on the left, mid-tier in the middle (typically a business tier when there are three tiers), and in this case, a reporting tier on the right. Server affinity for user sessions is likely to be

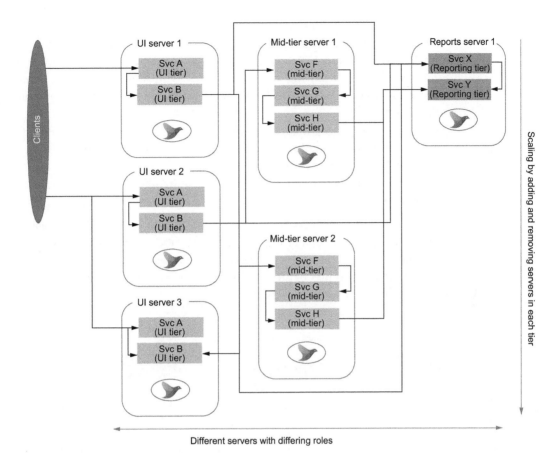

Figure 7.3 In this situation, the services are grouped by a common purpose to target scaling more efficiently. However, following the invocations, end to end is more complex.

less of an issue, so the same server may see the same user sessions for their fragment of a user event.

Ultimately, tracking the activities of a user's session end to end will require us to bring all the logs together to see the complete picture. Sometimes the complete picture isn't handled until all the logs reach an analytics platform and are periodically processed. This is fine, but we've already highlighted that we may wish to quickly react or be proactive and trigger actions from the log event processing. Bringing the logs through a centralized node presents several benefits:

– Dedicated node(s) for handling a workload allows resources to be tuned for that job.
– When configuration becomes complex, it's easier if the logic is more centralized, as deploying improvements and refinements involves a smaller number of deployments—even with automation, fewer nodes are generally better.

- Rather than lots of nodes needing credentials and access to a repository of credentials (such as Vault), we keep the access to such details restricted to a smaller set of servers. Therefore, it is harder for the details to be exploited. This is essential if storing credentials (or certificates when using mutual Transport Layer Security [TLS]) is handled in a less-sophisticated manner than Vault.
- It can be easier to demonstrate security if the number of points of origin for data is controlled. This is particularly true if the final destination of logs is outside the network, as it means the number of servers needing outbound access is constrained. It also makes it easier to handle when outbound proxy servers are involved.

Figure 7.4 illustrates how such a configuration could be deployed with the application servers having a relatively small-footprint Fluentd node. The outermost (top) instances of Fluentd are capturing log events (and maybe filtering out some of the low-value/unneeded log events) before passing log events onto an inner node (shown at the bottom) being fed by multiple Fluentd nodes.

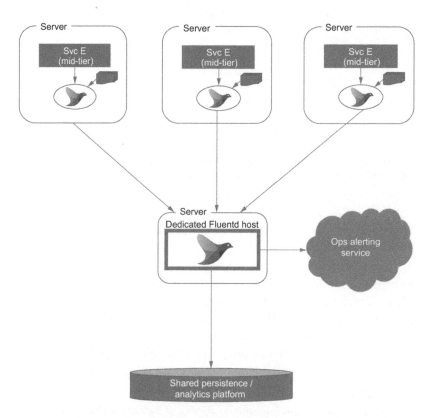

Figure 7.4   An example concentrator network deployment with multiple Fluentd instances feeding a central Fluentd instance on a dedicated server doing the majority of the work

It is common to illustrate a fan-in configuration with a single server in the middle; however, this could be a cluster of servers, particularly when considering hyperscale environments. What continues to characterize the model as fan-in is that the number of log event sources is far greater than those at the center doing the core log event processing.

FLUENTD CONFIGURATION FOR FAN-IN

Let's walk through the setup of this kind of concentrator network configuration. We will need two Fluentd configuration files, one of which will work for as many source servers as we want to represent using the `forward` plugin as an output. A second configuration uses `forward` as an input to process and direct traffic to a final destination. To keep things simple, we'll use the dummy source plugin rather than running the simulators. To make the origin node easy to identify, we need to incorporate something into the log event. Normally we could do that with the node hostname, but since we're running everything on a single machine, that doesn't help us. Another approach to this is to retrieve an environmental variable and use it for the tag name. As long as the environment variable scope is restricted to the scope of the shell used to launch the Fluentd instance, this will work. Figure 7.5 illustrates the configuration in more detail.

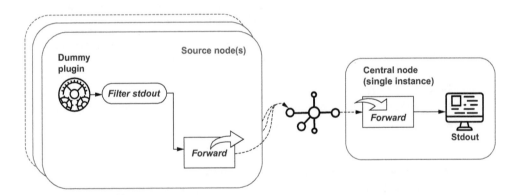

Figure 7.5   A detailed view of how multiple Fluentd nodes running the same configuration feed a single instance

To get the environment variable into the payload, we've added a filter into the source, which takes the tag value and is set using the Ruby command `"#{ENV["Node-Name"]}"`; this retrieves the value of `NodeName`.

Listing 7.2   Chapter7/Fluentd/dummy-foward1.conf—illustrating forward out

```
<system>
  log_level info
</system>
```

```
<source>
  @type dummy
  tag "#{ENV["NodeName"]}"              ◁──┐  Here, we are grabbing the
                                             environment variable to
  auto_increment_key counter                make each instance distinct.
  dummy {"hello":"world"}
</source>

<filter *>
  @type stdout                          ┌─  Puts the tag into
  <inject>                         ◁────┘   the log event record
    tag_key fluentd_tag
  </inject>
</filter>

<match *>                                ┌─  Declares the forward
    @type forward              ◁─────────┘   plugin output        ┌─  Buffers up events before sending; for convenience,
    buffer_type memory                                              we're limiting this. In the real world, you'd
    flush_interval 2s                                   ◁─────────┘  probably consider a longer duration.

    <server>                     ◁──────┐
      host 127.0.0.1                      Defines the target server
      port 28080                          to direct the log event to
    </server>

  <secondary>                     ◁─────┐ If we can't communicate with the central Fluentd instance, we
                                          need to send the log events somewhere. In this configuration,
      @type stdout                        we're just sending the events to the console if they can't be
  </secondary>                            handled. You'll probably want to do something more robust in
</match>                                  a production scenario, like writing events to a file.
```

Before starting Fluentd, the shell used to run Fluentd will need to `set` or `export` (Windows or Linux) `NodeName=Node1`. Each source node has a new number in the assignment. Then we can start up Fluentd with

```
fluentd -c Chapter7/Fluentd/dummy-forward1.conf
```

Repeat the steps of starting a shell, setting the environment variable, and launching the source Fluentd node to get a second Fluentd node generating log events and sending them to the central Fluentd node.

> **NOTE** If the environment variable is not set up, and if Fluentd is showing its configuration (at the info log level), you can see if the value has been properly inserted. If the value is absent, depending on the attribute, you'll observe a startup error at best; at worst, things will start up but not appear to do anything. This comes from the fact that a default value may be defined and taken. For example, the `port` attribute will be `0`.

We have used a filter to ensure that the tag is captured into the log event. In addition, we can also utilize the `stdout` plugin so the console from the sender will show us the log events that we should receive in the central node. Ideally, we need to run several shells and set the environment variable accordingly. Depending on how long it takes to start up the central (consuming) node, periodic network errors will be reported on the source nodes, as there is no response to the network calls.

This brings us to the consuming configuration, which is simply accepting the forwarded events and pushing them out to the console. We've seen much of this before, although the use of the `forward` plugin is new. For Fluentd to receive the events, we need to define a Fluentd source, which binds to a network address and port. This obviously needs to match the sender's configuration. We can see all of this in the following listing.

Listing 7.3 Chapter7/Fluentd/forward-stdout.conf—illustrating forward as a source

```
<system>
  log_level info
</system>

<source>                          Defines the use of the
  @type forward                   input forward plugin

  port 28080                      Network address to bind to (DNS
                                  or IP)—in our case localhost.
  bind 127.0.0.1                  This needs to match the sender.
</source>

<match *>                         Shows on the console what
  @type stdout                    log events have been sent
</match>
```

With the consuming Fluentd node defined, we can fire up a single instance (for the more common concentrator network). Once all the Fluentd nodes are communicating, we'll see all the log events in this node's console. So, let's start up the consumer node with the command

```
fluentd -c Chapter7/Fluentd/forward-stdout.conf
```

When you look at the console output now being generated, you should see that the node name included in the console output will vary. The variation reflects that the log events are from two different Fluentd nodes, as we made the tag values dynamic in the configuration.

> **NOTE** The application of the msgpack plugin will help reduce network traffic, as a formatter can be set to msgpack for the forward plugin. The receiving forward plugin can recognize msgpack-formatted events and automatically unpack them. As a result, Fluentd-to-Fluentd traffic is transmitted very efficiently.

7.2.2 *Fan-out and workload distribution*

We can see how we can increase the compute effort available to Fluentd processes by offloading work from a node collocated with the application workload to one or more dedicated Fluentd servers, as figure 7.6 illustrates. If we're simply offloading work, it may be worth using Fluent Bit as the application's collocated log collector. Fluent Bit

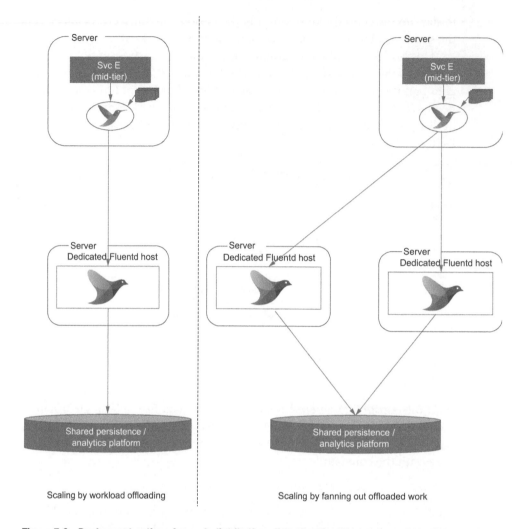

Scaling by workload offloading   Scaling by fanning out offloaded work

Figure 7.6 Deployment options for work distribution allow the allocation of more compute power to Fluentd's processing of log events without impacting the originating application(s), as we can route log events to more servers with dedicated capacity for Fluentd.

is smaller, and if it can collect the log events (remember Fluent Bit is more restricted in plugin options), it can easily forward to Fluentd. We then use the downstream Fluentd to do the hard work of processing the log events. Revisit chapter 1 to review Fluent Bit's differences from Fluentd.

The application of a fan-out pattern is unusual, at least in our experience. If you find yourself using unusual configurations, it is worth reviewing the situation to ensure there isn't a larger issue. For example, restrictive default resource allocation forces the need to fan out, but easing or removing the restrictions could eliminate some distribution complexity.

FLUENTD CONFIGURATION FOR FAN-OUT

With both fan-out and high-availability deployments, we need to have the ability to send workload to potentially multiple nodes. In the context of high availability, sending traffic to a different node will be triggered by communication loss, and in fan-out, the connectivity is driven by workload sharing. Let us examine both requirements, as there is some commonality in the configuration. As shown in figure 7.7, this time we will deploy only one node with the dummy source generator, but route log events to multiple consumer nodes that will output to the console.

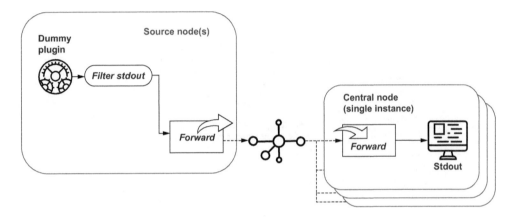

Figure 7.7 Our example configuration of Fluentd fan-out with one node passing log events to multiple nodes to process

The key difference between this and the previous source node configuration is that the configuration of the `forward` plugin will now need multiple servers specified. In high availability, which node should be considered the primary and which should be the standby must be addressed. For fan-out, we may want to weigh the workload in favor of one node over another. All of this can be done within the configuration through properties. For multiple servers, as shown in listing 7.4, we can simply declare multiple contiguous blocks of attributes for the server helper plugin `<server>`. As this is a basic fan-out, we have added a `weight` attribute to establish a ratio of workload between the servers. In our case, that ratio is 10:1. If unspecified, then all the nodes get the same weighting applied.

Listing 7.4 Chapter7/Fluentd/dummy-forward2.conf—illustrating forward to multiple servers

```
<source>
  @type dummy
  tag dummy-fanout-source
  auto_increment_key counter
  dummy {"hello":"world"}
</source>
```

```
<filter *>
  @type stdout
  <inject>
    tag_key fluentd_tag
  </inject>
</filter>

<match *>
    @type forward
    buffer_type memory      First server definition with
    flush_interval 2s       its differing ports so we
    <server>                can run on the same host

      host 127.0.0.1
      port 28080
      weight 10             Defining the weighting, which will
                            favor the first server configuration.
    </server>               If unset, this value defaults to 60.
    <server>
      host 127.0.0.1        Defines
      port 38080            alternate port
      weight 1              Weighting set to bias
    </server>              traffic away from this server

  <secondary>
    @type stdout
  </secondary>
</match>
```

As we're running everything on the same machine, the Fluentd instances forming the fan side will need to be configured to operate on different network ports to avoid conflicts. A production-like environment with the Fluentd instances is configured to run on separate servers but using the same network port. Utilizing the naming trick we saw in listing 7.2, we can make the value configuration-driven and avoid needing multiple configuration files with different values. As a result, each node will need an environment variable called `NodePort`, defining one of the ports used on the source side of the node configuration, as shown in the following listing.

Listing 7.5   Chapter7/Fluentd/forward-stdout2.conf

```
<source>
  @type forward
  port "#{ENV["NodePort"]}"     Setting the port number up
  bind 127.0.0.1                dynamically allows us to run
</source>                       the same configuration twice.

<match *>
  @type stdout
</match>
```

Let's see what happens with this configuration of nodes. Start the source node with the command

```
fluentd -c Chapter7/Fluentd/dummy-forward2.conf
```

Then we need to configure a shell with the command `set NodePort=28080` for Windows or `export NodePort=28080` in a Linux-based environment. Once this is set, we can start the Fluentd instance with the command

```
fluentd -c Chapter7/Fluentd/forward-stdout2.conf
```

We then repeat the steps again, replacing `28080` with `38080` in the set/export step.

Once everything is running, the log events should appear on the consoles of the Fluentd instances running the `dummy-forward2.conf` configuration. With the ratio set, we should see that the logs are heavily biased to the node running on port 28080. But if you count how many updates go to one console over the other, you're not guaranteed to see every output on the server using the 38080 port and ten on the other, as the ratio is calculated every time we want to send an output. The calculation then yields a value that will dictate on which side of the ratio it will fall.

ROUNDROBIN PLUGIN

Another way of distributing the workload is to leverage the *roundrobin* plugin. This plugin is a core Fluentd output plugin that works with the `store` helper plugin. This is illustrated in the following listing, with a `roundrobin` rotating the outputs to each individually identified server. As this is for a fan-out implementation, each `store` block will use a `forward` plugin, but that isn't mandatory.

> **Listing 7.6 Chapter7/Fluentd/dummy-forward3.conf—illustrating the use of roundrobin**

```
<source>
  @type dummy
  tag dummy-fanout-source
  auto_increment_key counter
  dummy {"hello":"world"}
</source>

<filter *>
  @type stdout
  <inject>
    tag_key fluentd_tag_roundrobin
  </inject>
</filter>

<match *>
    @type roundrobin    ◁——  To get the roundrobin behavior, we need to use
                              it as the output plugin. It will then use each
                              store helper plugin in turn, in the same way as
                              the copy plugin uses all the store helpers.

    <store>             ◁——  Declares the store configuration, but as we want
                              the roundrobin to use each target equally, the
      @type forward           configuration for a store can have only one server.
      buffer_type memory
      flush_interval 1s
      <server>          ◁——  The server definition
        host 127.0.0.1        for the destination
        port 28080
      </server>
```

```
      </store>
      <store>
        @type forward
        buffer_type memory
        flush_interval 1s
        <server>
          host 127.0.0.1
          port 38080          ◁─┐  The second server configured
        </server>                │  to be using a different port
      </store>

  <secondary>
    @type stdout
  </secondary>
</match>
```

Let's look at how the `roundrobin` behaves in comparison to the weighting. We need to start up as before; if the console for the two fan nodes doesn't have the variable set for `NodePort`, we need to reestablish the settings. We then start the event source Fluentd instance with the command

```
fluentd -c Chapter7/Fluentd/dummy-forward3.conf
```

Then start the two instances of the fan node using the same command:

```
fluentd -c Chapter7/Fluentd/forward-stdout2.conf
```

This time the output will consistently go to the alternate console outputs as the `round-robin` deliberately ensures the allocation is consistently even. The use of the `weight` attribute can also be applied, but this does undermine the `roundrobin` behavior.

7.2.3 *High availability*

The configuration for the high-availability arrangement is not that different from the fan-out. Rather than using the `weight` attribute to distribute the workload, we use the `standby` attribute and set one node to have the value true and the other false. An example of the server part of a match plugin can be seen here:

```
<server>
  name myserver1
  host 127.0.0.1
  port 28080
  standby false
</server>
<server>
  name myserver2
  host 127.0.0.1
  port 38080
  standby true
</server>
```

As the fragment shows, we have defined two servers; for example, using the forward output plugin would be two instances of Fluentd to send log events to. When the

Fluentd instance with this configuration starts up, it will try to send the log events using the server named myserver1, as it is marked as not being the standby. However, if this Fluentd instance experiences communication issues with myserver1, it will send the log events to the standby called myserver2.

In this fragment, we have used the name attribute. The name is normally used only for Fluentd logging and certificate verification. But as you can see, using the name attribute can also help you determine which server is which, particularly when IP addresses rather than meaningful DNS names are being used.

7.2.4 Putting a high-availability comparison into action

Your customer wants to see how a high-availability configuration differs in setup and behavior. Your team has agreed that configuration files Chapter7/Fluentd/dummy-forward2.conf and Chapter7/Fluentd/forward-stdout2.conf should be refactored to provide the comparison.

Once the configuration has been refactored, run the two configurations and shut down individual instances of Chapter7/Fluentd/forward-stdout2.conf. Note the resultant behavior to show the customer the differences.

ANSWER

The configuration to illustrate high availability based upon Chapter7/Fluentd/dummy-forward2.conf and Chapter7/Fluentd/forward-stdout2.conf can be found in Chapter7/ExerciseResults/dummy-forward2-Answer.conf and Chapter7/ExerciseResults/forward-stdout2-Answer.conf.

The only change of importance in the configuration is removing the weight attribute and introducing the attribute standby set to true or false in the relevant server configuration. The difference can be observed as soon as the nodes have started (it's best to start dummy-forward2-Answer.conf node using port 38080, so it doesn't immediately think the primary destination node is down and switch to the reserve). The console output will only show up on the node listening to port 28080. However, when this node is shut down, the log events will pass to the Fluentd instance working on port 38080.

7.3   Fluentd scaling in containers vs. native and virtual environments

So far, we've looked at how we can scale Fluentd from a pure Fluentd node-to-node perspective. In most cases where you're working in a virtualized or native hardware environment, you can use the configurations as shown with Fluentd or Fluent Bit instances deployed. These deployments can be described as having Fluentd collocated with the application running on a VM or server. Each node is capturing the application log events along with those from the host OS. As a result, scaling out the VMs or native servers will drive the scale-out of Fluentd.

We have more options and considerations for containerized environments such as Kubernetes, as containers are typically more finely grained (therefore, more containers are needed for a complete solution). We have an additional abstraction layer in the form of pods, and the orchestration is far more sophisticated. While we'll focus on Kubernetes, the principles aren't very different for OpenShift and other related products.

7.3.1 *Kubernetes worker node configuration*

Not only do your applications need to log content, but so, too, does the orchestration layer, such as Kubernetes, Apache Mesos, Docker Swarm, and others (including the container engine itself). As a result, the Kubernetes engine creates special services that it uses on each worker node. The deployment would then look as shown in figure 7.8. All the log events in the individual containers must be directed to stdout for this deployment to work.

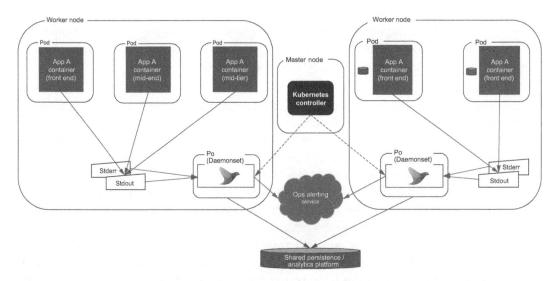

Figure 7.8   Illustration of Fluentd deployed as a daemon service in a Kubernetes context. Fluentd collects all the pod stdout and stderr outputs.

7.3.2 *Per-cluster configuration*

The per-cluster model looks a lot like the worker node configuration but is a little more structured. The structure is due to the containers writing to a defined location via mapping rather than simply trusting stdout and stderr and hoping something is listening in. It is also a little easier to segment the different types of logs and infer some meaning as a result. The containers now just need to mount the cluster-wide file system and write their logs to files as they would if running locally (mapping the local filesystem to shared storage is a Kubernetes configuration issue).

With logs being written to the filesystem, a pod with a Fluentd container simply uses the tail plugin(s) to capture and process the log files. With good directory and/or file naming, we can define specific details about the log file format. Knowing the log file origin determines the kind of things that are particularly important. This approach is illustrated in figure 7.9.

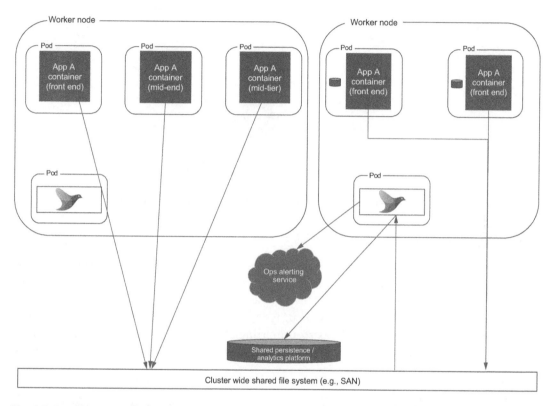

Figure 7.9 Kubernetes cluster shared log capture, where pods write to the file system and a Fluentd pod then gathers the files and processes

In figure 7.9, we reference SAN (storage attached network), which would be ideal for on-premises deployments. It will give you disk redundancy and, typically, storage allocating the physical disks, giving high performance. In a cloud context, you would implement this with block or file style storage and trust the quality of service and performance controls the cloud provider offers.

7.3.3 *Container as virtualization*

This reflects the simple idea of taking an existing environment and configuring it within a container, converting a virtual machine with its own OS to a container that delegates OS work to the shared host. So, a logical deployment could look like figure 7.10, with each container hosting the application and Fluentd, or, more preferably, Fluent Bit if it has the right adaptors and a smaller footprint.

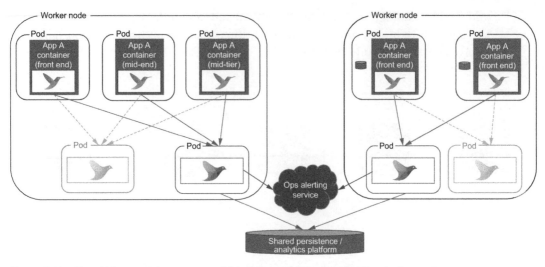

Figure 7.10   **Fluentd in a container, as you might do in a virtualized application deployment**

7.3.4   *Sidecar pattern*

Container-based technologies such as Kubernetes have pod design patterns, such as the *sidecar* (http://mng.bz/nYNK). The idea of the sidecar pattern is that within the pod of containers, there are containers added to provide support services; this can include a proxy layer supplying security to logging. This would mean a container with Fluentd or Fluent Bit would exist supporting all the other containers within the pod, as illustrated in figure 7.11. This is the most flexible and, for Fluentd, the easiest to

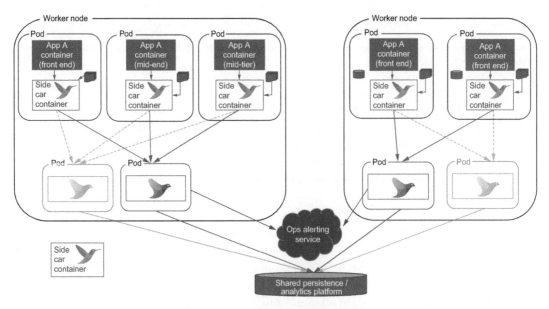

Figure 7.11   **Make Fluentd available to all the containers in a pod using the sidecar pattern illustrated here.**

configure but does require more sophistication in the configuration of containers and pods.

7.3.5 Options comparison

Having looked at the different deployment models, we should take the time to understand the pros and cons of the different approaches. In table 7.1, we've taken each of the patterns described and pulled out the pros and cons of both Fluentd and Fluent Bit.

Table 7.1   Fluentd deployment options in a containerized environment

Approach	Pros	Cons
Fluentd as part of the worker node	Simplest in terms of deployment, as it involves only the worker node. No need to change pods or containers to deploy patches to Fluentd.	Requires more work to translate logs back into more meaningful structures. To apply meaning to log events requires some context, such as an understanding of the application or service. The downside is that the application context resides outside the application domain (the services used). Fluentd patching configuration changes impact the entire worker node.
Fluentd in the application container	Isolates configuration to the smallest component.	A larger compute footprint, running lots of instances of Fluentd—this makes Fluent Bit a better proposition.
Fluent Bit in the application container	Isolates configuration to the smallest component. Smaller footprint than Fluentd.	Total compute effort increases compared to the other models. But smaller than Fluentd. Limitations in terms of types of inputs that can be consumed, as the plugin options are smaller. Fluent Bit is not as rich as Fluentd concerning available plugs, limiting the processes performed on the log events.
Fluentd as a sidecar	Minimizes the number of Fluentd instances within a pod. Service awareness is linked to an application's pod (e.g., intercepting specific log events). Potential to use a generic Fluentd container and leverage configuration to dynamically retrieve configuration.	More complex pod configuration. Fluentd patch process is more complex, as it has an impact on the pod. The container will be a bit larger than a Fluent Bit variant.
Fluent Bit as a sidecar	Minimizes the number of Fluentd instances within a pod. Service awareness is linked to an application's pod definition (e.g., intercepting specific log events). Smaller footprint than Fluentd. Log event handling is within the application context. Potential to use a generic Fluentd container and leverage configuration to dynamically retrieve configuration.	More complex pod configuration. Fluentd patch process is more complex, as it will impact each pod.

7.4   *Securing traffic between Fluentd nodes*

When communicating between Fluentd nodes, you'll likely want to provide some level of security. Using unsecured network traffic can result in credentials being exposed, not only as part of authenticating between Fluentd nodes, but also between Fluentd and source or targets such as Elasticsearch. We have made it very easy for someone to acquire the credentials when listening to network traffic. Not only are credentials exposed, but the communicated log information will also provide an attacker with the means to work out how your solution may work, harvesting sensitive data if the log events are for auditing, and so on. Using HTTPS encryption with TLS, the successor to SSL (Secure Sockets Layer), can mitigate these issues.

If your log events include PII data, a proactively secure configuration will be needed for the application and the log events during transmission and when stored. You have all of these considerations in addition to the possibility that log events may be communicated between clouds and data centers over insecure networks (i.e., the internet). But security should not come down to just adopting TLS or, better still, mutual TLS (mTLS), as we'll see shortly.

Setting up TLS is not the scary black art that it once was, possibly in part because we've moved past the idea of SSL/TLS termination at the network edge, and the compute overhead of encrypting and decrypting is not seen as being so onerous now. But configuring SSL/TLS is still rather context-sensitive and does require some basic understanding of TLS ideas (a subject addressed in depth in other books, such as *Securing DevOps* by Julien Vehent, available at www.manning.com/books/securing -devops). So rather than a lengthy process of going through a TLS configuration that will work for everyone, we'll take a brief look at the support provided. (Appendix E provides links to a range of resources that can help you apply TLS yourself.) With contemporary security approaches adopting a trust-no-one stance, it is worth investing time in establishing TLS security.

7.4.1   *TLS configuration*

When it comes to configuring network transport, we can provide a set of transport configurations. Some adaptors leverage the helper plugin directly, and as a result, sometimes offer slightly different attribute names. For example, `secure_forward` uses `tls_version` in the server part of its configuration. In contrast, the attribute is called `version` when using the transport helper directly (which can be provided in source, filter, and match directives). The transport construct is represented in the configuration within XML brackets and includes an element indicating the type of transport (`udp`, `tcp`, `tls`). For example:

```
<transport tls>
 . . .
</transport>
```

While we've been focusing on TLS and the plugins that abstract more of the network, we can process TCP (Transmission Control Protocol) or UDP (User Datagram Protocol) traffic. Still, these require more configuration effort to use.

> **More on TCP and UDP**
>
> For more information on how these protocols can be used, the following resources will help:
>   - www.vpnmentor.com/blog/tcp-vs-udp/
>   - www.cs.dartmouth.edu/~campbell/cs60/socketprogramming.html
>   - www.openssl.org/docs/

TLS VERSION AND ALGORITHM

The version of TLS that can be supported can be controlled through the Fluentd configuration. TLS 1.3 (published as RFC 8446; https://tools.ietf.org/html/rfc8446 in August 2018) is presently the latest version of the standard published. Currently, TLS 1.2 is the default version used by Fluentd, reflecting that TLS 1.2 is the most widely adopted. Industry practice recommends using the latest version of TLS possible (as it is the most secure) and accomodating lower versions only where necessary. The TLS compatibility and cipher options can be managed via the `version` and `ciphers` attributes.

SPECIALIZED FORWARD PLUGIN FOR SSL/TLS

There is a secured version of the forward plugin for both in and out actions, as previously referenced. This can be deployed like all plugins using gem. For example:

```
gem install fluent-plugin-secure-forward
```

This version of the plugin still requires certificates but simplifies the configuration and masks the transport layer configuration section.

7.4.2 TLS not just for encryption

Using TLS isn't just for providing an encryption key but can and should be verified as an authentic certificate from a certificate authority (CA) for the server using it. Typically, part of the handshake is when the client and server connect. If the effort in confirming a certificate's authenticity with the certificate authority is harming latency, then you might consider disabling the check if you're entirely within a trusted network environment (e.g., a physical private data center network, but not a cloud-hosted network). Switching such checks off does go against the concepts of security in-depth, so consider what risks this may bring. You'll need to go further if you use self-signed certificates, as there is no CA involved. Additional attributes—`tls_insure_mode` and `tls_allow_self_signed_cert`—are needed to prevent Fluentd from checking the certificate with a CA.

7.4.3 Certificate and private key storage

To use a certificate, we obviously need to be able to store it and the private key. This information is defined as several attributes and includes accommodating Windows store options (for more info, see http://mng.bz/vo6M).

Regardless of where the certificate is stored, we need to tell Fluentd where the certificate is located via `cert_path` (e.g., `cert_path ./myFluentd.crt`) along with the private key location, via `private_key_path` (e.g., `private_key_path ./myFluentd.key`). Ideally, certificates are provided by a public or private CA, which can be contacted to confirm the authenticity of a certificate being used. We can tell Fluentd whether or not it should make that verification via the `client_cert_auth` attribute (`true` or `false`). With a self-signed setup, this has to be false.

7.4.4 Security is more than certificates

Securing communications is more than simply the application of TLS. Some organizations will require more, such as passing a username, password, and tokens. The use of attributes like this and token IDs can provide additional assurance. If we're going to pass sensitive values like this, then the use of TLS should be considered mandatory.

7.5 Credentials management

We have the challenge that the Fluentd configuration doesn't have the means to encrypt and decrypt credentials in its configuration file. So, a username and password needs to appear in the configuration when Fluentd starts in cleartext. Any system administrator (sysadmin) aware of a file with cleartext credentials will not be happy, and if you work with an IT security officer, they will be even more concerned. Some strategies are available to limit this risk; these are the ones we've seen or adopted. The list is ordered in increasing strength of security:

1 Lock down the Fluentd file so access is very tightly restricted. Remember, this also means blocking or restricting the use of the Fluentd UI (illustrated in chapter 2), as well as the UI's credentials. This approach is really the bare minimum, and if sensitive data such as PII is involved, it is probably not seen as acceptable.

   This is likely to need localhost users to be set up and run Fluentd or Fluent Bit. Such a setup brings a range of other administrative considerations.

2 Use inclusions to separate the core configuration from the credentials. Then just the inclusion files need to be subject to the aggressive file access controls. This is an improvement, as it allows you to work with the configuration more freely. But this will prove to be fiddly if there are lots of credentials to handle and is unlikely to be considered acceptable if PII data is involved.

3 Wrap the Fluentd startup with a script that, before starting Fluentd, loads the credentials into environmental variables within the OS session and then start Fluentd. The Fluentd configuration then incorporates access to the environment variables, as we've previously illustrated. As a result, the configuration file has no sensitive values until Fluentd parses the file. But we can incorporate into the script a means to source and decrypt the environment variable. This allows you to then utilize standard OS security features. In a containerized environment, this may get messy, and in a world of multiple OS types, this means potentially

different configurations. Indeed, different scripts load the required credentials into memory.

4 Another component typically associated with the more cloud-native approach that can be equally applied in traditional deployment environments is the use of Vault (www.vaultproject.io) from HashiCorp. Vault comes in a free (open source) version and an enterprise edition with additional features (synchronized distributed vaults). We can then embed it into the configuration file and call the Vault to retrieve the credentials needed using the Vault CLI or API. This alleviates the issue of needing to load into the OS environment beforehand. We won't go into the detailed specifics of aligning application roles to credentials available in Vault, as the documentation provides an excellent explanation at www.vaultproject.io/docs/auth/approle.

If you're working within a Kubernetes environment, then, of course, you have an additional option in terms of using Kubernetes secrets (more about this at http://mng.bz/4j4V). Vault has a raft of plugins to work with other native credentials frameworks such as Kubernetes's Secrets, those from cloud vendors, or older standards like LDAP (Lightweight Directory Access Protocol).

7.5.1 *Simple credentials use case*

We can define username and password credentials as part of a security configuration between Fluentd nodes. This allows a Fluentd node receiving forwarded log events to have an increased level of trust.

The credentials are obviously associated with a server, so in the forward output configuration, we provide the attributes `username` and `password` in the `server` attributes set. In the following listing, we have taken the `dummy-forward.conf` and extended it to include the credentials.

Listing 7.7 Chapter7/Fluentd/dummy-user-forward1.conf with user credentials

```
<source>
  @type dummy
  tag "#{ENV["NodeName"]}"
  auto_increment_key counter
  dummy {"hello":"world"}
</source>

<filter *>
  @type stdout
  <inject>
    tag_key fluentd_tag
  </inject>
</filter>

<match *>
    @type forward
    buffer_type memory
```

```
  flush_interval 2s
  compress gzip

  <security>
```
Mandatory attributes need to be provided for security, which include a logical name and a common key.
```
    shared_key hello
    self_hostname source_host
  </security>

  <server>
    host 127.0.0.1
    port 28080
    username hello-this-is-a-long-username
    password world-of-security-likes-long-passwords
  </server>

<secondary>
  @type stdout
</secondary>
</match>
```
Provides the user credentials

Building on `forward-stdout.conf`, the consumer side also needs the same credentials to verify against. In listing 7.8, we show the additional attributes involved. The consumer side will need the username and password specified and an explicit indication in the `security` structure using the attribute `user_auth`. The server logical name should expect the forwarded log event to be defined using the attribute `self_hostname` and mandatory security attribute `shared_key`.

Listing 7.8   Chapter7/Fluentd/forward-user-stdout.conf receiving with credentials

```
<source>
  @type forward
  port 28080
  bind 127.0.0.1
  <security>
    user_auth true
    self_hostname destination_host
    shared_key hello
    <user>
      username hello-this-is-a-long-username
      password world-of-security-likes-long-passwords
    </user>
  </security>
</source>

<label @FLUENT_LOG>
  <match fluent.*>
    @type stdout
  </match>
</label>

<match *>
  @type stdout
</match>
```
Starts the security configuration

Tells Fluentd that we must apply user authentication

Declares how this node should be addressed by the client

Declares the credentials expected to arrive

We can run this configuration with one shell running:

```
fluentd -c Chapter7/Fluentd/forward-user-stdout.conf
```

Along with this, we need another Fluentd running. Before starting Fluentd, the shell used to run Fluentd will need to `set` or `export` (Windows or Linux) `NodeName` `=Node1`. Each source node has a new number in the assignment. Then we can start up Fluentd with

```
fluentd -c Chapter7/Fluentd/dummy-user-forward1.conf
```

Everything should run as it did when we ran without the user credentials. However, we are validating credentials on the consumer side. Stop the client side, change the password, and restart that Fluentd instance. This will now fail with reported password issues.

7.5.2 *Putting certification into action*

Your company needs the Fluentd deployment to span multiple data centers so that the security team can use their preferred monitoring tool across the WAN. Your chief security officer (CSO) is pleased that an element of security is applied for internode communication. But they are not happy that credentials could be communicated in cleartext. The CSO has approved the use of Fluentd nodes spanning the company-wide network as long as you can provide SSL/TLS configuration to encrypt the traffic. The data centers do not have direct internet connectivity to enable validating and direct distribution of certificates from a public CA. There isn't an internal CA at present, although there are discussions about one in the future. The infrastructure team has said that they will distribute self-signed certificates for you. Therefore, we will need to configure Fluentd using self-signed certificates. To demonstrate that the infrastructure team can meet certificates requirement and that they understand what is needed, it has been agreed that `dummy-user-forward1.conf` and `forward-user-stdout.conf` will be modified to include the use of self-signed certificates to prove the process.

ANSWER
Proof that the solution will work can be achieved by running the Fluentd nodes by replacing the certificate or key file with a dummy file. This should cause the data exchange to fail.

The example configuration can be found in the configuration files `Chapter7/` `ExerciseResults/dummy-user-forward1-Answer.conf` and `Chapter7/` `ExerciseResults/forward-user-stdout1-Answer.conf`. We have referenced dummy certificate files within the Fluentd configurations (if used, this will trigger a failure). For this to work, you will need to replace these files with proper certificates. As the certificates take details and have a lifetime, you should create your own certificates and replace the dummy file with the certificates you generate. This is because certificates can be linked to identities and have defined lifetimes. Guidance on how to do this using OpenSSL (www.openssl.org) can be found in the liveBook version of

Understanding API Security by Justin Richer and Antonio Sanso (Manning, 2017) at http://mng.bz/QWvj.

An alternative approach is to adopt Let's Encrypt, which will provide an automated mechanism to renew certificates (https://letsencrypt.org/).

In the configuration, you'll note that we have opted to switch from the standard forward plugin to the secure forward plugin, so we don't explicitly need to set the transport layer attributes. We have also assumed that the passphrase used in creating the key and certificate is `your_secret`. To change the configuration-held passphrase to align with what was used, you'll need to modify the `forward-user-stdout1 -Answer.conf`, which contains an attribute called `ca_private_key_passphrase` that will need the correct value.

To run the configuration, we'd need to start the Fluentd nodes with the commands

```
fluentd -c Chapter7/ExerciseResults/forward-user-stdout1-Answer.conf
fluentd -c Chapter7/ ExerciseResults /dummy-user-forward1-Answer.conf
```

As we've seen, Fluentd is very flexible for implementing scaling, distribution, and resilience. But with that comes the use of network connectivity. We should protect our network traffic as much as we work to secure individual servers or containers. This does mean handling certificates both for authentication and encryption. Certificate use can make things more challenging, but such issues will become a lot easier if a well-thought-out strategy is adopted, not just for monitoring but for the application communications as well.

Summary

- Fluentd performance can be tuned by using workers running individual CPU processes or through thread management constrained by how Ruby works.
- Workers do require some careful consideration to avoid mistakes like putting log events out of sequence. There are strategies to help determine how to configure workers so they don't introduce new problems.
- Workloads can be distributed using fan-out and fan-in patterns to distribute or concentrate the processing of log events.
- High availability can be implemented using a distributed deployment of Fluentd nodes.
- The same basic distribution principles can be applied within a microservices environment. The use of Kubernetes allows several different ways of deploying and using Fluentd.
- Communication between different Fluentd and Fluent Bit instances should be made secure by using SSL/TLS certificates and should be further enhanced with the use of credentials or tokens.
- Security should not only address communication between Fluentd nodes but should also extend to sending and retrieving the log events to other services, such as a Mongo database or Elasticsearch.

Driving logs with Docker and Kubernetes

Previous chapters have referred to Fluentd's relationship with Docker and Kubernetes, but we have focused on running Fluentd independently of these technologies to minimize complexity. This has helped underpin the point that despite the association with CNCF, Fluentd certainly is not restricted to cloud-native use cases.

In this chapter, we will now look at how Fluentd can be used with Docker and Kubernetes. We should recognize that the more advanced configuration of Docker and Kubernetes is not trivial; both technologies deserve and have many dedicated books. We can view the different technologies as layers of a "cake" that form a cloud-native microservice development platform—each layer adding increased sophistication, abstraction, and scaling. Typically, each layer assumes an understanding of the one preceding it. Operating systems provide a bedrock on which containers provide the first layer, commonly through Docker. The next layer is container orchestration—Kubernetes for us (but others, such as Mesos and OpenShift, exist). A further layer could be added to provide a service mesh like Istio or Linkerd. However, as they bring another layer of components from telemetry to mutual TLS, we've opted not to address this.

However, we want to look at a small slice through these layers to understand how logging fits into each technology layer in turn. To get this perspective, we will assume that you have a basic conceptual appreciation of Docker and Kubernetes. The explanations of Docker and Kubernetes will only be at a high level as we aim to provide insight into how Fluentd and the prebuilt solutions support logging can be applied. We'll keep the setup and illustration of the different points as minimalist as possible, so the approaches and considerations don't need a deep hands-on experience of every layer. By the end of the chapter, you will have grasped the ideas and seen how to deploy Fluentd to work with Docker and Kubernetes. If you'd like to know more about these technologies, appendix E provides recommendations for additional book resources.

8.1 Fluentd out of the box from Docker Hub

The previous chapter illustrated a range of deployment configurations, including patterns applicable in a Kubernetes environment. These use cases can be addressed directly using predefined containers provided by Fluentd and others and published in the central Docker Hub repository (https://hub.docker.com/r/fluent/fluentd/). The container has been configured so that it is possible to pass a location to write output log files—this allows appropriate mount points to be used and allows the logs to be accessed from outside of the container, avoiding the issue of losing logs when a container terminates. In addition to the location for log files, we can also pass in our own custom Fluentd configuration if the default is insufficient. The default settings include the following:

- Port 24224 is used for receiving logs using the forward plugin.
- Logs tagged with `Docker.**` are written to `/fluentd/log/docker.log`.
- All other logs go to `/fluentd/log/data.*.log`.

8.1.1 Official Docker images

The Fluentd has a single official image, according to Docker Hub. The official image means we can be assured the image is being maintained and can be found at https://hub.docker.com/_/fluentd (you will need at least a free Docker Hub account to access this). This isn't the only Fluentd-provided Docker image available, but the other images don't come with the same assurances. Other than the official image, the other image of particular interest is the DaemonSet, which was first referenced in chapter 2. The DaemonSet, as you may recall, provides the means to ensure each Kubernetes worker node (host machine) runs a pod that provides foundation services, such as logging and monitoring of infrastructure health. The Docker files are available in the Fluentd GitHub repository if you want to use them as a starting point.

If you search the Docker Hub for Fluentd, you will find hundreds of entries. This is because many organizations (including many vendors who want to make it easy for you to send log events to their product) use Fluentd and have their own image configurations. It is worth keeping in mind that the official Docker images only include the core plugins. To use your custom or community-contributed plugins, the Docker image needs to be modified to retrieve that plugin and install it, along with any dependencies. It is worth considering where the Docker image you elect to use has originated. Doing so will enable us to track whether the image provider maintains the image with the latest patches and releases to the OS and software, including Fluentd in the image.

8.1.2 *Docker log drivers*

The purpose of the log drivers is to capture the output streams for `stdin`, `stdout`, and `stderr` (i.e., the content you would expect to see on a console) and direct them to a suitable destination; otherwise, this information will "disappear into the ether." Docker supplies, out of the box, several bundled log drivers covering

- *Fluentd*—Communicates with the Fluentd forward endpoint, which must be on the host machine.
- *JSON file*—The default setting; stores events in a file using JSON format.
- *local*—A file-based storage custom to Docker and optimized for its operations.
- *Syslog*—Integrates with the Syslog product.
- *journald*—A daemon service that uses the same API as Syslog but produces a more structured file. This comes with systemd which provides a range of OS services beyond the Linux core (http://mng.bz/XWZ6).
- *GELF*—Graylog Extended Log Format; a format adopted by several logging frameworks such as Graylog and Logstash (https://docs.graylog.org/en/4.0/pages/gelf.html).
- *ETW logs*—Windows log events (http://mng.bz/y4vq).
- *Google Cloud Platform, AWS CloudWatch, Rapid7, Splunk*—Some of the vendors and platforms that have provided log drivers to their services.

In addition to these Docker-shipped log drivers, you can also build your own. But unless you want to tightly couple Docker logging to a product or platform, there are plenty of options without resorting to development.

8.1.3 *Getting set up for Docker log drivers*

To use Fluentd log drivers, we will need to get Docker installed (as well as Kubernetes for later parts of this chapter). As these technologies have significant differences between Windows and Linux, we will adjust our approach to accommodate both plat-forms (a practice that recognizes many people who work from a Windows machine but often work with Linux in production). Microsoft and Docker have made several significant advancements that allow Linux containers to run on Windows servers. This is through using the *Windows Linux Subsystem* (*WSL*), but this isn't available on all ver-sions of Windows OSes (but if you have the means to use WSL, it is a great way for-ward). For this chapter, we will focus on just Linux containers. This means working with WSL, *Hyper-V*, or *VirtualBox* for Windows users. In appendix A, we have provided the resources to help you get set up.

8.2   Using Docker log drivers

Docker provides the means to control what happens to logs. By default, Docker uses a JSON log driver that writes to `stdout` and `stderr` (i.e., our console unless you've overridden the routing of these outputs in your environment). There are two ways to control the log driver, either with additional parameters in the Docker run command or by modifying the Docker configuration. The difference is that the command-line approach means you can use alternative configurations for specific Docker contain-ers. The downside of the command-line approach is the parameters need to be pro-vided every time.

8.2.1   Docker drivers via the command line

For our first use of log drivers, we're going to use the command-line approach. It is the least invasive approach to tailoring log driver behavior; therefore, experimenting with configuration controls involves the least disruptive change.

We'll continue to run a configuration of Fluentd on our host computer to receive and output log events. First, we will run the `Hello-World` Docker image from within the Linux VM (virtual machine) established using the guidance in appendix A. If your host operating system is Linux, this may seem a little perverse, but this approach has the following benefits:

- Clear separation of network layers, as the virtualization layer will provide a sepa-rate network layer besides the network abstractions from the Docker layer.
- Keeps the number of VMs needed down and the resource overhead that virtual-ization creates.
- The outcomes will be the same regardless of the host operating system. This can be particularly beneficial if your host is Windows, as it helps to emphasize that Fluentd is platform-agnostic.

Personally, this is going to be done using my Windows 10 Pro host running Hyper-V with an Ubuntu 18 LTS VM. This means we will be using Ubuntu to run Docker con-tainers. We can visualize the deployment as shown in figure 8.1.

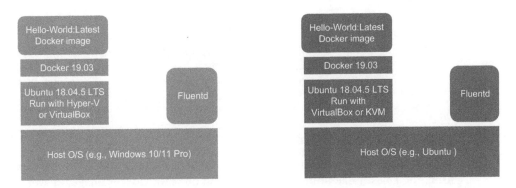

Figure 8.1 The layers of the operating system and virtualization and containerization being used to ensure our host environment isn't disturbed with just Docker

8.2.2 *A quick check of network connections*

Getting network configurations correct is a significant consideration for using Docker, Kubernetes, and virtual machines. This means it is always worth doing quick and easy checks to ensure the network connectivity works as expected, such as using curl or Postman to send HTTP log events to Fluentd. To help with this and use the Fluentd log driver, we have prepared a simple Fluentd configuration to send anything received to stdout. We can start Fluentd just as we have many times before using the command

```
fluentd -c Chapter8/Fluentd/forwardstdout.conf
```

Once Fluentd is running from the Linux environment, we can execute a variation on our "Hello World" test used in chapter 2. In the following configurations and commands, we need to replace `w.x.y.z` with the host computer's IP, as seen by the Linux guest. You can get the IPs of a machine with the command `ipconfig` on Windows and `ip addr show` on Linux hosts (`ifconfig` may also work but is deprecated). Our test command on the Linux VM or container has to be

```
curl -X POST -H "Content-Type: application/json" -d '{"foo":"bar"}' http://
    w.x.y.z:18080/test
```

This should result in the JSON details `{"foo":"bar"}` being displayed on the console where Fluentd is running on the host.

Strict bind controls

Strict bind controls can be an excellent thing. They allow us to apply security controls when dealing with components that may reside on machines with multiple network connections, regardless of whether those connections are physical or virtual (as is the case for Docker and Kubernetes environments). The bind configuration attribute for input plugins like `forward` will ensure Fluentd invocations will come through the

(continued)

relevant networks. But when Docker and Kubernetes create network addresses, we must be a lot more aware. When connections fail, it is easy to start looking at host firewalls, network configurations, and so on. The reality is that the target system is at fault for listening to only one specific network connection.

8.2.3   Running Docker command line

Having set and checked our deployment, particularly networking, we can move on to using the Docker daemon. Rather than build our own Docker image, we will retrieve a traditional "Hello World" one from the Docker Hub website. The `hello-world` Docker image is straightforward, and when people are finding their way with Docker, it's a good starting place. Details of the image are available at https://hub.docker.com/ _/hello-world.

We can stipulate a specific version through the use of tags. The tag is added after the name with a colon separator. As the `hello-world` Docker image has been tagged following the convention of using a `latest` tag for the most recent stable version, we can add `:latest` to the command. This can be done by running on the VM the Docker CLI command

```
docker pull hello-world:latest
```

We haven't made any changes to the Docker configuration, which means we will see the standard Docker log driver behavior when asking the Docker daemon to run our image. While the location of Docker logs can vary, typically we should locate them in the folder `/var/lib/docker`, where we will see a folder called `containers`. We can see this as highlighted in section 1 of figure 8.2, with each container instance having its own folder created using its unique ID. Of course, there won't be any containers present initially. With a local copy of the image now available, we should tell Docker daemon via the CLI to run the `hello-world` image using the command

```
docker run hello-world
```

If we now refresh our view of the folder `/var/lib/docker/containers`, the folder will have a new entry, highlighted in section 2 of figure 8.2. In the new container's folder structure, we will see a log file with a long name (Docker image instance; e.g., `b361e69a1...`). Navigating into a container's folder, we'll see the resources for that Docker instance, including a folder called `local-logs` (highlighted in section 3 of figure 8.2). Finally, navigating into the `local-logs` folder, we can see the container's log file called `container.log` (highlighted in section 4 of figure 8.2). The log file contents will be unreadable because it's stored in its own custom format (section 5 of figure 8.2).

To make things more practical, we want to configure Docker to log using a more consumable format. We can override the default settings, so Docker uses the Fluentd

Figure 8.2 Directory structures holding Docker and the folders per container instance, followed by the listing of a container and a container log, which is encoded in a custom manner (numbers in the screen shot are explained in the preceding text)

log driver. This is done by telling the Docker daemon to use an alternative with the parameter `--log-driver=fluentd`. We don't need to do anything more, as the Fluentd driver is bundled in the deployment of Docker. We also need to tell the driver where to find our Fluentd node to receive the log events. This and other configuration options are provided using the parameter `--log-opt` followed by a name-value pair separated by the equals (=) character. In our case, we need to give the address (just like the previous curl command) of our host machine's Fluentd. As the Docker log driver can use the forward plugin (and benefit from msgpack providing compression), we need to ensure the network address, including that port, is provided. This results in the command to run `hello-world` like this:

```
docker run --log-driver=fluentd  --log-opt fluentd-address=w.x.y.z:28080
    hello-world
```

The outcome of executing the statement will be to see log events from the Docker image being output on the Fluentd console. If the Docker command returns with an error message such as

```
docker: Error response from daemon: failed to initialize logging driver: dial
    tcp w.x.y.z:28080: connect: connection refused.
```

then something is wrong on the network or in Fluentd (e.g., it is not binding to the correct network). The order in which the docker image and the target Fluentd node are started up should also be noted. This will become particularly important when moving into container orchestration with Kubernetes, as it manages the order in which pods start up. In the event of such issues, we would recommend checking the Docker configuration values for network ports to ensure network traffic is allowed out of the container. If any port number mapping is happening, then that is fine.

The Fluentd driver can use any of the standard features Fluentd offers, such as making communication asynchronous (i.e., exploiting the memory buffer capabilities; more on this in chapter 9). But we'll look at more of these when we move to the complete configuration.

In figure 8.3, we can see the output generated from running our command. Notice how the log events include the following attributes:

- `container_id`—The complete 64-character ID of the container uniquely identifying an individual container.
- `container_name`—The name of the container when the container was started. Any renaming actions after the startup aren't reflected until restarted.
- `source`—Details whether the log came from `stdout`, etc.
- `log`—The content from the source (e.g., a line from `stdout`).

```
2021-03-14 17:01:22.000000000 +0000 9e2e208d5f1f: {"container_id":"9e2e208d5f1f439b63ac76595884bd8af650
d7eab91a45919aca9df1cbff1bcb","container_name":"/naughty_benz","source":"stdout","log":""}
2021-03-14 17:01:22.000000000 +0000 9e2e208d5f1f: {"log":"Hello from Docker!","container_id":"9e2e208d5
f1f439b63ac76595884bd8af650d7eab91a45919aca9df1cbff1bcb","container_name":"/naughty_benz","source":"std
out"}
2021-03-14 17:01:22.000000000 +0000 9e2e208d5f1f: {"container_id":"9e2e208d5f1f439b63ac76595884bd8af650
d7eab91a45919aca9df1cbff1bcb","container_name":"/naughty_benz","source":"stdout","log":"This message sh
ows that your installation appears to be working correctly."}
2021-03-14 17:01:22.000000000 +0000 9e2e208d5f1f: {"log":"","container_id":"9e2e208d5f1f439b63ac7659588
4bd8af650d7eab91a45919aca9df1cbff1bcb","container_name":"/naughty_benz","source":"stdout"}
2021-03-14 17:01:22.000000000 +0000 9e2e208d5f1f: {"container_id":"9e2e208d5f1f439b63ac76595884bd8af650
d7eab91a45919aca9df1cbff1bcb","container_name":"/naughty_benz","source":"stdout","log":"To generate thi
s message, Docker took the following steps:"}
```

Figure 8.3   The console output from Fluentd received from executing the `hello-world` container from Docker

8.2.4   *Switching to driver configuration through a configuration file*

With a parameterized solution proven, we can advance the configuration in a more readable manner and add further options that are relevant. Given all the possible configuration options, using a command line for an advanced configuration will make for a challenging maintenance task. By default, changing the Docker daemon configuration file will impact all Docker images being run. The Docker command line also allows us to point to a configuration file with the parameter `--config`, followed by the filename for alternate configuration.

The Docker daemon keeps its configuration, including the log driver configuration, in a file called `daemon.json`. The default location for the file is `/etc/docker/` for Linux setups. If you use an instance of Docker on Windows (rather than the indirect approach we've chosen to adopt), the location is `ProgramData\docker\config\` (`ProgramData` is typically found on the C drive root). It is possible that the file does not exist if the Docker setup is running entirely on default values.

In the daemon configuration file, we clearly want to include the setting of the type of log driver and connection to our Fluentd instance. To do this, we include into the JSON file the configuration version of the command line parameter `"log-driver":` `"fluentd"`. In the command line, we also provided the `fluentd-address` attribute. When it comes to the `fluentd-address`, we can provide the address as `tcp://` `w.x.y.z:28080` or as an explicit path reference to the relevant socket file (e.g., `unix:///usr/var/fluentd/fluent.sock`).

In addition to the address, we should also introduce several additional parameters directly related to the log driver and other general parameters relevant to logging. The general settings we've included are

- `raw-logs`—Should be set to either `true` or `false`. If specified as `false`, then a complete ANSI timestamp is applied (e.g., `YYYY-MM-DD HH:MM:SS`), and the coloring of the log text through the use of escape codes is switched off from any encoding.
- `log-driver`—As shown in the command line example used to set the log driver.
- `log-level`—The log filter threshold to apply to Docker daemon. The accepted levels are `debug`, `info`, `warn`, `error`, and `fatal`, with the default being `info`.

Within the configuration file, we can start an inner group of attributes called `log-opts`; these logging specific options include

- `env`—We can ask the driver to capture and include specific environment variables. This is done by defining a comma-separated list. For our purposes, we can use `"os, customer"`. This does assume that something has set such values. It is also possible to define a regular expression version of this by using the attribute `env-regex`.
- `labels`—This works very much in the same way as `env`, insofar as a list of labels (Docker metadata name-value pairs) can be specified, or a regular expression can be provided via `labels-regex`.
- `fluentd-retry-wait`—Each time a connection fails, a waiting period is applied before retrying again. The value needs to include the duration type (e.g., `s` for seconds, `h` for hours).

- `fluentd-max-retries`—The maximum number of connection retries before giving up. This defaults to `4294967295`—that is, `(2**32 - 1)`. We don't want things hanging for that many retries. Given that we have set retry to one per second, up to 10 minutes retrying would be plenty, meaning a value of `600`.
- `fluentd-subsecond-precision`—Allows us to get the timestamp precision to millisecond accuracy if the hardware is capable of it. While the default value is `false`, it is worth setting explicitly, even if it's to the default value. By explicitly setting the value, we're reminded that we won't have such precision.
- `tag`—The tag to associate with the log event record. This can be built using several predefined values (the complete list is in appendix A) using a notation defined by Docker. In our case, let's define the tag using the shortened ID and Image ID using the following representation: `{{.ID}}-{{.ImageID}}`.
- `fluentd-address`—As in the command-line configuration, this is the location of the Fluentd server to talk with. This, as with the parameter approach, needs to be tailored to the host IP of the Fluentd instance.

The outcome of addressing these other needs means we arrive at the code shown in listing 8.1. Running the Docker daemon process in debug mode is the easiest way to ensure that the configuration file is processed correctly. This means that as this is a daemon service, we need to stop the current process using the command

```
sudo service docker stop
```

Listing 8.1 Chapter8/Docker/daemon.json configuration for Docker Fluentd log driver

```
{
"log-driver" : "fluentd",        ◁── This tells Fluentd to use the
"log-level": "debug",                Fluentd version of the log driver.
"raw-logs": true,      ◁──┐ This is setting Docker to use raw logs, so the formatting
                           │ isn't used, and the ANSI timestamp is applied.
"log-opts": {
    "env": "os,customer",
    "labels": "production_status,dev",
    "fluentd-retry-wait": "1s",
    "fluentd-max-retries": "600",
    "fluentd-sub-second-precision": "false",   │ This tailors the tag to be
    "tag": "{{.ID}}-{{.ImageID}}",        ◁──┘ used in the log events.
    "fluentd-address": "w.x.y.z:28080"     ◁──┐ This specifies to the log driver
    }                                          │ where the Fluentd server is.
}
```

Once the service has stopped, we need to copy our modified daemon configuration file to the default location `/etc/docker/`. Then we can start the process manually with the command

```
sudo dockerd -D
```

This will launch Docker in debug mode, picking up the configuration from the default location. If there are any issues with the configuration file, the Docker daemon will almost immediately stop or generate warnings about not parsing the configuration. Messages will be displayed on the console, such as

```
unable to configure the Docker daemon with file /etc/docker/daemon.json:
    invalid character '\n' in string literal
```

Once the file is read okay, the Docker daemon will direct log events to our Fluentd instance, including the output when running the `Hello-World` docker image. As our previous command has started the Docker daemon in the foreground, we need to use an additional shell to run the docker image. We can use the same command as before:

```
docker run hello-world
```

If you're feeling brave, then you can jump straight to running Docker as a service again. This means terminating the current execution of the Docker daemon process in debug mode. Then execute the command

```
sudo service docker start
```

When you're confident about any further changes to the configuration file (daemon.json), rather than running the Docker daemon manually, we can adopt an approach of simply restarting the daemon to force it to pick up the latest config. This is done by replacing the `start` command with `restart`. For example:

```
sudo service docker restart
```

Suppose you want to verify that config attributes have been accepted by the Docker daemon. In that case, it is possible to run the command `docker --info`, which will display all the settings being used, including those defaulted values on the console.

8.3 *Kubernetes components logging and the use of Fluentd*

The nature of Kubernetes and the model making it highly pluggable means that the landscape can become complex. To illustrate this, if we look at the containerization aspect of Kubernetes, Docker may be the most predominant container technology today. Still, Kubernetes, through the API model, allows us to use other container technologies such as *containerd* (https://containerd.io/) and *cri-o* (https://cri-o.io/), both under the governance of CNCF. Some of the complexity is addressed through the *Open Container Initiative* (https://opencontainers.org/), also under CNCF governance, which helps abstract the interaction between the container implementation and Kubernetes's orchestration of containers. The essential question here is how does that impact us and the use of Fluentd?

   The important thing here is that, as we have seen, we can configure Docker to capture the events propagating through `stdout` and `stderr`; therefore, do the other containers support such a capability? Not all containers are as mature as Docker when it comes to logging. Many simply line up with Kubernetes's internal logging frame-work *klog* (https://github.com/kubernetes/klog), which adopts the logging approach of using *journald* when it is deployed, and otherwise logging to a default file location.

Klog's evolution

Klog goes back to the Google C++ libraries (https://github.com/google/glog). As Kubernetes is implemented in Go, C++ libraries aren't an option, and along the way, a Go implementation was developed (https://github.com/golang/glog). Since then, the Kubernetes developers determined that glog presented some challenges regard-ing containerization and thus forked the code base, leading us to klog. The APIs remain essentially the same. In all cases, the logging mechanisms are streamlined for optimal performance; thus, plugging and configuring logging is very much down to command-line options offered by an application using the library rather than a config-uration file.

8.3.1   Kubernetes components and structured logging

The application of structured logging today in Kubernetes components is an evolving journey. Not all components within Kubernetes have adopted structured logging yet (although this is changing). We should be prepared for the possibility that any addi-tional system components or extensions used in the future might not apply structure. This reinforces the recommendation that it is better to actively adopt logging and deployment patterns outlined in chapter 7 (Fluentd as a sidecar pattern, embedded with the application, etc.) rather than try to harvest logs out of Kubernetes.

8.3.2   Kubernetes default log retention and log rotation

When the logs come through to Kubernetes from a container because of the con-tainer configuration, Kubernetes will push the log entries into a log file for each con-tainer instance. To manage the size and log rotation, it is our responsibility to establish a log rotation tool, which can control how many log files and how frequently they are rotated.

Kubernetes doesn't have its own log rotator; it is the responsibility of the deployer of Kubernetes worker nodes to address log rotation challenges. That said, if the worker node is set up using a Kubernetes provided script (`kube-up.sh`, http://mng.bz/M25n), it will deploy the open source tool logrotate (https://github.com/logrotate/logrotate). Logrotate can be configured to retain a specified number of files. Some fla-vors of Linux will have logrotate deployed, so it is a matter of additional configuration. How logrotate is set up can vary across Linux flavors only because of how the Linux con-figuration is applied. Some flavors use systemd, and logrotate is provided as part of that. Where logrotate isn't already deployed, it is typical to be able to perform an indepen-dent installation via the Linux flavor's package manager of choice.

Logrotate is not cross-platform as a solution, so running Kubernetes on Windows needs another answer to achieve log rotation, which isn't obvious and more challenging when examining the Kubernetes discussions on the subject. Regardless of log rotation, logs generated by klog are automatically truncated when they reach 1.8 GB. So any log rotation needs to be established to occur before hitting that threshold.

Kubernetes will automatically delete all except the current log files when a container is removed. If the process of capturing such log events is too far behind, there is a risk of losing log events—something to be considered when establishing log capture.

The takeaway from this is that managing logs at the Kubernetes layer presents challenges with potential differences based on the deployment approach and infrastructure setup. As a result, our preference is to minimize the issues by focusing on log capture in the layers where we can see more consistency and the means to assert more control. We can't entirely ignore Kubernetes logs, but intercepting the log events elsewhere means the loss of Kubernetes log events isn't as critical.

Easing of deployments into Kubernetes

The easing of deployments into Kubernetes for solutions is necessary. Within the Kubernetes ecosystem, several tools, such as Helm (https://helm.sh) and Rancher (https://rancher.com), have been developed to ease the challenges. Helm (the more dominant solution) even refers to itself as the package manager for Kubernetes. Given Helm's dominance, the Fluentd committers have developed Helm configuration files (known as *charts*) to support Fluentd deployment. The charts consolidate and define the configuration details unique to deployment, and then Helm uses templates and scripts to complete the rest. The DaemonSet chart included in the GitHub Fluentd repository (https://github.com/fluent/helm-charts) provides a baseline start, leaving you to just apply configurations for your specific needs. If you're involved with the regular development of Kubernetes deployments, then we recommend investigating Helm and leveraging the Fluentd charts.

8.3.3 kubectl with logging

As you may well already know, *kubectl* is the primary CLI tool for interacting with Kubernetes. When Kubernetes understands where the logs are being written, we can utilize kubectl to perform various tasks, such as tailing one or more log files, forwarding logs to different ports, and supporting the everyday log file activities. Rather than describe kubectl log commands, all the details can be found in the kubectl command reference at http://mng.bz/aDJB.

8.4 Demonstrating logging with Kubernetes

We need to collect Kubernetes process logs and understand whether internal container processes such as Kubelet are logging errors. Kubernetes has plenty of mechanisms to help us check the health of containers. Still, understanding that everything is running without issue in Kubernetes is essential to knowing whether the containers are being cared for, or the nodes are slowly failing. If an application is logging into the console and events go to Kubernetes, where do we retrieve the events?

To address this, we will deploy a ready-built pod containing the LogSimulator, which is configured to direct the log events to `stdout`. The log events will propagate through the container mechanism and let Fluentd intercept them in the Kubernetes layer, so we will be capturing the Kubernetes and container internal logs. This may reflect the recommended setup described by the twelve-factor app (https://12factor .net/logs). But it does, in many ways, represent a worst-case scenario, as we have to invest effort in deriving the context (separating multiple log events in `stdout` that could have been from the platform or container versus the application, etc.) and restructuring the log events.

At this point, if you haven't followed appendix A to install minikube as our Kubernetes implementation, then now is the ideal time. Once complete, your environment will look like the layout shown in figure 8.4.

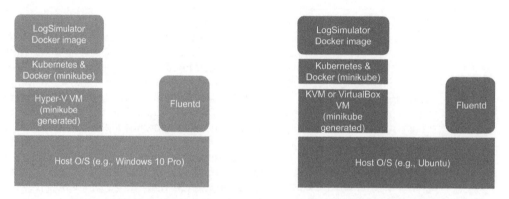

Figure 8.4   The layers of operating system and virtualization and containerization being used to ensure our host environment isn't disturbed with minikube

8.4.1   Kubernetes setup

To demonstrate the Kubernetes configuration to keep things nice and compact, we're going to use minikube. Minikube is a version of Kubernetes pared down to keep the footprint as compact as possible. If you haven't already followed the instructions in appendix A, that is the first step to perform on the Linux virtual machine. It also happens to be the Kubernetes implementation used in *Kubernetes in Action* by Marko Lukša (http://mng.bz/g4wE). Once minikube is installed, let's fire it up and use the Kubernetes dashboard to look around at the initial state. We do this with the following command for Windows:

```
minikube start --vm-driver hyperv --hyperv-virtual-switch "Primary Virtual
    Switch"
```

The Linux equivalent is

```
minikube start --vm-driver docker
```

This will establish a single node "cluster" of Kubernetes stripped down to the minimum. The download package for this chapter contains Linux shell and Windows batch scripts, which will perform this command (making it a lot easier than remembering or copying the commands every time). Then we can start up the dashboard with this command in either Windows or Linux:

```
minikube dashboard
```

This command starts a foreground process that will deploy the necessary pods to run the dashboard UI and provide the dashboard page URL. With the dashboard page open, we can navigate using the UI's left-hand menu to see what DaemonSets, Deployments, and Pods are currently deployed (as part of the Workloads section of the menu). As you can see in figure 8.5, there are no DaemonSets currently deployed. You will find the basic `hello-minikube` deployment and associated pod running.

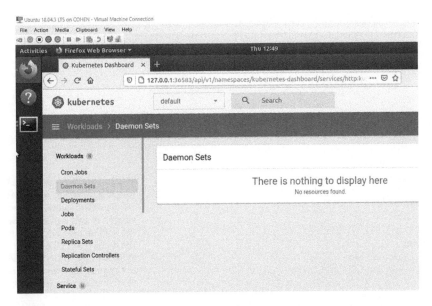

Figure 8.5 Kubernetes dashboard running on minikube, currently only showing the default namespace rather than the kube system or where most DaemonSets will be.

Simplify navigation with all namespaces

Simplifying the UI navigation can be done by setting the drop-down next to the Kubernetes logo to All Namespaces rather than default (as shown in figure 8.5); this will make seeing details easier. Otherwise, you will likely get tripped up when you navigate the UI, wondering why you cannot see expected information, such as the Fluentd DaemonSets. Within our environment, displaying everything (i.e., all namespaces) is not going to be problematic, although in a production setup, this is not something we would recommend.

8.4.2   Creating logs to capture

We first need an application to generate log events so we can observe a log DaemonSet collecting events from Kubernetes and the applications not logging more directly to an endpoint (i.e., they are simply sending logs to `stdout` and `stderr`). For this, we can use a containerized version of LogSimulator. The containerized version of this tool is, by default, configured to loop through a simple data set several times and then stop. Each log event is simply written to `stdout`; thus, log events will get collected by Kubernetes. When the LogSimulator pod completes its run, it will stop the pod, at which point, Kubernetes will intervene to restart the deployment. The LogSimulator Docker image already exists within Docker Hub. The Kubernetes configuration to use this Docker image within a pod is shown in the following listing, which can be retrieved from http://mng.bz/5KQB. As there is no need for any configuration or external facing endpoints, the YAML configuration is straightforward.

Listing 8.2   Chapter8/LogGenerator/Kubernetes/log-simulator-deployment.yaml

```
apiVersion: apps/v1
kind: Deployment
metadata:
  name: log-simulator
  labels:
    app: log-simulator
spec:
  replicas: 1
  selector:
    matchLabels:
      app: log-simulator
  template:
    metadata:
      labels:
        app: log-simulator
    spec:
      containers:
      - name: log-simulator
        image: mp3monster/log-simulator:v1    ◁──
```

This is the reference to the Docker Hub image, which, when deployed, will be downloaded. If a newer version of this pod needs deploying, the version reference at the end of the name (i.e., :v1) must be updated. Without this, Kubernetes will ignore the request as it already has that version of the LogSimulator.

To deploy this pod, you need to ensure the environment variable `LogSimulator-Home` is defined, which references the root folder of the LogGenerator that has been previously installed. Alternatively, edit the provided script (`deploy-log-sim-k8.bat` or `deploy-log-sim-k8.sh`), replacing the environment variable reference with the absolute path. If you use the script, it will always try to remove any possible existing pod deployment first to be safe. This means that if you want to keep redeploying, then just use the script. To issue the deployment command yourself, then, in a shell, issue the following statement:

```
minikube kubectl -- apply -f %LogSimulatorHome%\Kubernetes\log-simulator-
    deployment.yaml --namespace=default
```

Minikube should confirm the deployment as being successful.

Difference between minikube CLI and kubectl

The difference between kubectl and minikube commands is minimal. Minikube has wrapped the use of kubectl so that the minikube command can provide additional commands and the kubectl commands. If you have installed kubectl, it is possible to configure it to direct instructions to the minikube instance of Kubernetes. Then you can replace the first part of the commands, which appear as `minikube kubectl --`, with just `kubectl`. An alternate approach to this for Linux hosts is to introduce an alias into the Linux environment. This is done by using the command - `alias kubectl="minikube kubectl --"`. Now when you use the command `kubectl`, Linux will substitute it for the full expression. If you find yourself having to prefix a lot of the calls with `sudo` to ensure the privileges are correct, you could incorporate that into the alias as well.

UNDERSTANDING LOGSIMULATOR'S VIEW

Before we move on to look at the DaemonSet, it is worth taking a "little peek under the hood" to see things happening. As we've previously started the Kubernetes dashboard, we can use this to help us. We need to access the list of pods (left menu option); thus, we will see a list like the details shown in figure 8.6. We need to access the `log-simulator` pod instance, which can be done by clicking on the name that starts with `log-simulator`.

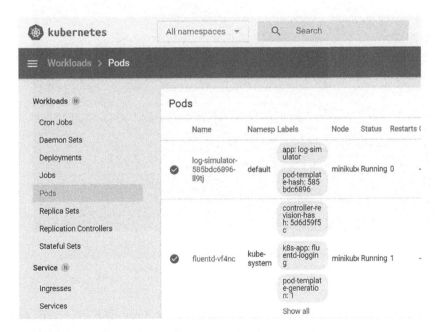

Figure 8.6 Kubernetes dashboard showing the instances of pods that contain our LogSimulator and Fluentd

This will display the details about the specific pod, and the top of the screen will look something like the details shown in figure 8.7.

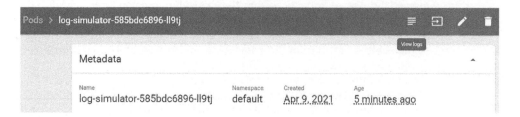

Figure 8.7   Kubernetes dashboard showing a specific instance of the log-simulator

As you'll note in figure 8.7, there are four icons in the top right-hand side of the image. Clicking on the first icon will display a view like the one in figure 8.8. The figure shows us the `stdout` being generated by the LogGenerator.

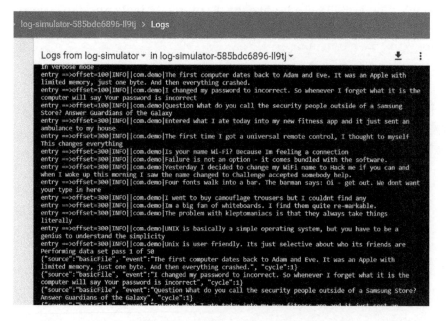

Figure 8.8   The console (stdout) of our instance of the LogGenerator with its simple configuration generating events to be collected by our Fluentd setup

While this is useful and confirms the container is functioning as expected, we need to know which file Kubernetes is pushing this output to, as we need to set up a tail input plugin against that file. Returning to the screen, we saw in figure 8.7 that we want to use the arrow-based icon (second from left), as this will provide us with a shell view into the container being executed.

It is also worth logging into a shell provided by this container image, because you will see the environment as your application will. Any container exploration needs to be quickly done—once the LogGenerator has completed generating log events, it will stop. As a result, our container will die, taking our session with it. If you try to see what logs exist, you shouldn't see anything, as the log events will be captured on the host running Kubernetes, not in the container. By doing this, we have clearly established the first of the requirements of our Kubernetes container—the fact that access to the host file system is needed to collect the logs generated.

8.4.3 *Understanding how Fluentd DaemonSets are put together*

Our first contact with Kubernetes was in chapter 2, where we looked briefly at using a DaemonSet provided by Fluentd. We've said Kubernetes configuration gets complex. However, it would be easy to question this given the `Kubernetes.yaml` we've used for the LogGenerator. Let's take a moment to step through what is involved with the Kubernetes and Docker resources for Fluentd. There are a couple of crucial repositories relevant to this, specifically the following:

- *Kubernetes DaemonSet in GitHub*—This is where most of the necessary implementation details are (http://mng.bz/6ZXo).
- *Docker file base images*—(https://github.com/fluent/fluentd-docker-image). These are the Docker base images, including the template mechanism used to help generate the different OS variations.
- *Docker Hub repository*—This is where the Docker images are pulled from for the Kubernetes configuration (https://hub.docker.com/u/fluent). One or more Docker images form a pod based on the configuration provided.
- *Metadata filter*—This is incorporated into the DaemonSet (http://mng.bz/oa2d). The metadata filter enriches the Kubernetes log records with additional context to help you better understand what is happening.

When you visit the GitHub repository for Fluentd's DaemonSets, you see a range of YAML files. The Fluentd community has provided a range of standardized configurations for capturing Kubernetes logging and sending the contents on to a single destination. The configurations range from forwarding the content to another Fluentd node, to sending to various cloud-native services provided by AWS, Azure, and Google, to dedicated services such as Graylog, Loggly, and the more common targets Elasticsearch and Syslog.

When examining the Kubernetes YAML configurations, you'll see they are all very similar in nature, with the following characteristics:

- Setting the image up, so it will be deployed in the kube-system namespace
- Referencing a suitable container image

- Defining environment variables that can be used in the relevant Fluentd configuration file to connect with the external service—typically details such as the host and port of the target solution
- Specifying the number of resources that should be allocated to the container
- Defining the host-file locations that need to be visible within the container—specifically `/var/log` and `/var/lib/docker/containers`—and how the path should be seen within the container.

What isn't shown in the configurations is that some additional environment variables can be set and passed through, further changing the container's behavior; for example, whether to try and interact with systemd. But we'll see this in more detail shortly. We can assume that the "real magic" occurs in the container, and therefore in the Docker file.

KUBERNETES DOCKER IMAGES

If you examine the README in the repository's root, you'll see a list of Docker pull commands, with one or more references for each type of daemon. Looking through the list, you'll note they have been broken into two major groups: `x86_64 images` and `arm64_images`. The need for this may not be immediately apparent until we remember that the Docker file has to ultimately reference binaries specific to the computer hardware. This is a downside of delivering virtualized or containerized solutions over using a more generic package manager. This means we have a lot of Docker images to maintain.

The Kubernetes Docker images are also generated using templates, but we can characterize the activities as doing the following things:

- Establishing a dependency on the relevant Docker image
- Setting up Ruby and Gem, including defining environment variables to the appropriate locations
- Installing various gem files
- Configuring files covering Fluentd, systemd, Kubernetes, Prometheus

Using an example such as https://github.com/fluent/fluentd-kubernetes-daemon-set/tree/master/docker-image/v1.12/arm64/debian-forward/conf, we can examine the configuration and file relationships in detail. Figure 8.9 also provides a visual representation of the file relationships:

- `Fluent.conf` is in the root container and uses the `include` mechanism to bring in the contents of other configuration files, as we saw back in chapter 5. This configuration file also has a single match that, in the case of the forward DaemonSet, matches all log events and sends them on to the target server. It is worth noting that the forwarding configuration does not include any security (no TLS, etc.); this isn't a problem if the logs are not sensitive. But if they are, then you will need to replace the configuration files with ones that include the necessary configuration. We'll see more of how this can be done later in the chapter.

The inclusion of the systemd and Prometheus configurations are subject to environment variable controls, specifically the existence of settings for `FLUENTD_SYSTEMD_CONF` and `FLUENTD_PROMETHEUS_CONF`.

The `Kubernetes.conf` is needed, so it is included. Finally, any configuration in the `conf.d` folder is included, so extending the configuration with any specific customizations is possible.

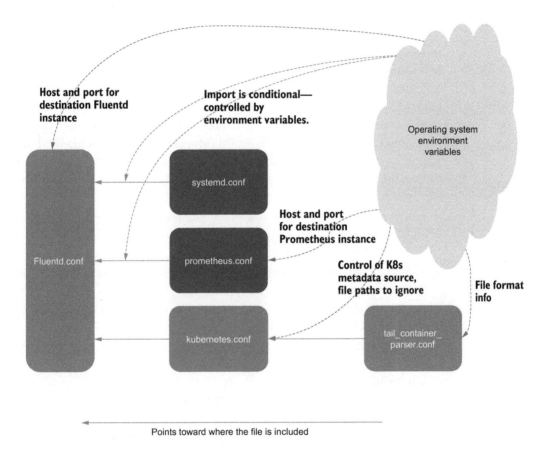

Figure 8.9 A representation of the relationship between the configuration files and how they are influenced by environment variables

- The `Prometheus.conf` file is straightforward. It defines the use of the input plugins for Prometheus and `Prometheus_output_monitor` to monitor Prometheus. Environment variables define the server addresses to `bind`, `port`, and a `path` if the metrics URI are different using the variables `FLUENTD_PROMETHEUS_BIND`, `FLUENTD_PROMETHEUS_PORT`, and `FLUENTD_PROMETHEUS_PATH`, respectively.

- The `Systemd.conf` file defines the sources for Docker, Kubelet (the Kubernetes node controller and bootkube service using the systemd source plugin). It is worth noting that this plugin is separate from the Fluent Git repository and has been separately authored (details at https://github.com/fluent-plugin-systemd).
- The `Kubernetes.conf` file is the most interesting of the inclusions in the configuration. Like systemd, it also uses an external plugin, this time a filter called `kubernetes_metadata` (the details of which can be found at https://github.com/fabric8io/fluent-plugin-kubernetes_metadata_filter). The filter's job incorporates or excludes additional metadata into the log events. This is done by communicating with the Kubernetes API endpoint using the environment variables `FLUENT_FILTER_KUBERNETES_URL` or combining `KUBERNETES_SERVICE_HOST` and `KUBERNETES_SERVICE_PORT`. This requires metadata from the log events for essential context to retrieve information from the Kubernetes API. The info can be drawn from the journald if being used or possibly from the log file names. Some of the attributes used with the plugin either assume the default values or are hardwired into the container. The controls that can be configured map to the plugin attributes as follows:
  - `KUBERNETES_VERIFY_SSL`—`verify_ssl` sets a flag indicating whether the SSL/TLS certificates should be checked. If your environment has a certificate authority for the certificates used, we recommend this be set to yes.
  - `KUBERNETES_CA_FILE`—This attribute provides the path to the CA file for Kubernetes server certificate validation.
  - `FLUENT_KUBERNETES_METADATA_SKIP_LABELS`—Don't retrieve the labels from the metadata if set to `true`.
  - `FLUENT_KUBERNETES_METADATA_SKIP_CONTAINER_METADATA`—If set to `true`, then the metadata relating to the container image and `image_id` will not be included.
  - `FLUENT_KUBERNETES_METADATA_SKIP_MASTER_URL`—If `true`, the `master_url` metadata will not be included.
  - `FLUENT_KUBERNETES_METADATA_SKIP_NAMESPACE_METADATA`—If set to `true`, then the metadata such as `namespace_id` will be excluded.
  - `FLUENT_KUBERNETES_WATCH`—When set to `true`, it tells the plugin to watch for changes in the metadata held by the Kubernetes API server for the pods.

For a filter to do anything meaningful, the configuration needs to include sources. In this case, the tail source plugin is used multiple times to capture any logs generated in the folders `/var/log/containers/*.log`, `/var/log/salt/minion`, `/var/log/startupscript.log`, `/var/log/docker.log`, `/var/log/etcd.log`, `/var/log/`

`kubelet.log`, `/var/log/kube-apiserver.log`, `/var/log/kube-controller-manager.log`, `/var/log/kube-scheduler.log`, `/var/log/rescheduler.log`, `/var/log/glbc.log`, `/var/log/cluster-autoscaler.log`, and `/var/log/kubernetes/kube-apiserver-audit.log`. You may have recognized these as the log files for the core Kubernetes processes. Based on this, we should see log events picked up as long as our container's log events get written somewhere in the `/var/log/containers/` folder on the Kubernetes host.

Fluent Bit in Kubernetes

We have primarily focused on Fluentd with Docker and Kubernetes as the main way to provide a flexible means to capture log events. But in a containerized environment, Fluent Bit, with its smaller footprint, should be considered, especially if the goal is to push the log events out to a dedicated Fluentd node or log analytics platform like Elasticsearch and perform the "heavy lifting" with these parts of your solution. It is worth noting that Fluent Bit has its own projects within GitHub to provide a Docker base setup and to extend Docker images for different environments and operating systems, such as Debian, CentOS, Raspbian, and Amazon Linux. The Docker images support some possible targets and a Fluent Bit configuration deployed as a Daemon-Set in Kubernetes.

8.5 Getting a peek at host logs

Earlier in the chapter, we peeked at what our LogGenerator container could see of the environment and established that it couldn't see any part of the host, and therefore any logs. This is because we didn't configure the container to mount a file system. A folder mount wasn't necessary, as we trusted the container to capture `stdout` and put the content in a suitable location. However, when we demonstrated that behavior, we had control of Docker. Now Docker will be managed by Kubernetes. Additionally, we need to think about how we monitor Kubernetes itself. A review of the prebuild Fluentd resources points to the log content residing in `/var/log`. Minikube provides a convenient tool that allows easy access to the host environment. Once we can access the host, we can examine the environment to locate the relevant log files and understand what needs to be captured. Using a new shell (Windows or Linux), we can use the command

```
minikube ssh
```

This will provide us with a secure shell into the host environment. Let's look at the folders we've seen in the current configuration using the command

```
ls -al /var/log/containers
```

The result is perhaps not as expected, given this is a folder of symbolic links to files in `/var/log/pods`, as shown in figure 8.10. Fortunately, everyone can see the links.

```
16677d7bb789e275b64ee1036bbb110b6.log -> /var/log/pods/kube-system_etcd-minikube_4c89ad65c4ce4aee35196e
ff03377b3a/etcd/2.log
lrwxrwxrwx 1 root root    83 Apr  9 16:41 etcd-minikube_kube-system_etcd-75a85367304d725e1d1bb11de61f093
7bc162af5c1dd506318df1166d796f1dd.log -> /var/log/pods/kube-system_etcd-minikube_4c89ad65c4ce4aee35196e
ff03377b3a/etcd/1.log
lrwxrwxrwx 1 root root    90 Apr  9 16:41 fluentd-vf4nc_kube-system_fluentd-118ffb7a0c30eaa7a4bfd0eabd5d
d7e468a99705d5d428e535138917179c7dc7.log -> /var/log/pods/kube-system_fluentd-vf4nc_fd42679f-aa07-4382-
b527-0d352daa43c0/fluentd/1.log
lrwxrwxrwx 1 root root    90 Apr 10 19:40 fluentd-vf4nc_kube-system_fluentd-ccfaeebb3d37f9f530aa4c1b978b
61415dce61e86e63fd2e5f3732d26ac00380.log -> /var/log/pods/kube-system_fluentd-vf4nc_fd42679f-aa07-4382-
b527-0d352daa43c0/fluentd/2.log
lrwxrwxrwx 1 root root   103 Apr  9 16:41 kube-apiserver-minikube_kube-system_kube-apiserver-3502a1a39dd
f932abd9f665ea36bc295ae78b7304601d85e37f4ef0faf74a8b8.log -> /var/log/pods/kube-system_kube-apiserver-m
```

Figure 8.10   The result of looking at the /var/log/containers folder—you can see the files listed as symbolic links to another file in the pods folder

If we follow the links to /var/log/pods, we see that each link resolves to a folder that reflects instances of the pods, as shown in figure 8.11.

```
$ ls -al /var/log/pods
total 52
drwxr-xr-x 13 root root 4096 Apr  9 19:03 .
drwxr-xr-x  6 root root 4096 Apr  8 14:12 ..
drwxr-xr-x  3 root root 4096 Apr  9 19:02 default_log-simulator-585bdc6896-vc7r4_d3e89dea-5518-44fc-aca
5-7abfb7091792
drwxr-xr-x  3 root root 4096 Apr  8 14:11 kube-system_coredns-74ff55c5b-txclg_bd0ee68e-7b26-4d13-889e-a
f380a9a9cba
drwxr-xr-x  3 root root 4096 Apr  8 14:11 kube-system_etcd-minikube_4c89ad65c4ce4aee35196eff03377b3a
drwxr-xr-x  3 root root 4096 Apr  8 16:43 kube-system_fluentd-vf4nc_fd42679f-aa07-4382-b527-0d352daa43c
0
drwxr-xr-x  3 root root 4096 Apr  8 14:11 kube-system_kube-apiserver-minikube_5a74edc10eb4e10bc9a6ad0ec
11e9c49
```

Figure 8.11   The result of looking at the /var/log/pods folder, which turn out to be directories

Examining one of the pod folders, such as log-simulator, previously deployed into the default namespace (hence the default_ prefix), we see a folder with incrementing log file numbers and another layer of symbolic links, shown in figure 8.12.

```
-aca5-7abfb7091792/ods/default_log-simulator-585bdc6896-vc7r4_d3e89dea-5518-44fc-
total 12
drwxr-xr-x  3 root root 4096 Apr  9 19:02 .
drwxr-xr-x 13 root root 4096 Apr  9 19:03 ..
drwxr-xr-x  2 root root 4096 Apr 10 20:14 log-simulator
-aca5-7abfb7091792//log-simulatorg-simulator-585bdc6896-vc7r4_d3e89dea-5518-44fc-
total 16
drwxr-xr-x 2 root root 4096 Apr 10 20:19 .
drwxr-xr-x 3 root root 4096 Apr  9 19:02 ..
lrwxrwxrwx 1 root root  165 Apr 10 20:11 36.log -> /var/lib/docker/containers/f1790bd6a20cb34263f3f9f42bd2b3d3a068b9b2bb029e0
0bd6a20cb34263f3f9f42bd2b3d3a068b9b2bb029e0f4d0ec116c17f9405-json.log
lrwxrwxrwx 1 root root  165 Apr 10 20:19 37.log -> /var/lib/docker/containers/b93dfafd0728f0983e5766677bda73001d1ef1f0ea05109
fafd0728f0983e5766677bda73001d1ef1f0ea05109f0e73308df9c5d484-json.log
```

Figure 8.12   The content of one of the pod folders in /var/log/pods, which again are symbolic links to another part of the file system

Following the link into `/var/lib/docker/containers` yields a new challenge—the privileges are greatly restricted, and we need to use a `sudo` command to list the folder's contents, as shown in figure 8.13.

```
$ ls -al /var/lib/docker/containers
ls: cannot open directory '/var/lib/docker/containers': Permission denied
$ sudo ls -al /var/lib/docker/containers
total 176
drwx-----x 44 root root 4096 Apr 10 20:19 .
drwx--x--x 14 root root 4096 Apr 10 19:40 ..
drwx-----x  4 root root 4096 Apr 10 19:40 01cfd3f4d55ed4fe28428262fa193e613ec9e93d6dfef43a6cb5353934efde2c
drwx-----x  4 root root 4096 Apr 10 19:41 01fafb73792166060507c53a234427a280c2d46fb1158d97fa5da35071311376
drwx-----x  4 root root 4096 Apr 10 19:40 08797bc4828281bcc73a50039e7de0adb510d5a0dc721748cc1870a7fe63b203
drwx-----x  4 root root 4096 Apr 10 19:40 118ffb7a0c30eaa7a4bfd0eabd5dd7e468a99705d5d428e535138917179c7dc7
drwx-----x  4 root root 4096 Apr 10 19:40 2f11db651a1a7dcb5ef3bc5c781c3387f50edb8b63e1e3115101448ec220cd1b
drwx-----x  4 root root 4096 Apr 10 19:40 3502a1a39ddf932abd9f665ea36bc295ae78b7304601d85e37f4ef0faf74a8b8
drwx-----x  4 root root 4096 Apr 10 19:40 35f7ac6912b14c782d4488d680921676bbb8bc298433f404811b17f1589c1a43
drwx-----x  4 root root 4096 Apr 10 19:40 36ef0aff09c48b2e1c574b3e171a91d0c64e12c5739480bd2f3211a22580f166
drwx-----x  4 root root 4096 Apr 10 19:40 37ad8f8f12bf3a653807a28ea782dbc166d90e7ffaa25503a089d00b00d68125
```

Figure 8.13 The restricted contents of /var/lib/docker/containers can be seen here; note the very restrictive privileges.

If we look inside one of these folders, we find the log files shown in figure 8.14. But the last couple of steps have worked only with elevated permissions. It also helps us understand the different file paths being used in the predefined configuration. This means that in the YAML file, we need to ensure that the mounts work with appropriate permissions. It also confirms that the paths inside the containers are the same as the host.

```
d6dfef43a6cb5353934efde2ccker/containers/01cfd3f4d55ed4fe28428262fa193e613ec9e93d
total 396
drwx-----x  4 root root   4096 Apr 10 19:40 .
drwx-----x 43 root root   4096 Apr 10 20:23 ..
-rw-r-----  1 root root 370027 Apr 10 20:24 01cfd3f4d55ed4fe28428262fa193e613ec9e93d6dfef43a6cb5353934efde2c-json.log
drwx------  2 root root   4096 Apr 10 19:40 checkpoints
-rw-------  1 root root   6201 Apr 10 19:40 config.v2.json
-rw-r--r--  1 root root   2210 Apr 10 19:40 hostconfig.json
drwx-----x  2 root root   4096 Apr 10 19:40 mounts
```

Figure 8.14 Having overcome the restrictions, we can see the contents of /var/lib/docker/containers, which include a genuine log file rather than another symbolic link.

We should also note that minikube's log access security is very coarse-grained, and as a result, if you can see one log, you'll be able to access them all if you interact with the host. In a production context, this is not very desirable from a security perspective. The takeaway is if you're sensitive about logs in a containerized environment, control the visibility more directly using patterns such as the sidecar, as discussed in chapter 7. Taking more active control of your container's log events means you won't be subject to how access controls are managed in Kubernetes.

Navigating through the file system makes it clear that the way Kubernetes is configured is not trivial. This brings us back to the point that the more we can monitor at the container and application levels, the easier things will be.

8.6   Configuring a Kubernetes logging DaemonSet

Given the overview, it would be reasonable to assume that we can copy the configuration YAML to establish the Kubernetes DaemonSet for logging. We can leverage the existing Docker images provided by Fluentd in our configuration. The YAML configuration will need to give specific environment variable values and mount the right parts of the file system. If we wanted the DaemonSet to also apply some customized configuration, we would need to map additional configuration files into the system.

Rather than set a lot of environment values to control the current Fluentd configuration, we can look at how we can point Fluentd to an alternative configuration file and inject the modified configuration. This also gives us a chance to address content layout in a Docker file that can impact downstream applications.

8.6.1   Getting the Fluentd configuration ready to be used

With the customized Fluentd configuration, we could deploy this by modifying the Docker build. However, a more elegant way is to exploit the features of the Kubernetes configuration. This means if we wish to alter the configuration, we only need to redeploy a configuration change rather than changing the Docker image and the subsequent steps involved in redeploying it. This is made possible because the Fluentd Docker files work by configuring Fluentd through environment variables and suitably placed additional configuration files that can be picked up through the includes statements.

With our Fluentd configuration established, we need to get it ready to be consumed by the container. We'll do this using a Kubernetes ConfigMap, which we'll explain a bit more shortly. We need to start by deploying the ConfigMap into Kubernetes, ready to be referenced. The ConfigMap can be included in our core Kubernetes YAML file, or we can use the Fluentd file, translate it to a suitable format, and deploy the configuration separately. This latter approach is more desirable, as we can check the configuration using the Fluentd dry-run feature we saw in chapter 3 to validate the configuration before deploying. If the configuration is embedded in the larger configuration file, the validation step won't be possible.

The Fluentd ConfigMap is associated with the kube-system namespace to match the fact that the standard Fluentd DaemonSet is deployed into that namespace. The use of this namespace makes sense; in this case we're configuring and deploying a Kubernetes-wide service. Listing 8.3 shows the Fluentd configuration that we want to introduce. As you can see, it sources logs from the containers and pods and sends the log events to a configurable target. We also need to note the name of the ConfigMap (`fluentd-conf`), as this will be referenced in the YAML file. As with the LogSimulator deployment, we've bundled a batch and shell script, removing any previous configuration (`deploy-config.bat` and `.sh`).

To deploy the configuration file, we need to use the minikube command:

```
minikube kubectl -- create configmap fluentd-conf -from-file=Fluentd/
    custom.conf --namespace=kube-system
```

If you want to confirm the deployment, use the dashboard to view the configuration and select Config Maps (from the left-hand menu). Then, in the center part of the dashboard, you'll see all the ConfigMaps, including our `fluentd-conf`. The content of the ConfigMap can then be displayed by clicking on the name of our ConfigMap. You may see each line terminated with \r; this is the Linux encoding of a carriage return and won't present any issues when the file is processed.

Listing 8.3   Chapter8/Fluentd/custom.conf overriding configuration for Kubernetes

```
<system>
    Log_Level debug
</system>

<source>
  @type tail
  path /var/log/containers/*.log
  read_from_head true
  read_lines_limit 25
  tag deamonset
  path_key sourcePath
  emit_unmatched_lines true
  <parse>
    @type none
  </parse>
</source>

<source>
  @type tail
  path /var/log/pods/*/*.log
  read_from_head true
  read_lines_limit 25
  tag deamonset2
  path_key sourcePath
  emit_unmatched_lines true
  <parse>
    @type none
  </parse>
</source>

<source>

  @type tail
  path /var/lib/docker/containers/*.log
  read_from_head true
  read_lines_limit 25
  tag deamonset3
  path_key sourcePath
  emit_unmatched_lines true
  <parse>
    @type none
  </parse>
</source>

<match *>
    @type forward
    <buffer>
```

This source is part of the secured file system and needs the privileges set to allow Fluentd to read.

We've set a very short-lived buffer so we can see the events flowing through quickly; given our deployment, the networking overheads aren't an issue.

```
      buffer_type memory
      flush_interval 2s
    </buffer>
    <server>
      host "#{ENV['FLUENT_FOWARD_HOST']}"      ◁──┐  Allows the addressing of the
      port "#{ENV['FLUENT_FOWARD_PORT']}"         │  server to be driven through the
    </server>                                     │  Kubernetes configuration file
  </match>
```

PASSING CONTENT TO THE CONTAINER THROUGH KUBERNETES

Kubernetes provides a range of ways to share content into a container as a mount path. The number of options is such that *Kubernetes in Action* has several chapters dedicated to the subject. Essentially, the different techniques can impact whether the container can modify the file system, whether the storage has persisted beyond the container's life, and so on. A ConfigMap is immutable (read-only), which is ideal for our scenario. The contents of a ConfigMap can be consumed through environment variables, command-line values, and files, depending upon the options used. However, they are limited in size, so they may not be suitable if you wish to pass over a log file to be replayed.

When sharing files into Kubernetes-managed containers, we must be mindful that any content already in the folder (volume) of the container receiving the shared folder will effectively get overwritten with the shared content from Kubernetes. So, pushing new configurations into the container needs to be done carefully. For example, replacing just the `Kubernetes.conf` file in the standard Docker setup wouldn't be wise because it shares a common folder with all the configuration files. By adopting the approach used in the containers of putting the new configuration files into a different location and modifying the path to the configuration file Fluentd picks up via the environment variable, we protect ourselves from such issues. This means if we wanted, we could include the standard Kubernetes and Prometheus configurations and then replace them when necessary.

8.6.2   *Creating our Kubernetes deployment configuration*

Let's adapt and deploy that standard Fluentd repository DaemonSet for our minikube environment. To do that, we need to download the file locally, as we need to make a couple of tweaks. This can be done by using either a `wget` command on the raw view (http://mng.bz/OGpE) or by using the `git clone` command. My preference is `wget` (it's the easiest way to retrieve lots of things in Docker files, etc.), which looks like

```
wget https://raw.githubusercontent.com/fluent/fluentd-kubernetes-daemonset/
    master/fluentd-daemonset-forward.yaml
```

We need to then make the following additions and modifications:

1 Set the values for the location of our Fluentd node that we want to forward the log events to. This means we should replace the text `REMOTE_ENDPOINT` with the address or IP of the host machine (e.g., `192.168.1.2`). The value for the

FLUENT_FOWARD_PORT also needs to be changed from 18080 to 28080. This is to reflect the port being used in our Fluentd node configuration.

In a production setup, we would always recommend this be a DNS address. That way, any changes in the environment or scaling Fluentd with load balancing are masked from the configuration. This will require understanding how DNS is handled within Kubernetes, which is not a subject for this book.

2 Add the environment variable FLUENTD_SYSTEMD_CONF into the env section of the YAML, and set its value to "FALSE".

3 Override the FLUENTD_CONF environment variable in the same section so that it points to our custom.conf file we've supplied via the ConfigMap.

4 Add a securityContext section to the container's part of the YAML file with the privileged attribute set to true to overcome the previously identified permissions challenge.

5 Add the volumeMount entry for our ConfigMap so that the path is defined as expected. This means adding to the volumeMounts section an additional name called config-volume, a mountPath of /fluentd/etc/custom.

6 We then reference the volumes section as an additional entry with the name of config-volume (linking the volumes and VolumeMounts) with an attribute of configMap, which is then referenced by name, which we previously set up as fluentd-conf.

As we have tailored the existing configuration, you will still reference the Docker image defined by the Docker file at http://mng.bz/p2dz. The actual Docker image will come from Docker Hub at http://mng.bz/QWvG. The result of tailoring the Kubernetes YAML file can be seen in the following listing.

Listing 8.4   Chapter8/Kubernetes/fluentd-daemonset.yaml modified for our requirements

```yaml
apiVersion: apps/v1
kind: DaemonSet
metadata:
  name: fluentd
  namespace: kube-system
  labels:
    k8s-app: fluentd-logging
    version: v1
spec:
  selector:
    matchLabels:
      k8s-app: fluentd-logging
      version: v1
  template:
    metadata:
      labels:
        k8s-app: fluentd-logging
        version: v1
```

```
spec:
  tolerations:
  - key: node-role.kubernetes.io/master
    effect: NoSchedule
  containers:
  - name: fluentd
    image: fluent/fluentd-kubernetes-daemonset:v1-debian-forward    ⟵

    env:
      - name:  FLUENT_FOWARD_HOST    ⟵

        value: "192.168.1.2"
      - name:  FLUENT_FOWARD_PORT
        value: "28080"
      - name: FLUENTD_SYSTEMD_CONF
        value: "FALSE"
      - name: FLUENTD_CONF    ⟵
        value: "custom/custom.conf"
    resources:
      limits:
        memory: 200Mi
      requests:
        cpu: 100m
        memory: 200Mi
    volumeMounts:
    - name: varlog
      mountPath: /var/log
    - name: varlibdockercontainers
      mountPath: /var/lib/docker/containers
      readOnly: true
    - name: config-volume    ⟵

      mountPath: /fluentd/etc/custom/
    securityContext:    ⟵

      privileged: true
    terminationGracePeriodSeconds: 30
    volumes:
    - name: varlog
      hostPath:
        path: /var/log
    - name: varlibdockercontainers
      hostPath:
        path: /var/lib/docker/containers
    - name: config-volume    ⟵
      configMap:
        name: fluentd-conf
```

We continue to reference the prebuilt Fluentd Docker image setup for managing logging for Kubernetes.

The IP and port for the log events to be forwarded to, set by using environment variables

Overrides the location of the configuration file to be used when Fluentd starts up

Defines the mount location that the container will see. This path is then mapped to a file system outside of Kubernetes, giving us assurance the logs can be safely retained.

The additional security setting so that the container can access the restricted folders and files we saw when exploring the host server

Maps the volume to the ConfigMap that was loaded into Kubernetes earlier

8.6.3   *Putting the implementation of a Fluentd for Kubernetes into action*

Using the understanding gleaned from chapters 3 and 7 and exploiting the existing Fluentd configuration files for the DaemonSet (see http://mng.bz/XWZv), construct a simple single configuration file that tails any relevant files from the Kubernetes cluster. As the log events are collected, forward them to the Fluentd node previously used with the Docker log driver configuration.

ANSWER

A simple Fluentd configuration has been provided in the download pack as shown in listing 8.4, which we will utilize for the following steps. Still, there is nothing to stop you from substituting your configuration into the next steps.

8.6.4 *Deploying to minikube*

Before deploying the DaemonSet, we should start our local Fluentd instance ready to receive log events. This is the same step as we have done many times before with the command

```
fluentd -c Chapter8/Fluentd/forwardstdout.conf
```

The next step is to deploy to Kubernetes our DaemonSet:

```
minikube kubectl -- apply -f Kubernetes/fluentd-daemonset.yaml --
    namespace=kube-system
```

Again, we've made a batch and shell script in the download pack called `deploy -deamonset.bat` or `.sh`, which will remove any preexisting deployment and push the current configuration into Kubernetes. You can confirm the DaemonSet's deployment for the other assets using the dashboard by selecting the menu option for Daemon Sets (in the left-hand navigation menu under Workloads); this should list `fluentd`. Clicking on the title will show the details of the pod containing our container.

If Kubernetes has been in a steady idle state, then we may not see any logs immediately. We can address this by redeploying our LogSimulator configuration as we had did earlier in the chapter using the script `deploy-log-sim-k8`. This will quickly result in various events from Kubernetes being sent across, including the `stdout` log events from the LogSimulator container. We can see an example of the output in figure 8.15.

```
-simulator-acf166434dbb1c045374664ea4872311ab79c79a59aa54c69bb6b0a9ea48330e.log"}
2021-04-08 18:49:53.908887040 +0100 deamonset: {"message":"{\"log\":\"{\\\"source\\\":\\\"basicFile\
\\", \\\"event\\\":\\\"Entered what I ate today into my new fitness app and it just sent an ambulanc
e to my house\\\", \\\"cycle\\\":22}\\n\",\"stream\":\"stdout\",\"time\":\"2021-04-08T17:49:53.29695
8959Z\"}","sourcePath":"/var/log/containers/log-simulator-585bdc6896-rrcrm_default_log-simulator-acf
166434dbb1c045374664ea4872311ab79c79a59aa54c69bb6b0a9ea48330e.log"}
2021-04-08 18:49:53.908888040 +0100 deamonset: {"message":"{\"log\":\"{\\\"source\\\":\\\"basicFile\
\\", \\\"event\\\":\\\"The first time I got a universal remote control, I thought to myself This cha
nges everything\\\", \\\"cycle\\\":22}\\n\",\"stream\":\"stdout\",\"time\":\"2021-04-08T17:49:53.597
461201Z\"}","sourcePath":"/var/log/containers/log-simulator-585bdc6896-rrcrm_default_log-simulator-a
cf166434dbb1c045374664ea4872311ab79c79a59aa54c69bb6b0a9ea48330e.log"}
2021-04-08 18:49:53.908889540 +0100 deamonset: {"message":"{\"log\":\"{\\\"source\\\":\\\"basicFile\
\\", \\\"event\\\":\\\"Is your name Wi-Fi? Because Im feeling a connection\\\", \\\"cycle\\\":22}\\n
\",\"stream\":\"stdout\",\"time\":\"2021-04-08T17:49:53.897848344Z\"}","sourcePath":"/var/log/contai
ners/log-simulator-585bdc6896-rrcrm_default_log-simulator-acf166434dbb1c045374664ea4872311ab79c79a59
aa54c69bb6b0a9ea48330e.log"}
```

Figure 8.15 The received log events in our receiving Fluentd node

8.6.5   *Tidying up*

Having run Kubernetes and retrieved various Docker images and minikube assets, you'll reach a point where you want to clear or refresh the environment. One of the simple but excellent features is that minikube will completely wipe the environment with a single command to release resources because you've finished, or reset and start again if you want to validate everything again. This is done with the command

```
minikube delete
```

8.7   *Kubernetes configuration in action*

We have established a basic configuration that gives us a sight of the log events within a Kubernetes environment. However, the configuration isn't enterprise-ready. To get to enterprise readiness, we will need to improve the configuration. Your challenge is to identify the changes necessary and take the provided configurations and amend them as necessary.

8.7.1   *Answer*

The changes you have identified should include the following points:

- The tail source is not recording its tracking position in the file; thus, a restart could duplicate log events.
- The recorded `pos_file` needs to be mapped to a mount point so that if the pod is restarted, the position information is not lost.
- The tail configuration needs to address this issue of log rotation being managed.
- The additional Kubernetes metrics and Prometheus information should be available and controlled through the configuration.
- The Kubernetes core components (in the kube-system namespace) should have their logs tagged separately to hosted applications and the receiving end separating out the tags.
- Exploit the Kubernetes plugin to tag the log events with the additional metadata.
- Tune the caching in Fluentd to be more production-friendly and take into account the resources provided by Kubernetes.
- The log level should be moved from debug to info.

8.8   *More Kubernetes monitoring and logging to watch for*

We have addressed the core logging considerations for Kubernetes, but there are additional areas you should be aware of that may need further consideration. Kubernetes is continuing to evolve and be extended rapidly. As a result, some features may not be provided, as the deployment being run on is not the latest iteration, or if you're using a managed service, the service provider may have implemented certain features differently as the different capabilities are typically API-led. And, of course, you may wish to overlay Kubernetes with a mesh framework, like Istio or Linkerd, that will have its own logs. We believe the following areas are the most valuable areas to track with core Kubernetes.

8.8.1 *Node monitoring*

So far, we have focused on the core logs involved with our containers. But you may wish to also address the monitoring of the health of the underpinning of the Kubernetes node. There are various options around this, including using Fluentd or Fluent Bit on the native node and monitoring the server's raw statistics. However, this may not be allowed in some environments. Kubernetes also provides an additional DaemonSet for a service called the *Node Problem Detector*.

The node problem DaemonSet is an optional add-on for minikube, and some other prebuilt Kubernetes clusters provided by cloud vendors and others take this approach. As a result, the DaemonSet needs to be enabled. The Node Problem Detector monitors the kernel log file and reports on specific issues based on the configuration, which can be overridden with a ConfigMap, in the same manner as we have modified the Fluentd configuration. The detector includes an exporter element that sends the information to different endpoints, including the Kubernetes API server and the Stackdriver, which integrates to our Fluentd Daemon.

More information on this service can be found at https://github.com/kubernetes/node-problem-detector.

8.8.2 *Termination messages*

Within the configuration of a pod, it is possible to configure the recording of information relating to a pod's termination. So in the event of an abnormal termination, it is possible to perform a retrospective diagnosis. Within a container configuration, Kubernetes can be given a path to where the termination messages are in a container using the property `terminationMessagePath` (which is defaulted to `/dev/termination-log`). We need to verify that the Kubernetes configuration ensures the log event is directed to a location picked up by Fluentd or that Fluentd knows how to retrieve this information from Kubernetes. More information on this can be found at http://mng.bz/y4aB.

Summary

- The default Docker log driver works in such a way that trying to track its log files directly using standard Fluentd plugins isn't possible (e.g., use of compression).
- Fluentd can be used as a log driver for Docker, making accessing and using Docker log events a lot easier.
- Fluentd GitHub repository includes predefined DaemonSet configurations. Alternative Fluentd configurations are also made available in prebuilt images to

accommodate OS differences and the possibility of routing logs directly to services such as Elasticsearch.

- Kubernetes configurations such as minikube are complex, with levels of indirection through symbolic links making it difficult to determine which files are the real logs if we want to monitor.

- Using the power of Kubernetes's ConfigMaps, it is possible to tailor or extend the out-of-the-box Fluentd configuration. So, a prebuilt Fluentd Docker image will capture log events and send them to a different Fluentd node.

Creating custom plugins

This chapter covers

- Developing custom Fluentd plugins for Redis
- Using Fluentd utilities to speed up development
- Implementing the Fluentd plugin life cycle methods
- Testing and packaging custom Fluentd plugins
- Creating documentation for the custom plugins

At various points in the book, we have referred to Fluentd's support for the development of plugins beyond those from the core product. The extensibility of Fluentd has led to a robust ecosystem of third-party plugins to make it easy to capture, filter, manipulate, and send them to many different systems and data stores. We have also discussed how custom plugins could connect to and monitor esoteric and legacy solutions when things cannot easily or efficiently be achieved with the existing plugins.

In this chapter, we will walk through the process of creating an input and output plugin that makes use of Redis's list capability. We will take a closer look at Redis and the rationale behind its use.

Developing Ruby

This chapter does call for some development experience. Still, you do not need to be a hardcore Ruby developer to take the information shown here and put it into action. Like most languages, once you have had some development experience with one language, you can use that understanding to start coming to grips with others. I count myself in this category given that I've come through a career of programming with Ada, C, C++, and then Java for the last 15 or more years. We are not going to write another Ruby book; others have done an exceptional job of this already, such as David A. Black and Joseph Leo III with *The Well-Grounded Rubyist*, 3rd edition (Manning, 2017). I have tried to provide just enough detail for you to understand what we are doing with Ruby and the code without first learning the language. After all, it is our goal to help you understand what is happening with Fluentd. In appendix E, we have included links to resources to help you learn the basics of Ruby and to better understand the tools used, or you might want to make use of them if you take on the exercises.

9.1   *Plugin source code*

Code for the plugin developed here is included with the download of the book or retrievable from our GitHub repository (http://mng.bz/M20W). If you want to build upon what is provided, we encourage you to fork the GitHub repository and develop it as you wish; enhancement opportunities you might like to consider include

- Moving to use the RedisTimeSeries feature (more on this in a moment)
- Developing support for Fluentd's block size-based buffering
- Increasing security on the connection to Redis (e.g., using SSL/TLS connections and credentials, such as username and password)

Whatever approach you take, all we ask is for you to acknowledge this book as the starting point in the code.

9.2   *What is Redis, and why build a plugin with the Redis list capability?*

Redis is an open source, scalable, in-memory storage solution built around name-value pairs. The ability to define details such as time to live (TTL; this means that the time to hold the data is defined, after which it is automatically deleted) on data elements held, making for an exceptional caching tool. (In appendix E, we have provided plenty of supporting references for Redis in addition to those for Ruby.)

Aside from using Redis to help demonstrate plugin development, there are some potential real-world benefits of developing such a plugin:

- Rather than using a small, embedded, in-memory cache, we can use a highly resilient open source option that can be far more effective in scaling and replicating the cached data across multiple servers (for more insight into the use of caches, check out https://techterms.com/definition/cache).

- It provides an additional option for enabling Fluentd nodes to collaborate efficiently.
- It creates integrations with Redis lists, such as the Ruby Resque (Ruby queuing implementation; https://github.com/resque), providing opportunities to support or use additional services.
- It provides a means to keep events held in order, as Redis lists support the first in, first out (FIFO) pattern; this allows us to keep log events in sequence (i.e., in time series).

Caching solutions such as Redis operate by storing the data within memory data structures rather than long-term storage like a conventional database. The structures handle the data as key-value pairs. The internal structures can be very sophisticated to allow the cache to quickly locate the correct bit of memory. In addition to this, the data can be handled as a time series of events. The data held can also have a TTL before being automatically removed from the store.

9.2.1 Redis list over RedisTimeSeries

At the time of this writing, Redis Labs has developed the high-performance Redis-TimeSeries, which handles data in a time-series format made of two 64-bit structures representing the time and a value (more at https://oss.redislabs.com/redistime series). Using it presents some challenges:

- There is no support for a Windows native option, and we want to keep things as simple as possible without needing to work through the different approaches to Linux virtualization.
- The data structure used by RedisTimeSeries cannot hold the log events in 128 bits, which means that to use this structure, the value part must act as a "foreign key" to another data structure. Taking the example solution to an enterprise-class capability may make this worthwhile, but it adds complexity related to Redis, not Fluentd, and therefore won't be beneficial to this book.

Given these points, we will stick with the vanilla Redis features.

9.3 Illustrating our objective using Redis CLI

Before we start looking at any development activities, let's simulate the behavior we want to achieve with the plugins. Simulating the behavior will make it easier to relate the development activities back to the solution. To do this, we first need to install Redis, using the details provided in appendix A. Once Redis is installed, we will use its command-line interface (CLI) to simulate the effect of the plugins we will build.

The Redis server needs to be started in its own shell. This can be done with the command

```
redis-server
```

Once we see evidence of that process running (Redis reporting to the console), the next step is to start the Redis CLI with the command `redis-cli` in a new console window. We can recognize when the command has worked, as the command prompt will look like

```
redis 127.0.0.1:6379 >
```

We can confirm that we have a proper Redis server connection by entering the command info. This will result in a lot of settings information, including the Redis version displayed in the console. With one `redis-cli` running, we need to repeat the process in a separate shell to simulate the effect of two different processes interacting with the cache. For the rest of this section, we will refer to these as CLI 1 and CLI 2. As we go through the simulation, imagine CLI 1 is acting as a Fluentd output plugin and CLI 2 as a Fluentd input plugin. In CLI 1, we want to run the following list push (`lpush`) commands:

```
lpush fluentd '{"tag":"demo", "timestamp" : 1606076261, "record" : {"blah" :
    "blah 1"}}'
lpush fluentd '{"tag":"demo", "timestamp" : 1606076263, "record" : {"blah" :
    "blah 2"}}'
lpush fluentd '{"tag":"demo", "timestamp" : 1606076267, "record" : {"blah" :
    "blah 3"}}'
```

Each time the command is issued, you will get a response looking like (integer) 1. To start with, we will see this response changing as the list depth changes. We can use the list length (`llen`) command

```
llen fluentd
```

to find out how many entries in the list exist. The reference to `fluentd` in these commands is the name of the list we are using. Notice how we need to use single quotes at the beginning and end of the record so that we can use double quotes in the JSON. Now, in CLI 2, issue the list pop (`lpop`) command:

```
lpop fluentd
```

As a result, you will see the first entry provided in CLI 1 displayed on the CLI 2 console. Repeat the command `lpop fluentd`, and the response will include the second record added. Add more entries on CLI 1 and continue popping on CLI 2 until you see a nil response. This means the list has been emptied.

CLI 1 is effectively our output plugin behavior in our simulation, and CLI 2 is our source plugin behavior. This can help our Fluentd setup by smoothing out the spikes in the activity. Fluentd input and output nodes are transient in nature (as may be the case of a containerized environment). In that case, we have efficient in-memory storage of log events (holding events in memory will not suffer the same I/O performance impacts of storage to disk).

9.4   *Preparing for development*

Before we can start any development, some basic preparation is needed. You need to have

- Prepared an installation of Fluentd and Ruby, or continue using the existing installation that has been used with the previous chapters (if you would rather start fresh, then all the necessary steps are detailed in appendix A).

- Prepared a simple installation of Redis, if you have not already done this (details for this are in appendix A).
- Chosen an IDE (integrated development environment) that can support Ruby and installed the IDE and any relevant extensions needed (we will be using Visual Studio Code). As this tends to be a personal choice, we will leave the choice and installation up to you.
- Installed the Redis Gem to write Ruby code to talk with Redis (detailed in appendix A).
- Established a folder for implementing our plugin; this may align with the folder structure created when you retrieved all the book's support files.

    We do not want to accidentally pollute the use of Ruby and the catalog of gems with our development efforts. One way to achieve this is to allow our development code to be picked up by Fluentd when we start it rather than require it to be packaged as a gem and deployed to test code. There are also ways to comingle development code with the gems file system, which we would not recommend.

For the rest of this chapter, we will assume that path starts as `c:\myDev\GitHub |LoggingInAction\Chapter9`. Once these components are in place, then we are ready to start.

9.5 Plugin frameworks

As you have seen throughout the book, Fluentd works with a strong foundation of plugins of different types—input, output, filter, parser, and formatter. Fluentd needs to impose some common mechanisms, including naming conventions and folder structure, to make plugins work and tell the core of Fluentd about the different plugins installed. To help with this, Fluentd includes some tools to help make sure plugin development complies with the required conventions. Plugins have a class hierarchy with classes to build upon for each plugin type. Figure 9.1 illustrates this class hierarchy.

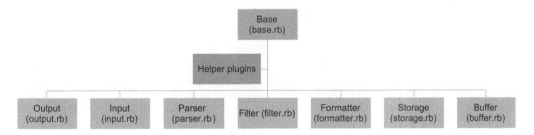

Figure 9.1 The foundation classes on which we can build our plugin, all of which are located within the lib/fluent/plugin folder of the source tree

9.5.1 Creating the skeleton plugin

Fluentd provides a tool for building the skeleton framework for our plugin. Before this is executed, you need to be in the correct location that you want to use for Fluentd development (e.g., the root folder for your own GitHub project), as it will use that folder as the starting point for all the artifacts. Once in the correct location, we can use the command `fluent-plugin-generate <plugin type> <plugin name>`. The plugin type represents the type of plugin (input, output, etc.) and the plugin's name. We are going to start with the output plugin. In our case, this makes the complete call:

```
fluent-plugin-generate output redislist
```

We have opted for the name `redislist`, as the plugin works specifically with Redis's lists capability. As with most data stores, there is already a general-purpose Redis plugin in existence (http://mng.bz/aDP7); you might want to build a plugin to monitor its health as well.

As a result of using the utility, we get a directory structure as illustrated in figure 9.2, which includes some skeleton configuration and code files. As we progress through this chapter, we will address each of the files.

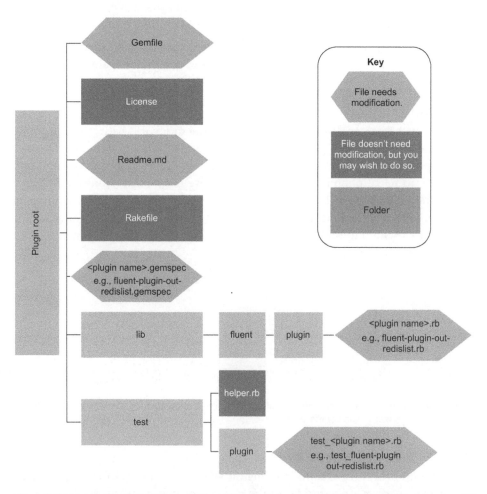

Figure 9.2   The directory structure and files generated when we run the fluent-plugin-generate utility. Colors indicate what needs to be modified to complete a plugin, as shown in the key.

The code we will develop for the plugin is shown in the `/lib/fluent/plugin` folder, as illustrated in figure 9.2, with the Ruby file based on the plugin name (e.g., `out_ redislist.rb`). The code we develop in the following few sections will go into this file.

9.5.2 *Plugin life cycle*

Plugins are taken through a life cycle, with each stage having a method that can be overridden if you need to implement the logic for that specific stage of a life cycle. As we will see during the development of our input and output plugins, we do not have to use every stage, but some are essential in nearly every case—for example, configure, start, and shut down. Each of these states also has a query function to determine whether that is the current state—for example, `after_shutdown?` Figure 9.3 illustrates the full life cycle that a plugin supports along with the goal of each stage.

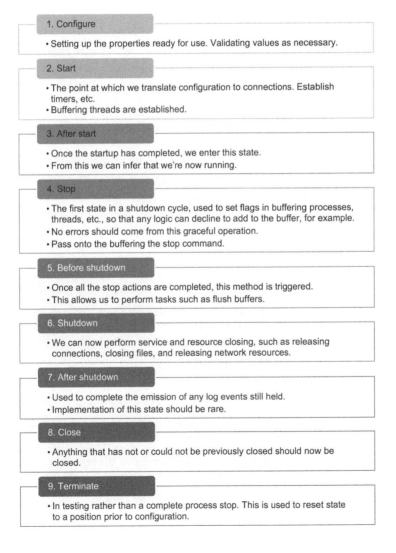

1. Configure
• Setting up the properties ready for use. Validating values as necessary.

2. Start
• The point at which we translate configuration to connections. Establish timers, etc.
• Buffering threads are established.

3. After start
• Once the startup has completed, we enter this state.
• From this we can infer that we're now running.

4. Stop
• The first state in a shutdown cycle, used to set flags in buffering processes, threads, etc., so that any logic can decline to add to the buffer, for example.
• No errors should come from this graceful operation.
• Pass onto the buffering the stop command.

5. Before shutdown
• Once all the stop actions are completed, this method is triggered.
• This allows us to perform tasks such as flush buffers.

6. Shutdown
• We can now perform service and resource closing, such as releasing connections, closing files, and releasing network resources.

7. After shutdown
• Used to complete the emission of any log events still held.
• Implementation of this state should be rare.

8. Close
• Anything that has not or could not be previously closed should now be closed.

9. Terminate
• In testing rather than a complete process stop. This is used to reset state to a position prior to configuration.

Figure 9.3 Plugins go through this life cycle with methods provided in the skeleton to be overloaded and implement specific logic needed at each life cycle stage. Not all states have to be overloaded.

9.6   *Implementing the plugin core*

We've generated the skeleton and taken a moment to look at the life cycle stages; now the plugin can inject any specific behavior required. We can now get down to writing the plugin code that processes the configuration and executes the handling of log events, and we'll cover connecting and disconnecting with Redis.

9.6.1   *How configuration attributes work*

With the plugin structured, the first step is to define the configuration attributes the it will use. This is achieved by using the `config_param` object, which takes the values for

- The attribute name as it would be used in the configuration file.
- The attribute's data type, which could be any of string, integer.
- The default value, if one can be specified.
- Whether the value should be kept secret when Fluentd performs a dry run or the startup output of its configuration. By default, this is false and therefore not needed. But to illustrate the behavior, we have included its use.
- The ability to define an alias for the attribute name. Aliasing can be helpful when a plugin changes over time.

We need to capture a port number, host address (a DNS name or IP), and the list's name held by Redis. To do this, we need to define several configuration attributes to be specified in the configuration file. The code is a sequence of `desc` and `config_param` statements, with the `desc` providing the description of the following `config_param` appearing in the code. We know the data types and potential default values mean we should exploit the available attributes to simplify data validation. This will also make the user's experience as simple as possible. As a result, we should end up with code as illustrated in the following listing.

Listing 9.1   Chapter9/fluent-plugin-out-redislist/lib/fluent/out_redislist.rb

> Providing the desc entry before each config_param means that tools can be used to generate the documentation for the plugin configuration, as well as provide documentation internally.

```
desc "specifies the port to connect to Redis with, will
➥ default to 6379 if not specified"            ◁─────────────

config_param :port, :integer, default: 6379, secret: false, alias:
➥ :portNo    ◁─┐
```

> This is an example of setting an integer configuration value and defaulting the value. We can also indicate to Fluentd when it generates the summary of the configuration at startup and outputs it; we can tell Fluentd with the secret parameter whether the value should be included. We have also told Fluentd that if it receives portNo as a configuration value, then use it as the port number source.

```
desc "Defines the host address for Redis, if not defined
➥ 127.0.0.1"
```

```
config_param :hostaddr, :string, default: "127.0.0.1",
➥ secret: false                                        ◄──────
```
As with the previous example, we are setting a default value. This time we are providing a string.

```
desc "Defines the name of the list to be used in Redis, by
➥ default this is Fluentd"
config_param :listname, :string, default: "fluentd"

desc "Defines the number of reconnection attempts before giving
➥ up on connecting to the Redis server."
config_param :reconnect_attempts, :integer, default: 2

desc "Defines the number of seconds before timing out a connection
➥ to the Redis server"
config_param :connection_timeout, :integer, default: 5

desc "Defines the number of log events in a chunk"
config_param :chunksize, :integer, default: 20
```

Once defined, we can refer to the values as class-level elements and use the Ruby @ notation (e.g., @port) within the rest of the code.

We should also hold the Redis connection as a class member, so we do not need to re-create the connection every time we interact with Redis. With the configuration details, we could also try to create the Redis connection now. Still, by the life cycle definitions, that would be incorrect, and if another plugin configuration failed, Fluentd might choose not to start our plugin. As a result, we would be consuming unnecessary resources, such as the network connection. But we need the Redis dependency incorporated into the code with require "redis" declaration at the top of the file.

> **NOTE** When it comes to coding style, I create the steps needed in the plugin as small functions. This may appear inefficient, but the optimizers in compilers, interpreters, and language virtual machines can usually optimize out these overheads. This approach does make for easier testing, and each step is easier to examine in isolation.

The framework provides a configure function, as seen in the life cycle (see figure 9.3). This gives us the chance to implement any additional custom validation needed. We can also use this method to define our own class-level variables. To illustrate this capability, we will implement code to check if the network port defined is the default Redis port. If it isn't the default port, log a warning message to remind developers that they need to ensure ports are deconflicted. This code is in the following listing, with both our check function and the implementation of the configure function, which uses any inherited behavior.

Listing 9.2 Chapter9/fluent-plugin-out-redislist/lib/fluent/out_redislist.rb

```
def check_port(conf)
log.trace "checkport invoked"
  port = conf['port']      ◄──┐
```
Retrieves the configuration value from the list of configuration attributes using the defined name

```
    if (port != RedislistOutput::DefaultPort)
    log.info ("Default Redis port in use")
    else
    log.warn ("Non standard Redis port in use - ensure ports are deconflicted")
    end
end

def configure(conf)

super
  checkPort (conf
end
```

We defined a constant in the class for the default port.

This is the method that is invoked as part of the plugin life cycle and triggers our check_port method.

Makes sure any inherited logic is executed first

Invokes our method, passing all the configuration data over

9.6.2 *Starting up and shutting down*

After the configuration, the most critical functions in the life cycle will be the start and shutdown functions for most plugins. These are the ideal moments to create or close connections, such as those to Redis. Since establishing connections to storage solutions is often relatively slow, we want to perform the task before actively communicating with the remote solution. Redis allows us to define time-outs on the connections and how many reconnection attempts we can have. We'll set these up as configuration values, but for now, let's hardwire them. If the connection fails to be established, we should make it easy to recognize during the plugin life cycle. We can do this by setting the connector to `nil` and logging the issue.

We need to incorporate the start and shutdown functions shown in the following listing into our plugin and our supporting functions to ensure that the required behavior is achieved.

Listing 9.3   Chapter9/fluent-plugin-out-redislist/lib/fluent/plugin/out_redislist.rb

Establishing the Redis connection, informing the connection parameters from values retrieved from the configuration properties and defined constants

```
def connect_redis()
  log.trace "connect_redis - Create connection if non existant"
  if !@redis
    begin
      @redis=Redis.new(host:@hostaddr,port:@port,connect_timeout:@connection_
      ↪ timeout,reconnect_attempts:@reconnect_attempts)
      log.debug "Connected to Redis "+@redis.connected?.to_s
    rescue Redis::BaseConnectionError, Redis::CannotConnectError => conn_err
      log.error "Connection error - ", conn_err.message, "\n connection
      ↪ timeout=", @connection_timeout, "\n connection attempts=",
      ↪ @reconnect_attempts
      @redis = nil
      return nil
    rescue => err
      log.error "Error connecting to redis - ", err.message,
      ↪ "|",err.class.to_s
      ↪ @redis = nil
      return nil
```

Handles Redis connection errors separately from the general catchall, as we can guide the user more effectively for these kinds of issues

```
      end
    end
  end

  def start
    super
    log.trace "starting redis plugin\n"
    connect_redis()

  end

  def shutdown
    super
    log.trace "shutdown"
    if @redis
      begin
        @redis.disconnect!
        log.debug "disconnecting from redis\n"
        @redis = nil
      rescue
        log.error "Error closing Redis connection"
      end
    end
  end
```

Establishes a connection to Redis as part of the startup once all the inherited activities are completed

Ensures any inherited tasks are completed

If we still have a Redis connection, then start the disconnection process.

9.6.3 *Getting the plugin to work with our Fluentd installation*

With enough code to prove we can get our plugin to at least start and stop, we can run a simple test with the full Fluentd. The Fluentd tooling includes extensions to help with unit testing, but it is always rewarding to see code firing up as part of something bigger, particularly when the startup is quick. To do this, we need to ensure Fluentd can pick up our plugin code.

We need a test configuration to be able to run Fluentd. We have prepared one for this job, and it can be retrieved from `Chapter9/Fluentd/dummy-plugin.conf`. Of course, you might like to choose to develop your own configuration, given everything you've learned in the book.

We have repeated using the dummy source Fluentd plugin to generate log events, as the content is not essential. The crucial element is the match configuration, as illustrated in the following listing.

Listing 9.4 Chapter9/Fluentd/dummy_plugin.conf

```
<match *>
  @type redislist
    portno 6379

  #<buffer>

  #  flush_interval 120
  #</buffer>
</match>
```

This is the declaration to use our plugin.

As we build upon the base class provided, the in-memory helper plugin is available if the use of the buffer attribute is defined. For now, we have the buffer configuration commented out.

Before starting Fluentd, we need to start the Redis server as we did earlier in the chapter. Eventually, we will want to package and deploy our plugin just like any other Fluentd plugin using the gem tools. But to start with, we do not want to go through the additional effort of deploying and undeploying a gem every time we make a change. To avoid the gem deployment issue, we can add parameters to the command line telling Fluentd to pick up the source code of our plugin from a Ruby file. For example, my copy of the plugin directory structure starts at

```
c:\myDev\GitHub|UnifiedLoggingWithFluentd\Chapter9\
➥ fluent-plugin-out-redislist
```

Then the extended Fluentd command will look as follows:

```
fluentd -c Chapter9\Fluentd\dummy-plugin-out.conf -p
➥ c:\myDev\GitHub|UnifiedLoggingWithFluentd\Chapter9\fluent-plugin-out-
➥ redislist\lib\fluent\plugin  -vv
```

Going forward, we will show the path as `<plugin absolute path>\Chapter9\ fluent-plugin-out-redislist\lib\fluent\plugin`, where you need to substitute `<plugin absolute path>` accordingly.

Combining the configuration file and extending the path to collect our plugin mean our command to start Fluentd will result in Fluentd displaying the configuration as it starts up. With the Redis server running at the command line, it will be possible to see Redis logging the number of connections it has as we start and stop Fluentd.

9.6.4   *Putting additional configuration validation into action*

Your objective is to restart the Redis server on a different port and create an alternative Fluentd configuration to connect to Redis on a different port. You need to confirm that our configuration check is performing correctly. To restart Redis on a different port, add `--port nnnn`, where nnnn represents the port number to use with the startup command.

ANSWER

The modified configuration file solution can be found at `Chapter9\Exercise-Results\dummy-plugin-Answer.conf`, where we have changed the port from 6379 to 16379. We also modified the log message generated by the dummy output plugin, although we will not see that yet.

When the Redis server is started, we need to add `--port 16379` to override the default. Our Fluentd startup command now becomes

```
fluentd -c Chapter9\ExerciseResults\Fluentd\dummy-plugin-Answer.conf -p
➥ <plugin absolute path>\Chapter9\
➥ fluent-plugin-out-redislist\lib\fluent\plugin
```

When Fluentd starts up, we should see the warning in the log output from Fluentd about using a nonstandard port. But the Redis server should report the connection.

9.6.5   *Implementing the Redis output logic*

Having proven we can configure, start up, and shut down the plugin, we can move to the next step of implementing the logic of sending the events to Redis. There are several ways the logic can be executed:

- *Synchronous*—Process each event by implementing the method `def process (tag, es)`. This is the most straightforward approach and the least performant for execution, as it does not use any buffering.
- *Synchronous buffered*—Output is implemented by the method `def write (chunk)`.
- *Asynchronous buffered*—Output is implemented by the method `def try_write (chunk)`.

Which implementation method is used is dictated by whether the configuration includes a `<buffer>` section or not, unless we configure some override to the standard behavior. For the first implementation, we will keep it nice and straightforward with the synchronous model.

Our implementation process needs to tag the event stream passed as `(es)` and iterate through the events. As the stream could contain multiple events, we can make the process a little more efficient by telling Redis to batch up executing the insertion of the events. This is done by telling Redis it will receive multiple transaction calls using the command `redis.multi`. Once we have iterated through the events, tell Redis it can execute the transactions using the call `redis.exec`. As we iterate through the log events, we need to perform the following actions:

- Build a JSON representation of the log event(s). If you have reviewed the output interface, you will note that there is a predefined formatter function. We have chosen not to override or use this, as we do not want to impact other applications of this method within the plugin's base classes; we can therefore format the presentation in any desired manner—for example, using msgpack.
- Perform a Redis list push function.

We should be defensive in our code to handle the scenario of losing the Redis connection before all the events have been committed to Redis.

We need to transform the log event to JSON for potentially three different functions; we should write the logic once and invoke it from the different plugin methods involved. The result of this is two methods, as shown in the following listing.

Listing 9.5   Chapter9/fluent-plugin-out-redislist/lib/fluent/pluginout_redislist.rb

This is our function that translates the log event into a JSON representation. We need to build our own JSON representation, as we need to capture all the log event attributes.

```
def redisFormat(tag,time,record)

  redis_entry = Hash.new
  redis_entry.store(RedislistOutput::TagAttributeLabel,
  ➥ tag.to_s)
```

By using predefined constants, these could be shared with the input plugin.

```
redis_entry.store(RedislistOutput::TimeAttributeLabel,
⇒ time.to_i)
redis_entry.store(RedislistOutput::RecordAttributeLabel,
⇒ record.to_s)
redis_out = JSON.generate(redis_entry)    ◁──┐

return redis_out
end
```

As the record, event time, and tag represent a flat structure, we can build a simple hash structure and then exploit the prebuilt operations to convert it to JSON. Note we don't use the formatter method, as this is used by other parts of Fluentd, such as the buffer, and we don't wish to confuse that logic with a variant representation.

```
def write(chunk)    ◁──┐  This is one of the
  log.trace "write:", chunk   standard functions used
                              by an output plugin.

  @redis.multi    ◁──┐  This tells Redis to accept multiple statements
  chunk.each do |time, record|   that should be executed in a single operation.
    log.debug "write sync redis push ", chunk.metadata.tag,
    ⇒ time, record, @listname @redis.lpush(@listname,redisFormat
    ⇒ (chunk.metadata.tag, time, record))
  end
  @redis.exec    ◁──┐  This releases the Redis library to send all the
end               statements to the Redis server as a single block.
```

9.6.6 *Putting the testing of synchronous output into action*

We have reached a state where we can confirm that we can write to Redis. Using the previously illustrated approach, restart Fluentd and use the illustrated Redis commands to review the list in Redis and pop entries in the list.

ANSWER

In repeating the Fluentd test, with the write method now in place, you should expect the Redis commands to show the list structure to grow with JSON content, looking something like this:

```
{"tag" : "dummy", "time" : "2014-12-14 23:23:38", "record" :
⇒ {"hello" : "world", "counter":1}}
```

The log events as they are generated will increment the counter value due to the source configuration. This will mean there should be a correlation between the counter attribute values and the Redis list length. This can be confirmed with the llen command in the Redis CLI. You will also be able to pop the entries from the list using the command lpop fluentd, as the configuration will allow the default list name to be used.

9.7 *Implementing the Redis input plugin*

Before implementing one of the other write methods, let's complete the circuit with the input plugin. We can use the same utilities that generated the output plugin to generate the skeleton folders and files for the input side. Everything is the same as before rerunning the utility, except that we specify the plugin as input, not output. This will result in the generated code extending a different base class (as we saw in figure 9.2); thus, we need to implement some different functions.

For Redis, the input plugin is effectively a polling activity, as most solutions don't support callbacks or webhooks (it is worth noting that Redis does have a webhook concept). This means we will need a configuration value as to how quickly the plugin needs to poll Redis. As with the output plugin, we will need the information necessary to connect to Redis. For this latter task, we can copy the code written for the output plugin. While this does not support the excellent coding principles of DRY (don't repeat yourself), there are plenty of opportunities to improve our code later.

Although we have some additional values to consider, the input plugin processes the configuration attributes just as the output plugin does. The two key functions that need to be implemented on the input plugin are to handle the `run` command and the `emit` function (as shown in listing 9.6). The run method will be responsible for starting our scheduling thread. The emit function handles calling Redis and emitting the log events to the next process in Fluentd defined by the configuration file.

As a source plugin, the framework will set the tag and timestamp values on the event to reflect the current time and the tag default behavior. Do these values make sense, as they do not truly reflect when the original event occurred? To address this, we are providing the means to determine whether the original tag and time are added to the event record or should be used in the core log event. It is probably best if we allow the person configuring the plugin to determine what should be replaced. If the values should be inserted into the log event, we must determine what attribute names to use. We can address this using the same mechanism for capturing plugin configuration attributes already used.

Listing 9.6 Chapter9/fluent-plugin-redislist/lib/fluent/plugin/in_redislist.rb

```
def emit
  log.trace "emit triggered"                    Determines whether a new
  if !@redis                                     connection is required
    log.debug "reconnecting Redis ",@hostaddr,":",@port
    connect_redis()
  end                                        Sets the loop controller up so we keep
                                             calling Fluentd until a shutdown process
  if @redis                                  changes the status of this flag
    keep_popping = true

    while keep_popping        Redis allows us to treat a list as first in, first out (FIFO) or last
      if (@fifo)              in, first out (LIFO). So we can use this configuration to control
        popped = @redis.rpop(@listname)   whether we want to operate the list in a FIFO or LIFO manner.
      else
        popped = @redis.lpop(@listname)
      end

      log.debug "Popped",@listname, ": ", popped
      if popped
        data = JSON.parse(popped)

        if (@use_original_time)
          time = data[TimeAttributeLabel]
```

```
      else
        time = Fluent::EventTime.now
      end

      if (@use_original_tag)
        tag = data[RedislistInput::TagAttributeLabel]
      else
        tag = @tag
      end

      data_record = data.fetch(RecordAttributeLabel).to_s
      log.debug "original data record=>",data_record

      if (@add_original_time && !(data_record.include?
➥       '"'+@add_original_time_name+'"'))
        data_record= inject_original_value(data,data_record,
➥         RedislistInput::TimeAttributeLabel,@add_original_time_name)  ◁
      end

      if @add_original_tag &&
➥       !(data_record.include? '"'+@add_original_tag_name+'"')
        data_record = inject_original_value(data,data_record,
➥         RedislistInput::TagAttributeLabel,@add_original_tag_name)
      end

      log.debug "Emitting -->", tag," ", time, " ", data_record
      router.emit(tag, time, data_record)   ◁
    else
        keep_popping = false
    end
    end
  else
    log.warn "No Redis - ", @redis
  end
end

def run
  log.trace ("run triggered")
  while thread_current_running?   ◁
    current_time = Time.now.to_i

  emit() if thread_current_running?
  while thread_current_running? && Time.now.to_i <= current_time
    sleep @run_interval   ◁
  end
  end
end
```

Determine whether the tag and date-time values should replace the new log event or simply be incorporated in their log event record.

This is when we tell Fluentd to pass the log event onto the next step of the process based on the configuration definition.

The thread handling for the run method, and for as long as the thread is allowed to run

Once we've decided the thread has legitimately been woken since the last cycle, we can use emit to send all the log events.

9.7.1 Testing input and output plugin execution

With our input plugin implemented, we can perform a simple test. We could easily incorporate both the input and output plugins into our single configuration (see

`Chapter9/fluentd/dummy-plugin.conf`); the problem would be that the log information for input and output would intermingle. We would need to extend the plugin path parameter to include both plugins, like this:

```
fluentd -c Chapter9\fluentd\dummy-plugin.conf -p <plugin absolute
➥ path>\Chapter9\fluent-plugin-out-redislist\lib\fluent\plugin -p <plugin
➥ absolute path>\Chapter9\fluent-plugin-redislist\lib\fluent\plugin
```

Alternatively, we can start two instances of Fluentd with each using their own configuration, so each process has one input. This will make seeing what is happening a lot easier. To do this, repeat the steps previously used to see the output plugin at work. Then, in another console window, we can adapt the command to reference our input plugin path and the `Chapter9\Fluentd\dummy-plugin-in.conf` that we have prepared already. The result should look like this:

```
fluentd -c Chapter9\Fluentd\dummy-plugin-in.conf -p <plugin absolute
➥ path>\Chapter9\fluent-plugin-redislist\lib\fluent\plugin
```

With everything running, you should see in one console messages showing the log events being added. Another shows them being removed and the Redis console displaying the two interactions of adding and removing from the list.

With the ability to write and consume log events with a Redis list now in place, let us go back to the write logic and extend the implementation with alternate ways of the output logic working, such as by using the buffer.

9.8 *Extending output with buffering*

As we saw in chapter 4, if the plugin supports a buffer, the I/O process can be optimized. We have already done some performance optimization by configuring the synchronous process to bunch the Redis push operations together, so the Redis connector executes them all at once if we receive more than one log event. But we can further accelerate the process by using the buffer to process larger groups into a single transaction in Redis.

As we saw in chapter 4, out of the box, there are two types of buffers for Fluentd using either a temporary file or memory. Supporting a file implementation does not make sense when our target is an in-memory solution that provides better performance than using physical storage such as disks. This means our solution should only allow the use of the memory buffer.

In figure 9.4, we can see how the log event passes through the different paths of the base Fluentd output class and the functions that need to be implemented, depending on whether buffering is used and whether buffering is synchronous or asynchronous in nature.

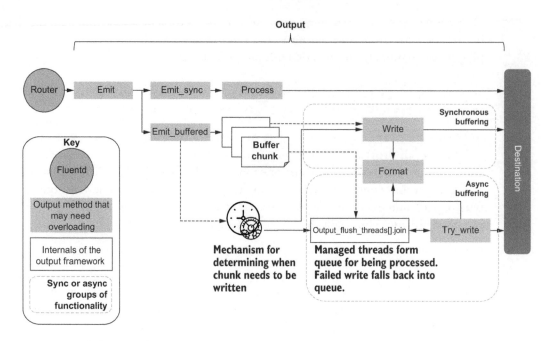

Figure 9.4   The different methods involved in outputting log events from an output plugin depending on the use and type of buffering

As shown in figure 9.4, to keep things simple, we will implement the synchronous buffered path to start with once we have plugins for input and output; then we will revisit to extend the plugin for the buffered use case.

The asynchronous path is largely the same as the synchronous path regarding how we interact with Fluentd. But we have to manage the additional logic that makes the behavior asynchronous and uses the buffer chunk data structures. With the buffering, we could offer either or both approaches to handling the buffer chunks. The options include the following:

- *Each chunk is controlled by the number of log events it can contain.* This is a simple mechanism and very efficient and predictable when log events are consistent in size. But if log events are variable in size, you can exhaust the available memory before filling a chunk.
- *Each chunk is controlled by allocating the same amount of memory.* With the size model, we have the responsibility to implement the logic around calculating the size of the log event, determining if the log event can fit into the current chunk or needs to be put into another chunk. Also, we must decide what to do if the log event is larger than the chunk size limit.

  The benefit of this model is that if log events are variable in size, we don't risk memory exhaustion scenarios, as we've capped the number of resources that will be used. The additional code complexity here is not about how

Fluentd plugins are written and more about understanding Ruby and how it works with data structures.

In the spirit of "keep it simple stupid" (KISS) and focusing on Fluentd, we will illustrate the number of log events per chunk model. The responsibility of understanding the log events and avoiding the risk of memory exhaustion is on the user. With our approach worked out, we should make it easy for the user by defaulting some of the buffer settings as we would like to have them. As a result, we can incorporate with the configurations the following code fragment:

```
config_section :buffer do
  config_set_default :@type, 'memory'
  config_set_default :chunk_keys, ["tag"]
  config_set_default :chunk_limit_records, @chunksize
end
```

As you can see, we have defined a chunk size configuration attribute, which has itself defaulted. As a result, we will default to the buffering approach without any configuration values unless explicitly overridden. We should also extend the `configure` function to consider the possibility of being supplied with configuration values that we do not recommend or are not supporting, as they are intended for the chunk size model of buffering.

The next step is implementing the write function, which takes a buffer chunk once complete and passes the chunk building up the Redis push calls. We can leverage the previous logic to generate the representation we want to use in Redis. Just as with the synchronous bufferless path, we want to brace the looping through the chunk with the instruction to the Redis connector to batch up all the Redis commands to execute in one go using the `redis.multi` and `redis.exec` functions. The new write method is shown in the following listing.

Listing 9.7   Chapter9/fluent-plugin-out-redislist/lib/fluent/out_redislist.rb

The function is called from the base class logic. We have implemented our own version. Unlike functions like configure, calling super would trigger a not-implemented exception.

```
def write(chunk)
  log.trace "write:", chunk

  @redis.multi
  chunk.each do |time, record|
    log.debug "write sync redis push ", chunk.metadata.tag, time,
      record, @listname
    @redis.lpush(@listname,redisFormat(chunk.metadata.tag,time,record))
  end
  @redis.exec
end
```

Instructs the Redis connector to group all the Redis statements that follow

As before, we need to take the log event, time, and tag to build a representation to be used in Redis.

Handles Redis connection errors separately from the general catchall, as we can guide the user more effectively for these kinds of issues

The chunk has a different structure to the stream structure provided in the unbatched path, so we need a different loop. This will iterate over each chunk entry.

We can rerun our test with a slightly different configuration to ensure we use the buffering behavior with this method introduced. This can be done with the following command:

```
fluentd -c Chapter9\Fluentd\dummy-plugin.conf -p <plugin absolute
➥ path>Chapter9\fluent-plugin-out-redislist\lib\fluent\plugin  -vv
```

With the test configuration provided, we should see the write method trace statements occurring periodically. The internal tracing writes log events to stdout in short bursts as the write function logs the details as it calls the Redis connector.

9.8.1   *Improving our scenario by putting maintainability into action*

Our proof-of-concept level implementation of the Redis list plugin has shown how we can deliver a new plugin. In the process of development, there is some commonality between the input and output code. As a result, we have received the go-ahead to make some improvements. Therefore, the first goal is to refactor the input and output to use a common base class.

9.9   *Unit testing*

The testing we have done so far is a manual process that we all know is not the best. In the real world, we would lead with unit testing and build up from there. Ideally, changes in the code should trigger a continuous integration and continuous delivery process, automatically running the unit tests and end-to-end testing.

We will not go into depth here, as unit testing is primarily an aspect of Ruby development, rather than Fluentd. The Fluentd team has built some support libraries that can be used with any major unit test frameworks, including *test-unit* (https://test-unit.github.io/), *RSpec* (https://rspec.info/), and *minitest.* Our example utilizes test-unit, as it is a well-adopted framework and feels like many other major unit test frameworks, such as *NUnit, JUnit,* and so on.

When we used the utility for generating the plugin skeleton and generated the main Ruby code, the tool also generated a folder structure test in the base plugin folder. This includes providing a skeleton class to help us get started. The test class has the same name as the plugin but with a prefix of test_. This is a small piece of helper code (helper.rb) in the base of the test path. This loads the framework's helper code into the test-unit tool.

To illustrate the possibilities, we have built a couple of tests for the output plugin, as illustrated in listing 9.8. These tests focus on validating the configuration-related logic that drives the behavior of our plugins. This is achieved using part of the Fluentd test framework that implements different types of drivers. The type of driver needed is dictated by the plugin type and mimics the core of Fluentd. We can trigger the necessary operations using the driver, including feeding in log events to the plugin. The driver also provides the means to retrieve and evaluate the results, such as how many times events have been through specific stages (e.g., emit, write). The evaluation can be done using the driver to access and examine the processed events, such as the output of the synchronous and asynchronous write operations, and to simply know how many events have been handled.

The driver capability can be extended to handle the impact of scheduled activities, such as events accumulating in a buffer. The test utilities can also capture standard out and process the text. Capturing such output allows you to verify that the processing of log events is being generated as expected. In our test for advanced config, we apply this technique. If log events are not going to `stdout`, but to a log file for Fluentd, it can also be interrogated, looking for how much log information is generated and whether specific log events have occurred.

Listing 9.8   Chapter9/fluent-plugin-out-redislist/test/plugin/test_out_redislist.rb

```
test 'advanced config' do                          ←─────┐ Declares the
    conf = %[           ←──┐ Creates a set of             │ unit test
    host 127.0.0.1         │ configuration values
    port 24229             │ to be passed
    ]
                                                   ┌─ Defines a variable to capture any
                                                   │  stdout generated within the
    captured_string = capture_stdout do    ←───────┘  following statement block
      d = create_driver(conf)
      assert_equal 24229, d.instance.port          ←──┐ Tests the values set in
      assert_equal '127.0.0.1', d.instance.hostaddr   │ the plugin for the port
    end

    assert_true (captured_string.include? "Non standard Redis port in use")   ←──┐

    d.shutdown    ←──┐ Shuts down                      Evaluates whether the
  end                │ everything cleanly              warning about no standard
                                                       port has been produced
```

(annotation left of `d = create_driver(conf)`) **Creates the driver using the test config provided**

To execute the unit tests, we simply need to follow the unit test framework's guidance. In the case of test-unit, that comes down to using Ruby to execute the unit test file. For example:

```
ruby Chapter9/fluent-plugin-out-redislist/test/plugin/test_out_redislist.rb
```

9.10   *Putting the development of unit tests into action*

Previously, we identified the need to test different configurations through running Fluentd with alternative configuration files. These should be replaced with unit tests. As the output plugin has restricted how we can use buffering, we need to further test configuration handling. This is best done with unit tests for the `configure` and `write` functions.

9.10.1   *Answer*

Within the `Chapter9/ExerciseResults` directory, we have included two child directories called `test-out` and `test-in`. These contain the directory structures and files with additional unit tests covering the configure and other operations that you can compare against.

9.11 Package and deployment

Having completed testing, we can think about packaging and deploying our plugins. This includes preparing the metadata files and documentation.

9.11.1 Documentation

Part of packaging up a solution includes providing the licensing information and documentation for the plugin. The template utility will have provided a standard license document and a basic README. The most important thing here is to ensure that the readme is clear and complete. Like any good product, the plugin's ability to be successfully used is predicated on people understanding how to use it, so good documentation will make a meaningful difference. In the download pack (and GitHub repository), we have provided a separate completed readme, so the initial generated state (`readme.md`) and final state (`readme-final.md`) can be compared. You may notice in the readme content some instructions for helping to complete the Gemfile, which we will come to in a moment.

The task of generating the documentation for the plugins is greatly simplified using another Fluentd-provided utility. The `fluent-plugin-config-format` utility takes the plugin type (in the same way that the utility that created the skeleton for us) and names the plugin's parameters. We can then tell the utility how we would like the documentation to be generated. In the following example, we have used mark-down (it makes it easy for GitHub and other Git-like repositories to render nicely, but other options include pure text and JSON). As we want to generate the documentation from the source, we need to provide the path to the Ruby plugin code. Using this utility with the following parameters will produce the documentation about the plugin configuration information:

```
fluent-plugin-config-format output redislist -f markdown -p lib/fluent/plugin/
```

The result of the utility is sent to the console rather than to a file, so we do need to cut and paste the output into our `readme.md` file (or use some shell/console tricks to pipe the output into the file). We have incorporated the output into the `readme-final.md` file.

USING RDOC OR YARD

In the directory structure shown in figure 9.2, we had a doc folder that was not generated by the Fluentd utility. This comes from running *RDoc* or *YARD* on the code, resulting in developer-level documentation being generated. In this case, we have opted to use YARD, as it provides some additional neat features over standard RDoc. To find out more about YARD and install it, see appendix E. Note that if you prefer to stick with RDoc, the metadata tags YARD uses will appear in the generated output.

With YARD installed, maintaining this document comes down to looking after the code, commenting, and running the commands from the root folder of the plugin:

```
yard doc lib/fluent/plugin/out_redislist.rb
yard doc lib/fluent/plugin/in_redislist.rb
```

This will update the documentation for you, but it focuses on general Ruby code and comments, not the specifics relating to Fluentd, such as the configuration values and their parameters.

9.11.2 *Complete metadata aka manifest*

The Gemfile needs to be updated as directed by the README in its defaulted content. Therefore, we need to add to the `gemspec` file the name of the gem we want to create. It takes the form of `gem <name of the gem>`—for example, `gem "fluent-plugin-out-redislist"`—for our input plugin.

The gemspec file will also need to be completed with additional information, including the summary, description, home page, license, contact details, and versioning (Semantic Versioning format is expected; https://semver.org). This also needs to include details of any dependencies. When set up, we installed several additional gems, such as the Redis connector. This means we need to add the dependencies into the `gemspec` file so they are retrieved when this plugin is installed:

```
spec.add_runtime_dependency "redis", "~>4.0"
```

This indicates that the Redis gem is needed at a version of 4.0 or later. The gemspec standard does allow for complex rules to be defined for what versions can be used.

9.11.3 *Building the gem package*

Once complete, we can do this using the RubyGem tooling that we previously installed. This means we can use the gemspec tools to create the final package. But be careful where you execute the command from, as the gemspec file includes scripting, which uses relative paths to locate all the files that need to be included. We can switch on the verbose mode using the `-V` parameter to the command to make it easy to see what is going on. To complete the task, we use the command to create the gem file:

```
gem build in-redislist.gem --config-file ./fluent-plugin-redistlist.gemspec -V
```

With the gem file is created, we need to install it into our local library of gems. Once complete, we can then use the gem without providing the path to the actual Ruby code. This can be done with the command

```
gem install ./fluent-plugin-out-redislist-0.1.0.gem
```

We can confirm that the gem is in place by executing the command

```
gem search -l redis
```

This should yield a list including our gem.

9.11.4 *Rerun without the plugin paths*

With the plugins built and the gems created and installed, we can rerun our test scenario. This time the test can be run without referencing the Ruby code directly, as we have made the code available via the gems we created to ensure we don't accidentally run using the -p parameter in the Fluentd command line. As a result, we can see our plugin working, but the execution commands reflect the conventional way of working that we would see in production.

9.12 *Extending to be an enterprise-class solution*

The plugin development has been successful and has met all our requirements. But it doesn't yet reach the level at which we could call the solution suitable for enterprise-class use cases. To bring things up to a suitable standard, we recommend some changes:

- Credentials used on the Redis connection—configure the plugin to optionally use an authenticated connection with Redis. This should be done to allow the credentials to be injected from a secure source, such as Vault.
- Using an authenticated connection to Redis means passing credentials. We do not really want to be doing that with an HTTP connection with the credentials in cleartext. So, the connection to Redis should be implemented securely with SSL/TLS certificates.
- One of the features within Redis, and what makes it such a good cache solution, is the inclusion of TTL. By incorporating TTL, we can control the size of the Redis buffer, and if we cannot keep up, then events will simply expire.
- As events are handled, some basic stats could be generated that could potentially be consumed by Prometheus.
- Extend and enhance the unit testing to achieve a target of greater than 60% coverage.
- Develop the prebuilt *Rakefile* to include and execute all the unit tests. Also, incorporate activities such as
  - Lint code analysis.
  - Maintaining the additional documentation using of *RDoc* or *YARD*. Currently, the doc folder is generated using YARD.
  - Generating `fluent-plugin-config-format` output and determining if there have been any changes since the last build.
- Incorporate the process into a continuous integration tool suite.
- Consolidate the `readme.md` documentation rather than using the `readme - final.md`

If you wish to develop your plugin development skills or use this as a practical opportunity to develop your Ruby development skills, we would encourage you to try implementing these suggested improvements. As you won't be following our steps when implementing these features, we would recommend that you adopt your preferred development tool(s). We do not have a reference solution to this, but running the test scenarios as you implement your solution to this exercise will confirm a successful outcome functionally.

Summary

- Fluentd plugin tooling provides the means to create the skeleton code to develop both input and output plugins.
- Fluentd's skeleton supports asynchronous and synchronous buffering output plugin functions.
- Fluentd input plugins need to be able to set the time and tag details. The input plugin implements this logic.
- The plugin framework includes defining, creating, and defaulting the configuration properties for the plugin loaded from the configuration file.
- Fluentd plugins are typically made available as RubyGems. The utilities provided by Ruby and Fluentd make this easy to achieve.

Part 4

Good logging practices and frameworks to maximize log value

Software is only as good as the data it processes. Likewise, log processing is only as good as the logs generated. Perhaps we should look at it this way: good information enables good insights and effective decisions. To gain benefits from capturing, manipulating, and routing log events, we need log events that are clear and precise in meaning. The more directly software can get log events to Fluentd, the lower the overheads and the less opportunity for ambiguity to creep into monitoring.

In the remaining chapters, we will focus on ensuring the log content has maximum value and meaning. In short, what makes a good log event? When are logs oversharing or not sharing enough? Is the context of the log event clear?

Many applications these days use logging frameworks either as part of the language or from third parties. What should we look to gain from such frameworks? What should we look for when choosing a framework? What options exist if there isn't a framework or a specific means to connect to Fluentd? Fluentd provides a range of additional utilities and libraries that can help, so what is available? These are all questions we'll engage with in the last part of the book.

Logging best practices

This chapter covers

- Applying log levels to filter and prioritize actions
- Identifying characteristics of good logs
- Easing operational activities with good logs
- Understanding the impact of legislation on logs
- Coding practices for improved logging

The technology used is only as good as the log events themselves, regardless of how log entries are generated, whether applications write to stdout, stderr, OS event frameworks, or logging frameworks. To maximize the technical investment, we need to make the log events and their creation as effective as possible.

We have delved deeply into the technology, so we need to do the same for log events. This chapter will explore what should and should not be logged in terms of business data, and it will examine what information can make log events more helpful. With that, we'll identify some practices to help get values from the log events. The business data our systems process can be subject to a wide variety of contractual and legislative requirements. So we'll look at some of the better-known legislation needs, some options to mitigate their impact, and sources that can help us identify any other legislative requirements that can impact the use of logging.

10.1   Audit events vs. log events

When is an event an audit event, and when is it a log event? Let's start with defining what the two events are (figure 10.1):

- *Audit events*—These are typically a record of an action, event, or data state that needs to be retained to provide a formal record that may be required at some future point to help resolve an issue of compliance (such as accounting processes or security). Many of these actions will be user-triggered.
- *Log events*—These record something that has occurred; the log event will be provided for a technical reason, ranging from showing how a transaction has been handled to reporting unexpected circumstances to show how code is executing.

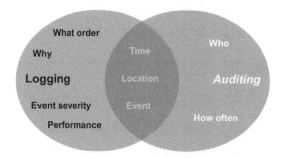

Figure 10.1   Venn diagram showing the relationship between logging and auditing

From the description, you can see a fair degree of overlap. The overlap comes from the fact that logging as a technical mechanism can be used to meet auditing requirements, and both have a common core of data. Audit events are often informed by well-structured content with a bias to security-related events, such as logging in and out. The question is more about whether the tool the events are routed to is suited to audit-related tasks. This all points to the fact that a log unification tool like Fluentd can support audit needs; we need to concentrate on ensuring the information in the event is suitable and that we send it to a suitable tool for analysis.

10.2   Log levels and severities

Going back to chapter 1, we talked about how log messages will support different roles at different times, whether you work in a DevOps organization (the development team is also operationally responsible) or on a classic separated operation and development team. Some logs help development and testing, others help with troubleshooting, and still others help with forgetting audit, security, and performance tracking. The simplest thing that can be done is to attribute every log with a log level or severity reflecting the impact of what the log event represents. Typical log levels are *trace, debug, info(rmation), warn(ing), error,* and *fatal.* The idea of event severity and these severity levels goes back to the '80s and Syslog development. Many aspects of how Syslog does things have become standards with the IETF (Internet Engineering Task Force; https://tools.ietf.org/html/rfc5424). But there is a correlation between these levels on the associated activities, as we'll see in a moment.

> **NOTE** Should log events be described using terms such as *severity* or *log levels?* The IETF talks about severity; however, this carries connotations suggesting the log information is linked to something bad. However, logs should legitimately be generated to indicate that everything is running as expected. As a result, many people, including myself, use the term *log level* to avoid the connotations that come with the word *severity.*

Of course, the key to this is a common understanding of what the log level represents. Misclassification of log entries is a common mistake with log events, which is why we've mentioned the possibility of correcting those issues using Fluentd in previous chapters. But it also means we should be explicit and that teams agree on the meaning of the levels. The following sections provide a common set of log level definitions.

10.2.1 Trace

Primarily for development activities, the execution can have simple events written to the log to indicate what method is executing. This allows us to confirm/validate that execution paths are as expected.

When it comes to the ideas of *open tracing* and *open telemetry,* we do need to separate these from the classification. These technologies collect "trace" information showing how a "transaction" has flowed through our environment. Open tracing depends on the granularity of the tracing implemented. If the trace reflects the technical steps of what is executed during the transactional flow, for example, in and out of components, functions, and so on, then we will see a fine-grained and comprehensive trace, and it should be logged using a trace categorization. If the tracing reflects the business perspectives (e.g., executing all the actions related to getting goods into a warehouse), then we're going to see coarse-grained details, and this is best logged at an information level.

10.2.2 Debug

This level is intended for sharing logging data to support any development and debugging activities. This logging level should be information-rich to make troubleshooting easy or to re-create an operational issue, since it will yield the most insight into what the software is doing. The content of such information should be produced with both developers and those involved in more detailed troubleshooting. We often see this level of logging being used rather than trying to use an IDE debugger and attaching it to running software.

These log messages are the most vulnerable to accidentally logging too much information (e.g., personal or financial data), as whole data objects can be easily logged. This shouldn't be an issue in non-production environments since the data is likely to be synthetic. This also means it is easy to overlook the risks for production.

The risk of logging sensitive data could be addressed by

- Developing standards that include details to address what data is or isn't logged and testing processes to ensure synthetic event data isn't logged.
- Putting a blanket ban on enabling debug-level logging in production (production should never have debug-level logging). In the event of a serious operational issue, the temptation to help diagnose a significant operational issue will be high, and the consequences of setting debug-level logging are overlooked until it's too late.

10.2.3 *Info(rmation)*

This is the typical threshold for logs in everyday operational environments. It should provide sufficient log information that diagnostic tasks can be undertaken if a system doesn't appear to be behaving correctly. The information recorded should include details like

- Software versions, and so on, logged during startup and deployment.
- Audit logging, such as what and who, through details like session IDs (this brings challenges involving personal data security, which we'll discuss in more depth later).
- Data values that influence decision logic.
- Interaction with sources and targets, such as URIs for other services, databases.

10.2.4 *Warn(ing)*

When things are not working as expected, there is a risk of an error, but the software can continue to execute. For example, database connections fail, and the code supports a rollback or a successful retry operation. This may result in a warning to say that it failed to connect, and then an error if it retries, or a complete rollback and the transaction being abandoned.

Warnings should not require immediate intervention but should be indicative of the possibility of remediation being needed. This should include handling unexpected paths, and therefore assuming an action.

Warnings ideally are linked to operational guidance documentation such as advising that maintenance processes may need to be performed sooner than the maintenance schedule would lead us to expect, or that mitigation actions have been automatically taken, such as scaling up a resource. Other warning actions may include reviewing how a transaction has been completed as the system hasn't processed it conventionally or the code has assumed something incorrectly.

We should also think about our solutions being defensive, checking if things are getting close to dangerous thresholds, and creating warnings. For example, this might include ensuring there is disk capacity to cope with the current rate of data growth.

Other defenses should include validating data received, even if it originated from a trusted source.

10.2.5 *Error*

This is used to record an event that will require intervention; for example, performing an operation on an empty data structure that is assumed to always have a value can trigger a null pointer exception. This will likely create a situation where a process does not complete cleanly and thus needs to reflect as an error. For logging to help with error resolution, the log events need to clarify the error cause. The location in the code where the error occurred is crucial in order to enable improvements to be effectively applied. This means a developer needs consumable information in an error log event to help implement improvements, and Ops need details to determine what remediation is needed.

　　When errors occur, not only do we need a fix, but the errors also need to have operational corrections applied to data (e.g., dividing by zero results in a calculated value not being updated). Therefore, the information must also be clearly understood by Ops people and the development/support team. Error codes can be beneficial, as the remediation steps can be documented without swamping code with lots of text.

　　Errors should try to fail gracefully—that is, they are handled and minimize the disruption (e.g., record the requested transaction and then allow subsequent transactions to be processed without being tainted if possible).

10.2.6 *Fatal*

This kind of error should only be used in exceptional circumstances, such as when the application has to terminate unexpectedly. The termination is likely to be ungraceful. As with errors, the information needs to be as comprehensive as possible. However, with a fatal error, there may be limitations on the information that can be gathered—for example, a fatal error because of a failed file system will limit the ability to grab related data values that may have influenced the cause of the problem.

　　Again, error codes can be helpful, both to direct recovery tasks and by providing indications to underlying causes without resorting to having to build nice error messages.

10.2.7 *Extending or creating your own log levels*

These definitions do not mean you can't formulate your own levels, but they have significant implications in using a framework and ensuring common understanding. For example, from time to time, I have wondered whether the error level should be split—some errors demand immediate intervention, as they are a precursor to a fatal event if you don't intervene. And some errors mean a bad outcome, but they can wait until regular operating hours to be resolved. Consider an overnight payroll run—the calculation of the pay for one individual has failed because the formula didn't allow for someone being paid for 0 hours one month, triggering an error such as dividing by zero. While this is an error and needs addressing, should it stop the payroll run for everyone?

The log levels have a hierarchy of severity, and with that comes a frequency of occurrence. Trace logs are likely to be pretty pervasive, but fatal log events should be very rare. We can see this in figure 10.2. If we add a new log level, how does it fit into the hierarchy?

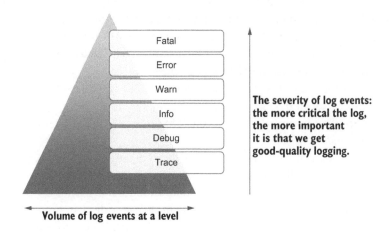

Figure 10.2 **Log levels as a hierarchy of severity and occurrence**

While creating additional or different log levels is possible, I have concluded that changing log levels from industry norms is like swimming against the tide and have settled on clearly worded definitions of log levels. If you're considering customized log levels, the bottom line is to be prepared for a considerable amount of effort, from communicating the log-level details to figuring out everything impacted to determining the log framework settings.

Should audit events use log levels, given the overlap previously described? Typically, audit events should be benign in nature and as a result should be logged at the info level, as indicated in section 10.2.3. However, if your auditing includes financial considerations, then failed transactions such as credits/debits to an account balance should form part of the audit trail and reflect the event's significance. As such, events may require manual intervention, which will create subsequent audit events showing possible interventions. It is worth considering the possibility of linking the log events together to enable better insight.

10.3 *Clear language*

Writing log entries can at times feel tedious, and searching through log files is unexciting. It is tempting to include jokes (or worse) in the messages, making logs more entertaining, or add random keywords that are easy to search for when it's our code rather than simple, straightforward language. The problem is that there will be a time when you will no longer be the person looking at these messages. There is a fair chance that someone who needs to work with the logs may not have the language you are using as their first language, so the message's meaning will not be understood. Logging things like Geronimo... or one giant leap for code when logging about raising an exception is lighthearted for most, but it may cause confusion or, worse, may offend someone in the future—so, sorry, it's time to be boring, simple, and direct. Using wording to make log searches easier is good but not at the price of risking understanding.

In the same vein as this, we should carefully choose the words we use in log messages. This is important, as we do often overload the meaning of words. For example, when using API, some treat the term as just the interface specification, as you would see with technologies like OpenAPI, Blueprint, and Swagger. Others actually mean the code that implements the logic behind the Swagger, Open API, or Blueprint definition. This problem isn't just an IT issue; it happens within the business domains we are using or in writing software.

10.4 *Human and machine-readable*

Calling out the need for logs to be both humanly readable and machine-readable may seem rather obvious. But when we're writing log event entries, it is easy to focus on what reads well for us humans and forget that perhaps we want to make the log event actionable downstream, which means we should ensure the log event is as structured as possible. For example, if I had a log entry that said "received 12345678 date-time for the schedule that is in the past," that could become {"Incorrect-Data": "12345678", "AttributeImpacted": "schedule", "DataType": "date-time", "Reason": "date past"}. It may require a little more cognitive effort to read the log message, but the latter format can be subjected to many possibilities in processing, from the error cause to the way we represent values.

10.5 *Context is key*

Understanding any log event requires context. When we're developing and using trace and debug logs, the context will, to an extent, be known to us, perhaps implicitly, as the position in the code will be part of the context or the test scenario being run will be the context. But when we come to production, the context is not likely to be implicit, so we need to make it explicit. The key to the context is how well we're answering the following:

- *What*—What is being reported, an error or just a trace?
- *When*—The date and time. This is the easy bit if you're using some form of logging framework.
- *Where*—Where in the code and where in the infrastructure the source of the log event is.
- *Why*—When it comes to log levels of info and higher, why we provide the information is essential. Is there a problem about to occur, or are we reporting something you want to track, like a login action?
- *Who*—Who triggered the action? Whose data could be impacted?

Let's explore these points in a bit more detail.

10.5.1   Context: What

The log event's "what" is partially addressed by the log level being included in the event. For trace log events, the fact that the event is logged is probably enough when combined with where. For info log level and above, we're going to provide some additional detail: Is the info record for audit purposes? What kind of error has occurred? What does the warning relate to (e.g., shortage of storage)? The "what" is best supported with details that allow a transaction to be identified, including the type of transaction. The transactional data or a proxy, such as a unique ID for a transaction (so we can look up the actual transaction data), should provide sufficient insight; for example, if the transaction is missing a reference to associated data, we need to see that value isn't set.

10.5.2   Context: When

Logging frameworks address most of this for you without any effort but are likely to go back to the server's system clock. In chapter 2, we highlighted the implications of time zones, clock skew, and so on. These can catch you out if you're looking for a solution that is running in a time zone that applies daylight saving time (because someone is looking at the timestamp and it appears to be out because they're applying daylight saving time but the log isn't) or the solution is globally distributed. So you need to know which time zone the server is in. One option is to configure the logging framework to include the time zone in the log, but better still, align all servers to UTC (Coordinated Universal Time).

   When trying to align a log analysis with a user error report, you will need to be clear about which time zone the user is working in and whether the error report is recorded against their time or system time.

10.5.3   Context: where

Naming the code location requires some awareness of how the code is handled. This is especially important when the code is deployed for a commercial solution where *obfuscation* and *minifier* tools are likely to be used, particularly on script-based solutions such as JavaScript. As a result, relying on reflection to get details of where the code is can be unhelpful. Although there are tools, some obscurification providers will include mapping information to identify the original code given the correct information.

> **NOTE**   For more information on code minifying and obscuring, check out the following resources:
>
> - The liveBook version of *Web Performance in Action* by Jeremy L. Wagner (Manning, 2016) at http://mng.bz/g4RV
> - http://mng.bz/p26z

Applications are typically either multithreaded (e.g., Java) or context switched on an I/O wait (e.g., Node.js) and they are single-threaded. The context switching means we don't handle one transaction at a time, so understanding whether log events preceding or following the event of interest are related can become challenging. This can be overcome by incorporating transaction IDs or session IDs, or by leveraging open tracing or open telemetry IDs as part of the log event. Some logging frameworks will help you capture a thread or process ID in their configuration. For example, in Fluentd, we can utilize the *WorkerId* in log file output.

"Where" can also be influenced by software versions. We can have multiple versions of the same logic in production at one time to support activities such as

- Operating A/B deployments to help evaluate whether one implementation improves user interaction
- Operating with high availability, so software updates require rolling updates to occur

Here's another way to look at it: you spot an image that has not been rendered very well in this book. You contact Manning. To help you, we need to know which figure is faulty. What if the issue has been seen before and been fixed in a new edition of the book? This isn't saying that every log event needs to publish every aspect of version information, but we do need to make it easy to supply sufficient information. Perhaps when we log errors or worse, this information is written into the log. This is an area where injecting into log events can be helpful. If a log event is identified as reposting something abnormal in the software, such as an error, then Fluentd could retrieve the version of the software running and inject it into the logs for future reference.

10.5.4 *Context: Why*

This comes down to why an event has occurred—is it an error or just a signal to show where the code is (trace) or the application's current state (debug)? As we move to the higher levels (warning, error, and fatal in our classification), "why" becomes more important and less evident from just the log level. The information-level log events could be an audit or a periodic snapshot of the system's current state regardless of whether things are good or bad—for example, logging how deep a message queue is. However, the log event consumer needs to be able to understand why the event is being generated. With a bit of thought, this is easily solved.

A simple attribute, such as "current status" or "audit action," could be included along with the shared data. We are, in effect, providing a secondary classification in many cases for the log event. Given that we provide additional metadata, we might structure it as long as we are consistent within the development organization.

When it comes to reporting warnings and errors, the why comes back to what triggered the warning or error. Is it the primary error, or has something occurred as a by-product of a previous issue? Trying to indicate whether an error is cause or effect is difficult. If we can be certain, we should be clear; if it isn't, we can perhaps give the log event consumer some hint about the possibility. Coding such information can be complicated and hard to test. But it is easy to link to an error code and provide steps to confirm cause or effect.

The record we generate with the event needs to clearly provide the information to help perform a diagnosis, not just operationally, but also whether something in the code may be needed, such as a more defensive code or better data validation. As the solution is now on an unhappy path, we should not be afraid to be generous with the information—as long as it doesn't raise sensitivity issues, which we'll look at shortly. For error-handling paths, we're in a place where performance should not be a consideration, as this part of the codebase should only execute infrequently. Generally, too little information is a lot worse than too much.

10.5.5   *Context: Who*

Logging of "who" can be tricky. As we'll see a little later, logging information that is identifiable to an individual will make our log processing subject to legislative, contractual, and commercial requirements. Still, we will explore this a bit more later in the chapter. The important thing is to consider when the "who" is necessary and whether we can safely use other data as a proxy for the true identity. For example, perhaps the "who" is relevant only during the logged-in session, so we just need to carry the session ID and use that. If we need to attribute the actions in a session back to a specific individual, we record that separately in a secure way. That session ID could equally be a transaction or order ID, and so on.

When recording events such as failed logins, or application interactions that do not require a specific individual, we may still need a value for who, such as an originating IP address. For example, a single server ping may be harmless (alive service reporting is likely to just do this), but a really rapid repeated occurrence from the same location is not good. However, having that IP means it is possible to determine that it was the same system calling and therefore who to block.

"Who" context in action

Working with a client's DevOps team, we discovered the client's security team employed a third-party organization to regularly run probes across all their internet-facing servers. We figured out what was happening, as we'd see our API gateway servers reporting illegal requests originating from one of several IPs on a regular frequency. Once we identified the pattern and the logged details like the IP origin, time, and the HTTP request, we raised our suspicions with the security team, who confirmed the use of a third party.

Don't forget that the "who" could be a system or application component. For example, when processing payroll, that activity is triggered by a scheduler. So it is helpful to know which schedule or scheduler triggered the process.

10.5.6   *a practical checklist for capturing context*

Addressing what, when, where, why, and who can be a little abstract. Personally, I try to address it using the following questions:

- Where in the code is the event coming from?
- If there is a chance that there are multiple versions of your code in production? If so, then which version becomes important.
- How is the transaction handled? This is especially important if the impact of a problem needs to be remediated in the data later.

- Which server, process, or thread experienced the problem? If the issue is infrastructure-related, you need to know which server, virtual machine, or container it relates to.
- Is the cause of the error identifiable (e.g., divide by zero as an error identifies the values involved in the error)? Can the error log be tracked back to a location in the code? At a minimum, express the nature of the error and, if practical, the data values associated (e.g., a divide by zero error—say what was being divided by zero and the values involved).
- What data values led the execution in a specific path?

10.6 *Error codes*

As developers, we tend to write log details with ourselves in mind. This is fine in a DevOps organization, where the development team also handles the ops. But many larger organizations may choose to operate an *Information Technology Infrastructure Library (ITIL)* approach to error- and problem-management, or you may have a product that people are deploying in locations beyond your reach; we need to think further ahead. One of the important aspects of ITIL for us is its definition of a known error:

> *A Known Error is a problem that has a documented root cause and a Workaround. Known Errors are managed throughout their lifecycle by the Problem Management process. The details of each Known Error are recorded in a Known Error Record stored in a Known Error Database (KEDB). As a rule, Known Errors are identified by Problem Management, but Known Errors may also be suggested by other Service Management disciplines, e.g., Incident Management.*

> More information can be found at http://mng.bz/enpQ

In simple terms, an organization will keep a record of errors with resolutions. This is why we assign errors with error codes. An error code allows us to provide a simple lookup for an error that can be linked to the appropriate documentation. The documentation should describe the error and provide details, including a remedial set of actions to perform (this is essential if this involves bringing the system back to an optimal state without corrupting or losing data). If, of course, the log event is recorded and acted upon before things really go wrong, then the actions could be preventative in nature.

The cause of the error could be either from a user action or a bug in the application that has been caught; either way, we should add error codes to the log information. It is best not to pop up error codes in a UI, as you're likely to undermine user confidence in your product. But that shouldn't stop you from linking error codes to messages suitable for users when a user action triggers a problem.

Error codes make it straightforward to enable customers to look up error codes, descriptions, and recommended responses to incorporate into a KEDB (Known Error Database). Building such error code content may seem very demanding; this can be far from the case. While developing the software, the simplest solution is to have a collaborative spreadsheet that allocates error IDs, ensuring the IDs are unique. Then capture the expected cause with a brief description from the developer. Building out resolution documentation can always follow later.

One of the benefits of using error codes is that it becomes pretty easy to standardize and internationalize the documentation about the errors. The error codes are language- and locale-agnostic; once you have the code, you can then look up the code documentation in an appropriate language.

There are all sorts of additional tricks that you can incorporate into the software development processes, such as including the documentation into the code management tool. Hence, you release the document with the code so the details are linked to your release process. Code quality tooling could look for error or fatal log entries and apply a regular expression to see if an error code is linked to it, and so on.

Error code numbering

A few tips for creating your error code numbering:

- Don't use leading zeros in the number unless prefixed with an alpha character—this risks getting truncated if handled numerically or creates additional work for formatting (e.g., number string with stipulated length and prefix character). Then, if that number is converted back to a string, it won't match as a key for information lookup anymore.
- Don't start at 1; it's best to start with the lowest digit for the full range (e.g., 1000).
- Make the error code easy to find using search tools (e.g., 1000), as a code is less likely to be indexed than AppErr1000. For example, Oracle prefixes their DB error codes with ORA, and WebLogic starts with BEA; thus, they're more likely to be indexed and more unique in searches.
- It is tempting to simply document all the error codes within a piece of code (class, interface, header file, depending on your language); after all, there is one place to go, and documentation can be generated from the code. But this is not recommended. You will end up with code on which everything will become dependent and constantly changing while the system is being developed. Each addition to the error code makes a code change with an enormous dependency impact. Code changes with that much impact will give rise to concerns (even if they're not justified) and resistance to the change.

  Better to compile the details in a shared knowledge repository, such as a wiki or collaborative knowledge base that everyone can maintain without consequence. Note that defining a local subset of errors in the code is fine—this applies the DRY principle. For example, error codes relating to a specific module could be defined together, as adding an error code is likely to go hand in hand with the module development.
- Group error codes together into families, as seen in the HTTP RFC, but be pragmatic about it; an error code may logically belong in two groupings (e.g., with a DB connection error—is that a DB issue or a network connectivity issue?).
- This doesn't necessarily mean reserving ranges of numbers. Still, the codes could be prefixed or postfixed with a shortcode to provide a scope at the product or subsystem level; for example, BEA-00000 and ORA-00000 denote error codes for two different Oracle products (WebLogic and Oracle Database).

- If you use the same error code from different exceptions, try to differentiate the point of origin in the supporting information.
- Consider the error code consumer; an error may come from a single location but have different causes, so use different error codes for the causes. This will make the support team's job or remediation easier.

10.6.1 Using standard errors

Some technologies provide codes to indicate success and errors, which have been well documented, such as those for HTTP (RFC https://tools.ietf.org/html/rfc7231# section-6); others include SMTP (email services), Oracle WebLogic Server, and so on. Using such codes in our logs helps provide more context through a common meaning and understanding as long as they are used correctly. For example, the temptation to simply do everything through the standard HTTP 200 or 400 codes doesn't help. Using an HTTP 413 code to tell the requester they sent too much data is far more effective and meaningful, not to mention that this will show up in the logs for any network routing devices.

The use of predefined error codes does need to be judged with care, as exception classes in software can be considered a special form of error code. But, as we'll see later in the chapter, these circumstances could lead to a loss of clarity.

10.6.2 Codes can be for more than errors

Error codes are the most important messages to be uniquely identifiable. The principle of associating codes to documentation for operational processes (rather than user ones) means that you can hook the event back to specific operational recommendations that could range from performing database optimization processes to archiving log files.

10.7 Too little logging or too much?

What to put into a log can be tricky. It is easy to dump whole data structures/objects into a logging event on the off chance that it is all relevant. This approach raises two challenges:

- The volume of data being logged could become very substantial as a result, excessively increasing the computational and storage workload.
- The chances are that you may end up logging sensitive details.

When it comes to the point of taking too much effort to process logs, there is nothing to stop the code from applying conditional controls, so when we need a lot of information, we can get it. What is worse—configuration controlling the information logged or modifying code to get enough information? The bottom line is tuning log framework configurations to avoid over-chatty logs is preferable to modifying code, if for no other reason than that the change cycle will most likely be quicker for a configuration file.

Software change governance controls will likely demand greater diligence in the release, slowing the task that the log files will be supporting.

The problem is that logging whole data structures can result in the logs incorporating sensitive data, such as personal or credit card data, both of which have strict rules about protecting anything that contains this kind of data. The important thing is to provide enough context in the log without writing to log any sensitive data. If the event is logged early into secure storage, such as a database, we have the possibility of attributing an ID to that event. Then the rest of the logs can be implemented by logging the recorded event ID. If necessary, this allows you to go back to the data context without the values being spread across logs.

Part of this problem extends beyond just how we write application logging to the design of our solutions. The best illustration of this is the handling of HTTP calls. Before the HTTP calls reach our application server, the HTTP traffic will pass through firewalls, load balancers, proxies, network routers, and other infrastructure elements when we're implementing a web application. Even if you have the best HTTPS configuration ever, header information must be readable to route the traffic to its destination. Typically, these components will log the URIs and often all of the HTTP headers. The headers may contain details about handling the request and response (e.g., headers contain attributes instructing infrastructure as to whether content can be cached). The net result is that if you put sensitive values into payload URIs or headers, the sensitive information may accidentally end up being logged.

If you have a local log file capturing sensitive data and there is no means to rectify the code, we need to contain the issues this can create. An approach to this is to use Fluentd to process the log events with some logic to strip out the sensitive data. Implementing this kind of logic before sending the logs on or simply writing the logs to a separate local file can help contain the impact (some might say the "blast radius" of sensitive data being logged). This strategy can be further helped by configuring the application's logging so that it is as short-lived as possible, and the original logs are never backed up or copied anywhere.

10.7.1 *What qualifies as sensitive?*

Deciding what data is sensitive can be tricky, as it can be driven by a multitude of factors:

- Business valuation of data
- Legislative demands
- Consequences of information becoming available in the public domain

Many of the complexities come from the patchwork of legislation, not only internationally but also within nations. For example, in Europe, all the countries have ratified *GDPR* (*General Data Protection Regulation*), and a growing list of countries have adopted similar legislation (e.g., Australia). But within the EU, some countries have additional legislation, so compliance to just GDPR may be insufficient. In the United States, controls are both federal and state-driven, with California having taken the lead and adopted GDPR-like legislation, but not all states have followed this.

Given that GDPR appears to be the starting point for many, it's worth examining what it seeks to achieve and what impact it can have. The central principles are the following:

- Principle of lawfulness, fairness, and transparency
- Principle of purpose limitation
- Principle of data minimization
- Principle of accuracy
- Principle of storage limitation
- Principle of integrity and confidentiality
- Principle of accountability

These principles cascade down to several entitlements for those we retain data about:

- Individuals are entitled to know why their personal data is held and what it will be used for.
- Individuals are entitled to ask for the information that is stored about them.
- Individuals can require the correction of any inaccuracies in the data.
- Individuals can exercise a right to "be forgotten," which will mean all data is erased.
- Individuals can ask for their personal data to be restricted in its use.

In addition to this, organizations must be able to justify their actions to the body responsible for overseeing GDPR compliance (the *Information Commissioner's Office* in the UK); for example:

- How long data is stored.
- Demonstrate that actions that ensure integrity and confidentiality are taken.

As you can see, this has some far-reaching implications. For example, if your system is processing payroll data, then when the data regarding someone's pay was logged, the log file would become subject to a large number of security requirements. If this was your own personal data, you'd want it to be treated just as securely as the copy in the application. In some countries, there is a legal right to be forgotten (i.e., have all records of an individual removed from all systems). This would not only create tasks to remove the data from the applications—the easy bit—but it could also extend to having to locate and delete log entries for an individual from any server that could have executed the processing, along with backups, and so on. Just finding such details alone would be very time-consuming. This is in addition to the requirements of addressing the need to make sure log files are secured and that access to log files is defensible.

All of this leads to the argument that while log data is important for problem diagnosis, audit, and so on, we need to minimize the sensitive data put into the logs wherever possible. Control the logged data, and we eliminate those logs from needing to comply with all the rules.

If sensitive data is needed to be kept, then keep it separate if you can. When you can't keep it separate, don't use staging logs between the log data source, and secure the final destination. In terms of Fluentd, this means securing the "data in-flight" by using the forward plugin configured in a secure manner (e.g., implement TLS, control access to keys and certificates). If the data is stored in temporary or staging files, then the setup for the security of the staging files ("data at rest") is a lot more involved. This would cover things like access controls for the file system, applying appropriate encryption of the files, and all the work of creating and managing the encryption keys. The potential challenge could go as far as needing to put in place formal processes to manage the disposal of the physical drives storing the data, even if it was temporary. Don't forget that this would also apply to files created when a file-based buffer is being used.

Going back to the ideas of log analytics and log unification, the underlying principle is to log sensitive data only when it is necessary, and only keep it in locations that are adequately secured. Minimize the number of "touch" points in the log events transmission. Treat logs just as you treat the actual data.

> **NOTE** A global view on data protection law can be freely viewed from global law firm DLA Piper (www.dlapiperdataprotection.com). Appendix E contains several links to resources to help jump-start finding what legislation might impact your logs (or application, for that matter).

10.7.2 GDPR is only the start

National legislation isn't always about where data is being processed or the nationality of the company or citizen the data represents. It can come from other sources; another well-known origin of security requirements is Payment Card Industry (PCI) Data Security Standards (DSS). PCI is focused on the handling of payment cards such as credit cards. The level of security required is based upon the total value of transactions handled, with specific, detailed requirements that cover infrastructure, software, and operational processes. If card data gets captured in a log, there is no doubt that the logs will need to comply with PCI rules. Like personal data, the rules also apply to the hardware on which the logs reside, the applications that process the logs, and the visibility of log information to users (i.e., developers and operations).

Many organizations have taken steps to define sensitive data and statements of what they consider to be acceptable use (part of compliance). This is a good port of call for specific environments. Where a service is provided, the terms and conditions may also determine what is deemed sensitive. But as a rule of thumb, the following is considered sensitive:

- Any data that makes an individual uniquely identifiable, such as personal addresses or social security numbers (aka *personally identifiable information*, or *PII*).
- Any data that could have a financial impact on an organization or individual, as the information leaking could do serious harm. This covers data such as charge and credit cards, bank accounts, and fiscal reporting (such information becoming known early could result in insider trading on stock exchange–listed companies).
- Any clinical data relating to an individual.

So far, we have looked at logs from the viewpoint of trying to minimize their security impact. Logs, when well defined and managed, can contribute to showing compliance to commercial and legislative requirements—for example, logs recording who accessed information and when, and, probably more importantly, when access was rejected. This information can be used to demonstrate correct controls and can be made operationally actionable.

To illustrate the point, the following are just a few examples of other legislation or standards where the use of log events can provide an audit trail to address aspects of compliance to legislative requirements:

- Sarbanes Oxley Act (SOX) (http://mng.bz/Bxl8) and variants such as J-SOX (Japan), C-SOX (Canada), and TC-SOX (Turkey).
- Health Insurance Portability and Accountability Act (HIPAA) (www.hhs.gov/hipaa/index.html).
- ISO/IEC 27001. While not a legislative-driven set of rules, this is a best-practice set of standards that can be certified (www.iso.org/isoiec-27001-information-security.html).

> **Data risks: An analogy**
>
> The risks around handling sensitive data are a little abstract, so let's look at an analogy. Think of it as venomous; how sensitive the data is reflects how dangerous the venom is. If you like to visualize it, consider a nonvenomous snake as a low-risk data item, and very sensitive data like government IDs as jellyfish. Yet, with the right equipment, environment, and expertise, the risk of a bite or sting is small. A nonvenomous snake bite may be painful and possibly a source of infection if left untreated; more venomous stings or bites are serious, but if you are prepared and have the antivenin, you'll survive if treated quickly. The problem is not just how venomous the data is; it's how much venom (how many bites or stings) there is—in other words, the amount of data. We can limit the amount and the sensitivity of data being handled in log files; the lower the risk, the simpler the necessary precautions.

10.8 Log structure and format

By applying structure to the messages, it is possible to make the information more actionable because the logic processing the logs can derive meaning from the data. Suppose we experienced an error with a database connection, which produced a structured log event. It wouldn't be hard to implement a parser expression to retrieve the database connector error code and the database details. This could be done by Fluentd, and therefore a signal could be sent to the relevant database team. The log analytics tool could act on the same data, but the alert would be later, and more problems could have occurred. But the log analytics could help us by examining histories to determine if the problem was reoccurring, and, if so, at what frequency and if there was a commonality to the nodes(s) registering the problem.

The structuring of logs goes further than that, as we need to also have a structure around details such as timestamps, log levels, location, thread IDs, and so on, that help provide context. There are some industry-recognized formats. Figure 10.3 provides details of ones typically associated with application logic.

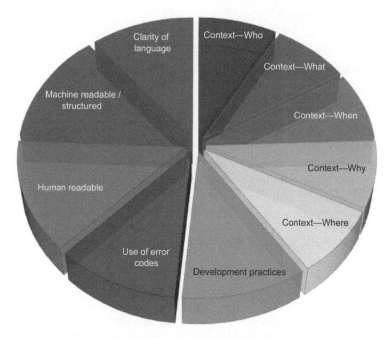

Figure 10.3   The aspects that, when combined, will provide excellent log events and robust mechanisms to use them as necessary

10.8.1 *Putting making log entries ready for application shipping into action*

As part of a development team, your server-based application reaches the point of being sufficiently well featured. The beta and early adopter customers are successfully using your software. The management team recognizes that to provide cost-effective support, documentation needs to be provided to avoid frustrated system administrators and unnecessary support calls. Also, good support documentation will help prevent support requests from coming back to the development team. You've been asked to identify what needs to be achieved and how long it is likely to take to implement, as well as if there is anything that can be done to minimize the time before sales can ramp up activities.

ANSWER

There are a great many things that could be done, and there is no single correct answer, except to build on what this chapter has discussed. When estimating such a task, the simplest thing is to search the currently active code base for log events and record the type of event. Then estimate the effort to evaluate the log events against the different factors illustrated in figure 10.3. Being pragmatic, if the estimates are squeezed, it is best to adopt a top-down approach (see figure 10.2.)

With the estimated effort of working through the code checking and amending the log events, you also need to estimate the effort to produce the supporting documentation. If you provide the documentation through channels such as a website rather than embedding it in the code, the software release can start before this documentation is complete. Obviously, there is a temptation to not complete this task and focus on the following product version with this approach. Conversely, not addressing this will directly impact the number of support calls, including those that get escalated back to the developers, even in a more traditional organizational arrangement.

10.9 Use frameworks if you can

Most programming languages provide logging frameworks, either as part of the base language or as libraries (we will explain these in more depth in chapter 11). Adopting a framework for logging can help in several ways to improve your logging. Potential benefits include the following:

- Consistency in the log data.
  - Consistency in log levels
  - Structure of log entries

- Additional contextual information managed for you (e.g., if the framework understands OpenTracing, it can pull trace context values).
- The framework can allow us to control what is looked at through configuration, making it easier to determine how much or how little logging is needed.
- Importantly, when logging in a containerized environment, we can save a lot of effort if we don't have to reparse text outputs to apply context and meaning. This saves processing power, and many log frameworks allow us to direct output mechanisms that can help avoid this overhead.

Using one of the many third-party or language native solutions is preferable, as they will be tried and true. Even a simplified piece of your own code that helps drive consistency is valuable. The mission-critical systems I started my career working on fell into this category. If you go down the route of using Homebrew, we would strongly recommend adopting one of the industry-standard formats to make ingestion into other tools a lot easier.

10.10 Development practices

We've seen a number of things we can do to positively improve the situation. But there are some common development practices that can be negative in nature, even if the intent is presented positively.

10.10.1 Rethrowing exceptions

Catching and rethrowing exceptions (the act of having a catch block in code and then using throw statements to raise the exception again) is a bad practice that can have undesirable impacts on logs, given that typically, when an exception is caught, it is logged. This means if you catch and rethrow an exception, the odds are you'll end up with multiple log events for the same problem. When it comes to analyzing what is wrong, you've increased the workload for determining which log event was the first actual occurrence of a problem and have doubled up on the number of alerts, moving another step closer to a "notification storm."

Notification or alert storms

Notification or alert storms are something to watch out for if you link your log events to a notification mechanism such as email or Slack. If you keep getting the same error, such as when logic keeps getting stuck in an infinite loop of trying to do something (e.g., writing to a file with no storage space available), then you end up with the same message saturating the notification channel. The net result is that everyone switches off and unsubscribes to notifications; worse still, systems think your application generates spam and it gets blocked. Fortunately, there are techniques for suppressing such scenarios, such as filters in Fluentd (http://mng.bz/OG6E) or in the logging framework itself. For example, Log4j2 provides a BurstFilter (http://mng.bz/YgKA), and Log4Net has an extension that does the same sort of thing (http://mng.bz/GG1O)

10.10.2 Using standard exceptions and error structures

My position on using standard exceptions from programming languages is possibly a more contentious point, as I don't agree entirely with the assertion that standard exceptions should be thrown. For example, Joshua Bloch's *Effective Java* (Addison-Wesley Professional; 3rd edition, 2017) advocates that if you have defensive code, and a value you receive is null (nil in Ruby) but shouldn't be, then your code should use the language's own `NullPointerException` or `IllegalArgumentException`. The argument made is that you can benefit from code reuse and that someone reading your API will understand the API more easily. While the reuse consideration may have merit, using a language-predefined exception class because it will lend to the understandable definition is about good naming conventions, not insight into the code.

The real problems come when looking at log events; it becomes tough to determine whether this exception resulted from defensive coding or a potential bug. The difference is that defensive coding points to a possible upstream issue. If someone has put in defensive checks, then the chances are someone considered the possibility of a problem and how to leave things in a recoverable state.

While my example and reference to best practice have focused on Java, the foundation principles apply to languages that support exception frameworks, Python and Ruby being two examples. Other languages, like Go, have error structures and the ability to handle the return of different structure types. So the question begs, what is the answer to this?

Going back to Java for a moment, from my perspective, there is nothing wrong with creating a simple one-line class that extends a base class with a clear, meaningful name (e.g., class `IllegalBufferConfigurationException` extends `Illegal-ArgumentException`). After all, this is how languages apply inheritance for the native exceptions in Java (e.g., `NullPointerException` extends class `Exception`). Ruby's approximate match is `ArgumentError`, which extends `StandardError`, which in turn extends `Exception`. If an exception is well named, it will be clear as to why the exception is thrown. It also will tell the reader what specific scenarios are being defended against and what the API caller should or should not be doing. So when we see a generic exception, like a `NullPointerException`, we're likely to be looking at a more fundamental problem and one that has not been considered. If we have considered a problem, we probably know what the remediation might be.

10.10.3 String construction as a reason not to log

When logging, we sometimes need to construct a log message by combining several elements to produce a practical level of information. Casting data to strings and concatenating them together takes a little bit of CPU effort. Let's assume for a moment that we're creating an info-level log message, so there is a chance the log message will get filtered out if someone has set the log filter threshold to a warning. In this situation, the CPU effort constructing the log message is effectively wasted. This has been used as an argument for not bothering implementing logging in the code since the log message construction consumes processing effort for no gain.

This argument attempts to rationalize not investing in evaluating where logging will help implement appropriate code, at least from my perspective. There are technical means by which we can minimize the cost. But perhaps, more importantly, the cost of a small number of CPU cycles compared to the cost of a developer's time trying to investigate and understand what is going on with someone else's code does weigh in favor of helping the developer. I'm not advocating writing grossly inefficient code. Still, the extra costs in compute cycles for having supportable and maintainable code (which includes sensible logging) are far smaller than the money saved in developer effort.

Coming back to the practical technical means to avoid waste, every logging framework I know of provides the means to query the logging level currently set, allowing the code to decide whether there is any value in constructing the logging payload. These are sometimes referred to as "guard" functions and can be applied like this:

```
Logger.ifDebug
{
  myLogMessage = '{"attribute:" + aStringValue + ","
    + aArrayOfKeyValues.toJSON + "}"
  Logger.debug (myLogMessage)
}
```

Obviously, the precise code will differ based on the framework in use and the language-specific syntax, but you see the point.

Over the last 5 to 10 years, we have seen most mainstream languages develop to support Lambda or lazy execution capabilities. This means we can now write code, so the guard is implicit and if the implicit condition resolves, only then are the subsequent expressions evaluated and executed. For example:

```
LOGGER.atDebug().log('{"attribute:" + aStringValue + "," + aArrayOfKeyVal-
    ues.toJSON + "}")
```

The result is negligible compute cost and optimization without losing the existence of the logging code. Add to that the performance improvements seen with compilers, virtual machines, and interpreters. We're gaining performance—consider GraalVM and Quarkus as examples of this. When you consider this, we're seeing more efficiency gains that will far outweigh those from not writing log statements.

For more about Quarkus and GraalVM

- Quarkus and microservice development: See the liveBook version of *Kubernetes Native Microservices* by John Clingan and Ken Finnigan (Manning, 2022) at http://mng.bz/zQ5Q.
- GraalVM introduction: See the liveBook version of *The Well-Grounded Java Developer,* 2nd ed by Benjamin Evans et al. (Manning, 2022) at http://mng.bz/0w96.
- GraalVM home page: www.graalvm.org/
- Quarkus home page: https://quarkus.io/

Summary

- The application of clear, simple language and, when appropriate, attributing the log event with error codes will make it significantly easier to understand a log and apply any necessary actions as a result of a log event.
- Good log events will include contextual information beyond just log levels, including details such as indicating on which server the relevant process is running.
- Legislation can impact log events, particularly when the log generation includes such things as PII or credit card data. As a result, extensive additional security controls and restrictions are imposed on log data.
- Some organizations will also classify internal data such as commercial values (e.g., margins on a product or service). It is important to understand organizational sensitivities when creating or transferring log events so that the organizational requirements relating to such data being logged are observed.
- The value of using error codes with log events is significant, from identifying which part of a system the issue originated to making remediation instructions easily identifiable.
- The application of industry standards to the content logged can accelerate understanding of data and its meaning.

Logging frameworks

In the previous chapter, we looked at how we can create log events that can be used to give the most meaning and value. Another significant way we can easily derive more value from logs is by using logging frameworks for our application development. Most programming languages these days will be able to use a logging framework. In some cases, the third-party ones predate the language native feature and become something of a de facto standard. Other logging frameworks have come as part of an application container or platform to address weaknesses perceived or proven in the native solutions.

This chapter will explore the logging framework landscape, as there is a range of commonalities in their capability and in design. A general understanding of this will help us appreciate the "art of the possible" and make informed decisions when choosing a framework. We will also look at whether the more dominant frameworks for different languages can support the ability to connect directly to Fluentd. Fluentd has also helped us in this space by providing logging libraries for multiple languages, so we'll look at those to understand how they may fit into the options we have.

If frameworks or Fluentd libraries aren't an option, we can obviously have our applications write to files. We've seen that Fluentd can consume such information. But connecting via a file is less efficient than connecting the application directly. If you are working with a Function as a Service (FaaS) like AWS Lambda and Functions services from Oracle Cloud, Microsoft Azure, and Google, or even self-hosted functions via Fn Project (https://fnproject.io/), you'll recognize that the services are very transient. As a result, these very transient services are more challenging to efficiently log from. Trying to connect to storage can be more complex to configure and slower to connect, and therefore more suited to network-based logging. So, we will explore how it is possible to communicate with Fluentd more directly.

11.1 *Value of logging frameworks*

Regardless of the genesis of the logging framework(s), they all address the following key themes to a greater or lesser extent:

- Providing an easy way to output log events using a log level classification
- Allowing the control of log events sent via configuration
- Directing the log events to different output forms, such as files, stdout, HTTP, etc.

While log levels can be traced back to Syslog standards (RFC 5424, https://tools.ietf.org/html/rfc5424) for application development (as opposed to OS-level tooling that led to the definition of RFC 5424), one of the strongest influencers on logging libraries is *Apache Log4J.* This influence could be attributed to the fact that the Apache Software Foundation ported the design and implementation to several different languages. But its influence goes further than that. While it is possible to arrive at very similar or even the same answers based on the same needs, you can see very similar if not the same APIs and features in the logging frameworks for many other languages. Some logging frameworks not linked to the Apache Software Foundation openly acknowledge drawing on the design principles of Log4J. To be open and transparent, my entry into open source was when I started developing with Java 1.2, so my perspective may be a little biased.

The beauty of following the Log4J route is the ability for third parties to implement certain parts of the framework, so the application doesn't see any difference. Still, the configuration could change behaviors, such as how the logs are stored, from flat files to databases. We'll see this in more detail in the next couple of sections.

> **NOTE** References to Log4J can cause some confusion, as there are two versions—Log4J and Log4J2. When referencing Log4J today, you can assume it refers to version 2. Version 1 was declared as being at the end of its life in

2015. Versions 1 and 2 aren't radically different in terms of ideas. But version 2 was rewritten to address some weaknesses of the version 1 implementation; this meant the implementation could be written to utilize new language features.

11.2 Typical structure of a logging framework

Given the Log4J influence across many logging frameworks and languages, it is best to start by examining the Log4J structure. We can easily understand and master other frameworks. Figure 11.1 illustrates this structure and the relationships with the different classes (we've used UML class notation with a couple of tweaks, as the key shows; www.omg.org/spec/UML/). We can see that the classes or modules involved are the *Logger Context, Configuration, Filter, Logger, Logger Config, Formatter,* and an *Appender.*

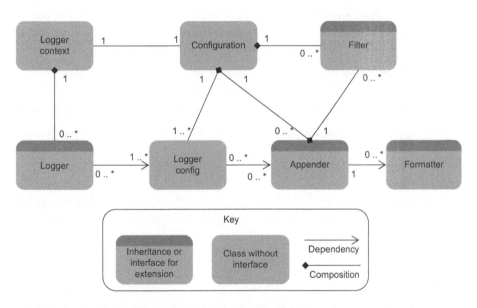

Figure 11.1   Common logging structure represented using UML class notation, including indicating the quantities in the relationships, such as 0 or 1 to many

In the following sections, we'll describe the role that each of these components plays. We have ordered the components based on how much their logic impacts the use and behavior of the logging framework.

11.2.1 Logger context

This is the foundation of the framework within your application. It takes responsibility for holding the references to specific logger objects. It will process any configuration files, creating the necessary logger objects as necessary.

The logger context typically forms a "one-stop shop" for all your logging elements; within the application, this class is used to retrieve an object that will handle the relevant processing of log events (represented by an instance of a logger object). When a request is made on the logger context for a logger object, it can derive or use parameters to determine which logger object to provide. If no specific logging configurations are associated with the identifier provided (usually a logical name or classpath), then a default logging behavior will be provided.

Depending on the implementation, it may also orchestrate any details such as connection pools, and so on. This is the only point where there is a certainty of having a single object, making it the root for all Log4J configuration values.

11.2.2 Appender

The appender's task is the easiest to relate to and is key to processing log events. Depending upon the specific logging framework implementation, the appender may be called an *adaptor* or *transport*, as this layer is responsible for taking the log events and sending them to the appropriate destination. For example:

- Transmitting them using techniques such as TCP/IP messages
- Using API calls to services such as Logstash
- Writing or appending the log event to the end of a file (hence the name)

Each appender will make use of filters to control which log events it may need to append. An appender can also use a formatter to convert the internal representation of the event to how it should be outputted; this can range from JSON to tab-separated rows. Some types of appender can only emit log events in a specific way; this relationship can sometimes get simplified and combined into a single class or module.

Within the configuration of a logging framework, it is possible (and expected) to see several different appenders configured to address sending some events to multiple destinations with different log levels.

11.2.3 Logger

It is possible to define multiple loggers (or just the context defaults) so that different application parts can use logging in different ways—for example, a separate logger for recording official audit events versus generic application audit trails. The official audit events may need to be sent to the database, and all events, including the audit, should be sent to the logging framework. These loggers can then be selected within the code. There will be different configurations with different loggers, such as which appender to use, which filters to apply, and so on.

By having multiple loggers, we benefit from varying the configuration for different parts of the code base and even having multiple configurations for parts of the application (e.g., log errors to stdout and log everything to file).

11.2.4 Filter

The filter determines which log events should be emitted, primarily by determining whether the log event is at a level above or below the threshold set in the configuration. As filters are associated with appenders, different log destinations can be configured with different log levels. For example, I could set the console appender to have a log level of Warning and a file appender set to Info. The result is that only Warning and Error events go to the console, but more details are included in the file.

11.2.5 Formatter

As described by the appender, the formatter's task is to construct the appender output so that the log entry is presented as wanted or required (e.g., time in a 12- or 24-hour format). Some appenders will allow flexibility (e.g., file appenders).

11.2.6 Configuration

Typically, we want to drive the logging of an application through configuration rather than code, as this allows the logging to be configured without necessarily making invasive code changes. This also makes for a quicker turnaround in the verification of configurations. It allows us to change how logs are processed, depending upon the deployment context. For example, we could have a configuration that sends everything to stdout for our development machines. However, in test and production environments, the configuration is set to send the logs to Elasticsearch.

11.2.7 Logger config

The logger config is a subset of the total logging configuration for a particular logger (see section 11.2.3). This will track the relevant configuration section and translate it into the correct objects in the code. This may include using things like factory design patterns.

11.3 Appender structures

Typically, appenders are built through a hierarchy of inheritance or encapsulation so that each layer of sophistication can leverage simpler operations. Ultimately, this will depend on a standard interface definition so that regardless of appender, they are orchestrated the same way, just as Fluentd does with its plugins. In figure 11.2, we can see how Log4J has organized its appenders through inheritance from a base class that realizes an interface and provides common logic, which is then extended to provide a set of basic appenders, such as the console appender. From this layer of derivation, we see the layering build an increase in specializations. This is most notable with the AbstractOutputStreamAppender, which is then used for general socket use cases and is further specialized for sending logs into a Syslog compliant solution.

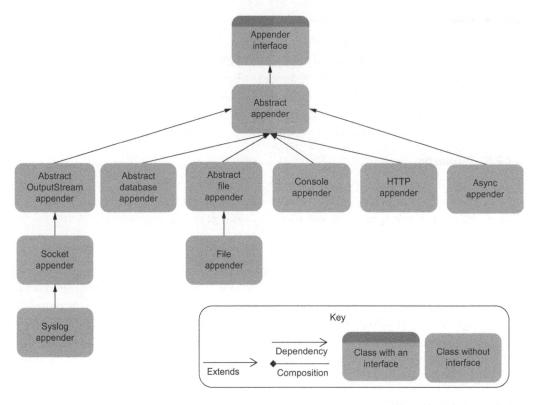

Figure 11.2   UML representation of how some of the appenders of Log4J are related

11.4   *Logging framework landscape*

The number of logging frameworks is substantial, with most languages having a native capability and open source frameworks. In appendix E, we have pulled together a list of logging frameworks for a range of languages commonly used. We also provide some details about the dominant frameworks, some of which are the language-native options and where to obtain more information.

In addition to logging frameworks, some libraries provide a programmatic interface and a mapping between the API and several different popular frameworks. Those familiar with Log4J will probably have heard of *SL4J* (www.slf4j.org), which abstracts Log4J, the Java native logging framework, and another called Logback. As a result, it is possible to switch the logging frameworks transparently. With these abstractions, a means to instantiate the desired logging framework is needed. This can be achieved by implementing a factory (http://mng.bz/KB00) or dependency injection (http://mng.bz/DxZw) pattern. Another example of this abstraction is .Net native logging (more detail can be found at http://mng.bz/9KV1).

11.5 Choosing a framework

When evaluating a logging framework to adopt, some things should be considered to help select the most appropriate framework. We have developed a set of questions that will help you evaluate your needs and select a framework to meet those needs. By reviewing these questions, it will help you determine your priorities in terms of a logging framework. Once the questions have been given some form of priority, it becomes easier to evaluate the frameworks against the questions to see how well they match your needs. The questions are the following:

- What appenders are available? Are they limited to one type of appender, such as files? Are there out-of-the-box appenders that can work with your log unification solution, such as Fluentd or Logstash?
- Can the appender behavior be tailored or optimized? For example, are log rotation or network ports and addresses configurable?
- Is it possible to tailor the output of log events based on the different parts of the application? For example, log thresholds for the application framework, such as Spring or Core .Net, are set to `Warning` and `Error`, but your custom logic can have thresholds set to `Info`.
- How easy is it to tailor the logging configuration (without using code)? You may wish to tune logging, and if there is an operational issue, ideally you can update or override the default logging configurations to selectively get more information.
- How much information does the framework derive for you (e.g., providing method and class names for tracepoints) with correctly structured timestamps?
- Can you tailor the log output formatting (e.g., JSON, XML)? This question reflects the previous chapter where the best logs have a structure allowing the log event to be both humanly readable and machine-readable.
- How compact is the footprint (this is important in IoT use cases)? For the IoT and mobile solutions, we need to have a tight footprint to limit resource use.
- Can you make the log output secure—use TLS, encrypt files, and so on? Is the security good enough for the data being handled?
- Will the framework have a material impact on my application's throughput/performance, particularly the final I/O phase? Can logging end up being a thread-blocking mechanism?
- How easy is the logging framework's API to work with? If the calls within the application code are difficult to use, developers may avoid creating log events. Ideally, the interfaces will be intuitive, but having good supporting documentation to reference can be invaluable, particularly for those starting their development careers.

Rather than evaluating every possible option, it is worth trying to narrow the field of options. The details in the appendix E, table E.11 can help here, as they reflect what we believe are the most important and/or most dominant logging frameworks.

11.5.1 *Putting optimizing application logging into action*

The adoption of Fluentd in your organization is going well, and you have been asked to determine whether the current logging framework in use is up to the job going forward or whether the success of Fluentd allows supporting a case of changing logging frameworks. Using the factors described, evaluate the current solution being used by your development team. Compare this with an alternative (examine appendix E to see if an alternative option has been offered).

ANSWER

As we clearly cannot give you a specific solution for this exercise, we hope you have found that you are already using a logging framework, and it fits well with your needs. If your logging framework is not a great fit, you will probably have recognized the issues already. If you haven't pinpointed the issues with your current framework, this list of considerations should have helped qualify the problems.

11.6 *Fluentd's own logging and appenders*

What happens if the logging framework being used does not provide support specific to Fluentd? There are several possibilities to overcome this. One approach is through the use of Fluentd-provided libraries.

Depending upon the language, the Fluentd logging library implementation may have some or all of the structures described earlier, such as appenders and filters. These implementations may work with and extend the native language logging library, as is the case for Python and Ruby. In other cases, the Fluentd libraries do not align with a framework, often when there is no native language logging library or an established dominant solution. In these cases, the library will be more straightforward and will need to be used directly from your code.

You may have established the use of a logging framework with no feature for connecting to Fluentd, and the Fluentd-provided library does not automatically plug in to a framework. In these situations, it may be possible to find additional open source software to wrap or extend the Fluentd library to allow its use within a framework structure. We can change how the log events are handled using configuration alone and not impact application code. Of course, you could create the code that bridges the gap. Depending on the combination of language, Fluentd library, and framework, the trickiest part of this will most likely be how to supply configuration values into the Fluentd library.

In table 11.1, we can see how Fluentd supports different programming languages with libraries. We have also suggested other open source options that will allow the logging code to communicate with Fluentd.

Table 11.1   Where Fluentd can integrate into a native or commonly used framework directly or indirectly

Language	Has native logging library	Fluentd logger library	Alternate open source solution
Erlang	Y	https://github.com/fluent/fluent-logger-erlang	
Go	N	https://github.com/fluent/fluent-logger-golang	
Java	N	https://github.com/fluent/fluent-logger-java	Log4J: https://github.com/tuxetuxe/fluentd4log4j
Node.js	N	https://github.com/fluent/fluent-logger-node	Directly integrates with Log4JS
OCaml	N	https://github.com/fluent/fluent-logger-ocaml	
Perl	N	https://github.com/fluent/fluent-logger-perl	Log4perl: https://metacpan.org/pod/Log::Log4perl::Appender::Fluent
PHP	N	https://github.com/fluent/fluent-logger-php	https://github.com/Seldaek/monolog
Python	Y	https://github.com/fluent/fluent-logger-python	
Ruby	Y	https://github.com/fluent/fluent-logger-ruby	
Scala	N	https://github.com/fluent/fluent-logger-scala	Via Logback compatibility with SLF4S

If you don't have a suitable logging framework or wrapper layer, then there is the option to use the Fluentd logging library directly within your core application code. As with all things, there are pros and cons to such an approach. To that end, in table 11.2, we've called out the pros and cons of using the libraries directly to help you make informed decisions.

Table 11.2   Pros and cons of using Fluentd's own log framework

Pros	Cons
Small footprint, as it is only providing for output to Fluentd.	Locked into using Fluentd. For packaged solutions, you had better not try to force its logging to work differently from the options it provides. This is where it may be better to consider a custom plugin or find a compromise configuration.

Table 11.2   Pros and cons of using Fluentd's own log framework *(continued)*

Pros	Cons
The Fluentd logging library provides the same programmer interface as other frameworks, giving a comparable development experience. But the Fluentd server offers significantly more sophistication than a logging framework for handling the log events.	
Communication to Fluentd is over the network. Using msgpack compression means efficient communication and can limit hosting complexities (e.g., external storage for containers, complexities of storage for FaaS).	

The final possible option for logging directly to Fluentd is to leverage a framework's plugins to communicate using TCP/IP or HTTP(s) and send log events using those protocols. These routes mean you have no library dependencies (assuming your programming language can provide basic networking).

11.7   Illustrations of an application logging directly to Fluentd

Having now looked at logging framework structures, the considerations involved in selecting a logging framework, and the possibility of logging directly to Fluentd without a framework, let's see how the different approaches for direct logging can look in reality. Each illustration will move further away from the ideal abstracted connection to Fluentd but will show how direct communication can be realized. In each case, we're going to transmit a simple log message to Fluentd.

For these illustrations, we've chosen to use Python because it

- Supports using the Fluentd library with its native logging framework to show the most ideal option
- Is a widely adopted language, and the language constructs are easy to read and map to other languages
- Is a scripted language, so no additional effort is needed to set up and run a compilation process first (compared to Java, C#, etc.)
- Is a different language from the implementation of Fluentd and so helps illustrate the language-agnostic use of working with Fluentd

11.7.1   Python with logging framework: Using the Fluentd library

In most situations, having the Fluentd library plugging directly into the logging framework is ideal, as we can configure different ways to log without any code changes. Let's start with the code that creates the logging framework driven by the configuration file; our application then uses the framework to record a log event. To achieve this illustration, we need to establish some code and configuration, which we will review in the coming listings:

- A simple Python test application to use the logging framework and generate a log event
- A configuration file telling the logging framework how and what to log
- A Fluentd server and configuration so it can receive the log events

In the code shown in listing 11.1, we can see the Python test application, which creates a configuration object from the configuration file and passes this into the logging context, and then requests a logger object. With the logging object ready, we could use that object as many times as we like. In our example, we then construct content in the log message—here, the date-time string representation. Then the logging framework is called twice, once as a text message and again as a JSON construct. When you review the code, note the complete absence of Fluentd references. This is all handled in the logging framework for us based on the configuration.

Listing 11.1 Chapter11/clients/log-conf.py—Test Python client—configuration only

```
import logging
import logging.config
import yaml

with open('logging.yaml') as fd:           ◁──┐  Loads the configuration
    conf = yaml.load(fd, Loader=yaml.FullLoader)    file, which will describe
                                                    the logging setup wanted

logging.config.dictConfig(conf['logging'])  │  Gets the correct logger object; by
                                            │  not providing a specific name, we
log = logging.getLogger()               ◁──┘  will be given the default setting

now = datetime.datetime.now().strftime("%d-%m-%Y %H-%M-%S")  │  Generates
log.warning ('from log-conf.py at ' + now)              ◁──┘  log event
log.info ('{"from": "log-conf.py", "now": '+now+'"}')                        ◁──┐
```

It would be preferable to create JSON for the log event being passed to the library. But building JSON objects first distracts from the point we're trying to make.

The configuration shown in listing 11.2 is the detail loaded in the application and interpreted by the logging framework to establish the desired ways of logging. Only the configuration will drive logging to communicate to Fluentd directly through the definition of *handlers* (or appenders, using the naming we described earlier). Note how the configuration entities relate back to the structure illustrated in figure 11.1, with loggers referencing a handler (appender) by name and the handler referencing a formatter implemented to work with Fluentd. Here the filters are not decoupled but specified within the loggers and handlers using the `level` attribute.

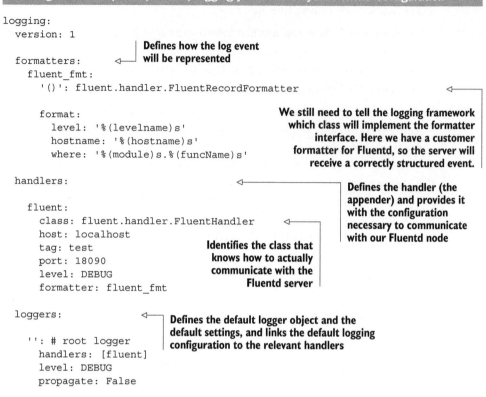

Listing 11.2   Chapter11/clients/logging.yaml—Test Python client: configuration

```
logging:
  version: 1

  formatters:          Defines how the log event
    fluent_fmt:        will be represented
      '()': fluent.handler.FluentRecordFormatter

      format:
        level: '%(levelname)s'
        hostname: '%(hostname)s'
        where: '%(module)s.%(funcName)s'

  handlers:

    fluent:
      class: fluent.handler.FluentHandler
      host: localhost
      tag: test
      port: 18090
      level: DEBUG
      formatter: fluent_fmt

  loggers:

    '': # root logger
      handlers: [fluent]
      level: DEBUG
      propagate: False
```

We still need to tell the logging framework which class will implement the formatter interface. Here we have a customer formatter for Fluentd, so the server will receive a correctly structured event.

Defines the handler (the appender) and provides it with the configuration necessary to communicate with our Fluentd node

Identifies the class that knows how to actually communicate with the Fluentd server

Defines the default logger object and the default settings, and links the default logging configuration to the relevant handlers

For Fluentd to work with the examples, we have provided a configuration file. If you review the configuration file in listing 11.3, you'll see two sources configured. The source using the `forward` input plugin will receive the log events. You can confirm that by comparing the port number in the configuration to the logger YAML file; we will see the other source put to use shortly.

Listing 11.3   Chapter11/fluentd/http.conf—simple HTTP source

```
<system>
    Log_Level debug
</system>
<source>
    @type http
    port 18080
    <parse>
      @type none
    </parse>
</source>
```

Sets the logging to debug to help us understand what is happening. Given that HTTP is highly configurable in its behavior, let's ensure that assumed configurations are compatible.

Let's not worry about the expected structure at this stage and process the log event as a single string received over HTTP.

```
<source>
    @type http
    port 18085
    <parse>
        @type json
    </parse>
</source>
```

Using a different port, we can take the log event using HTTP in a JSON structure.

```
<source>
    @type forward
    port 18090
</source>
```

Using the forward plugin, we can receive the payload as JSON text or compressed with msgpack.

```
<match *>
    <format>
        @type json
    </format>
    @type stdout
</match>
```

To start things up, we'll need two shell windows; having navigated to the folder with all the provided resources, Fluentd can be started with the following command:

```
fluentd -c Chapter11/Fluentd/http.conf
```

This is followed by navigating to the `Chapter11/clients` folder and executing the command

```
python log-conf.py
```

Once executed, you will see that the Fluentd server will write the generated log event to the console in a JSON format.

11.7.2 *Invoking Fluentd appender directly*

Let's now look at how the code may appear using the Fluentd Python library directly from our application instead of a logging framework. While this is the Python implementation, the logger libraries work similarly for most of the supported languages. Obviously, each implementation may have differences because of the constraints of how the programming language works. For example, Go doesn't have classes and inheritance like Python and Java, but rather has modules and types.

To make it easy to compare the direct calls to the Fluentd logging library approach using the logging framework, we have created a new Python test client shown in listing 11.4. The first immediate difference is the client we need to explicitly import the Fluentd library into our code. Our code no longer establishes the logger context and logger object but interacts with a sender, which is a specific implementation of an appender (or handler, as Python calls it). The sender object is constructed with the configuration needed to connect to Fluentd (you could, of course, retrieve this data from a generic configuration file). As before, we're constructing the time to put into the log event message. Then, finally, we can use either the Fluent library's `emit` or `emit_with_timestamp` functions to transmit the log event. The emit functions require the payload to be represented as a hashmap (or dictionary, using Python's naming).

Listing 11.4   Chapter11/clients/log-fluent.py—Direct Fluentd library use

```
import datetime, time                              The import making a direct
from fluent import handler, sender       ◄──┘      dependency on the Fluentd library

fluentSender =
    sender.FluentSender('test', host='localhost', port=18090)    ◄──┐  Creates an
                                                                     │  instance of the
now = datetime.datetime.now().strftime("%d-%m-%Y %H-%M-%S")          │  Fluentd handler
fluentSender.emit_with_time('', int(time.time()),
🡒{'from': 'log-fluent','at': now})                  ◄──┐ Sends the
                                                        │ log event
```

To see this scenario run, restart Fluentd as we did in section 11.7.1. This means that the log events will, when received, be displayed in Fluentd's console session. Then, in the second shell, we need to run the command (from `Chapter11/clients` folder)

```
python log-fluent.py
```

11.7.3   *Illustration with only Python's logging*

In the examples so far, the logging has used the Fluentd logging library directly (using its sender object) and indirectly (using the Python logging framework and configuration). This time, we're going to look at how we can work without using the Fluentd library at all. If you examine the code of the Fluentd library, you will find the library uses the msgpack compression mechanism that we encountered in chapters 3 and 4. Msgpack is part of Fluentd, not the native Python logging itself. As a result, when working with only the native layer, we don't benefit from the compression provided by msgpack. The only way to overcome this would be to implement our own formatter code that uses msgpack.

Without resorting to developing your own version of the Fluentd library, the next option is to use a prebuilt Python logging handler (or, as we have called it, an appender) to talk to Fluentd directly. The value of this approach for Python is nonexistent. But it may be necessary if you wanted to use a comparative approach in another language.

As not all languages benefit from the Fluentd library, let's look at how things need to be implemented without that help. In this case, we will exploit the prebuilt `HTTPHandler` (most languages have a comparable feature). As with the preceding illustrations, we have provided another client implementation shown in listing 11.5. For this to work, we instantiate a Python `HTTPHandler` for logging, with the necessary connection details. Note that in the connection, we provide both the server address and a URL path separately. Fluentd will expect a path rather than an attempt to talk to the root address. We have provided a custom formatter and attached that to the handler. We then go through the same formatting process to form part of the log event and invoke the logger object with the log event string.

Using the prebuilt HTTPHandler means that the Fluentd configuration will need an HTTP source plugin to be included, which we have already done.

Listing 11.5   Chapter11/clients/log-simple.py—Direct Fluentd library use

```
import logging, logging.handlers        ◁──┐  Needs to import the core classes
import datetime                              └─ for both logging and the handlers
testHandler = logging.handlers.HTTPHandler('localhost:18080',
  ➥ '/test', method='POST')   ◁──┐ Creates the HTTPHandler and provides the
                                  │ details; in a secured production environment,
custom_format = {                 │ this would include the use of certificates as well.
  'host': '%(hostname)s',
  'where': '%(module)s.%(funcName)s',
  'type': '%(levelname)s',
  'stack_trace': '%(exc_text)s'
}
myFormatter = logging.Formatter(custom_format)
testHandler.setFormatter(myFormatter)
                                        ┐ Creates the logger to use
log = logging.getLogger("test")   ◁──── ┘ if it doesn't already exist
log.addHandler(testHandler)                        ◁──────┐ We add the log
now = datetime.datetime.now().strftime("%d-%m-%Y %H-%M-%S")│ handler we created
log.warn ('{"from":"log-simple", "at" :'+now+'"}')  ◁──┐  │ to the root log object
                                                       │  │ ready for use.
                Invokes the handler. When implementing a
                language-specific version of this code,
                ideally you would use a library to generate
                the JSON rather than manually inject it.
```

To run this example, open two shells as done previously. Navigate the root folder, and then start up Fluentd. Once running, execute the Python script in each shell using the following commands (from the `Chapter11/clients` folder for the Python script):

```
fluentd -c Chapter11/Fluentd/http.conf
python log-simple.py
```

11.7.4   *Illustration without Python's logging or Fluentd library*

While there is no reason to stop using the Python logging framework in the real world, it may not be an option in other languages, so let's see how that might look. For continuity and ease of comparison, we'll demonstrate what this could look like with Python. Most languages provide the means to interact with HTTP services without any dependencies. We can interact with the Fluentd HTTP source plugin, as we eliminated Fluentd's logging library. But we are now responsible for constructing all the HTTP headers, handling the HTTP connection to keep things open, and closing the connections, as shown in listing 11.6. This listing follows the same previous pattern of a client file to make it easy to make side-by-side comparisons.

As you can see, code populates the header with details such as the content type and content length. This should feel familiar, as, in many ways, these few lines of code are exactly the same as how we configured Postman in our "Hello World" scenario in chapter 2. As this is using the HTTP connection, we again don't benefit from the msgpack compression.

Listing 11.6   Chapter11/clients/log.py—logging without any support

```
import httplib, urllib
import datetime                                          Manually populates the
                                                         HTTP header attributes
message = '{"from":"log.py", "at":"'+datetime.datetime.now().strftime
    ("%d-%m-%Y %H-%M-%S")+'"}'
headers = {"Content-Type": "application/JSON", "Accept": "text/plain",
    "Content-Length":len(message)}
conn = httplib.HTTPConnection("localhost:18085")                    Creates the
conn.request("POST", "/test", message, headers)       Sends the      connection
                                                      log event
response = conn.getresponse()
print response.status, response.reason      We're responsible for
conn.close()                                closing the resources.
```

Assuming that the Fluentd server is still running from the previous examples, then all we need to do is run the command (from the `Chapter11/clients` folder)

```
python log.py
```

As before, we should expect to see the log events being written to the Fluentd server console.

11.7.5 *Porting the Fluentd calls to another language into action*

The company you work for is trialing some smart devices with some custom functionality in your manufacturing facility. The trialed smart devices are currently known to support several core languages, including Java, Python, and Ruby. The idea has been put forward that the smart devices already call the central server when they need or have to send data. Doing so allows battery power to be conserved by not powering wireless until it is needed. That principle could be applied to logging any issues that the smart devices experience. To keep the software footprint as small as possible, you have been asked to not add any additional libraries. You have been asked to provide a proof of concept as to whether the devices could talk directly to your current Fluentd infrastructure rather than needing a custom solution that acts as a proxy between the smart device and Fluentd.

ANSWER

Our primary languages are Java and Groovy (Groovy running on the Java Virtual Machine). We have built a small Groovy example using native HTTP calls to a Fluentd server. This can be found in `Chapter11/ExerciseResults/native-fluentd .groovy`. Groovy does bring an overhead but allows us to produce the proof quickly, as we don't need to set up a build and package setup (and we've previously introduced a Groovy setup in the book).

You should have produced a similar outcome with your preferred language and demonstrated the result using our simple Fluentd configuration or one of your own.

11.7.6 *Using generic appenders: The takeaways*

As you have seen, working with common protocols is possible, but it does increase the development effort. Additionally, without more effort, you do not gain the benefits of msgpack and knowing that the library has been proven. So, if you cannot use a prebuilt Fluentd library, consider looking for or developing a wrapper that will translate the way the logging framework works with the interface provided by the Fluentd library.

Summary

- There are efficiencies to be gained if the logging of events can be sent directly from the application without having to resort to using an intermediary, such as a file.
- Many logging frameworks have a common set of characteristics, although they are often called different things. These include an abstracted mechanism to send logs to a type of consumer (referred to as an *appender, handler,* or *sender*). Another common element is a decoupled formatter, which translates the log event to be represented in a manner that can be understood downstream.
- When reviewing logging frameworks, a number of questions need to be asked about the framework to determine suitability: Does it have a native appender for Fluentd or other components used? Is it possible to fall back to writing to files? Can you transmit log events over HTTP(S) or TCP/IP?
- Fluentd provides a series of logging libraries that support various programming languages, including Ruby, Java, Python, and others. These libraries can, in some cases, integrate with the language's native logging framework.

appendix A
Installation of additional tools and services

A.1 Tool installation overview

This book uses components and tools in addition to those necessary to run Fluentd. These help illustrate how Fluentd can work and integrate with other capabilities, such as MongoDB and Elasticsearch. Chapter 2 looks at the installation and configuration of Fluentd and Fluent Bit, as they are central to this book, including Fluentd's dependency on Ruby and the use of the LogGenerator. If you wish to try the scenarios described in the book, you will have to download and install the tools described in this appendix.

The following sections provide enough details to install the tools to support the examples in this book. If an installation value is not stated, then the default value should be assumed. To get the installations to production class deployments, you will need to look to additional resources, many of which are in appendix E.

Although we have worked to ensure that we cover both Windows and Linux installations, there are many Linux flavors and package managers (yum, apt, etc.) associated with them, complicating things. To test the Linux instructions, we used Ubuntu 18 LTE. This does mean you may need to tweak the steps for your specific Linux flavor. Please feel free to share those tweaks through social media or online Manning forums if you have access.

> **NOTE** As you probably know, Linux and Windows directory and file paths differ in using forward and backslashes. A number of the tools used in the book work with the same commands regardless of the OS. As a result, we have not provided the same command for both types of OS. It has been assumed that you will recognize when to reverse the slashes as appropriate for your platform.

A.2   *Creating environment variables and amending PATH*

Setting up environmental variables and extending the PATH environment variable is a common requirement. Let's summarize how this can be done using the setting of JAVA as an example. Subsequent installations will reference this section. To check whether the PATH might need amending, we can see its values with echo %PATH% on Windows and echo $PATH on Linux.

A.2.1   *Windows*

The following needs to be done with care, as it represents a system-wide change. Within the following command, replace <path addition> with the new path—for example, c:\java\bin:

```
setx path "%path%;<path addition>"
```

For more documentation on setx, see http://mng.bz/jyAP.

Within Windows, you can make the change through the settings UI and search for environment variables. This will locate the UI element used to manipulate the PATH and other environment variables. The precise steps will vary slightly between Windows versions. If you use this approach, any shell windows will need to be restarted to see the changes.

A.2.2   *Linux*

Depending on your version of Linux, if you have a desktop UI installed, it is more than likely to offer a UI-based solution to updating the PATH. However, given the diversity of UIs available, there isn't a standard answer, but it is a common need, so a web search should yield the answer.

In the following command, replace <path addition> with the relevant path (e.g., /etc/java/bin). This will add the directory into the path for the shell that executed the command:

```
export PATH="$PATH:<path addition>"
```

To make the change work system-wide, add the previous command into a shell script (e.g., setup-for-fluentd.sh), and save the shell script in the folder /etc/profile.d. Make sure the shell script is executable (if necessary, run chmod a+x setup-for-fluentd.sh). More information on manipulating PATH in Linux can be found at https://bit.ly/SetLinuxPath.

A.3   *Java and Groovy*

The core details for these two elements are covered in chapter 2, as they are essentials for using the LogSimulator. If you wish to work outside of a package manager, retrieve the appropriate installer resources here:

- Java: www.java.com/en/download/manual.jsp
- Groovy: https://groovy-lang.org/install.html

If you wish to use the LogSimulator as a Groovy utility, then it is recommended that you observe the compatibility details with Java, particularly as the Java release cycle is faster. Not all releases are long-term editions and therefore tested for compatibility.

A.4   *Postman*

In chapter 2, we used Postman to send basic HTTP log events. Postman can be used in a simplified browser manner by accessing https://identity.getpostman.com/login; it does require a free account to be set up. Alternatively, a desktop solution can be installed from www.postman.com/downloads.

A.5   *Elasticsearch*

This section looks at a basic setup of Elasticsearch. Elasticsearch is a commonly used repository for performing log analytics activities, and therefore an important target for Fluentd. We only cover enough to allow us to work with Fluentd, so for a more comprehensive look at Elasticsearch, check out *Elasticsearch In Action* by Radu Gheorghe, et al. (Manning, 2015) at https://www.manning.com/books/elasticsearch-in-action.

A.5.1   *Core Elasticsearch installation*

The binaries can be downloaded for Elasticsearch, which can be retrieved from https://www.elastic.co/downloads/elasticsearch. This includes both package manager versions for the different Linux versions in addition to the zip and tar formats. For this, we'll use the zip or gzip/tar, depending on the platform. Once downloaded, unpack the compressed file. For Windows, we'll assume `c:\dev\elasticsearch` as the target and a similar path such as `/usr/bin/elasticsearch`. The Windows installation has a prerequisite of installing Microsoft Universal C Runtime Library (downloadable from http://mng.bz/W7M1).

To make things easy, add the Elasticsearch bin folder (e.g., `C:\dev\elastic-search-x.y.z\bin`), where `x.y.z` is the release number in the `PATH`, as explained in section A.2. Elasticsearch provides a comprehensive set of instructions at http://mng.bz/8l2w if you run into any issues.

To start Elasticsearch, we can run the shell script `elasticsearch` bat or bash script. Alternatively, it can be added, removed, and controlled as a service using the `elasticsearch-service` script with the following parameters:

- Install
- Remove
- Start
- Stop

The Linux equivalent of a daemon service is `elasticsearch -d -p pid` with the `pid` representing a file to hold the service details. The Elasticsearch installation and startup can be verified using `Postman` executing a GET call on `localhost:9200`. A successful result will return a JSON payload reflecting the status of the Elasticsearch server. This is illustrated in figure A.1.

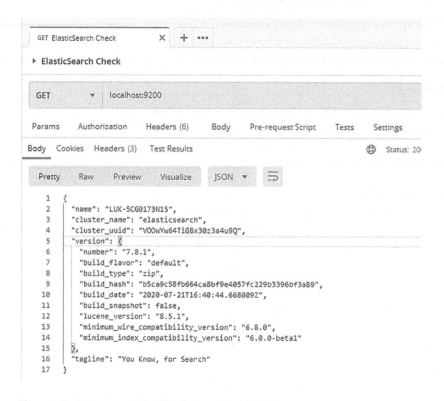

Figure A.1   Postman verifying Elasticsearch installation

A.5.2   *Elasticsearch UI installation*

To review the contents of Elasticsearch, rather than formulating expressions using Postman, we can utilize one of the available UIs. For the purposes of this book, we found Elasticvue to be both easy to use and incredibly simple to install. Elasticvue can be obtained from https://elasticvue.com and provides installation as a browser extension for Chrome, Firefox, Microsoft Edge, or as a web app or Docker image. We've adopted the Chrome extension, as it requires no configuration and runs locally to accommodate localhost addressing. This installation requires you to follow the link from the Elasticvue website into the Chrome store and then click the Add to Chrome button.

Once you've started Elasticsearch and opened the extension, you simply need to confirm the server you wish to connect to (http://localhost:9200). Once connected, Elasticvue provides stats about the server, and selecting the Indices menu will show the indexes. This will include those we use once the examples are run.

A.5.3 *Fluentd plugin for Elasticsearch*

The `td_agent` version of Fluentd includes the elastic search plugin `out_elastic-search`. However, the unmodified version of Fluentd does not. Therefore, it is necessary to install the plugin manually with the command `fluent-gem install fluent-plugin-elasticsearch`.

A.6 *Mongo database*

We first used MongoDB in chapter 4 as an alternative output destination. MongoDB is available with Enterprise and Community Editions. We will stick with a Community Edition, as this provides the features we need and is not subject to commercial licensing. In addition to the core MongoDB, we want to have the MongoDB GUI (graphical user interface) *Compass*, which also has variants. We will be using the free edition.

A.6.1 *Mongo DB installation*

MongoDB provides an MSI installer for Windows and other package management tools for Linux and macOS (RPM, DMG), and so on. You can download the current version by going to www.mongodb.com/download-center/community.

> **NOTE** RPM stands for *Red Hat Package Manager* and DMG stands for *disk image.*

We will assume the latest stable release using the MSI installer, ideal for setting up in development environments because of the simplicity and speed. While in production, you are more likely to adopt different installation strategies depending on your infrastructure and use case—for example, Docker in a microservices context or retrieving native binaries and manually crafted configuration files to exploit networked storage solutions such as SANs (storage area networks).

Depending on your OS privileges, you will likely need to run MongoDB as a local administrator in Windows or with root-based privileges (using `sudo`) for Linux. In standard OS configurations, this will undoubtedly be the case.

With the MSI downloaded, start the installation. The installer is self-explanatory; make sure you choose the recommended *Complete* setup. A couple of further steps, and the installer provides the option of installing Compass; make sure this option is ticked.

A.6.2 *MongoDB configuration*

Compass should be started once the installation is complete, and it will provide a button to connect (if your package manager installation doesn't begin Compass, please do so). Compass will display a screen with the basic setup. Click the Connect button, as shown in figure A.2.

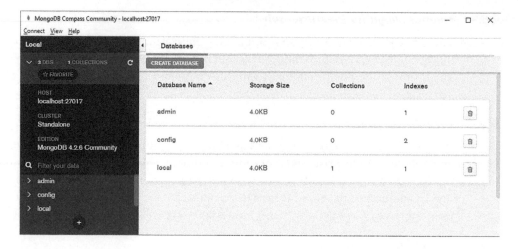

Figure A.2 MongoDB database viewed through Compass UI tool

The final step is to establish a database to be used to store the log events. Click the CREATE DATABASE button, as shown in figure A.2. This action takes us to a pop-up screen that will ask for a database and collection name. For our purposes, we will call them both `Fluentd`, as figure A.3 shows.

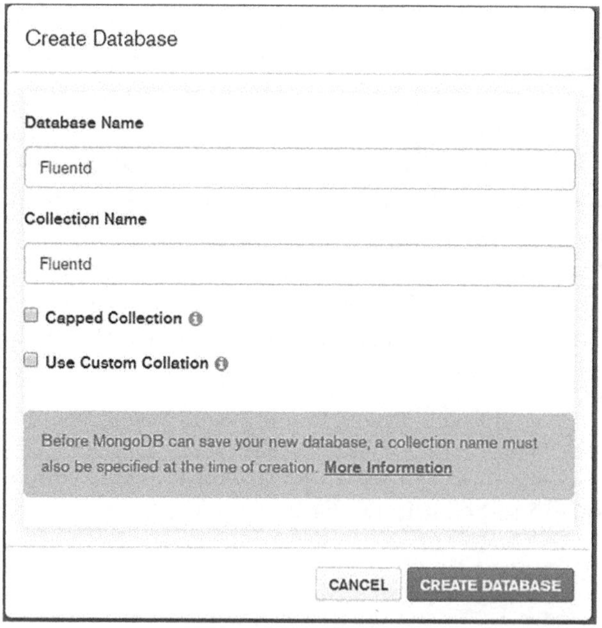

Figure A.3 MongoDB Compass Create Database pop-up—the simplest way to define a DB for our examples

We do not want to specify any MongoDB restrictions (Capped Collection) or customization for the Collection. This means ensuring the tick boxes are not set. With this, we have the setup for MongoDB and you can click CREATE DATABASE.

Once complete, you will see the addition of a Fluentd database in the list and the default databases provided as part of the installation (admin, config, and local) which can be seen if figure A1. If you click on the Fluentd database, you will get a view of the database collection.

The last step is to add the MongoDB binary to the `PATH` variable to run some simple commands to quickly refresh the environment. The precise path will depend on the version installed and any installation configuration values changed from the installation defaults you may have provided. A typical location would be `C:\Program Files\MongoDB\Server\4.2\bin`, where `4.2` is the MongoDB version number. The steps to apply this change are detailed in section A.2. Setting up the `PATH` on Linux will need a path to the installation location of the MongoDB binaries, which will be in a folder using the following form: `mongodb-linux-x86_64-4.2.0/bin`. The location of this folder will be more dependent on the package manager, but `/usr/bin` would be the convention.

A.7 *Slack*

Slack (https://slack.com) cloud service has a free use tier, which can be used as your private Slack workspace. We would recommend you set up your own space for the work with Fluentd to keep things simple. It also means that you will not have any issues if there are restrictions in the privileges when setting up application tokens if you're trying to use a work-related Slack workspace.

If you are new to Slack, you will find that the web UI is sufficient, but having the app installed on a device (phone, tablet, or desktop) gives a better experience (https://slack.com/downloads), particularly for putting the app into the background instead of keeping another browser tab open.

The next step will be to set up your token needed by Fluentd. Using the Fluentd web UI option, Add Features and Functionality, select Incoming Webhooks > Bots > Permissions, and click Save Changes.

With a personal Slack workspace, we need to use the Slack administration UI to configure an application to get an application token. The easiest way to do this is to jump directly to https://api.slack.com/apps once signed into Slack in the browser. Click the button Create New App, as shown in figure A.4. We need to provide an App Name (which we recommend you also use for the `username` attribute in the plugin configuration) and ensure that your workspace is selected for the Development Slack Workspace option; then click Create App. The UI will prompt you to enable the webhooks. Once done using the left-hand menu, we need to select OAuth and Permissions. In the lower part of the screen is the configuration for Scopes. We specifically want to modify the Scopes for Bot Tokens. The list of available API scopes adds `chat:write` and `chat:write:public` and ensures that the `incoming-webhook` is already included. Once this is complete, you will be shown two tokens at the top of the page. We need to copy the Bot User OAuth Access Token, as it is required when working with Fluentd. Then click the Reinstall App button. The configuration of Slack for our output is now complete.

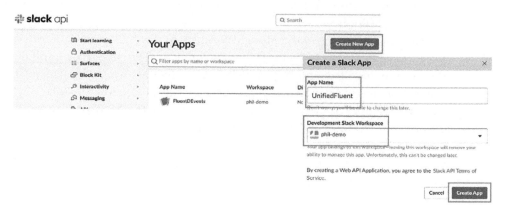

Figure A.4   Slack UI to create an "app," and the corresponding form with required values highlighted

A.8   *Setting up Docker and Kubernetes*

This section covers the installation of Docker and Kubernetes to support chapter 8. This section is a little tricky because Linux OSes differ in package management and what is already installed. For the purposes of this section, when it comes to Linux, we're going to assume Ubuntu 18.04 or later. This does mean some prerequisite steps are needed for Windows users.

If your Linux version isn't Ubuntu (e.g., Fedora, Debian), the steps may differ slightly because of the package manager, and so on. In this situation, there are a couple of options:

- Set up a containerized instance of Ubuntu using tools such as Docker and connecting to the container, which, in many ways, will probably be like Ubuntu anyway.
- Adapt the commands yourself to work on your Linux flavor.
- Follow the Linux version of the VirtualBox setup, which will be explained.

Chapter 8 used a virtual machine for working with just Docker and also used minikube, a CNCF-supported small footprint deployment of Kubernetes for running the Kubernetes aspects of the chapter. By actioning the Docker-related activities within a virtualized environment, we don't accidentally pollute the Kubernetes setup or any existing work you might have with Docker already.

Adopting minikube also means we have the same approach for local deployments as the book *Kubernetes in Action* by Marko Lukša (Manning Publications, 2017). Depending on your environment and deployment approach, minikube will use

VirtualBox or Hyper-V if you're operating on a Windows platform and Docker if operating on a native Linux environment.

A.8.1   *Windows Prerequisites*

The prerequisites will depend on the Windows version being run. Your choices are limited for Windows 10 and 11 Home or older Windows versions, and will mean installing and using VirtualBox as described in the next section. Windows 10 Pro or better offer a couple of options:

- Use the Windows Hyper-V Manager and create a Ubuntu VM; Microsoft's documentation to do this is available at https://docs.microsoft.com/en-us/virtualiza tion/hyper-v-on-windows/quick-start/quick-create-virtual-machine.

   If this approach is adopted, you may also need to take additional steps to ensure that you can copy and paste between the Windows Host and the Ubuntu VM. The solution to this is detailed at https://docs.microsoft.com/en-us/troubleshoot/windows-server/virtualization/copy-paste-not-work-hyper-v-vm-vmconnect-enhanced-session-mode.

- The alternative (and my preference) is to leverage the Windows Subsystem for Linux (WSL) 2. This provides a far easier way to switch between Windows native and Linux. The steps to set this are more complex, as you will need to install Docker Desktop (www.docker.com/products/docker-desktop) and download and install several additional components from Microsoft. The steps for this are detailed at https://docs.microsoft.com/en-gb/windows/wsl/install-win10.

   When setting up WSL and the Ubuntu distribution (our recommendation), we have observed that when it comes to running the Docker commands, like the `docker --version` to validate installation, not everything reports correctly. It has been reported that the configuration with Docker Desktop can be incorrect, but in the UI, it looks correct. In this situation, we've disabled the WSL2 option within the Docker Desktop, saved the change, and then, without Ubuntu running, gone back into the Docker Desktop settings and re-enabled WSL2. Next, we started our Ubuntu instance; once running, things have resolved themselves.

A.8.2   *VirtualBox approach*

VirtualBox (www.virtualbox.org) is an Oracle-supported open source project to provide virtualization on desktops covering Windows, macOS, and Linux. It does require the host to have an AMD or Intel chipset. VirtualBox won't work on Windows if you're using Hyper-V virtualization, and it can be sensitive to BIOS/UEFI settings. More information on this subject can be found at www.howtogeek.com/213795/how-to-enable-intel-vt-x-in-your-computers-bios-or-uefi-firmware.

The first step is to download VirtualBox from the downloads page (www.virtualbox.org/wiki/Downloads), providing access to a Windows executable as an installer or the relevant package for your Linux flavor. Once downloaded, run the installation process to get set up. With the core of VirtualBox installed, installing the Extension Pack is recommended and available on the download page.

The next step is to get the Ubuntu guest OS built. This can be done by either

- Downloading a prebuilt virtual image from the VirtualBox website, although the image provided for Ubuntu is old. Alternatively, use a site such as OSBoxes (www.osboxes.org/ubuntu-server/), which offers prebuilt images that can then be imported into VirtualBox. Using this route means you need to ensure you have the credentials for a user with root privileges.
- Creating a guest image using VirtualBox is detailed at http://mng.bz/Ex0O.

A.8.3 Ubuntu image preparation for working with Docker

With the image organized, it is recommended that you log into your Ubuntu image and run the following commands to ensure that the package manager is up to date:

```
sudo apt-get update
sudo apt-get upgrade
```

Next, let's verify whether or not the `curl` utility is available using the command

```
curl --version
```

If the response comes back positively with version information, then we're all done. If not, then the following command is needed to get `curl` installed:

```
sudo apt-get install curl
```

Next up in our installation needs is Docker. This can be done with the shell command:

```
sudo apt-get install Docker.io
```

If you have any preferred utilities, Linux shortcuts, and so on, this is the best time to configure them.

At this stage, we recommend that you stop the VirtualBox guest VM and Export the VM to have a ready start state available if going back to a clean state is required. This means if you wish to abandon the current VM and start afresh, it is simply a case of stopping the VM you're currently using, deleting it, and importing the exported image.

A.8.4 Kubernetes installation

This installation process isn't needed until you start working with Kubernetes but will need the Docker steps to be executed in advance, as they establish some of the prerequisites. In terms of computing power, you're going to need at least 2 CPUs, 2 GB of RAM, and 20 GB of storage. The more resources you can give over to minikube, the better the experience.

We had looked into the possibility of running minikube within the virtual machine, so the steps would be the same regardless of the host being Windows or Linux. But it makes for a more complicated setup for most users who are not likely to need it.

MINIKUBE ON WINDOWS

If you're going to deploy minikube onto a Windows platform, we'd recommend using the *Chocolatey package manager*, and this is how we're going to deploy minikube. Other approaches are detailed on the minikube site at https://minikube.sigs.k8s.io/docs/start/.

> **NOTE** Chocolatey (https://chocolatey.org/) provides a Linux package manager-like experience for Windows. For applications that aren't bound to a formal Microsoft installation experience (such as MSIs), it is worth using it to take care of things like setting environment variables, dealing with dependencies, and cleaning up, which is far better with Chocolatey than trying to remember the manual install steps to reverse. The process of installing Chocolatey is clearly explained at https://chocolatey.org/install.

The steps need to be performed using a `cmd` shell running as an administrator (right-clicking on the `cmd` option in the start menu to get the Administrator option). In the `cmd` shell, we need to install the core of minikube using the command

```
choco install minikube
```

Next, we'll need the Kubernetes command-line interface (CLI) known as *kubectl*, which can be installed using the command

```
choco install kubernetes-cli
```

These two steps have established minikube into the environment. As minikube uses Hyper-V when used on a Windows host, you may wish to set up an additional virtual network within Hyper-V to avoid any network conflicts with any other virtualization setups that presently exist. To implement this, the Hyper-V Manager can be started from the Start menu or with the command line using the command

```
Virtmgmt.msc
```

We need to click the Virtual Switch Manager option on the right of the Hyper-V Manager UI, as shown in figure A.5.

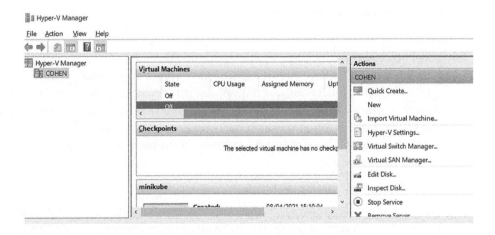

Figure A.5 Hyper-V management UI with Virtual Switch Manager option

When the Virtual Switch Manager UI is displayed, we use the New virtual network switch option at the top of the list of switches to create a new switch. The new switch settings are displayed on the right. The switch needs to be set to the Internal option. Once the switch is created with the name Primary Virtual Switch (the name is essential, as when you create the minikube cluster, we will reference this), the configuration should look like the details shown in figure A.6.

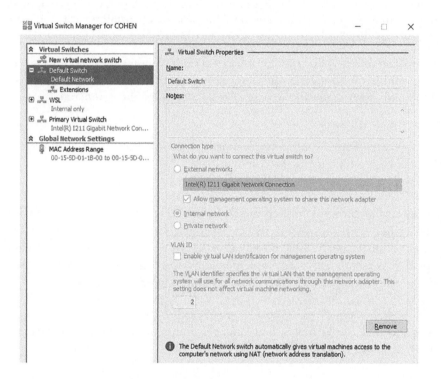

Figure A.6   Configuration of the virtual switch

MINIKUBE FOR LINUX

For Linux, the OS will need the appropriate Hypervisor installed, such as KVM (kernel-based virtual machine). As this process can change for different flavors of OS, we would recommend checking details with your OS documentation. The following describes the steps for Ubuntu, which are common to many Linux flavors.

First, we need to check that the hardware can support virtualization; this can be done with the command

```
egrep -c '(vmx|svm)' /proc/cpuinfo
```

A result of 1 or greater means that the computer hardware can support virtualization. You may wish to perform some checks to determine whether or not the host will perform well by examining whether the OS is 32-bit or 64-bit and how many resources are available. We're going to assume that this is not an issue. The next step is to install the virtualization features. These can differ slightly over Linux versions, but for Ubuntu 18.10 or later, the command is

```
sudo apt-get install qemu-kvm libvirt-daemon-system libvirt-clients bridge-
    utils
```

The next step is to ensure you have the privileges to use the virtualization; this is done with the following commands:

```
sudo adduser 'id -un' libvirtd
sudo adduser 'id -un' kvm
```

Each of these commands will confirm the addition of your user. The next step is to log in again for the changes to take effect. The installation and configuration can be checked with the following commands, which will indicate the ability to connect to the Hypervisor and access the `libvirt-sock`:

```
virsh list --all
sudo ls -la /var/run/libvirt/libvirt-sock
```

We need to ensure that the ownership and permissions for the folder `/dev/kvm` are correct. This is done with the command

```
sudo chown root:libvirtd /dev/kvm
```

Again, a login cycle is needed for the changes to take effect. The final step comes down to whether you want to use the Virtualization GUI; this can be installed with the command

```
sudo apt-get install virt-manager
```

With the virtualization successfully set up, this process is a little simpler, as it only uses Docker and doesn't create an additional virtualization layer. The first steps are to use `curl` to retrieve the Debian package and then install the downloaded package with the commands

```
curl -LO https://storage.googleapis.com/minikube/releases/latest/
    minikube_latest_amd64.deb
sudo dpkg -i minikube_latest_amd64.deb
```

We need to install the `conntrack` service and ensure that `apt-transport-hous-ings` packages that support connection management within the Linux OS are installed. This can be done with

```
sudo apt-get install conntrack
sudo apt-get install apt-transport-https
```

It is helpful to have the Kubernetes key command-line tools in the form of `kubectl`. We can get this installed with the following commands:

```
curl -LO "https://dl.k8s.io/release/$(curl -L -s \
https://dl.k8s.io/release/stable.txt)/bin/linux/amd64/kubectl"
sudo install -o root -g root -m 0755 kubectl /usr/local/bin/kubectl
kubectl version --client
```

The final step is to install minikube. This can be done with the following commands:

```
wget https://storage.googleapis.com/minikube/releases/latest/minikube-linux-
    amd64
sudo cp minikube-linux-amd64 /usr/local/bin/minikube
sudo chmod +x /usr/local/bin/minikube
```

We should be able to verify the minikube installation with the following command:

```
minikube version
```

A.9   *Support Ruby development libraries and tools*

For chapter 8, where we implement a custom plugin, we recommend installing additional RubyGems to help with the development. RubyGems can be added using the command

```
gem install <name of ruby gem>
```

You just need to replace `<name of ruby gem>` with the following recommended additions:

- `test-unit`
- `ruby-lint`

If you want to know more about these tools, the links are provided in appendix E, along with all the other helpful resource information.

A.10   *Redis*

Chapter 8 used Redis to demonstrate the development of a custom plugin. It is one of the leading in-memory cache solutions. The installation for our requirements is minimal. Redis can be installed in a couple of different ways on a Linux platform:

- Follow the Redis Quick Start guide (https://redis.io/topics/quickstart), which will take you through the process of downloading the source code and run the make tool to generate a suitable executable.
- Or follow the steps at https://redis.io/download to retrieve a package manager solution. In either case, you want to be using the latest stable release. Alternatively, Redis can be installed using the apt-get package manager (e.g., Ubuntu) or Snapcraft (https://snapcraft.io/).

For Windows to adopt this approach, you'll need to be using Windows 10 Pro with the WSL. There is a pure Windows port that can be retrieved via https://github.com/ServiceStack/redis-windows. There is also a popular community port available at https://github.com/dmajkic/redis/downloads; this is very dated, but it has the features for our needs. The alternative is to run the Docker prepackaged solution, which will make some of the steps needed more complex as we need to use the Redis CLI.

Once this is downloaded and built/installed, you will need to add the location of the binaries to your path, as described in section A.2. This should pick up both the server and the CLI.

A.10.1 Redis gem

In addition to the core Redis server, we need a Ruby library that can talk to Redis. This can be retrieved and installed very quickly using the command

```
gem install Redis
```

This will download and install the latest stable gem into your gem library, ready for use. If you want to know more about this, the documentation of this gem can be found at https://github.com/redis/redis-rb.

A.11 Python

In chapter 11, to illustrate how default adaptors can be used, we used Python. Installation of Python depends on your OS. For Windows, the most straightforward approach is to download the MSI from Python.org. For Linux, the OS package manager will be the best approach for installation.

When it comes to using Python 2.x or 3.x, many people are still using Python 2.x, even though it has reached its end of life. We would advocate for the adoption of Python 3; we have checked the small apps with both versions. For Windows, we would recommend using the Python Switcher utility (more details at http://mng.bz/Nx51) to allow the switching between different Python versions. For Linux, the best option, if required, is to utilize the Alternatives facility (a Linux generic description can be found at www.lifewire.com/alternatives-linux-command-4091710, and an Ubuntu detailed explanation can be found at http://mng.bz/DxDw).

With Python installed, two additional libraries will be needed, which can be installed using the *Package Installer for Python* (PIP), using the commands

```
pip install pyyaml
pip install fluent-logger
```

Depending on your preferred way of viewing files, you may wish to install or add a plugin to your preferred IDE to make it easier to work with Python and YAML files.

A.12 Vault

Within the book, we refer to the use of HashiCorp's Vault. While it is not necessary, you might consider trying it out with Fluentd. HashiCorp has produced an excellent installation guide that breaks the process down to a few pretty straightforward steps. The details can be found at http://mng.bz/laJ8. As the steps are relatively simple, we will summarize them here, and if you need more information, refer back to the Vault tutorial for the dev mode setup:

1 Download the correct binary for your OS from www.vaultproject.io/downloads.
2 Unpack the zip file into a suitable location (e.g., `c:\vault` or `/usr/bin/vault`).
3 Add the installation location to the `PATH` environment variable (see section A.2).
4 Run the command `vault -install-autocomplete`; this will add any command-line utilities it can to your environment.
5 Start Vault server in development mode using the command `vault server -dev`. Note that the output near the start of the command execution will display a key and token on the console. You'll need to note these, as the root token will be required in a minute.
6 Set up two environment variables using Windows set command or Linux's export:
   - `VAULT_ADDR=http://127.0.0.1:8200`
   - `VAULT_TOKEN=<Root Token>`

With these steps complete, you can verify the status of the setup with the command `vault status`. Note that every time Vault is restarted, the token will change, and the secrets held will be empty. This behavior is occurring because Vault is running in development mode, where development mode is nonpersistent.

appendix B
Processing times and dates, regular expressions, and other configuration values

B.1 Expressing relative time

Some configuration attributes of Fluentd require us to express time in a relative manner, (i.e., how long from now). Such values in a readable form are best done using simple integers and time types—seconds, minutes, and hours. The following table shows how this is done in Fluentd.

Interval	Character	Examples
Seconds	s	10s → 10 seconds 0.1s → 100ms
Minutes	m	1m → 1 minute 0.25m → 15 seconds
Hours	h	24h → 24 hours 0.25h → 15 minutes
Days	d	1d → 1 day 0.5d → 12 hours

B.2 Expressing dates and times

The date representation for input and output is driven by how Ruby can parse custom formatted date-times. The following table shows the mapping of character codes to the values they resolve to. In several cases, the lowercase and uppercase of

the same character represents truncated and full versions of the same value (e.g., a%
and %A). The lowercase form represents the truncated format. We have put these
cases together in the same row to make them easier to spot.

Code	Date element description	Example
%a %A	Three-letter abbreviation of the day of week. Full name of the day of week.	Mon Monday
%b or %h %B	An abbreviated version of the month name. Full month name.	Feb February
%c	Shortcut to locale default representation.	%a %b %e %T %Y The exact format is driven by the locale settings.
%C	Century in numeric form.	2021 would result in 20 (Ruby derives this value by rounding down the result of the year divided by 100.)
%d	Day of the month as a two-digit number 01 . . . 31.	06
%D	Shortcut for %m/%d/%y (month/day/year).	01/01/21
%e	Day of the month, but days less than 10 have a single-digit representation.	6
%F	A shortcut for %Y-%m-%d, which aligns to the ISO 8601 for- mat (more on the ISO format standard can be found at www.iso.org/iso-8601-date-and-time-format.html). Often documented as YYYY-MM-DD.	2021-12-31
%H	Hour of the day represented in the double-digit format against a 24-hour clock.	02
%I (capital *I*)	Hour of the day using double-digit 12-hour clock, so 01 could be 1 a.m. or 1 p.m. The alternate form is %l (lowercase *L*).	01
%j	Three-digit representation of the day of the year starting at 001	211
%k	Hour of the day (24-hour format 0 . . . 23); single digits rep- resent morning hours	3
%l (lowercase *L*)	Hour of the day using one digit for hours < 10, double-digit for the remaining. This uses the 12-hour clock, so 1 could be 1 a.m. or 1 p.m. The alternate form is %I.	1
%L	Millisecond part of the time in the three-digit form.	021
%m	The month of the year in the double-digit form.	08
%M	Minute of the hour in the double-digit form.	09

(continued)

Code	Date element description	Example
%N or %9N %6N %3N	Fractions of a second in nanoseconds (9 digits). Fractions of a second in microseconds seconds (6 digits). Fractions of a second in milliseconds (3 digits).	012345678 012345 012
%p %P	Meridian indicator: AM or PM (uppercase). Meridian indicator: am or pm (lowercase).	PM p.m.
%r	Shortcut for 12-hour clock time representation—same as using %I:%M:%S %p.	01:02:06 PM
%R	Shortcut for time representation using the 24-hour clock—equates to %H:%M.	15:01
%s	Number of seconds since epoch (i.e., 1970-01-01 00:00:00 UTC); also known as POSIX time or Unix time.	1588115129
%S	Number of seconds in the minute using a two-digit representation.	05
%T	Shortcut for %H:%M:%S—time to the second precision using the 24-hour clock.	01:59:11
%u	Day of the week in a numerical form, with Monday being 1.	7
%U	Week number in the current year in two-digit format, with the first Sunday counting as the first day of the first week: 00 . . . 53.	52
%V	Week number as defined by ISO 8601 (alternate to %U).	01
%W	Week number calculated from the first Monday.	00
%w	Alternate numeric representation of the day of the week, where the first day is Sunday (0).	6
%x	Alias for %D.	01/01/21
%X	Alias for %T.	01:59:11
%y %Y	Year as a two-digit number (i.e., century is omitted). Year including century.	21 2021
%z	Time zone offset is expressed as a positive or negative four digits relative to UTC. For example, New York is 4 hours behind UTC, so it is -0400. The first two digits represent hours; the second represents minutes. For example, Australian Central Standard Time is 9.5 hours ahead of UTC.	+0930
%Z	The time zone is represented by its name. A complete list of time zones and their codes can be found at www.timeanddate.com/time/zones/.	BST

B.3   Expressing sizes

Some attributes allow you to express data sizes in terms of bytes up to terabytes. However, we do not recommend you entertaining terabyte sizing.

Size	Character	Examples
Bytes	-	100 → 100 bytes
Kilobytes	k	12k → 12 kilobytes (Kb)
Megabytes	m	5m → 5 megabytes (MB)
Gigabytes	g	3h → 3 gigabytes (GB)
Terabytes	T	1t → 1 terabyte (TB)

B.4   Regular expressions

Regular expressions are a common means by which we can process strings of text to find specific patterns or break the strings into parts. Unfortunately, Regular Expressions (often REGEX for short) can differ slightly between implementations. For reference, the following sections highlight the most useful aspects of Regular Expressions as implemented by Ruby (and as Fluentd is implemented with Ruby) and used by Fluentd.

B.4.1   Escape Codes

Escape codes provide the means to use predefined groups of characters.

Regex code	Explanation
.	Any character except a newline, unless multiline options are enabled in the parser
\d	A digit character ([0-9])
\D	A nondigit character ([^0-9])
\h	A hexdigit character ([0-9a-fA-F])
\H	A non-hexdigit character ([^0-9a-fA-F])
\s	A whitespace character [\t\r\n\f\v] (i.e., space, tab, carriage return, new line, vertical tab, or form feed)
\S	A non-whitespace character [^ \t\r\n\f\v]
\w	A word character ([a-zA-Z0-9_])
\W	Any non-word character (i.e., inversion of \w)

B.4.2   Repetition/selection

These characters allow us to define different reoccurrence patterns and define ranges of acceptable values.

Regex code	Explanation
*	Zero or more times
?	Zero or one time (optional)
[n,m]	Defines a choice of accepted values
[n..m]	Defines a range of values—the content is impacted by ASCII encoding and can contain multiple ranges by a repetition of n...m (e.g., [a..zA..Z0..9])
^	Within a range
{,m}	m or fewer times
{n,}	n or more times
{n,m}	At least n and at most m times
{n}	Exactly n times
+	One or more times

B.4.3 Anchors, groups, and alternates

Anchors are metacharacters that match the zero-width positions between characters, anchoring the match to a specific position. Groups allow us to define atomic groupings, which could be seen as the mathematical use of brackets.

Regex code	Explanation
$	Matches to the end of the line.
(	Starts a grouping.
(?	Starts a group without capturing the content.
(?<NAME>	Define capture groups with a name. NAME is replaced with the name of choice.
)	End of grouping for both capture and non-capture groups.
\A	Matches the beginning of a string.
\G	Matches the first occurrence of the defined character.
\k<NAME>	Allows named groups to be back referenced (i.e., referenced once defined).
\Z	Matches end of the string. If the end of the line is a newline character, this is ignored.
\z	Matches end of the string.
^	Matches to the beginning of the line.
|	Separates two values or expressions, which can be treated like this or this—for example, for (a|b), the value could be a or b.

B.5   *Docker tag customization*

Within the log-opts configuration of the Docker log driver, it is possible to tailor the tag element of its output. This is done by setting the tag part of log-opts to equal a configuration string using the predefined template markup, as shown in the following table.

Markup	Description
{{.ID}}	Initial 12 characters of the container ID
{{.FullID}}	The complete 64-character container ID
{{.Name}}	The name of the container at the startup
{{.ImageID}}	Initial 12 characters of the image ID
{{.ImageFullID}}	The image's complete ID
{{.ImageName}}	Name of the image being used by the container
{{.DaemonName}}	Name of software daemon running the container (i.e., Docker)

Using this table, if we provided an additional configuration, such as `-log-opt tag="{{.ID}}-{{.ImageID}}"`, then the tag would look something like `"myid12xxeerr-mynamefluent"` with the hyphen coming from our separation of the two tag parts in the configuration as we specified.

appendix C
Plugins summary

We have looked at several types of plugins within the book but have not addressed all the available plugins available out of the box. This appendix addresses that. We have provided a summary of all the core plugins and some open source ones that warrant attention.

C.1 Formatter plugins

Plugin name	Summary	Fluentd core
csv	Covered in chapter 4. Basic comma-separated values, although the separator can be changed through the configuration attributes.	Y
hash	This translates the log event record to a representation that Ruby can handle in a hash format. It is possible to embed Ruby code fragments into some plugin configurations, hence its inclusion.	Y
json	Covered in chapter 4. Allows us to output the log event contents in a JSON format. For more information on JSON format, see www.json.org.	Y
ltsv	Covered in chapter 4. Label tab (character) separated values—rather than depending on positioning in the list to get the correct value meaning, we can include a label. See http://ltsv.org/ for more resources and information.	Y
msgpack	Covered in chapter 4. A formatter ideal for compressing log events to communicate between Fluentd and Fluent Bit. For more information on msgpack, see https://msgpack.org/.	Y
out_file	Covered in chapter 4. This formatter prints out the named log event attributes, which can be listed using a delimiter.	Y
single_value	The single_value formatter is a little like the CSV formatter in that it is possible to select from the log event record and output that content. However, it is only possible to identify one part of the log event record, using the message_key attribute in this case.	Y

C.2   *Extract and inject plugin support*

The out-of-the-box source and match plugins support for extract and inject are as follows:

Source	Inject	Extract
dummy	No	No
exec	No	Yes
forward	No	No
http	No	No
monitor_agent	No	No
syslog	No	No
tail	No	No
tcp	No	Yes
udp	No	Yes
unix	No	No
windows_eventlog	No	No

Match	Inject	Extract
copy	Yes	No
exec	No	No
exec_filter	Yes	Yes
file	Yes	No
forward	No	No
http	No	No
null	No	No
relabel	No	No
round_robin	No	No
secondary_file	No	No
stdout	Yes	No

C.3   *Filter plugins*

Plugin name	Summary	Fluentd core
add	Interesting as it provides an effortless way to add a UUID (universally unique identifier) and other additional name-value pairs. Unique IDs are helpful when log events pass through multiple Fluentd nodes. More information can be found at https://github.com/yu-yamada/fluent-plugin-add.	N
anonymizer	Anonymizer can be configured to perform a one-way hash of the contents of an element in a log event using the selected algorithm. This is ideal for masking sensitive data. More can be found at https://github.com/y-ken/fluent-plugin-anonymizer.	N
autotype	Applies typing to the log event attributes based on analyzing the payload. Ideal for handling numeric values, as it removes the need to effect a manual typecast.	N
filter_ parser	Combines the capability of parser plugins with the filter.	Y
fluent- plugin- fields- autotype	This plugin is ideal for parsing the log event structure and selecting the correct data type to evaluate the attributes. This is also a variant of fluent-plugin-auto-typ. More information can be found at http://mng.bz/AxlK.	N

(continued)

Plugin name	Summary	Fluentd core
`geoip`	This plugin exploits the fact that internet providers publish the internet protocol (IP) addresses they have been allocated along with the physical location at which these IPs connect to the "internet." This information is then aggregated together by several organizations. By knowing the IP of the request, it is possible to look up a location. This is beneficial, as it allows data to be more effectively routed and filtered. For example, you could have a global network of Fluentd servers. Using GeoIP will enable us to direct the logs to the nearest Fluentd server to aggregate the log events. This can be very helpful when working with high volumes of logs in distributed use cases such as • Internet of Things (IoT) deployments • Global multi-region and multi-cloud solutions More information can be found at https://github.com/y-ken/fluent-plugin-geoip.	N
`grep`	Provides the means to define rules about log event attributes to filter them out of the stream of events. Multiple expressions can be specified to create cumulative rules.	Y
`record_modifier`	A variant of `record_transformer` has been changed to make the plugin more efficient: http://mng.bz/ZzoO.	N
`record_tran sformer`	The most sophisticated built-in filter and provides a diverse set of options for manipulating the log event.	Y
`stdout`	Sends all events to `stdout`, without removing the event from the flow.	Y

C.4 *Tag manipulation plugins*

Plugin name	Summary	Fluentd core
`rewrite` http://mng.bz/2jad	This enables tags to be modified using one or more rules, such as if an attribute of the log event record matches a regular expression. As a result, performing specific tasks based on the log event becomes very easy.	N
`rewrite-tag-filter` http://mng.bz/1jMV	With one or more rules in the match directive, the log event has a regular expression applied to it. Then, depending on the result, the tag is changed to a specified value. The rule can be set such that you can choose whether the rewrite is applied to a true or false outcome from the regex. The log event is re-emitted to continue beyond the match event using the new tag if a successful outcome is achieved.	N
`route` http://mng.bz/PWx9	The routing plugin allows tags to direct the log events to one or more operations, such as manipulating the log event and copying it to intercept it by another directive.	N

C.5 *Preventing alert storms*

Some resources can help control or prevent possible alert storms if a continuous stream of errors is generated.

Plugin name	Summary
Log suppression filter http://mng.bz/J1lO	The Fluentd plugin keeps a list of previous log entries based on named log event attributes if they reoccur more than a defined number of times within a certain period.
Log4J2 plugin http://mng.bz/wnPq	Suppresses log events within the Log4J2 framework to prevent too many log events from being emitted that match a set of rules.
Log4Net http://mng.bz/7W19	A .Net variant of the Log4J2 solution.

C.6 *Analytical and metrics plugins*

Some plugins can help create analytics or metrics values within Fluentd or use tools to help generate metrics.

Plugin name	Summary
Fluent-plugin-prometheus http://mng.bz/mxJr	This bundles six plugins together, covering the following: ■ `prometheus` input plugin provides a metrics HTTP endpoint to be scraped by a Prometheus server on 24231/tcp(default). ■ `prometheus_input` plugin collects internal metrics in Fluentd, a bit like the monitor agent. ■ `prometheus_output_monitor` plugin collects internal metrics for output plugin in Fluentd. ■ `prometheus_tail_monitor` plugin collects internal metrics for the tail plugin in Fluentd. This allows us to provide assurance that the tail plugin is running as intended. ■ The output and filter plugins instrument the log event with additional metrics, such as the number of occurrences of a value based on the configuration attributes.
Fluentd Elasticsearch plugin http://mng.bz/5K1B	Plugin to send log events to Elasticsearch. The plugin provides a very rich set of configuration attributes.
Fluentd data counter http://mng.bz/6Z1o	Count log events that match any of the specified regexp patterns in the specified attribute: ■ Counts per min/hour/day ■ Counts per second (average every min/hour/day) ■ Percentage of each pattern in total counts of messages The `DataCounterOutput` emits messages containing results data, so you can output these messages (with the `datacount` tag by default) to any outputs you want.

(continued)

Plugin name	Summary
Fluentd numeric counter http://mng.bz/oaJd	Plugin to count log events that match numeric range patterns and emits its result (like `fluent-plugin-datacounter`): ▪ Counts per min/hour/day ▪ Counts per second (average every min/hour/day) ▪ Percentage of each numeric pattern in total counts of log events

C.7   Plugin Interfaces

The following tables summarize the functions that can or should be implemented when developing your own plugins. You can see the details by reviewing the Fluentd code as well at https://github.com/fluent/fluentd/blob/master/lib/fluent/plugin, but we hope these tables will make life easier.

Input

Function prototype	Description
`def emit`	This overloads the Fluent::Input class methods for our requirements.
`def run`	Set up the loop thread, and if there's nothing to emit, then go to sleep.
`def configure(conf)`	This method is for processing the configuration values so that they can be validated, particularly if values can conflict.
`def start`	A life cycle event to start the creation of connectivity. Start the timer to nudge the logic to see if any I/O is needed.
`def shutdown`	Start the process of releasing assets such as connections to resources.

Output

Function Prototype	Description
`commit_write(chunk_id)`	Once a chunk can be written, this method tells our implementation which chunk ID to write. On return to Fluentd, the chunk is purged.
`def configure(conf)`	This method is for processing the configuration values so that they can be validated, particularly if values can conflict.
`def format(tag, time, record)`	This serializes the code for holding in a chunk. The `tag`, `time`, and `record` represent the three parts of a log event, with the time in seconds from the epoch. The record at this stage is a hash to allow JSON manipulation. Will throw a `NotImplemented` error if this isn't overloaded.
`def formatted_to_msgpack_binary?`	To indicate custom format method (#format), returns msgpack to binary or not. If #format returns msgpack binary, override this method to return `true`. By default, it returns `false`.

Output *(continued)*

Function Prototype	Description
def multi_workers_ready?	False
def prefer_buffered_processing	Override this method to return false only when all of these are true: • The plugin has both implementations for buffered and non-buffered methods. • The plugin is expected to work as a nonbuffered plugin if no `<buffer>` sections specified `true`.
def prefer_delayed_commit	Override this method to decide which is used, `write` or `try_write`, if both are implemented.
def shutdown	The shutdown is the opposite of the Start event. At this stage, we should be releasing resources such as network connections.
def start	This is one of the important life cycle events; we should start consuming or allowing events to be sent on receipt of this.
def try_write(chunk)	This method is for implementing the asynchronous I/O. The base class will throw a `NotImplemented` error if this isn't overloaded but is expected to be implemented.
def write(chunk)	This takes a chunk and writes it out synchronously. The base class will throw a `NotImplemented` error if this isn't overloaded but is expected to work.
extract_placeholders(str, chunk)	Used to extract a string value from `str` using the chunk information. A string is returned.
process(tag, es)	This method is used for synchronous output. Will throw a `NotImplemented` error if this isn't overloaded. The `tag` is the tag that applies to all the events in the `es` structure. The `es` parameter represents one or more log events to be written.
rollback_write(chunk_id)	The plugin can control rollback and retries for the writing of chunks using this method.

appendix D
Real-world use case

D.1 Fluentd use in a real-world use case

Throughout the book, we have focused on explaining how to use Fluentd. The explanations have focused on specific areas rather than providing a holistic view. This appendix seeks to redress that by providing a more holistic picture.

This appendix has taken several similar real-world scenarios and blended them to avoid giving any client information away. Blending the cases together has allowed us to also incorporate more lessons. We won't go into the specific configuration details, as they're covered in the core of the book, but this should help you understand why we value some features.

D.2 Setting the scene

Our organization started about 30 years ago as a single-country retailer that has grown rapidly. The growth has been driven by the following:

- Acquiring its own manufacturing capabilities, as its offerings are custom to each client.
- Expanding its retail scope to related product lines reflecting changes in the market.
- Commercially the retail units are established as businesses in their own right and are either wholly owned by a subsidiary of the main corporation or are co-owned (with store directors); there are also a few traditional franchisees. This structure gives the stores a degree of autonomy and individual accountability. This has meant independent retailers can become part of the group, and external investment (share cost in co-ownership or franchise) has helped growth.
- Technology adoption has been driven by goals to streamline processes and, therefore, more retail throughput. This has meant growth in mobile device adoption and, more slowly, engagement with internet-based sales channels.

- International expansion has been driven in Europe, Asia Pacific (including China), and North America in the last 20 years.

Internally, the organization is split in terms of geographical business and operations. Within each organization, there are vertical domains of

- Retail
- Manufacturing and distribution
- Corporate (which covers marketing, accounting, external supply chain sourcing, etc.)

A central IT function supports corporate systems, core solutions used at a regional or manufacturing site level, and retail IT solutions. Still, the level of autonomy the verticals have creates conditions where shadow or gray IT exists. This is further compounded by the regional operations having their own IT teams aligned to the regional businesses. Corporate HQ and the primary IT operations, including software development, are based in Europe.

Some IT solutions reflect the organization's age and growth; some corporate solutions have seen years of cumulative extension, patching, and customization and are clearly aging and brittle. This has led to hesitancy to make changes and some significant programs having been started to replace some of the legacy with a COTS (commercial-off-the-shelf) or SaaS approach. Shadow IT has meant local pockets of SaaS and "integration" have sprung up. European IT is dominated by its own on-premises data centers. Still, the newer geographic regions are more quickly adopting cloud rather than seeking the capital outlay for their operational IT and support centers. Retail currently is an on-premises proposition, as wide area network communications are not considered robust enough to allow retail locations to continue operating in the event of an outage. In some parts of the world, the stores simply don't have sufficient network quality, reliability, and bandwidth to support all the demands of hosting solutions remotely.

In addition to COTS, solutions developed in-house for retail and manufacturing often embody corporate IP or streamline business processes. The organization sees increasingly connected devices in the manufacturing and retail spaces. The connectivity is coming either because of the natural IT evolution or because of parts of the organization commissioning third parties to build solutions or unique customizations of standard commercial offerings delivered by tablets.

Much of the system integration has been achieved via messaging, shared databases, or FTP. The retail and manufacturing capabilities are the most message-based, as store orders to manufacturing are time-sensitive and reflect dynamic stock allocation (reflecting these solutions have been bespoke built).

The rollout of software changes tends to be slow, often coming from nervousness about brittle legacy solutions. Delays outside non-European geographies have been compounded by the lack of understanding of software change and operational support challenges that made people resistant to change. Ironically, this has compounded problems, as outward pressure from Europe for upgrades to be rolled out means the rollout often entails a lot of change.

Existing operational and monitoring maturity depends upon geography, with Europe being the most established and mature. However, monitoring is primarily an infrastructure-only engagement. Monitoring at the application level is weaker. Business-level monitoring comes through classic retail and supply chain reporting metrics (sales and orders) rather than from more contemporary views of how many tasks are at different stages of their process.

Some of the problems have come from the continual drive for growth in terms of geography and market leadership (market share, innovation, regulation change). These pressures, at times, don't help with keeping on top of the nonfunctional considerations as they evolve with the growth and technical debt. This isn't unusual for many established organizations, but the continued growth embedded into the organizational DNA increases the pressure. IT momentum is typically measured through new functional capability and certainly creates some challenges in addressing debt until debt impacts delivery.

As you can see, this is not a cloud-born organization, but it was starting to feel its way into the cloud and needs to understand how to solve monitoring both for on-premises and when dealing with the cloud.

D.2.1 *The operational challenges*

It's worth looking at some of the operational problems that the organization has struggled with. Addressing such issues will bring business value that can be gained through the delivery of monitoring improvements, including the adoption of Fluentd.

Third- and fourth-line support for core systems comes from the IT development in Europe that doesn't provide 24/7 support. Regional operations working in different time zones have to provide their own support for their own regional retail. Central support provided often comes down to organizational politics and the goodwill of staff to provide out-of-hours support.

European development, which could effectively support local geographies using basic DevOps practices, had an insufficient appreciation for the needs of other regions. DevOps often was a reason not to write things down, so locally, understanding was very much through verbal and collaborative behaviors. The different geographies not being an active part of the development process and not benefiting from the collaborative knowledge transfer meant they lacked understanding of in-house solutions. This has resulted in problems arising from people using solutions in a way they were not expected to be used. Fast and dirty processes to recover from problems resulting in the loss of insight into operational failures (no logs retained or environment imaging/snapshots) made it very difficult for European IT to investigate and develop preventative measures.

It can be challenging to gather relevant information for operational support needs and problem data in a highly distributed environment. Not only is the distribution a challenge, but there are also network constraints (bandwidth, compliance, and security) between different geographic regions and organizational entities restricting what is retrieved to get a rich global picture of the problems and operational health. If the global IT operations can't retrieve the details of an operational issue and the regional teams aren't actively capturing the necessary information when an operational issue occurs (i.e., logs, software versions, host machine state, etc.) before resting systems or processes, then the challenges of resolving possible bugs, implementing preventative actions, and updating operational guidance are going to compound.

D.3   *Introducing monitoring*

The IT systems effectively formed a series of star structures from the store to regional operational hubs and from regional hubs to the corporate center. This can be seen in figure D.1. The manufacturing and distribution are also connected directly to hubs and to the global center. This lends itself to adopting monitoring as a series of concentrator networks. This also fits well because most of the hubs have the most significant volume of events/transactions passing through, meaning problems in these areas have the most significant commercial impact.

Figure D.1   The key "actors" in the business and their relationships (and flow of information) across the organization

The first goal was getting regional hub systems aggregating and unifying their log data. Working on an 80/20 principle, we looked for standard technologies and common systems (often those originating from the central IT capability) to create standardized log event capture configurations. Metrics data collection was also implemented with simple threshold alarms. Alarms reflected significant threshold breaches (before they went critical) and had log events generated. When investigating a problem through the logs, we could see historically that there might have been a performance issue of some sort (typically the most severe being disk storage exhaustion).

While aligning infrastructure logs with the application logs would have shown us these measures, wanting to combine infrastructure monitoring led to conflicting politics, as the infrastructure teams felt their monitoring was mature. They weren't the source of the problems. This wasn't helped by the fact that IaaS activities didn't see the infrastructure teams being involved.

We pressed development teams to catalog exceptions and use error codes as a first step to building better support documentation. This provided a vehicle for the regional teams to attach and share their own operational processes. Over time, we got CI/CD code quality checks to detect the allocation of error codes and gamified the adoption.

Traction with unifying the logs progressed, and we had a better understanding of what might be happening in the different deployments—some of the warning signs of problems had been identified and weren't being recognized until too late. Therefore, alerting was provided through the log monitoring for the well-understood indicators by using group emails.

Other candidate indicators started being watched, which triggered a script to gather more diagnostic information, such as message queue depths, capturing the last access time to a queue.

As confidence grew that the monitoring was producing results, with both local operational teams and central IT resources better seeing what was going on, the acceptance of extending monitoring was implemented. Forwarding specific events to the central IT team also helped confirm when data distribution processes from the corporate center became the source of issues. Some of the problems started to be identified by examining logs for what was expected to happen. Along with the incorporation of the capacity, flags were things like

- Housekeeping wasn't being run on time.
- Software deployments weren't always followed as recommended by the central teams. As a result, automated processes didn't fire when they were expected or needed to.
- Manual housekeeping wasn't consistently practiced, often because the additional housekeeping steps were passed around by email, which didn't reach everyone, or were not added to documentation as a more structured process.
- Some business processes took days or weeks longer than expected in different geographies. As a result, staging data built up more than was expected, creating issues.

- Indications of warnings were not addressed when they needed to be.
- Some application logic wasn't very defensive, allowing users to do things that weren't expected in other parts of the enterprise—for example, product images were GBs in size when the communication infrastructure assumed such data would only be a few Kb.

Some of these findings certainly had to be handled with a great deal of care, as the mistakes and issues of communication gave anyone with an organizational agenda fuel, and often a lot of finger-pointing could occur.

D.3.1   Extending monitoring

With good progress with the geographical hubs and labs, the same approach was repeated for retail operations. This had to be done with more care, as anything perceived as impacting retail operations was a sensitive issue. One of the key challenges was sending sufficient information back to the hubs to provide suitable value while not consuming precious bandwidth.

The log aggregation focused on the store's server-side solutions rather than the mobile platforms with device-native applications. Understanding native applications to get meaningful insights ended up being an issue separated from the core monitoring efforts. As the store applications handled PII data, the store servers were tightly locked down and experienced the occasional erroneous entry to a UI of data that shouldn't be there, resulting in PII data occasionally finding its way into log entries. The subsequent need to filter log events further led to applying data masking for log events, even locally.

D.3.2   Finessing of monitoring

With the operational insights starting to flow back to central IT teams, some development teams switched from using Java logging to files to logging directly to the Fluentd agent. Where this was adopted, we used a configuration during development that ensured the log events got written to a file rather than to a central log storage capability. Log centralization varied based on willingness to allow additional software to be deployed and who would deploy it. This meant developers didn't see the introduction of Fluentd early in the process as a disruption, because they were used to looking at their log files to help confirm code was working as expected. But this also helped promote improvement in logging, as we could still put filters in to highlight potential issues, such as accidentally logging sensitive data items.

D.4   Cloud dilemma

While cloud impact was very much a SaaS or IaaS issue, increasingly the challenge we are seeing with matured PaaS is the use of Cloud Native services, rather than a "low code" style of PaaS, such as MuleSoft, Dell Boomi, and Oracle's Integration Cloud, which are closed ecosystems, to varying degrees. AWS, Azure, Oracle, and Google all provide cloud native services that offer Fluentd-like capabilities for their Kubernetes services. Therefore, when building with AWS's Kubernetes or Oracle's Blockchain, should we use the vendor implementations or explicitly instantiate Fluentd and configure Kubernetes to use our Fluentd, not the out-of-the-box logging and monitoring? We can see this clearly in figure D.2 with a cloud host natural solution using cloud native technologies and a cloud host-aligned approach.

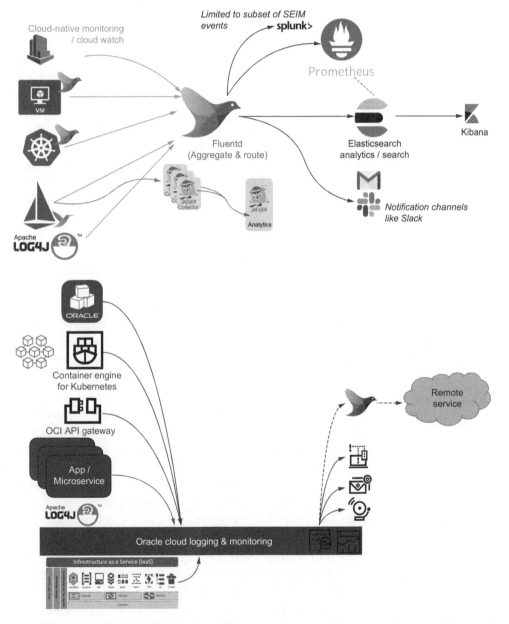

Figure D.2 This illustrates the difference between a cloud-neutral approach to logging using cloud-native solutions (top), where you will need to accommodate in the infrastructure as code the networking needs, versus a vendor-specific model, where all the log events will go into a transparent monitoring layer handled by the cloud vendor.

It isn't necessarily an easy question to answer. If we use the services provided and benefit from integrating, self-scaling, auto-patching, and so on, we must accept the consequential vendor lock-in. Or we must go the IaaS approach and deploy Fluentd ourselves, meaning any IaaS cloud vendor can be used, but we have to patch and scale ourselves. We've settled on answering this with several questions:

- What value do you gain by being cloud vendor–agnostic?
- For software vendors, the benefit is obvious—maximum potential in terms of the consumer base. But the reality is that you'll probably eventually incorporate adaptors into the clouds you support the most, as this benefits the customer. There are the high-profile stories of Zoom being able to switch cloud vendors quickly to realize substantial savings and Dropbox's decision to move off AWS as they reached a scale that meant private data centers offered a better economy.
- Are you likely to need multiple cloud vendors or operate in a hybrid manner?
- For truly global solutions, today's reality is that you are likely to need to deploy to multiple clouds. This is simply because not every vendor has a substantial presence in every geography. You may bump up against specific country data restrictions, which may mean using a particular vendor (e.g., Azure at the time of writing doesn't have a presence in Eastern Europe, and Google doesn't have a presence in Africa).
- Also, unless you're a significant customer with deep pockets, you won't be using the cloud in your data center solutions such as AWS's Outpost or Oracle's Cloud at Customer, where the entire cloud platform is deployed onto provided racks of servers that live in your data center. This means multiple implementation and configuration issues. This may not be an option if you want to operate in China, as many IT vendors have restrictions on where and what they will offer.
- How big and capable is your IT team?
- The more variations in how the same problem is solved, the more skills an IT team or department will need. Suppose your IT organization needs to be very lean in terms of people. In that case, a standard set of technologies has a lot going for it. The team can develop their expertise with a smaller, focused set of tools. Master those to greater depth and maximize the investment. We're not suggesting that all monitoring problems can be answered by Fluentd, but why master three or four log unification tools if one is enough?
- Are your monitoring needs or strategy likely to take you into specialist situations?
- For those specialist situations, where a restrictive solution is likely to need a lot of working around or you're pushing the boundaries of what is possible with standard tools, then a service model from the cloud vendors is likely to create more problems than solutions. You won't be able to tailor their platform around your unique circumstances like you can when you have complete control of both code and deployment.

Exploring these questions will undoubtedly reveal whether adopting Fluentd or something like the ELK stack is the way to go.

D.5   *Solution*

The solution that we arrived at on a regional hub level looks like the diagram in figure D.3. The corporate monitoring would look pretty similar, although the number of sources grew significantly over time as monitoring became more standard practice.

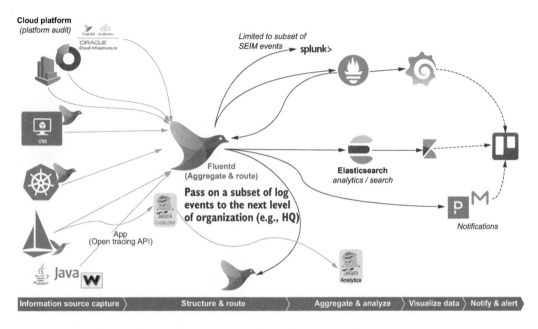

Figure D.3   Overview solution for monitoring laid against the log event life cycle

The stores and manufacturing centers would have some similarities, albeit a great deal simpler than the hubs, as they didn't use containerization and had a smaller suite of systems in action.

D.6   *Conclusion*

Hopefully you'll see from this that several of the Fluentd techniques we cover in the book helped deliver value to an organization with some challenges. You'll have noticed that the application of Fluentd was not bound to any specific type of platform or technology. While Fluentd does come under the governance of the CNCF, this reflects the fact that it can help with modern cloud challenges, not that it was designed exclusively for this context.

One of our biggest takeaways from this lesson is the need for the organization implementing the monitoring capability to ensure that the culture and approach to implementing monitoring is ready and able to embrace the changes necessary. While hardware monitoring is taken as the norm (after all, you've made a significant capital outlay, so you want to ensure it is paying for itself), application monitoring and the use of logs often don't get the same treatment. In the cases that formed this example, things had to become significantly problematic before a significant commitment was made to address them.

appendix E
Useful resources

E.1 Helpful Fluentd resources

These are resources directly related to Fluentd and supported by the Fluentd community.

Name	URL	Description
Fluentd official documentation	https://docs.fluentd.org/	The official GitHub documentation for Fluentd
Slack	https://slack.fluentd.org	Fluentd community on Slack
Stack Overflow for Fluentd	https://stackoverflow.com/questions/tagged/fluentd	Stack Overflow's content relating to Fluentd

E.2 Helpful Fluentd third-party tools

Fluentd is built with Ruby, and if you're writing Fluentd plugins, these resources will be of great help.

Name	URL	Description
Fluentular	https://fluentular.herokuapp.com/	Utility to help validate regular expressions in Fluentd configuration.
Grok parser	http://mng.bz/nYJa	This uses a Grok-based approach to pulling details from a log entry. It includes multiline support.
Microsoft's Visual Studio Code	https://code.visualstudio.com/	Free IDE that can support a wealth of languages and syntaxes through the use of a plugin framework.

(continued)

Name	URL	Description
Multiformat parser	http://mng.bz/vo17	Attempts to use different format patterns in the defined order to get a match.
VS Code—Fluentd plugin	https://github.com/msysyamamoto/vscode-fluentd	Search in Visual Studio Code for msys-yamamoto.vscode-fluentd.
A website version of the VS Code plugin	https://regexper.com/	Provides a visual representation of a regular expression. Helps resolve correct groups, etc.

E.3   Helpful logging practices resources

The key to effective use of logs is good logging. We have provided a lot of insight into recommended practices. But if you wish to find out what others think, then these resources may help.

Description	URL
Logging best practices from Logz.io.	https://logz.io/blog/logging-best-practices/
Loggly guide to logging—covers multiple language perspectives.	https://www.loggly.com/ultimate-guide/
Loggly's *The Pragmatic Logging Handbook.*	http://mng.bz/4j1w
National Institute of Standards and Technology (NIST) Guide to Computer Security Log Management.	http://mng.bz/QW8G
This defines the standard for Syslog; in addition to helping you better understand Syslog, it also contains some good ideas for logging practices.	https://tools.ietf.org/html/rfc5424

E.4   Common log formats and descriptions

The industry has developed several de facto or formalized industry standards for log file structures. The following are references to these industry specifications.

Log format	Reference for definition
Apache HTTP logs	https://httpd.apache.org/docs/2.4/logs.html
Common Event Format (CEF)	http://mng.bz/XW5v
Graylog Extended Log Format (GELF)	http://mng.bz/y4QB

(continued)

Log format	Reference for definition
Nginx logging	http://mng.bz/M2BW
Syslog	https://tools.ietf.org/html/rfc5424
Systemd Journal	https://systemd.io/JOURNAL_FILE_FORMAT/
W3C Extended Log File Format (ELF)	www.w3.org/TR/WD-logfile.html
WinLoG (Windows native logging)	http://mng.bz/aD17

E.5 *Helpful Ruby resources*

The bulk of Fluentd is built with Ruby, and if you're writing Fluentd plugins, you may need these resources.

Name	URL	Description
Explanation of Global Interpreter Lock	https://thoughtbot.com/blog/untangling-ruby-threads	Ruby uses a Global Interpreter Lock, which impacts how threading is managed and how to tune Fluentd.
Gem spec	http://mng.bz/g4BV	Defines the details of the gemspec file needed to package custom-developed plugins.
Gemspec vs. Gemfile	http://mng.bz/5Kwa	Explains the difference between the Gemspec and Gemfile.
Minitest—Ruby Unit Testing framework	https://github.com/seattlerb/minitest	Another popular unit testing framework. This resource includes information that helps differentiate it from the other commonly used frameworks.
Rake	https://github.com/ruby/rake	Provides a build process that can be incorporated into a CI/CD pipeline.
rbenv	https://github.com/rbenv/rbenv	This open source tool makes it easier to ensure that different applications can be worked on with different Ruby versions.
RDoc	https://github.com/ruby/rdoc	The standard Ruby-Doc generation. If you need to generate documentation but don't want to use the extensions from Yard, then RDoc is standard.
RSpec Ruby Unit Testing framework	https://rspec.info/	RSpec is an alternative to Ruby unit testing, which supports a test-driven development (TDD) approach to development.

(continued)

Name	URL	Description
RuboCop	https://docs.rubocop.org/rubocop/installation.html	Lint tool for Ruby. Worthwhile if developing custom plugins.
Ruby API	https://rubyapi.org/	Ruby documentation tool.
RubyGems	https://rubygems.org/	Catalog of RubyGems along with the RubyGems manager.
RubyGuides	www.rubyguides.com	A set of online guides to implement specific capabilities with Ruby.
Ruby in Twenty Minutes	www.ruby-lang.org/en/documentation/quickstart/	An excellent introduction to Ruby using Hello World.
Ruby in Practice	www.manning.com/books/ruby-in-practice	*Ruby in Practice* is a second book from Manning Publications taking a different approach to teaching Ruby development.
RubyInstaller	https://rubyinstaller.org/	Windows installer for Ruby.
Ruby Language Specification and Documentation	www.ruby-lang.org/en/documentation/	Includes summary pages of how Ruby differs from other languages such as Java.
ruby-lint	https://rubygems.org/gems/ruby-lint/	When developing custom plugins, lint tooling will help keep the code tidy and, importantly, help spot any potential errors.
Ruby threading	https://thoughtbot.com/blog/untangling-ruby-threads	A more detailed look at Ruby's threading.
Ruby unit test framework	https://test-unit.github.io/	Fluentd provides additional supporting resources to make it easy for plugins to be tested using the test-unit tool.
test-unit	https://github.com/test-unit/test-unit	An xUnit-based unit testing solution for Ruby.
The Well-Grounded Rubyist, third edition	www.manning.com/books/the-well-grounded-rubyist-third-edition	Manning bible on Ruby development.
VSCode Ruby plugin	https://marketplace.visualstudio.com/items?itemName=wingrunr21.vscode-ruby	Syntax-aware highlighting for Ruby in Microsoft's Visual Studio Code.
YARD	https://yardoc.org/	RubyDoc-compliant documentation generator, but also supports a tagging notation that helps provide more comprehensive metadata.

E.6   *Docker and Kubernetes*

Docker is the most used containerization technology and is usually used with Kubernetes. Kubernetes and the adoption by CNCF have been influential to Fluentd adoption. If you want to know more about Kubernetes generally, then these resources will help.

Name	URL	Description
Docker	www.docker.com	Home of the Docker ecosystem.
Docker Hub	https://hub.docker.com/	Repository of Docker images, including Fluentd images and other images used by this book.
Docker plugin for Visual Studio Code	http://mng.bz/6ZDA	Plugin to help understand Docker files and the file syntax.
Home of Kubernetes	https://kubernetes.io	The official Kubernetes website.
Kubernetes log (klog)	https://github.com/kubernetes/klog	The implementation and documentation of the Kubernetes klog component. Klog is being adopted by Kubernetes as the default native logger.
logrotate	https://github.com/logrotate/logrotate	Logrotate is an open source tool for handling log rotation. Depending on how Kubernetes is set up, this is deployed to manage Kubernetes log rotation.
Kubernetes in Action, Second Edition	http://mng.bz/oa1p	Manning's definitive guide to Kubernetes.
Kubernetes secrets	http://mng.bz/nYW2	Kubernetes's approach to sharing with pods and container credentials.
Open Containers	https://opencontainers.org/	A standard supported by Docker and several other container development organizations to standardize how Kubernetes interacts with containers.
Alternate Containers to Docker	https://containerd.io/ https://cri-o.io/	Several alternate initiatives to develop containerization, with input from organizations like Intel, IBM, Red Hat, and other Linux vendors such as SUSE, to name a few.
Deployment tools	https://rancher.com https://helm.sh	Deploying pods and configurations to Kubernetes can be complicated. Several solutions have been developed, such as Helm and Rancher, representing the leading solutions in this space.

E.7   *Elasticsearch*

Elasticsearch is one of the common targets for log aggregation. The Elasticsearch plugin is not part of the standard set of plugins for the open source deployment of Fluentd (although it is for the prebuild Treasure Data agent version). For pure Fluentd, the agent needs to be installed.

Name	URL	Description
Elasticsearch Stack	www.elastic.co/elastic-stack	Details for the ELK stack (Elasticsearch, Logstash, Kibana). While Logstash can be seen as competition to Fluentd, Fluentd is often used with Elasticsearch and Kibana.
Elasticvue	https://elasticvue.com	A UI tool for looking at the contents of Elasticsearch.
Fluentd Elasticsearch plugin	https://docs.fluentd.org/output/elasticsearch	A plugin that allows you to integrate Elasticsearch.
Elasticsearch plugin source	http://mng.bz/von4	Repository for the Fluentd Elasticsearch plugin.
Manning, *Elasticsearch in Action*	www.manning.com/books/elasticsearch-in-action	Manning's guide to using Elasticsearch.

E.8   *Redis*

Redis can be used by Fluentd to provide an in-memory cache solution. These resources will provide additional detail, downloads, and so on.

Name	URL	Description
Home of Redis	https://redis.io/	Provides the basic documentation and the downloads for Redis. In addition to the commercial offerings, we will use Redis in our custom plugin development.
Manning, *Redis in Action*	www.manning.com/books/redis-in-action	While *Redis in Action* goes beyond what we need to know for caching, this guide to Redis is helpful.
Redis RubyGem	https://github.com/redis/redis-rb	This is the Ruby Redis library for connecting and using Redis operations. We will use this when building our custom plugin.

E.9   *SSL/TLS and security*

The ability to use SSL/TLS when operating in a distributed manner is indispensable. The following are helpful links on the matter of using SSL/TLS.

Name	URL	Description
Certificate Authority	https://jamielinux.com/docs/openssl -certificate-authority/	A look at establishing your own certificate authority.
Introduction to TLS	www.internetsociety.org/deploy360/tls/ basics/	An Introduction to TLS.
Let's Encrypt	https://letsencrypt.org/	Let's Encrypt is a service developed by the Linux Foundation that provides free certificates with a short shelf life. The service includes some excellent automation to automate recertification.
OWASP TLS Cheat Sheet	https://cheatsheetseries.owasp.org/ cheatsheets/Transport_Layer_Protection _Cheat_Sheet.html	Provides practical, helpful information about TLS and how it works from the Open Web Application Security Project.
Self-Signed Certificate	https://dzone.com/articles/creating-self -signed-certificate	Explains how to create a self-signed certificate.
SSL and TLS	www.hostingadvice.com/how-to/tls-vs -ssl/	This site explains the differences between SSL and TLS.
Vault	www.vaultproject.io	Vault is a tool for managing secrets, including details such as usernames and passwords. It includes the means to safely distribute information from a master node.
OpenSSL	www.openssl.org	Open source full-featured toolkit for the Transport Layer Security (TLS) and Secure Sockets Layer (SSL) protocols. Adopted by many products, including Fluentd.

E.10   *Environment setup*

The following resources are useful additional sources of information that can be used to set up environments for Fluentd.

Name	URL	Description
Browserling Tools	www.browserling.com/tools	A set of online tools to help with format conversion, etc.
Chocolatey	https://chocolatey.org/	Chocolatey is a package manager for Windows. It provides a user experience with more Linux-like package managers such as rpm, yum, and others.
Clang	https://clang.llvm.org/	Libraries to support compiling the platform-native elements.
GCC	https://gcc.gnu.org/	The GCC compiler tools, needed if you build the OS native features for the source.

(continued)

Name	URL	Description
GraalVM	www.graalvm.org/	Next-generation multi-language virtual machine, supporting Java and other languages. It is capable of creating platform-native binaries.
Linux Package Manager Summary	http://mng.bz/4jDj	Provides information about the different package managers and the commands to use depending on your package manager.
NTP (Network Time Protocol)	https://doc.ntp.org/	The official site for the NTP definition; includes software and white papers on the subject.
Quarkus	https://quarkus.io/	A Java-based stack using OpenJDK capable of creating Kubernetes native solutions.
Semantic Versioning	https://semver.org/	A standard form for versioning artifacts.

E.11   *Logging frameworks*

The following is not an exhaustive summary of all logging frameworks, as maintaining such a list would be a full-time job in its own right. This list does provide coverage with links to both language-native logging frameworks and open source frameworks that we believe are active.

Name	Language	URL	Description
N/A	PHP	https://www.php-fig.org/psr/psr-3/	The PHP community has developed various standards (PSRs), including logging frameworks (PSR-3). PSR defines an interface standard for logging, so any framework supporting this will be compatible. A wide range of PHP frameworks supports this specification, from Zend to Drupal. Frameworks such as Magneto provide PSR-compliant logging that supports communication to Fluentd.
Django	Python	https://docs.djangoproject.com/en/3.1/	Django is a web application framework that leverages native logging and provides some additions. This means the Fluentd extension can be incorporated.
Language native	Java	http://mng.bz/QWPv	This is part of the Java language; however, it isn't the definitive logging solution. Many still prefer using other open source solutions.

(continued)

Name	Language	URL	Description
Language native	C#—Language Native Library	http://mng.bz/XWNa	This is the C# native framework provided by Microsoft. It supports JSON configuration file controls and injection of loggers driven from the configuration.
Language native	VB.Net—Language Native Library	http://mng.bz/y4Qd	This covers the Microsoft provided capabilities for logging in Visual Basic using .Net.
Language native	Ruby—Language Native Library	https://docs.ruby-lang.org/en/2.4.0/Logger.html	Ruby provides a native logging class with logging levels. The output is limited in choice. The language basics could be extended to support more destinations.
Language native	Python—Language Native Library	https://docs.python.org/3/library/logging.html	The Python native language features form the foundation for several logging frameworks that extend the capabilities, including a number of the Python frameworks that bring value with the addition of appenders. This includes the Fluentd Python library.
Language native	Go—Native Logging	https://golang.org/pkg/log/	This is Go's native logging package. Compared to many other logging mechanisms, this is quite simple and best seen as a set of helper methods for sending log events in a more structured way to stderr.
lgr	R	http://mng.bz/M2BB	A logging framework for the R language, drawing its design principles from Log4J. The number of appenders provided is smaller and focused on databases (understandable, given that this is a data analytics-focused language).
Log4cplus	C++	https://sourceforge.net/p/log4cplus/wiki/Home/	Based on the Log4J framework.
Log4Cxx	C++	https://logging.apache.org/log4cxx/latest_stable/	Port of Log4J as part of the Apache Log4J family.
Log4J2	Java	https://logging.apache.org/log4j/2.x/index.html	Apache also provides several JVM-related language facades for Kotlin and Scala.
Log4Net	C# & VB and other languages supported on .Net framework	https://logging.apache.org/log4net/	Log4Net is the port of the Log4J framework by the Apache Foundation, which developed the original framework.

(continued)

Name	Language	URL	Description
Logrus	Go	https://github.com/Sirupsen/logrus	Logrus is now in a maintenance-only state, as the developers feel it has reached its extensibility limits without breaking compatibility. However, it is referenced as it is commonly used.
Monolog	PHP	https://github.com/Seldaek/monolog	Monolog is just a logging framework supporting the PSR-3 specification. It includes a formatter for Fluentd, which can be combined with a handler for socket-level communication to Fluentd.
NLog	C# & VB and other languages supported on the .Net framework	https://nlog-project.org/	HTTP appender included in the framework extension.
Pino	Node JS	https://getpino.io/	Pino lends itself to being integrated into various Node.JS frameworks, such as Express. It uses the concept of transports to send logs to other systems, including some native cloud vendor solutions. It does support sockets and HTTP endpoints, so these could be used to communicate with Fluentd.
Serilog	C# & VB and other languages supported on the .Net framework	https://serilog.net/	Serilog is an open source framework that promotes stronger structured logging. It provides a wide range of destinations for output, including Fluentd.
SLF4J	Java	http://www.slf4j.org/	Simple Logging Facade for Java (SLF4J) is not a framework, but an abstraction layer so that different logging frameworks can be used using the same foundations; for example, Logback and Log4J2.
Twisted	Python	https://twistedmatrix.com/trac/	This is another Python framework with an event-driven model. It provides a logging mechanism that integrates into the broader ecosystem. From there, Twisted can be used to send log events to a small set of native publishers or to send log events via Python's native logging capability.
Winston JS	Node JS	https://github.com/winstonjs/winston	Winston has many characteristics of a logging framework, with features such as log levels and appenders (called *transports* in Winston). The range of transports is limited compared to some, but a framework for building your own is provided.

E.12 *Information portals on legislation*

The moment we log sensitive information, such as identifiable individuals, credit cards, and many other things, our logs and log storage can become subject to a raft of legislation. The following are a few resources we have looked at in the past to help further our understanding.

Common name	URL	Description
DLA Piper Data Protection	www.dlapiperdataprotection.com	DLA Piper is a global law firm that has developed and maintained a website that provides good insight into individual country positioning on data protection.
GDPR	▪ https://gdpr-info.eu/ ▪ https://ico.org.uk/for-organisations/guide-to-data-protection/ ▪ https://oag.ca.gov/privacy/ccpa	GDPR (General Data Protection Regulation) was developed by the European Union to strengthen personal data protection. All the EU countries have ratified this legislation and some national legislation that builds upon it. A wide range of countries and US states have developed their own derivative legislation; for example, California's California Consumer Privacy Act (CCPA).
HIPAA	www.hhs.gov/hipaa/index.html	Health Insurance Portability and Accountability Act (HIPAA) covers the detailing of health care–related information.
ISO/IEC 27001	www.iso.org/isoiec-27001-information-security.html	Many organizations look for ISO/IEC 27001 compliance; while not a legislative-driven set of rules, it is a best-practice set of standards.
PCI DSS (Payment Card Industry Data Security Standard)	www.pcisecuritystandards.org/	A standard adopted by all payment card operators defining a range of requirements from infrastructure to development practices.
Sarbanes-Oxley Act (SOX)	www.govinfo.gov/content/pkg/STATUTE-116/pdf/STATUTE-116-Pg745.pdf	The Sarbanes-Oxley Act (SOX) was developed in the United States to address corporate legal reporting. But as a byproduct, it set down practices for security, including the handling of data. There are other national variants such as J-SOX (Japan), C-SOX (Canada), and TC-SOX (Turkey).
United Nations Conference on Trade and Development (UNCTAD)	http://mng.bz/aD1m	UNCTAD provides a similar resource to DLA Piper but is focused on e-commerce considerations.

E.13   *Other handy sources of information*

Name	URL	Description
Converting different time representations	www.epochconverter.com/	Converts timestamps to and from their second or millisecond epoch representations as used by Linux/Unix systems and languages such as Java.
Examples of documented error codes	• HTTP codes: https://datatracker.ietf.org/doc/html/rfc7231#section-6.1 • Email codes: https://www.rfc-editor.org/rfc/rfc5248.html • WebLogic server: https://docs.oracle.com/cd/E24329_01/doc.1211/e26117/chapter_bea_messages.htm#sthref7	An example of good error code documentation. Covering HTTP and email from IETF and WebLogic Application Server.
ISO 8601 Date Time Standard	www.w3.org/TR/NOTE-datetime	This describes the different industry-standard ways to define date and time.
ITIL (Information Technology Infrastructure Library)	www.axelos.com/best-practice-solutions/itil	An industry-standard set of recommended practices and processes for things like ITSM (IT service management)
Payment Card Industry (PCI) Security Standards Council (SSC)	https://www.pcisecuritystandards.org/	The organization that defines PCI DSS (Data Security Standard)—the security standards for processing payment card data.
Regular expression development	www.regular-expressions.info/	This website gives a detailed insight into the use of regular expressions.
N-tier architectures	https://stackify.com/n-tier-architecture/ https://livebook.manning.com/book/the-cloud-at-your-service/chapter-6/point-12033-14-14-1	Provides an explanation to N-tier architectures and the value proposition they make.
TCP and UDP Network protocols	www.vpnmentor.com/blog/tcp-vs-udp/ www.cs.dartmouth.edu/~campbell/cs60/socketprogramming.html	Explanation of TCP and UDP and their differences.

E.14 Supporting Fluentd resources

The following table provides links to additional resources provided by the Fluentd community related to getting log events to Fluentd.

Name	URL	Description
Fluentd-supplied logging libraries	https://github.com/fluent/fluent-logger-java	Fluentd provided a library for direct logging from Java.
	https://github.com/fluent/fluent-logger-ruby	Fluentd provided a library for direct logging from Ruby.
	https://github.com/fluent/fluent-logger-python	Fluentd provided a library for direct logging from Python.
	https://github.com/fluent/fluent-logger-perl	Fluentd provided a library for direct logging from Perl.
	https://github.com/fluent/fluent-logger-php	Fluentd provided a library for direct logging from PHP.
	https://github.com/fluent/fluent-logger-node	Fluentd provided a library for direct logging from NodeJS.
	https://github.com/fluent/fluent-logger-scala	Fluentd provided a library for direct logging from Scala.
	https://github.com/fluent/fluent-logger-golang	Fluentd provided a library for direct logging from Go.
	https://github.com/fluent/fluent-logger-erlang	Fluentd provided a library for direct logging from Erlang.
	https://github.com/fluent/fluent-logger-ocaml	Fluentd provided a library for direct logging from OCaml.
msgpack	https://msgpack.org/	Compression library implemented in multiple languages that Fluentd can utilize. Used when the forward plugin is sending or receiving events.

E.15   *Related reading*

Fluentd, as you will have observed, crosses many boundaries in its potential application. The following table reflects this. The books listed might help you extend and leverage those linked services.

Name	URL	Description
Core Kubernetes	https://www.manning.com/books/core -kubernetes	Fluentd is often used within the context of Kubernetes and is just one aspect of a Kubernetes setup. This book and *Kubernetes in Action* will cover much of what you'll need.
Design Patterns	https://refactoring.guru/design -patterns/catalog	The details of the core patterns first described by the Gang of Four (GoF) and their book *Design Patterns: Elements of Reusable Object-Oriented Software*. The Gang of Four are Erich Gamma, John Vlissides, Richard Helm, and Ralph Johnson. Here we have provided a link to a brief guide to each of the patterns.
Docker in Action	http://mng.bz/g4Bv	Docker is the typical tech to implement a container. When we do not need the sophistication of Kubernetes, we'll use Docker more directly. This book covers the core of the building and running containers.
Effective Unit Testing	www.manning.com/books/effective-unit-testing	In chapter 9, when we implemented our custom plugin, we looked at unit testing. Ideally, the unit testing built for production use is extensive. This book, while focused on Java, will provide insight into the best practices.
Elasticsearch in Action	www.manning.com/books/elasticsearch-in-action	This book can be handy when working with Elasticsearch and Fluentd.
Groovy in Action, Second Edition	http://mng.bz/en1V	Our logging simulator was built using Groovy, making it extremely easy to bolt on enhancements to effectively simulate different sources. If you are interested in digging further into Groovy, this is the book that will help.
Kubernetes in Action	http://mng.bz/p2PK	This book covers a lot of details about Kubernetes and the way it works, giving more insight into container orchestration.
MongoDB in Action, Second Edition	http://mng.bz/OGxw	We use MongoDB as an output target. This will provide all the information likely to be needed relating to MongoDB.

(continued)

Name	URL	Description
Operations Anti-Patterns, DevOps Solutions	http://mng.bz/Yg1z	Getting your operational processes and logging is an integral part of achieving a DevOps way of working. This book looks at the potential pitfalls (or anti-patterns) you could end up facing.
Redis in Action	www.manning.com/books/redis-in-action	We used Redis as part of our example of building a custom plugin. This book will give more insight into Redis.
Ruby in Practice	www.manning.com/books/ruby-in-practice	More practical guidance on working with Ruby.
Software Telemetry	www.manning.com/books/software-telemetry	*Software Telemetry* is about the idea of getting metrics, logging, and certain types of business application state data and using them to provide you with a health perspective. Fluentd can be a crucial part of a telemetry solution.
The Well-Grounded Rubyist, Third Edition	http://mng.bz/GGyD	If you're considering getting under the hood of Fluentd or developing your own custom plugins, then this is a great read.
Securing DevOps	www.manning.com/books/securing-devops	Looks at the needs and techniques for securing cloud environments.
YAML	https://yaml.org/	The official site for YAML includes details of its syntax.

index